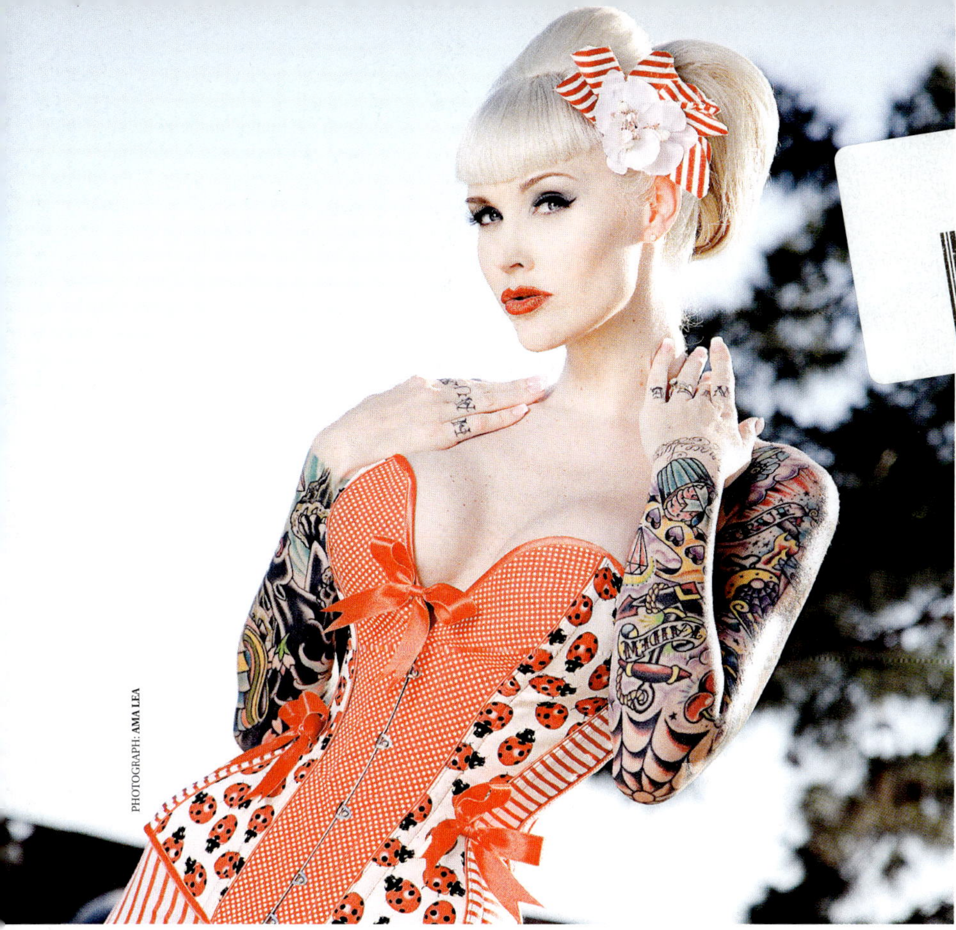

PHOTOGRAPH: AMA LEA

CONTRIBUTORS
Paula Hardy Kangelos, Marya Garcia, Ihsan Kemal, Ama Lea, Miss Missy, Tammy Nguyen Le, Marya Garcia

COVER MODELS
Main image: Kandy K (photographed by Robert Alvarado) **Cover grid:** (l-r) Sabina Kelley - Brian Brown, Zoe Suicide - Owen G Richards, Paula Hardy Kangelos - Anne Burns, Laura - Ihsan Kemal, Lady Kitty Meoww - David Garnier, Cindy Frey - Cindy Frey, Nina Kate - Ihsan Kemal, Lucy Kinsella - Ihsan Kemal, Kat Kalashnikov - Corrupt Image Data. **Back cover:** (l-r) Miss Ivi - Artstyle Photos, Hollywood Horror - Tammynize Glamour, El Wood - Ihsan Kemal, Hollie - Jay Mclaughlin, Ruca - Miss Missy, Sophie Paranoid - Marya Garcia.

SPECIAL THANKS
Special mention must be made to all of the contributing photographers without whom *Tattoo Vixens* would be little more than a blank colouring book. The same must be said of the models also. Both parties have been massively accommodating by answering emails and phone calls at exceptionally stupid hours of the night and I take my hat off to your professionalism in the face of an editor up against the clock.

To Kandy for giving advice where needed – an extra special thanks. To Eleanor and my children who are probably wondering where I've been mentally for the last couple of months – sorry, I'll be home for Christmas.

Thanks must also go to the team behind the scenes of Gareth Evans and David Gamble who have ridden shotgun on this trip and read the map well. May the Gods have mercy on my soul if I left anybody out!

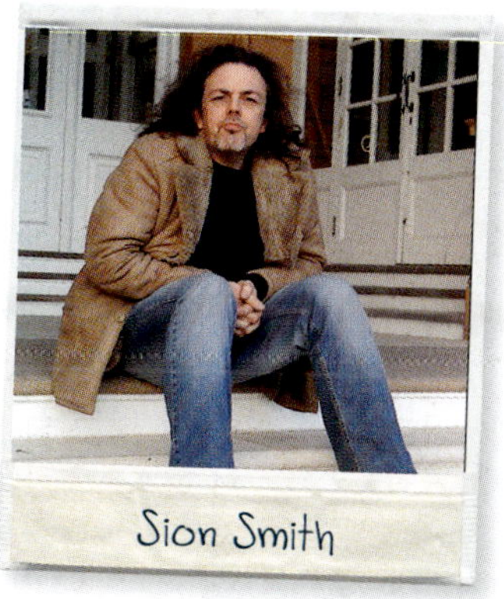

Sion Smith

WRITER & EDITOR
Sion Smith
sion.smith@skindeep.co.uk
Telephone: 01244 663400 ext. 299
ART EDITOR
Gareth Evans
gareth@jazzpublishing.co.uk
Telephone: 01244 663400 ext. 204
GRAPHIC DESIGNER
Owen Moran
owen.moran@jazzpublishing.co.uk
Telephone: 01244 663400 ext. 203
PRODUCTION MANAGER
Justine Hart
justine@jazzpublishing.co.uk
Telephone: 01244 663400 ext. 235
ACCOUNTS & ADMIN MANAGER
Emma McCrindle
accounts@jazzpublishing.co.uk
Telephone: 01244 663400 ext. 207
ADMINISTRATION
Jan Schofield
jan@jazzpublishing.co.uk
Telephone: 01244 663400 ext. 219
Katie-Marie Challinor
katie@jazzpublishing.co.uk
Telephone: 01244 663400 Ext. 220
CREDIT CONTROL
Pam Coleman
pam@jazzpublishing.co.uk
Telephone: 01244 663400 ext. 215
EVENTS MANAGER
Shelley Bond
shelley@jazzpublishing.co.uk
Telephone: 01244 663400 ext. 303
ADVERTISING ENQUIRIES
Dee Skinner
advertising@skindeep.co.uk
Telephone: 01244 663400 ext. 301
CIRCULATION & PROMOTIONS
Katy Cuffin
katy@jazzpublishing.co.uk
Telephone: 01244 663400 Ext. 237
PUBLISHER
David Gamble
david@jazzpublishing.co.uk
Telephone: 01244 663400
MANAGING DIRECTOR
Stuart Mears
stuart@jazzpublishing.co.uk
Telephone: 01244 663400
PRINTED BY
Warners Midlands plc

Contents

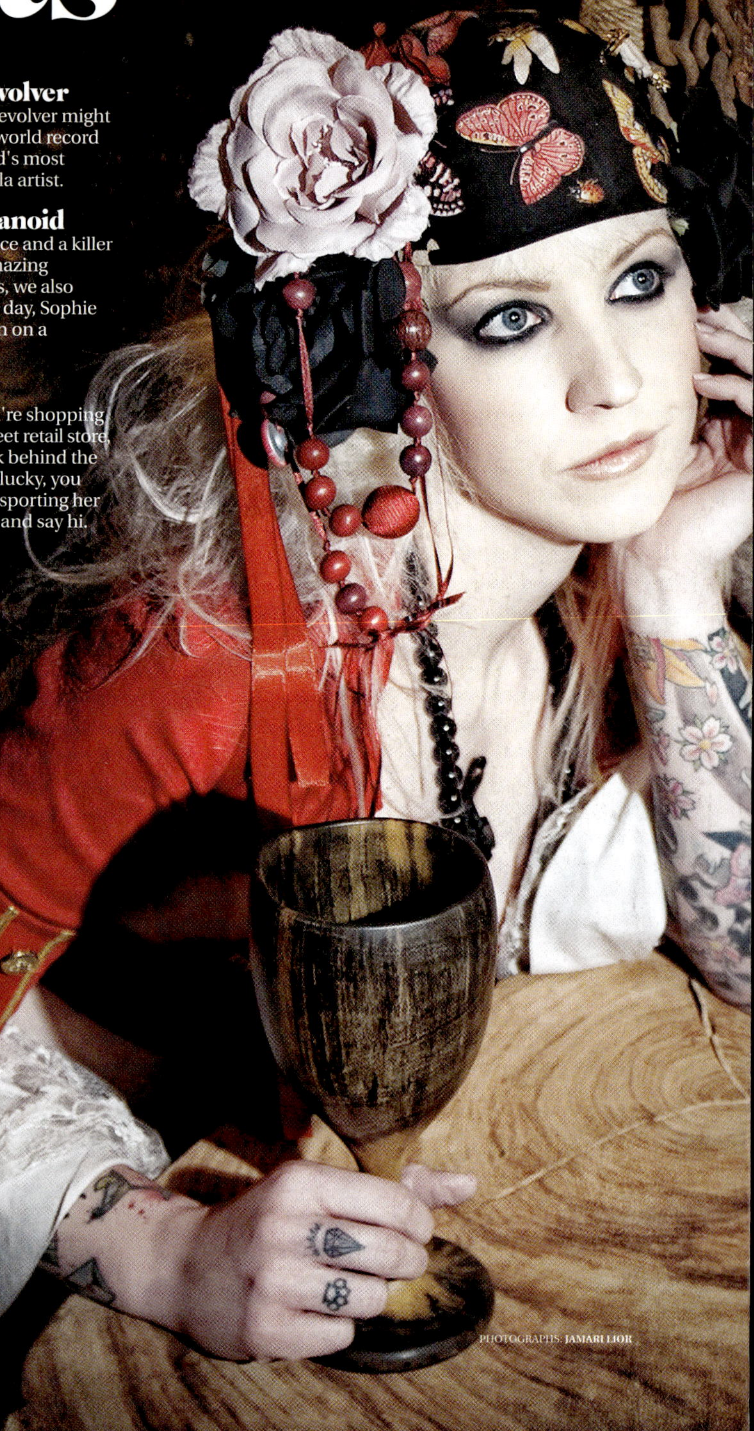

PHOTOGRAPHS: JAMARI LIOR

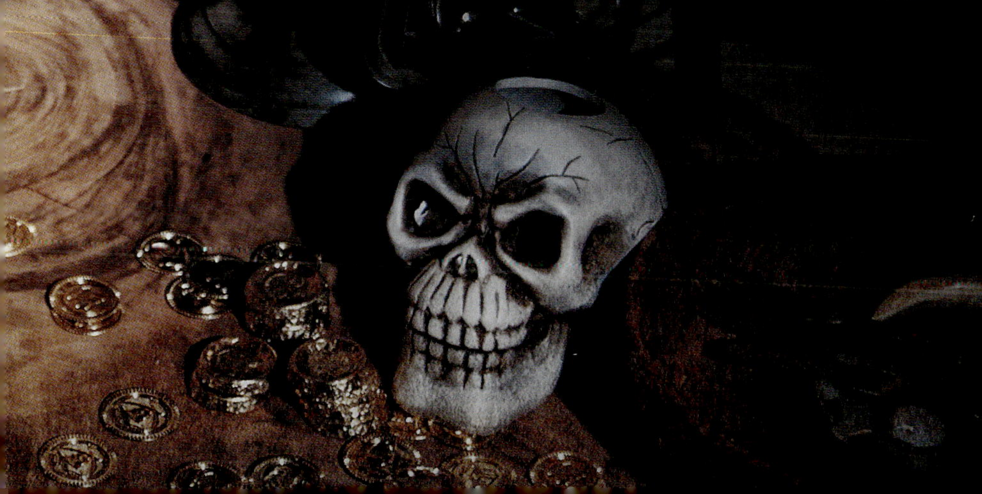

Foxy Foxy

We've come a long way from the circus sideshows when the tattooed lady was a principal attraction – or have we? With the sideshow no longer a commodity to be used in this way, time has had its wicked way and the "tattooed lady" can now be found in all walks of life. Some are professional tattooed models, some hold down regular jobs and some just are, but the one thing they all have in common is a love for the art:

Before we begin, I feel it is important to state up front that I am a pop culture writer and not an anthropologist. According to Wikipedia - the font of all knowledge so long as it doesn't need to stand up in court - the generic term 'pop-culture' embraces "*the totality of ideas, perspectives, attitudes, memes, images and other phenomena that are deemed preferred within the mainstream of a given culture, especially Western culture of the early to mid 20th century... heavily influenced by mass media, this collection of ideas permeates the everyday lives of the society.*"

As you can imagine, by its very nature, the lines between anthropology and pop culture blur every single day. In taking on authorship of this beautiful book, I'm not seeking to discover the why and wherefore of an entire generation of ladies who have chosen to heavily tattoo their bodies and display them to the world at large (or not as the case may be sometimes), I'm here to catalogue it, comment - sometimes inanely - on it and enjoy it with them.

As human beings, we often enter into certain behaviour simply because it's there to join in with – we get drawn in to the very culture of the culture itself.

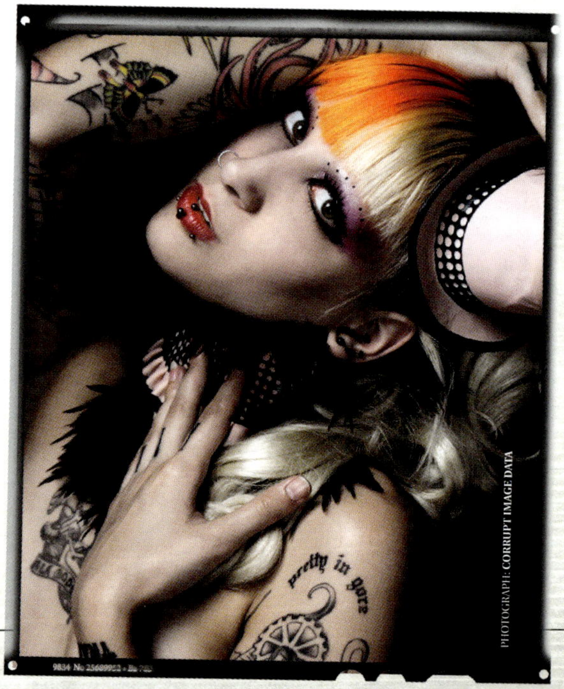

PHOTOGRAPH: CORRUPT IMAGE DATA

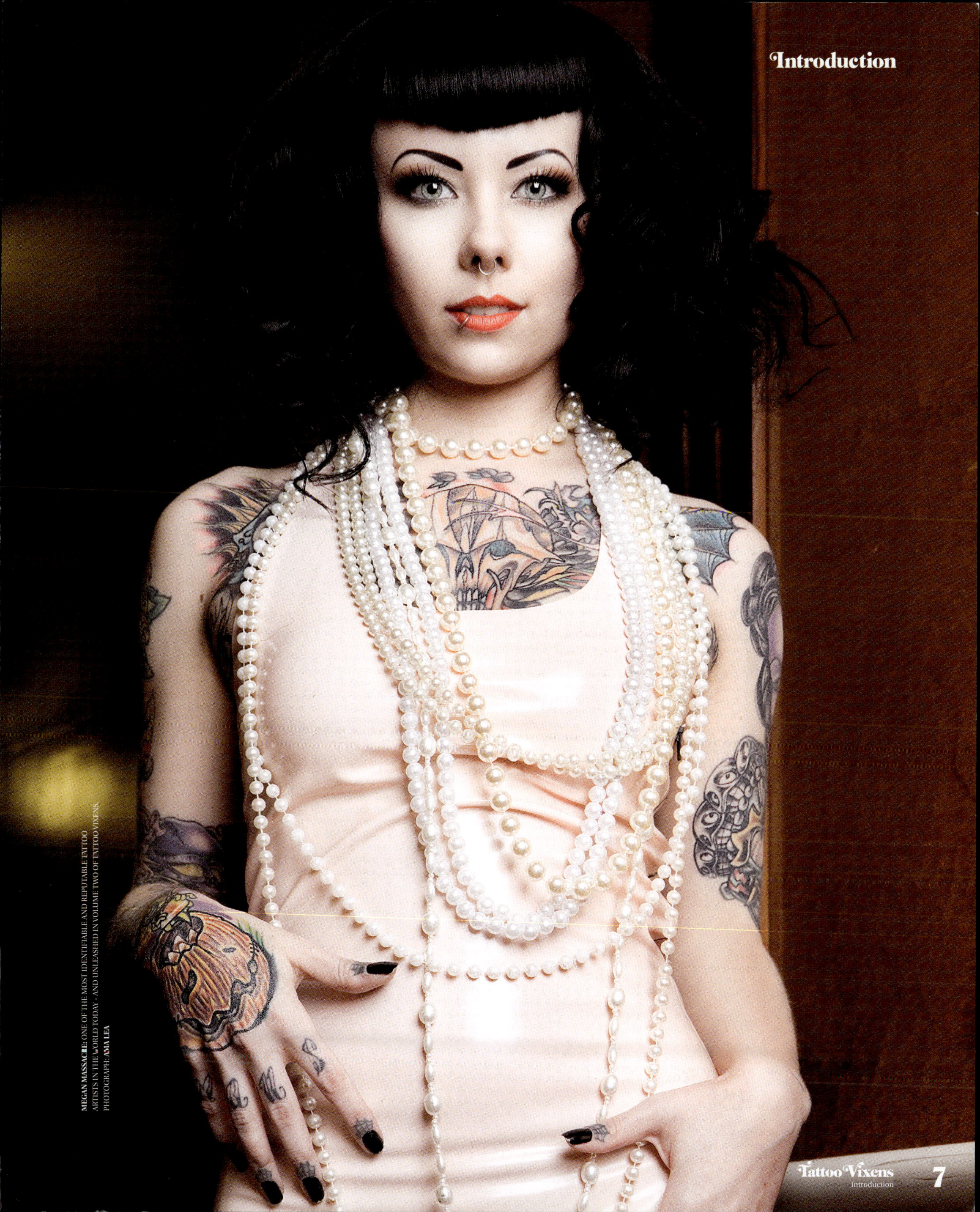

MEGAN MASSACRE: ONE OF THE MOST IDENTIFIABLE AND REPUTABLE TATTOO ARTISTS IN THE WORLD TODAY - AND UNLEASHED IN VOLUME TWO OF TATTOO VIXENS. PHOTOGRAPH: **AMA LEA**

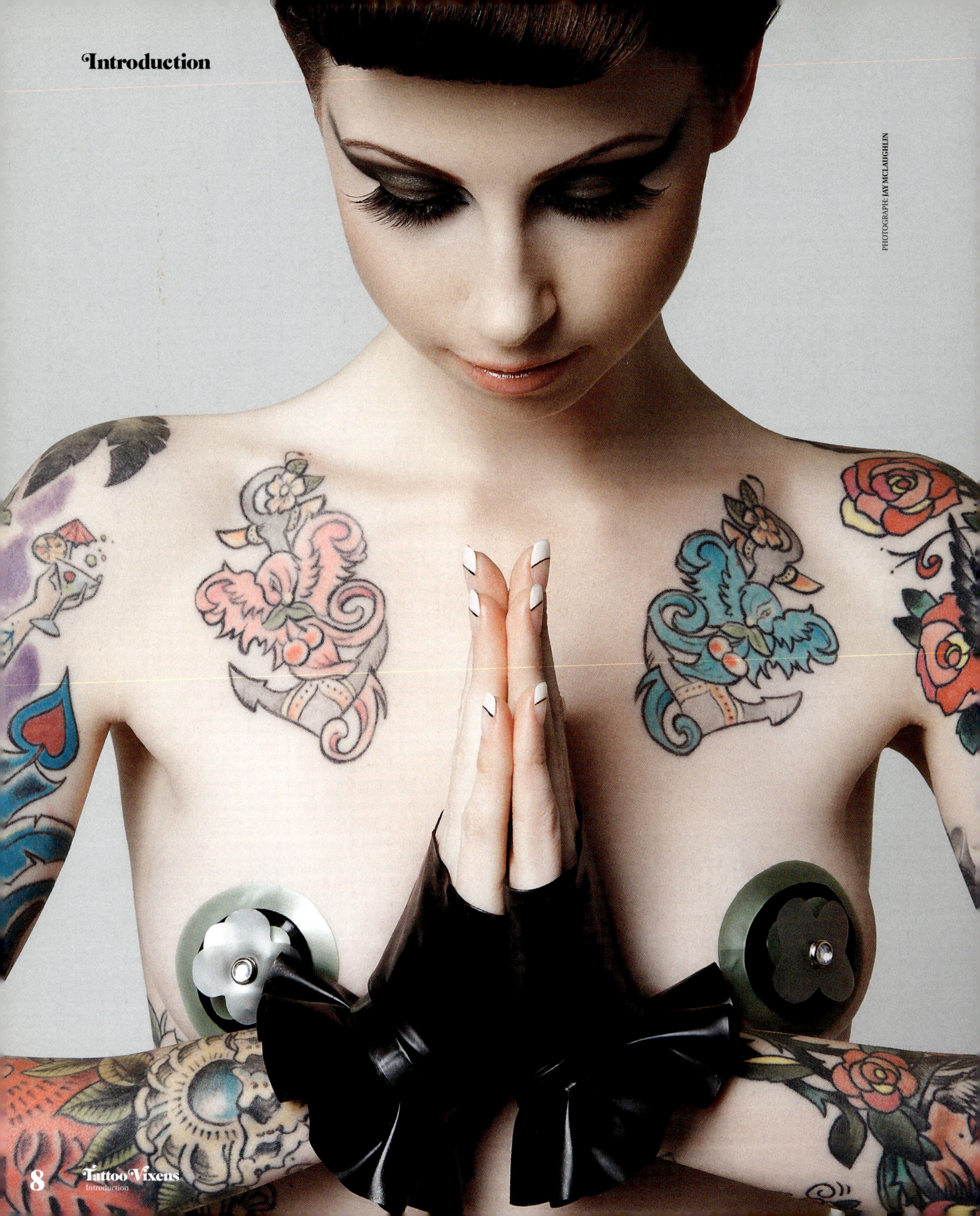

PHOTOGRAPH: JAY MCLAUGHLIN

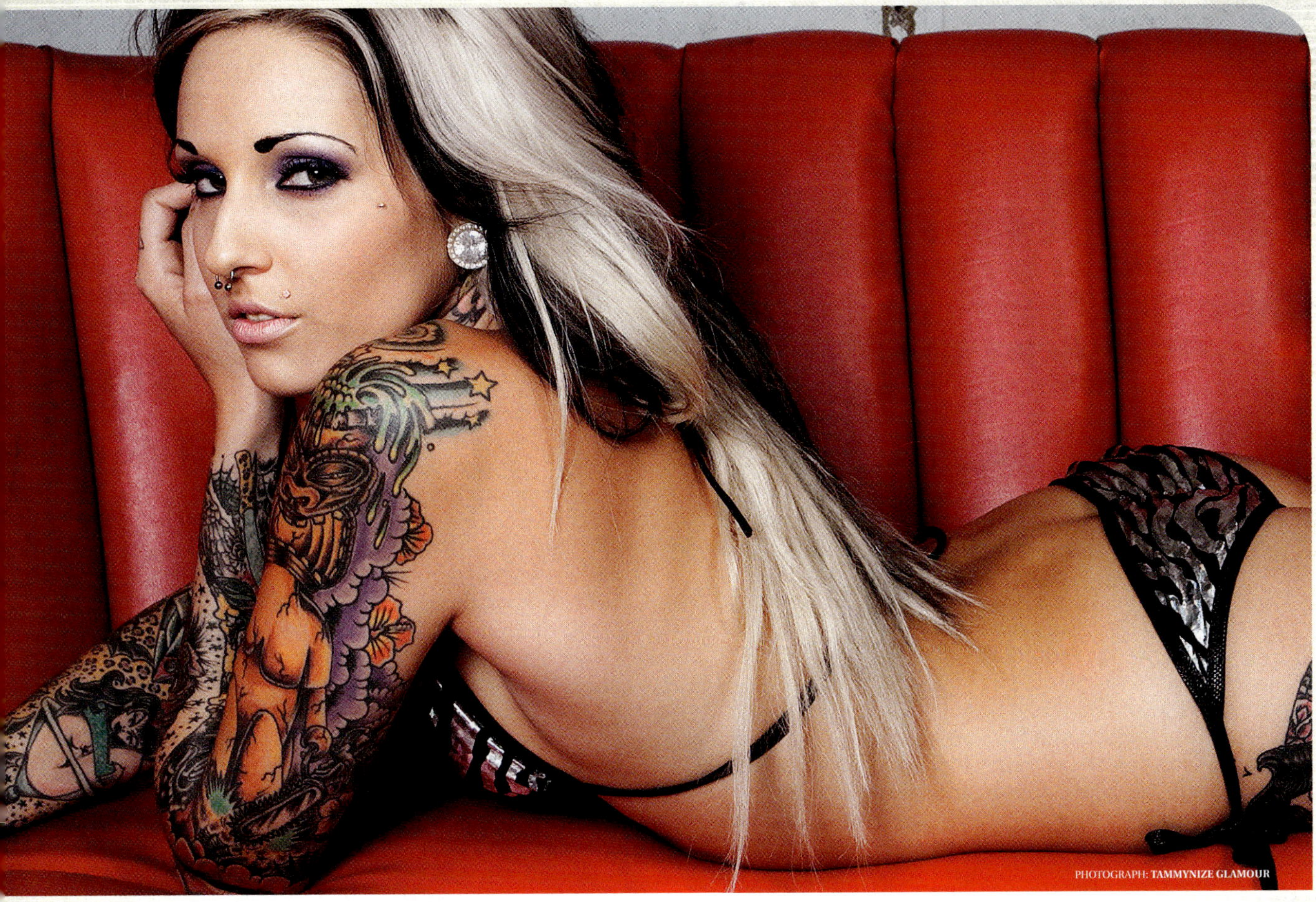

PHOTOGRAPH: TAMMYNIZE GLAMOUR

Where those who study humanity would be concerned with the psychology of why women would choose to illustrate themselves in this way, I understand that as human beings, we often enter into certain behaviour (for want of a better word) simply because it's there to join in with – we get drawn in to the very culture of the culture itself. This is how the Western world operates whether we are talking about television, music, fashion or indeed, tattooing. To dig deeper than this would require a university degree of some description and would also be totally pointless because as you will see, sometimes, even they don't know why. That's not to say no thought has gone into it – far from it – but there doesn't always have to be a deeper meaning to art. Such is the beauty of it. At its very best, art just 'is'.

'In the same way that tinkering with your car at the weekend does not make you a mechanic or getting together with some friends and playing your instruments does not automatically qualify you to be on the bill at Glastonbury, the same rules apply here.

As editor of Skin Deep tattoo magazine, I am approached daily with multiple requests to feature the tattooed bodies of women. Some of these are professional or part-time models. More often than not, it is the "girl next door" who will send in a picture – usually taken by their boyfriend in the kitchen. From this perspective, I feel that I have a responsibility to let them know that simply having a lot of tattoos does not make you an "authentic

It's not a flash in the pan attempt at becoming famous quickly. The hours are long, the pay isn't as great as you may think and conditions aren't always as luxurious as you might imagine either.

tattooed lady" – or indeed a model. I often think this may be hypocritical of me – after all, who am I to judge beauty that *really is* only skin deep? But in the same way that tinkering with your car at the weekend does not make you a mechanic or getting together with some friends and playing your instruments does not automatically qualify you to be on the bill at Glastonbury, the same rules apply here.

Every single woman in this book works damn hard at what they do. It's not a flash in the pan attempt at becoming famous quickly. The hours are long, the pay isn't as great as you may think and conditions aren't always as luxurious as you might imagine either. Which is a good place to take a moment to acknowledge all of the photographers in this book who all work hard on making those conditions as best as they possibly can.

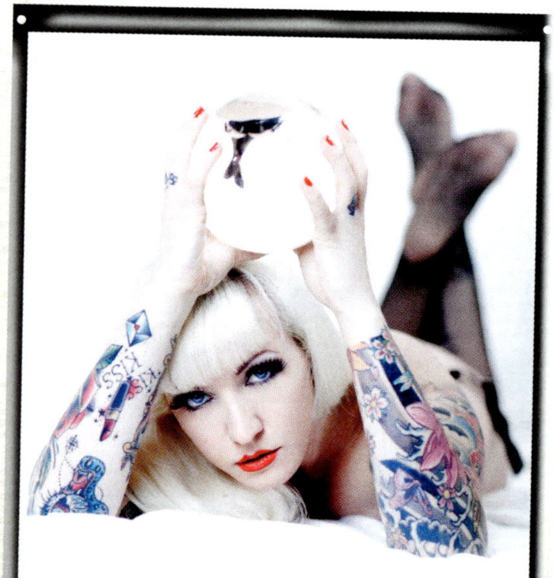

There's a certain swagger that goes with being a Vixen (do women swagger?). The ink is only half the story. The other half is how you live your life, how you portray yourself to the world at large. Somebody once commented to me that it was the most extreme form of burning your bra that a woman could ever go through. I don't know if that's what any of them actually think, maybe I should have asked, but it's certainly the impression I get. During the process of compiling Tattoo Vixens, I have found each of them massively independent that's for sure, but equally, each of them has gone out of their way to make sure our final product is as great as it can possibly be without being a diva about it.

So what does Vixens hold in store for the reader? Is it worth me laying it out on the table even! It will be a cold day in hell when you read this introduction before you've studied every single one of the Vixens themselves, but you may come back here afterwards.

We have full-time models who have reached a place in which they can make a living out of their bodies. This in itself is a major achievement. Not so many years ago, this would probably have been unfeasible but through hard work and determination, they have carved a niche out for themselves. There are also part-time models, although I really don't think they see themselves as this. Many are serious tattoo collectors who don't model in the true sense of the word but are well known simply for collecting. There are also collectors who have gone beyond the lens and taken on the role of photographers and collectors who combine being tattooed as part of their other lives as burlesque artists, nurses and well… you name it, there's a Vixen probably doing it somewhere.

When we started this project, it was difficult to know what to call it. It went through many different titles before we settled on Tattoo Vixens. This didn't go down well in all corners of the community and many whom we wished to feature backed out of the concept, deeming it something of a derogatory term, but it certainly was never intended that way. It's more of a collective and affectionate term and hand on heart, I can honestly say that it fits perfectly.

Thus, I present to you, the finest selection of Vixens we could find. Don't be surprised if this sign of the times is followed up by subsequent volumes – this rolling stone is showing no sign of slowing down now.

Sion Smith
Editor

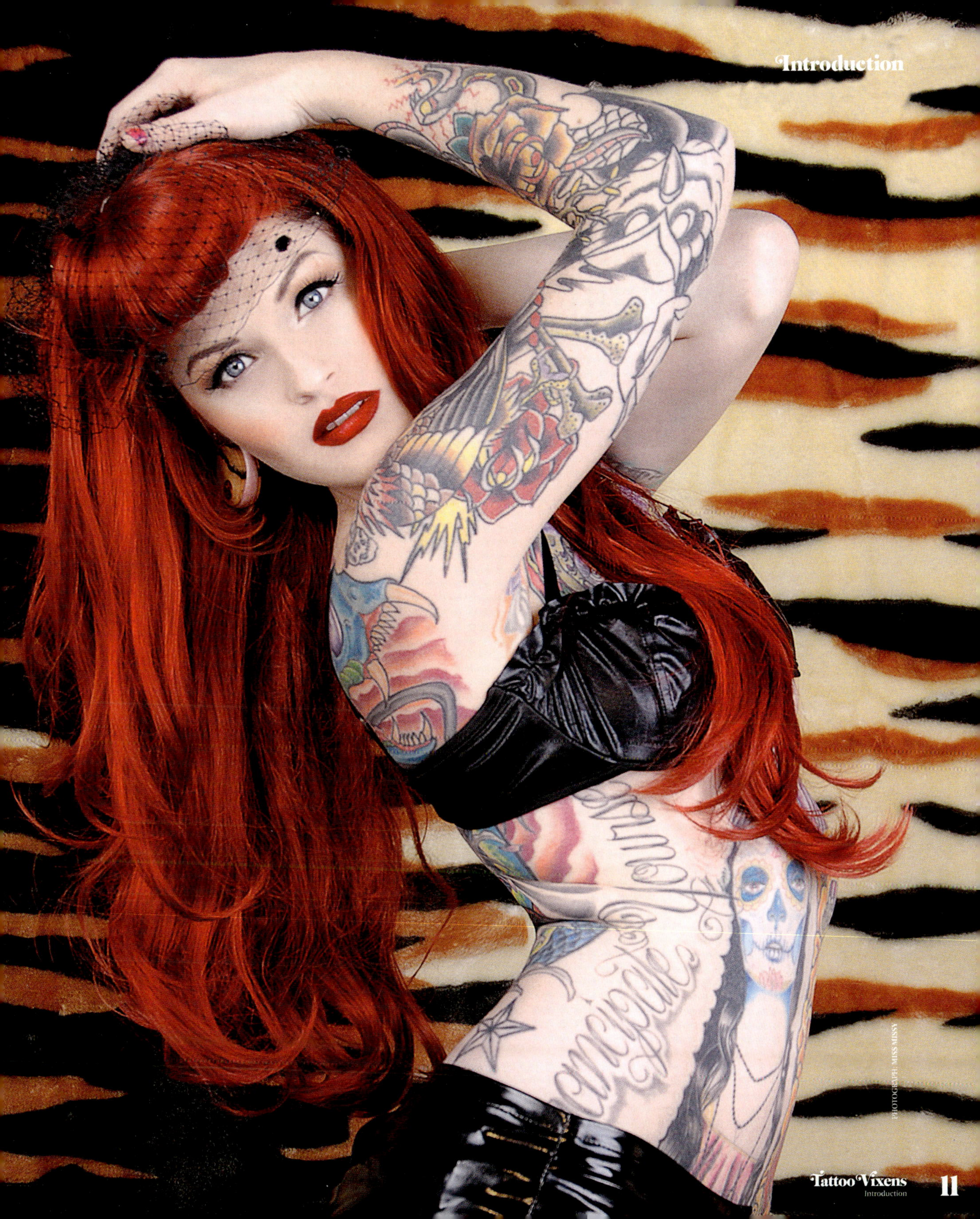

PHOTOGRAPH: MISS MISSY

The Girls Next Door

PAULA HARDY KANGELOS

The tattoo is a powerful talisman, imbibed with mystery, historical significance and undeniable power. Those that dedicate their bodies and lives to the ancient art carry with them that mystery.

While tattooing in general is hugely popular, large-scale tattoos on women remain somewhat rare and thus the idea of the tattooed lady remains special. From legendary sideshow performer to modern-day icon, tattooed women are a special kind of tattoo enthusiast. Once we were to feared and bravery was required before you dared to peep at the circus lady, now we are enviable, strong symbols of independence, unafraid to reject conventions and fearless in the face of perceived permanence.

The idea of the collecting is one that everyone is familiar with, most of us had a childhood obsession, mine was scented rubbers in ridiculous shapes and collecting tattoos is not so different to stamps or classic cars.

The tattooed lady's body continually ignores the most basic requirements of posterity, for there is the paradox of the tattoo. The mark is permanent, but the canvas is not. It is only with an eye beyond our own mortality that we can be freed from the fear of the indelible, to be tattooed is to say I'm living in the present, embracing the here and now. This anthology of tattooed ladies is perfect for the contemporary moment.

Having a tattoo and being tattooed are quite different but the defining factor is not necessarily quantity –rather, it's a feeling or an attitude, you don't need two full sleeves and a back piece to be a tattooed lady and although many of us do have near-to-total coverage, it's not a requisite for entry to our ranks - all you need is for your tattoos to be a love affair, a passion - for them to be a huge part of your day-to-day existence.

The idea of the collecting is one that everyone is familiar with, most of us had a childhood obsession, mine was scented rubbers in ridiculous shapes and collecting tattoos is not so different to stamps or classic cars. You need contacts and research and a constant ear-to-the-ground mentality, you must be willing to act as soon as a desired item becomes available - only rather than watching an online auction, the tattoo collector must scour magazines and convention listings for the prized piece.

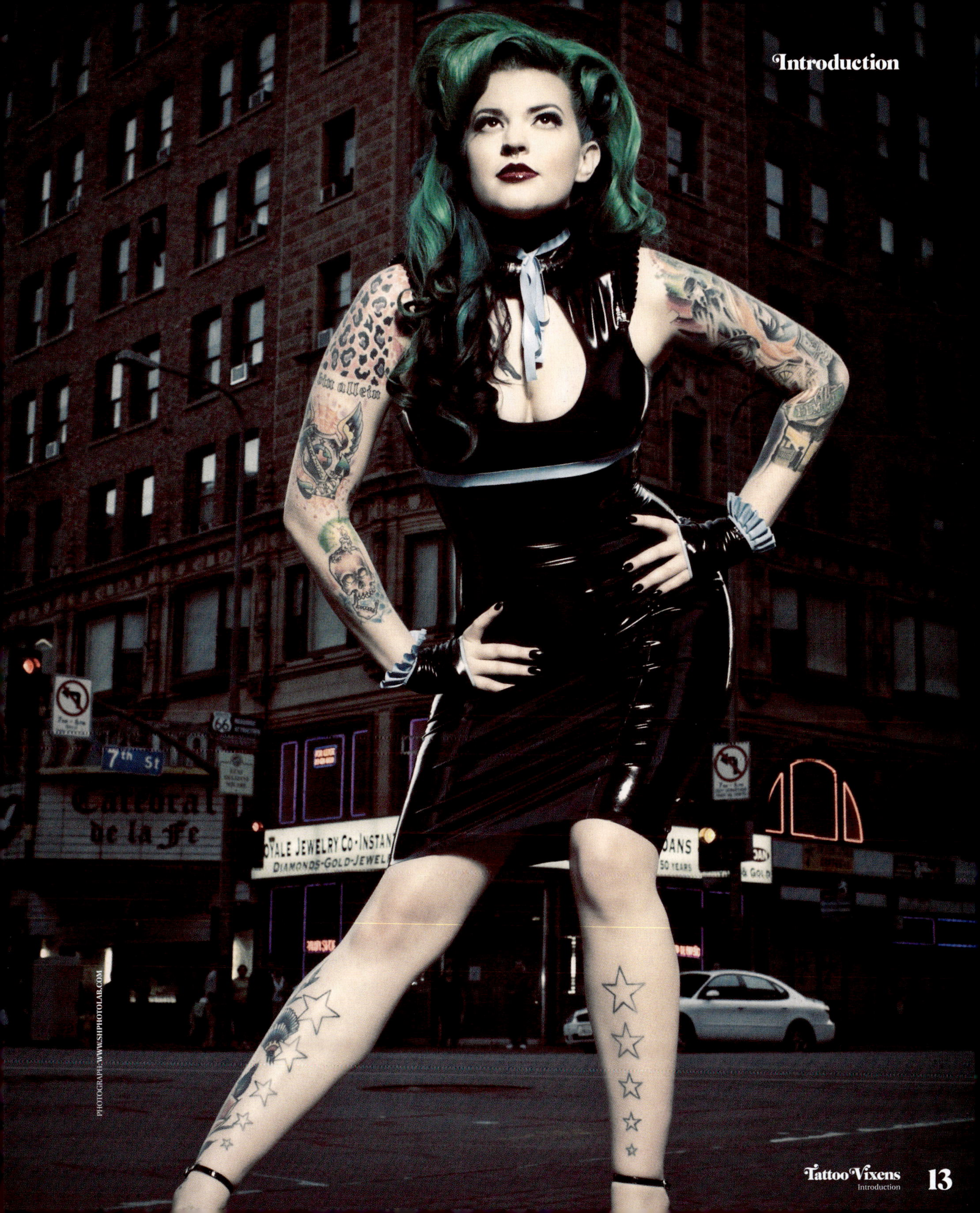

PHOTOGRAPH: WWW.SHIPHOTOLAB.COM

The tattoo is the connector between inside and outside, body and mind, so our decorative choices can reveal our joys and sadness, favourite music and images, our families and our hopes and dreams, we can etch our secret selves onto our public bodies, showing everyone who we really are.

Tattoo collecting involves many resources, time, dedication, money, endurance – many of us forgo expensive cars and far-flung holidays in order to sport the very best in ink, it's a commitment, a lifestyle, it's a big, big love.

So why have women embraced this commitment with such fervour? It's a complicated question and it's not possible to generalise such myriad people in a paragraph, tattooed women are varied and complex, but perhaps we have things in common.

Historically women have been the makers of family albums and scrapbooks, the organisers of a familial visual anthology. We've also felt societal pressure dictate on how we should look, what we should buy or wear to be pretty – so combining a beauty rebellion with a scrapbook, of the personal – to become tattooed seems natural, desirable. For if the gaze is fixed upon us, our tattoos create a defiant statement that returns that gaze, questions it and returns it.

All bodies, like albums, start as a blank; it is through accumulation, collecting and experiencing that the blanks are filled. The body, like the scrapbook is a repository for autographs, the names of lovers are etched onto us through memory, whether we choose to make the mark visible or not, those that touch us, the mistakes we make and the paths we choose are indelible marks upon ourselves and to make our life choices into tattoos is to embrace them and own them. To display them is to show pride.

The tattoo is the connector between inside and outside, body and mind, so our decorative choices can reveal our joys and sadness, favourite music and

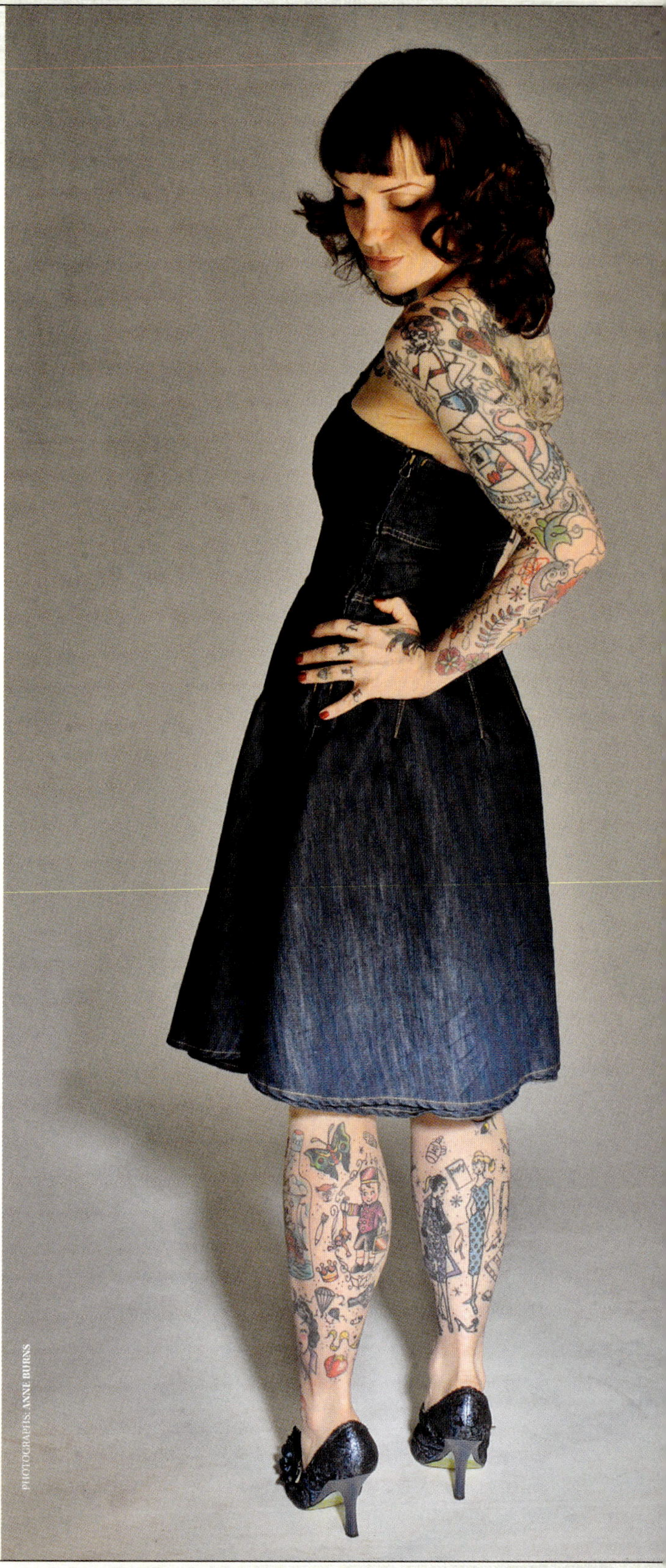

PHOTOGRAPHS: ANNE BURNS

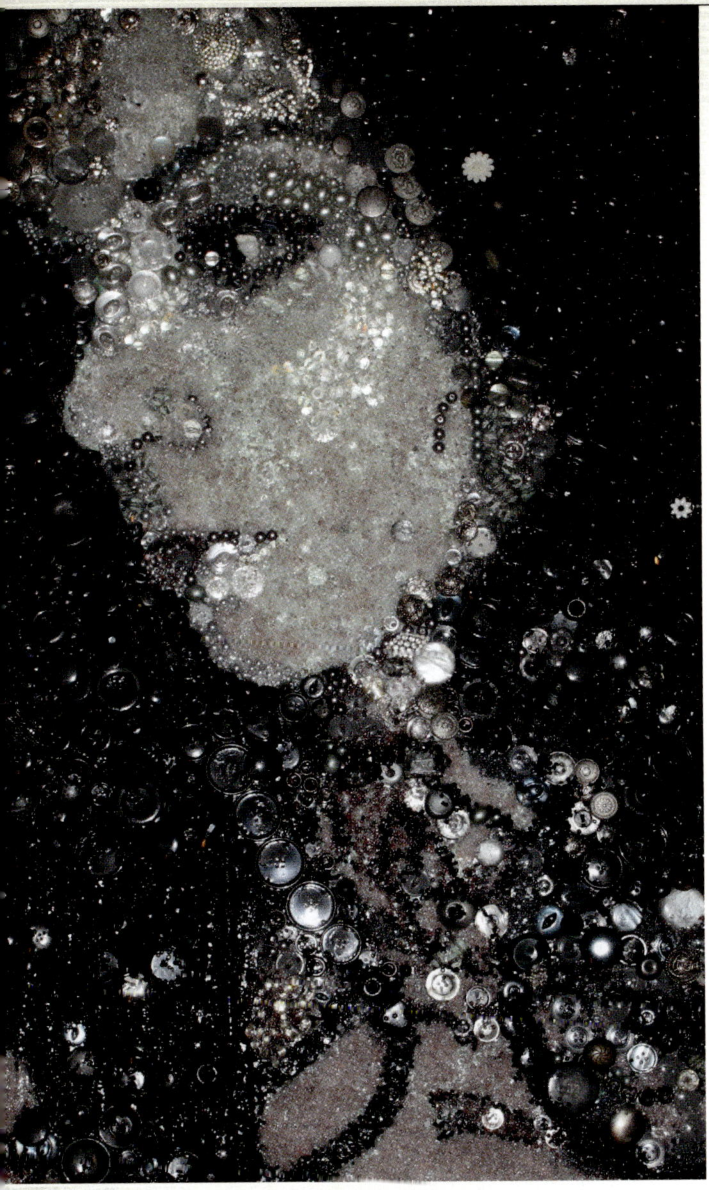

images, our families and our hopes and dreams, we can etch our secret selves onto our public bodies, showing everyone who we really are.

Being a tattoo collector, curating images on skin the way an exhibition is put together has never been a male preserve. Despite the sailors and criminals association, women have always modelled body modifications, from tribal pasts through circus sideshows and onto and into every high street, PTA and profession. Nurses, teachers, stay-at-home mums, boardroom executives, together we navigate our artwork through our everyday existence answering questions and locking eyes with those that challenge us.

Of course, it's still not always appropriate to be out and proud with our skin art. Some us must hide our tattoos to work in a professional environment, revealing them only during our personal lives or at the occasional staff party. Other tattooed ladies have found a way for their tattoos to co-exist peacefully with their careers, and some of us have transformed our passion into our jobs, tattooed ladies are out there making tattoos, writing about tattoos and forging alternative modelling careers where beautiful ink and large-scale coverage is a bonus, not a drawback.

All of the women featured here have rejected notions of mainstream beauty, some outright, some choosing to play with and subvert the bombshell stereotype. Tattooed ladies are a wide-ranging group with just one thing in common, we're not afraid to walk outside of the parameters of the ideal. I'm proud to be introducing this book; my sisters in ink are interesting and independent, talented and beautiful, out of the ordinary and into the amazing.

Tattoo Vixens presents an opportunity for everyone to discover the bodies and minds of the ladies that dedicate themselves to decoration.

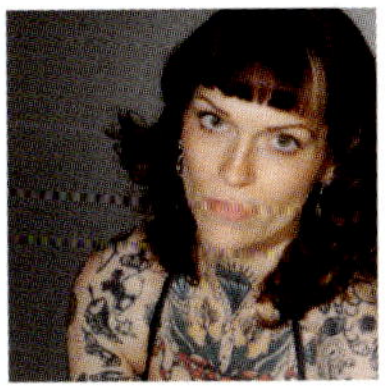

Paula Hardy Kangelos has studied Fine Art at Goldsmiths College (BA) and Manchester School of Art (MA). Born in Hertfordshire in 1976 she lives and works in Manchester where she avoids making artistic statements by telling stories and talking about things she likes, such as tattoos and haberdashery.

Working almost exclusively with images of tattooed women, Paula utilises found objects, such as beads and buttons and images found on social networking sites to make painstaking "paintings" of tattooed ladies worldwide. This time consuming practise reflects the endurance required during the tattooed subjects own transformative process and the use of found objects is indicative of the culture of collecting.

Paula is inspired by tattoos and tattooed people, childhood stories, random collections, things left at bus stops, her Sunday School teacher and the mice in Bagpuss and has said that she wishes her work to be as authentic as the tattooed mark. She believes that the body is the ultimate found object.

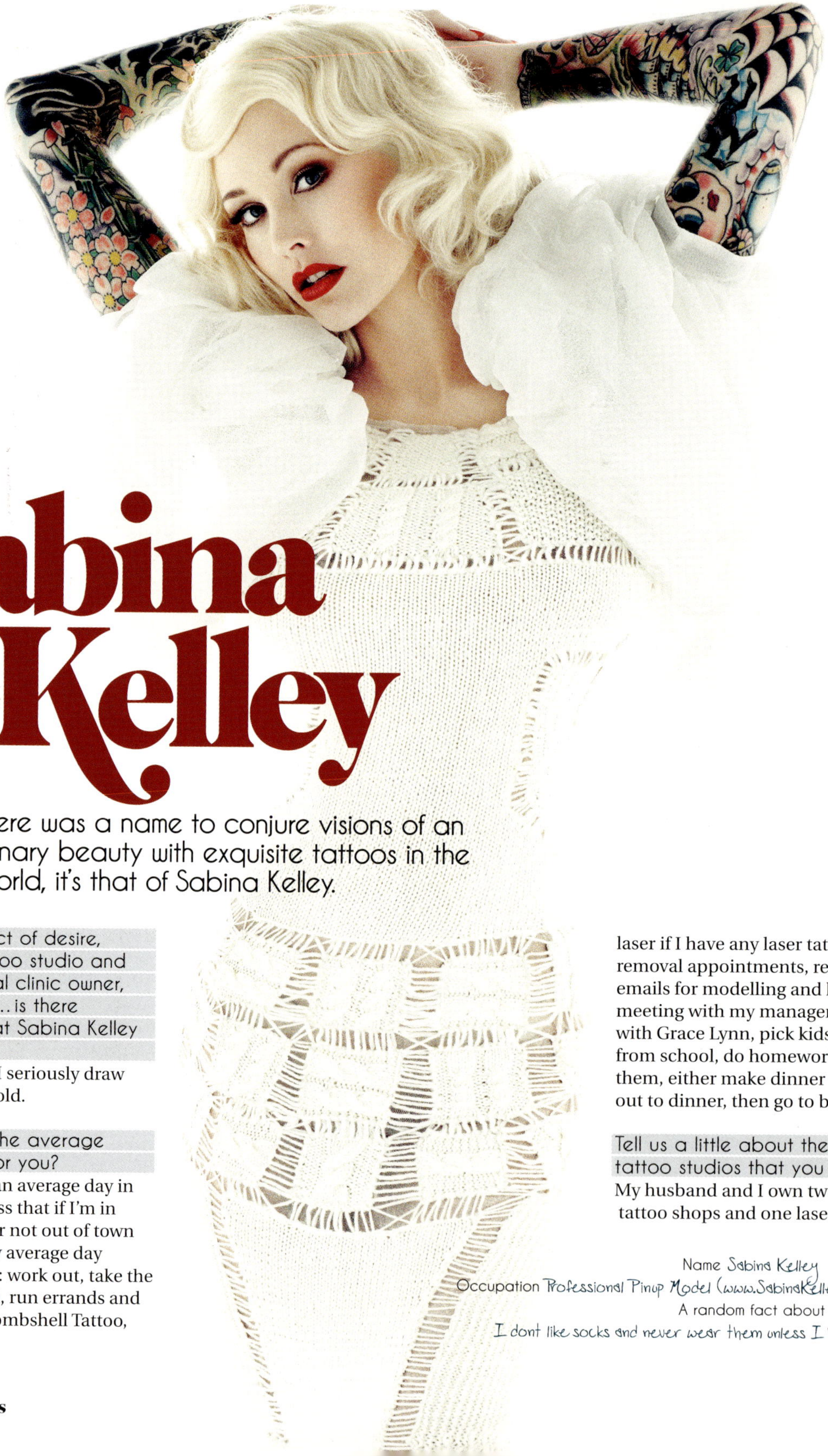

PHOTOGRAPHER: JASON LERACE

Sabina Kelley

If ever there was a name to conjure visions of an extraordinary beauty with exquisite tattoos in the pin-up world, it's that of Sabina Kelley.

Pin-up/object of desire, dancer, tattoo studio and laser removal clinic owner, mother, wife... is there anything that Sabina Kelley can't do?
I can't draw! I seriously draw like a 5-year-old.

What does the average day entail for you?
I never have an average day in my life. I guess that if I'm in the country or not out of town modelling my average day would be this: work out, take the kids to school, run errands and check in at Bombshell Tattoo, laser if I have any laser tattoo removal appointments, return emails for modelling and have a meeting with my manager, play with Grace Lynn, pick kids up from school, do homework with them, either make dinner or go out to dinner, then go to bed.

Tell us a little about the tattoo studios that you own.
My husband and I own two tattoo shops and one laser

Name Sabina Kelley Age 32
Occupation Professional Pinup Model (www.SabinaKelley.com)
A random fact about yourself
I dont like socks and never wear them unless I have to.

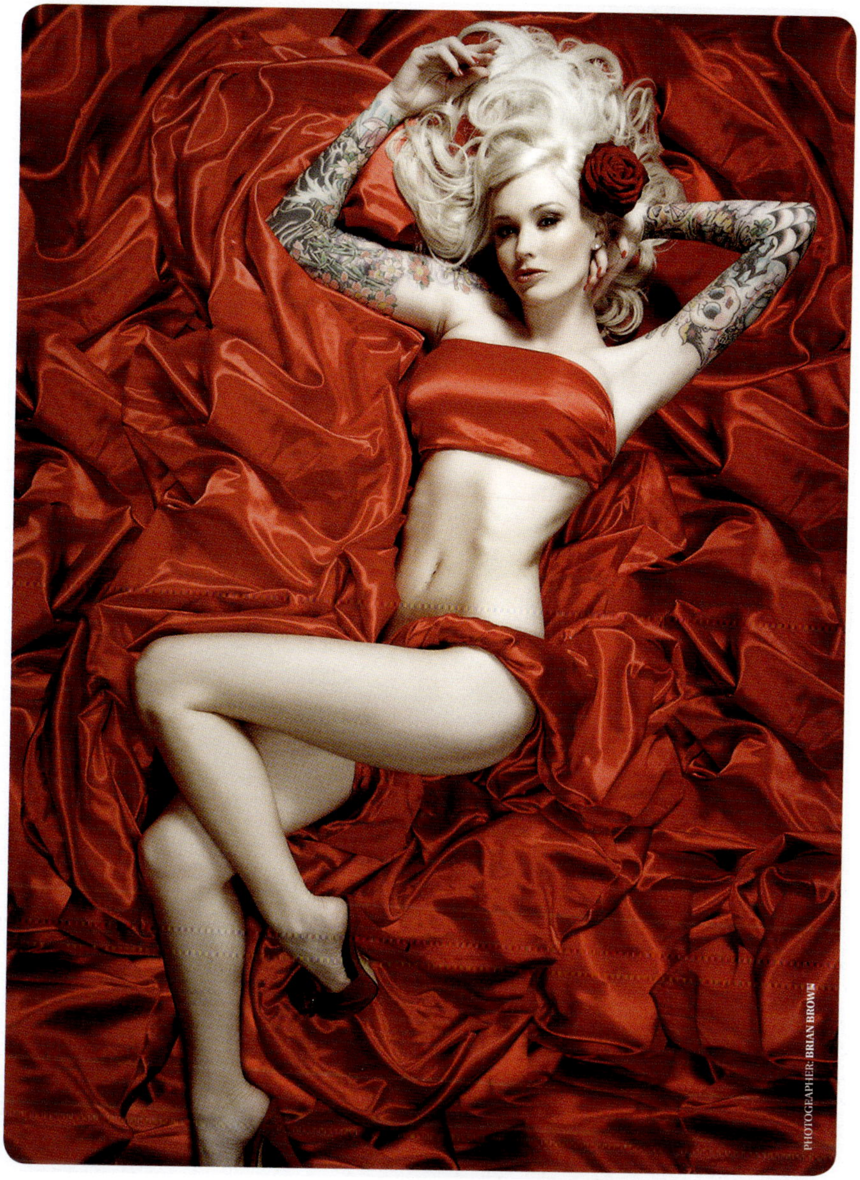
PHOTOGRAPHER: BRIAN BROWN

My career as a model really took off about 8 years ago. I began doing a few pin-up shoots and doing some covers and my career just snowballed and kept getting bigger and bigger.

tattoo removal shop. My husband runs Staytrue Tattoo Parlor (*www.MySpace.com/StaytrueTattooParlor*) which is an appointment-only shop and usually only does large tattoos. Then I run Bombshell Tattoo Parlor (*www.BombshellTattooParlor.com*) which is in the Fashion Show Mall in Las Vegas, inside the Bettie Page Clothing store. My shop is more of a walk-in shop. Then I do laser tattoo removal at Carey Hart's warehouse (*www.BombshellTattooRemoval.com*). I only work there one day week, appointments only. I just got awarded Best Tattoo Removal place in Vegas.

How did your career as a model take off?

My career as a model really took off about 8 years ago. I began doing a few pin-up shoots and doing some covers and my career just snowballed and kept getting bigger and bigger.

Did being sleeved make it more difficult to pick up modelling work in the early days of your career?

Yes, having tattoos definitely made it harder to get modelling jobs. Tattoos were not as acceptable then as they are now. I used to have photographers threaten they would not shoot me anymore if I got more tattoos. When I first started modelling, I only had one quarter sleeve, so photographers could pose me to look like I had no tattoos, or Photoshop them out. I listened to no one and did what I wanted, and got more tattoos and broke a lot of boundaries shooting with photographers and companies that would normally not shoot with tattooed models. I've been really lucky and really successful, which is not normal if you are heavily tattooed. In NO way did my tattoos make my modelling career easier.

Do you still partake in a lot of burlesque work, or have modelling commitments got in the way of late?

My modelling has taken over the last few years and burlesque got put on the backburner. I have just recently started rehearsing again, and will be performing again before you know it. Dancing was my life before modelling and I really miss it.

The images from the photo shoots you did whilst pregnant are simply incredible. Are you still really pleased that you did those shots?

I love the images I shot when I was pregnant. I definitely did not think I looked too cute being pregnant, but it is pretty neat to have photos of myself during that time to show the kids when they grow up.

You've attended the London Tattoo Convention a few times: what did you think of the UK's take on tattooing?

I have been to the London Tattoo Convention three times

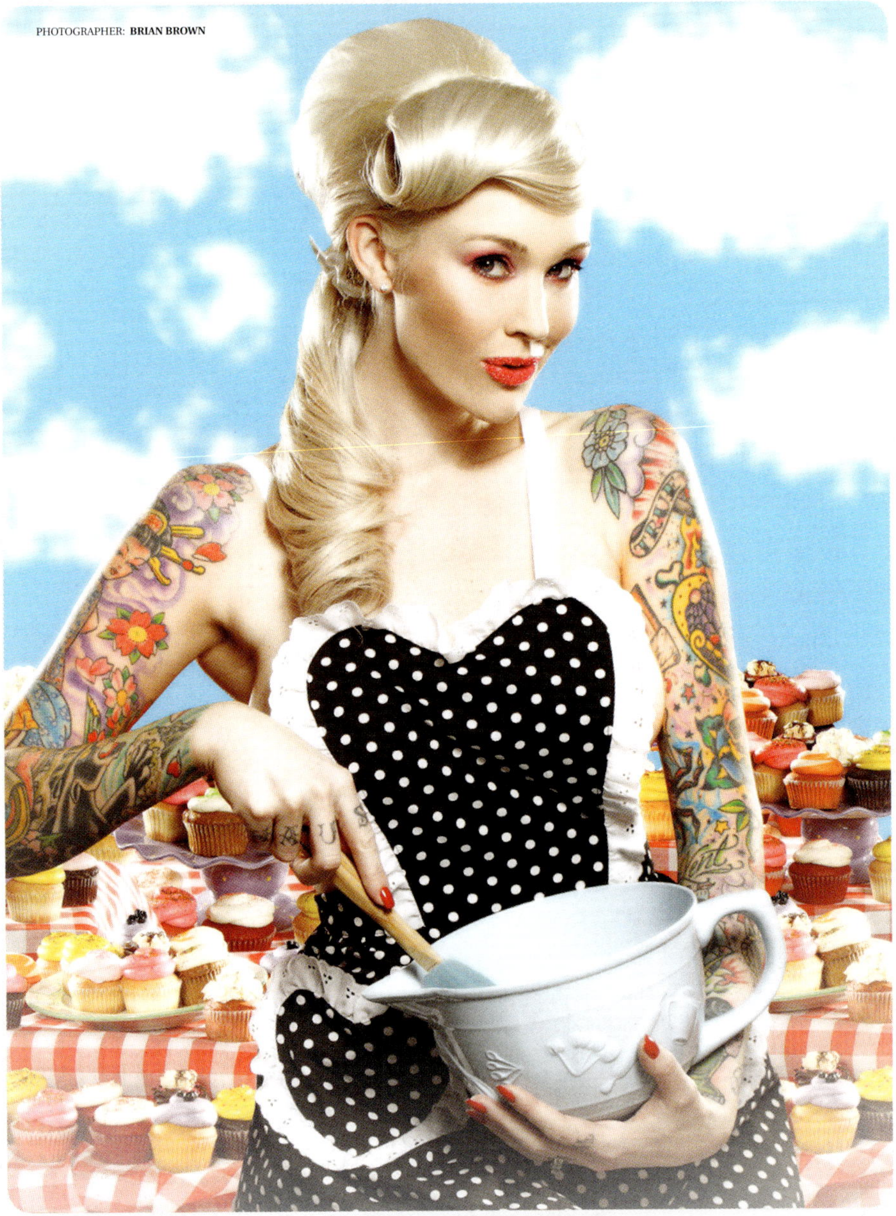

PHOTOGRAPHER: **BRIAN BROWN**

I've been really lucky and really successful, which is not normal if you are heavily tattooed. In NO way did my tattoos make my modelling career easier.

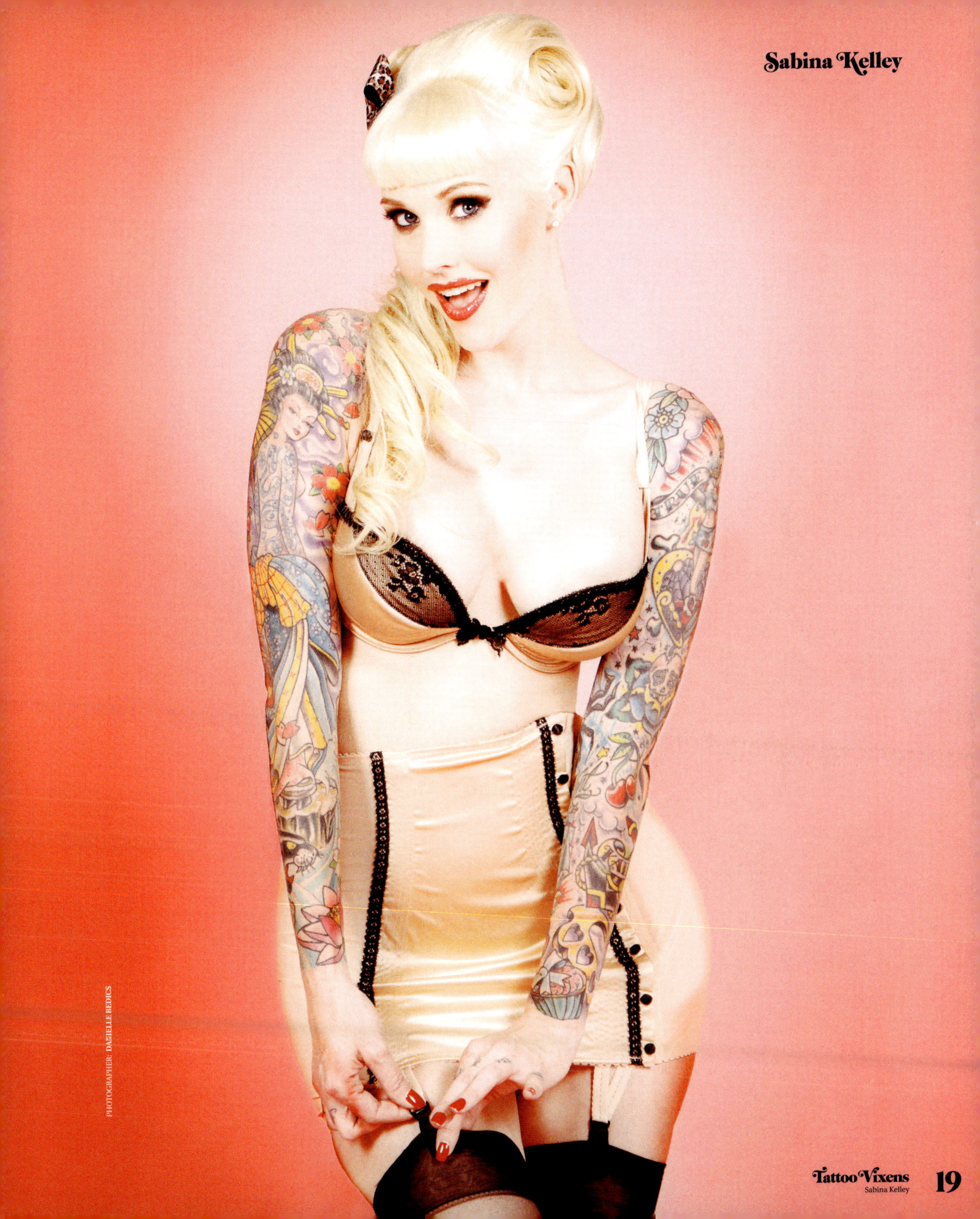

PHOTOGRAPHER: DANIELLE BEDICS

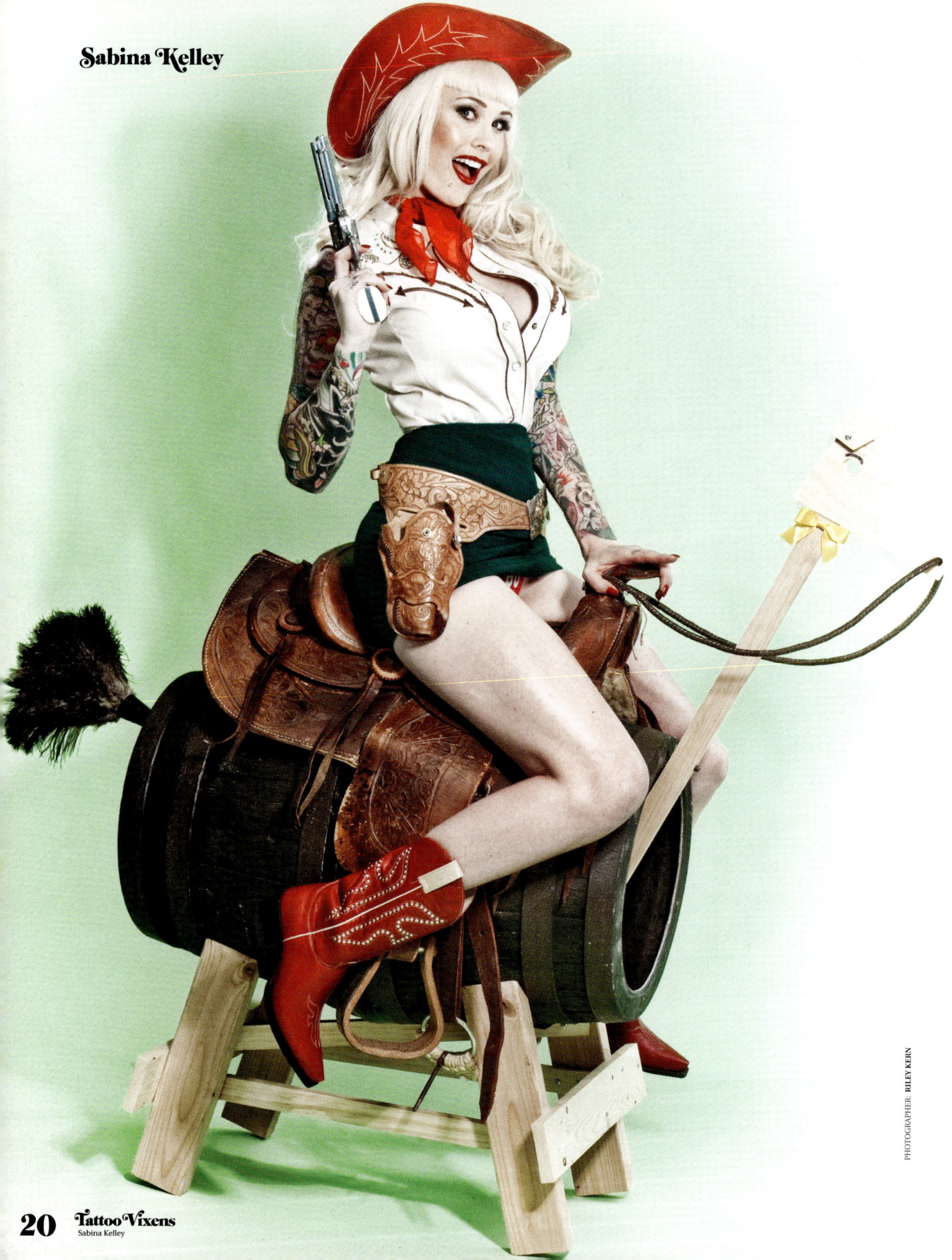

PHOTOGRAPHER: RILEY KERN

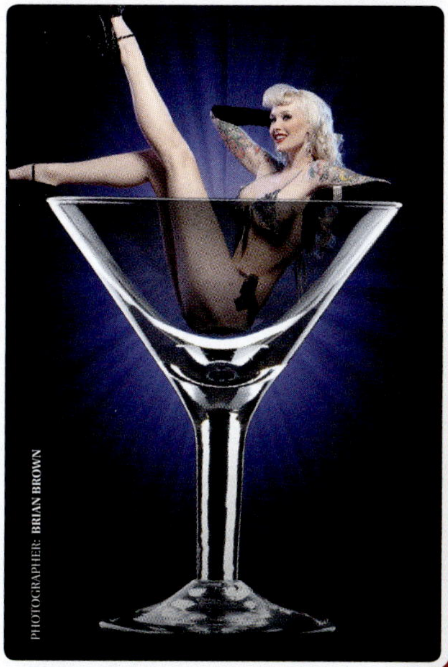
PHOTOGRAPHER: BRIAN BROWN

I would like to get some more work from my incredible husband Kent Kelley and then maybe some more work from Mister Cartoon.

now. I was first there as the calendar girl in 2006, then as the awards girl in 2007, then the awards girl again in 2009. I love the London Tattoo Convention. It is one of my favourite tattoo conventions in the whole world. That convention always has the best and biggest name artists, plus Miki Vialetto that puts it on is amazing!

Which tattoo artists do you hope to collect work from in the future?
I would like to get some more work from my incredible husband Kent Kelley and then maybe some more work from Mister Cartoon.

You are undoubtedly one of the world's sexiest women - do you have any words for your legions of admirers?
I want to thank all of my family, friends, and fans. You are all so amazing and I could not have done all of this with out your love and support. I love you all!

If you had a day off, how would you spend the time?
I would hangout with my kids and eat lots of ice cream.

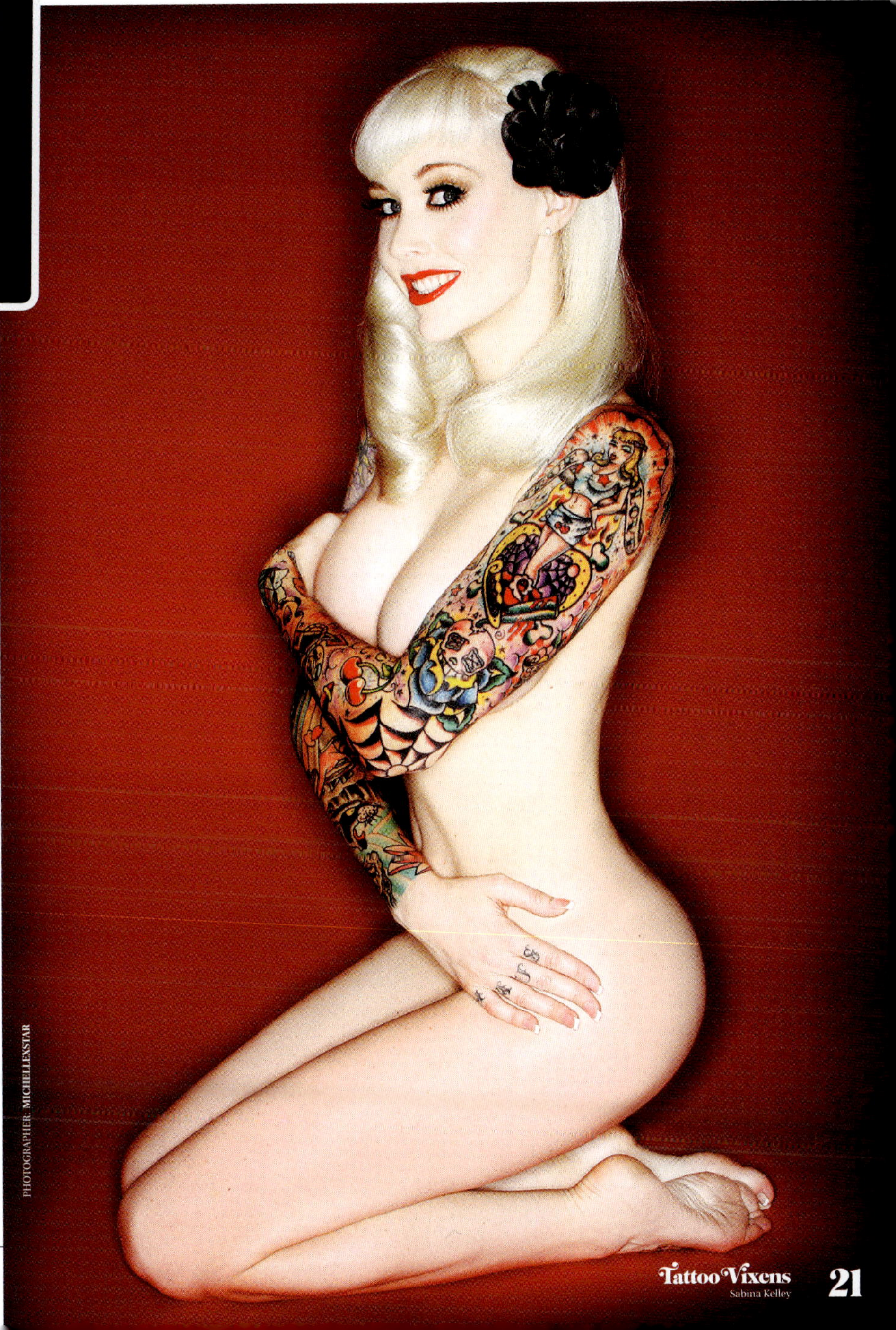
PHOTOGRAPHER: MICHELLEXSTAR

Lady Kitty Meoww

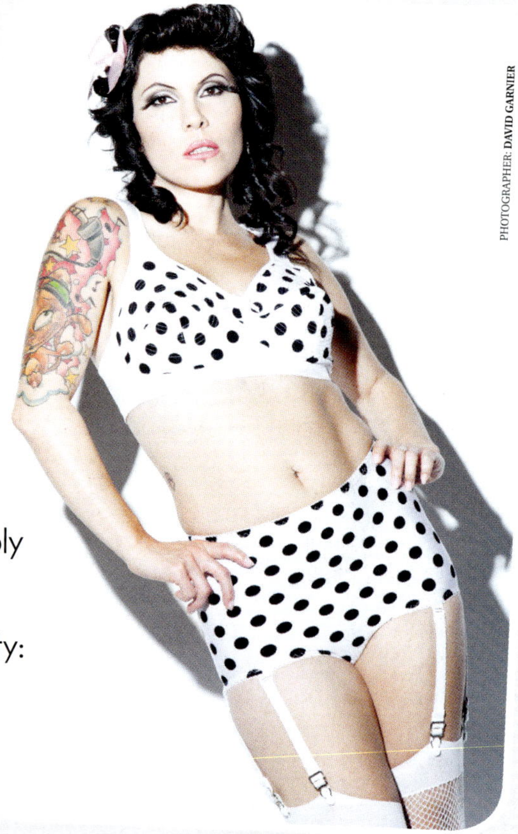

PHOTOGRAPHER: DAVID GARNIER

When it comes to class and style, there will probably be no argument that Paris is a world leader in this arena - so it came as no surprise when we came across the French/Vietnamese bombshell that is Kitty:

Can you tell us your story – how did your journey with tattoo art start?

Oh well it's a long way back. I was working in England in a cosmetic factory at the time and I was getting bored and nothing was happening, so one lunchtime I decided to go and have a look at the tattoo shop. I went for a stroll and ended up coming back with my first little tattoo on my foot, that was the beginning of the whole spiral! It was a small Chinese sign which mean't "Tiger" and the addiction then started!

Are you a big music fan?

I have been in the music scene from a very young age, I was going out clubbing in the eighties and music at that time was a big deal, it still is now but it's simply not the same anymore. Later, I became a DJ and played at many small events, parties, and festival but this didn't really last – I got bored of it all and moved on. Then I got into producing music and I released a track on an American label 2 years ago. I was also a PR for two music labels (Techno – House) which are still working strong.

Talking of stories – what's with the squid photograph?

Oh that "Squid"! I don't think there was any thought behind this idea, my head is always full up of ideas, projects, creations to be done and the squid was a part of them. In fact I was supposed to shoot in Vegas with a photographer who makes great imagery but he canceled so I think in my head I had to do it anyway. Bear in mind that I did this concept already years ago with another photographer, this time it was more like a little blink to the Vegas idea. I hate unachieved concepts, so that's the reason – or maybe I just have a fetish for smelly, squishy, slimy animals.

Where do you plan to go next with your art? Are you done? Is that enough for you or are you on waiting lists around the world to get the rest of you filled in?

I thought I was done with this for now but in fact I want a little bit more, so I will have a piece by Davee Von D from Poland. I'll try to have the full sleeve in colors – I can't wait, his art is so amazing and then I will have some more work done by Olivier Julliand from Glamort Tattoo Parlor in Montréal, the tattoo artist who did my arm of course when he comes over to Europe and has some spare time for me. I love his art, he's also really kind and talented and then I think I might stop after that. But maybe not!

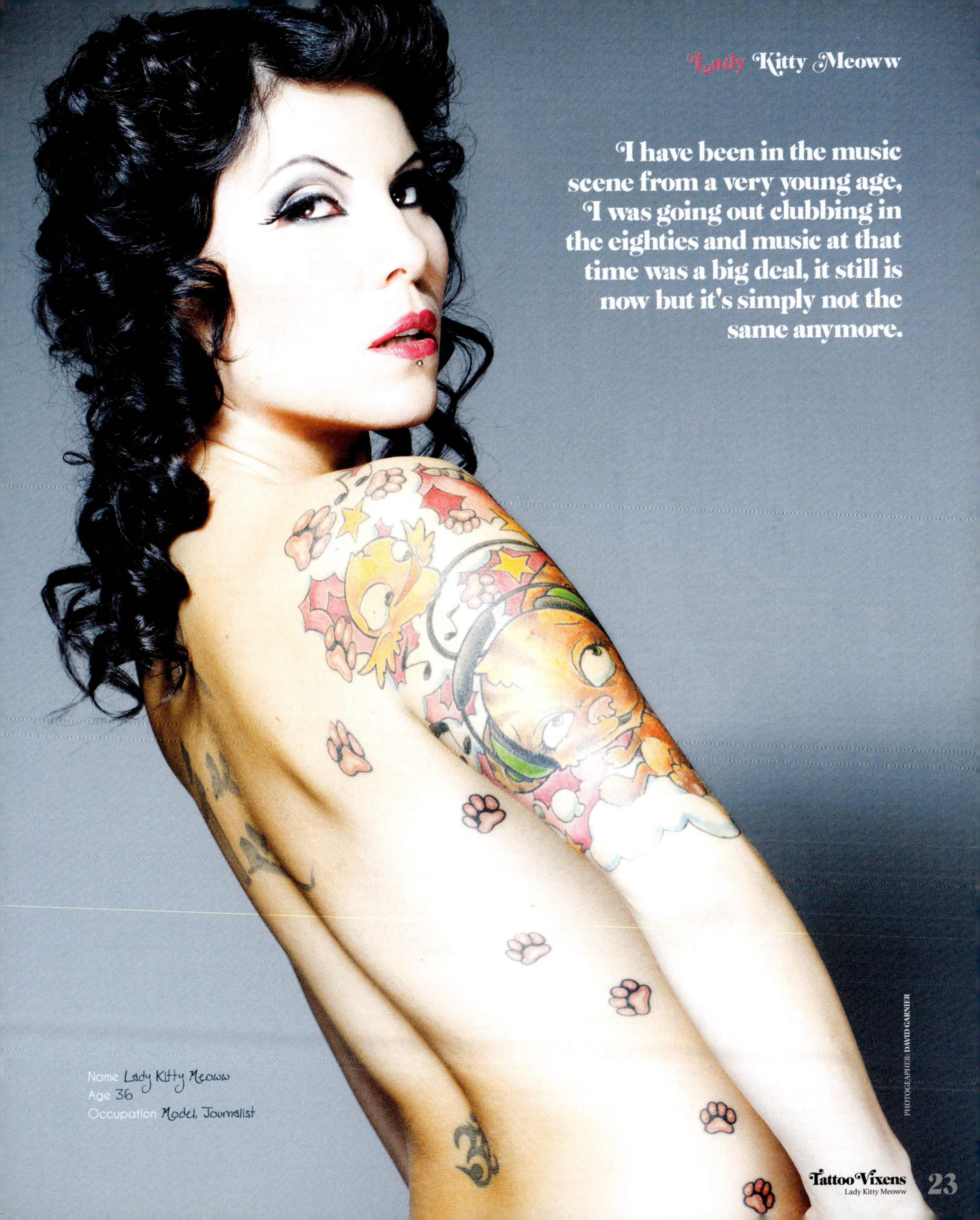

Lady Kitty Meoww

I have been in the music scene from a very young age, I was going out clubbing in the eighties and music at that time was a big deal, it still is now but it's simply not the same anymore.

Name Lady Kitty Meoww
Age 36
Occupation Model, Journalist

PHOTOGRAPHER: DAVID GARNIER

I get bored and need to constantly find some new things to do like meeting new people and seeing exciting landscapes and horizons...

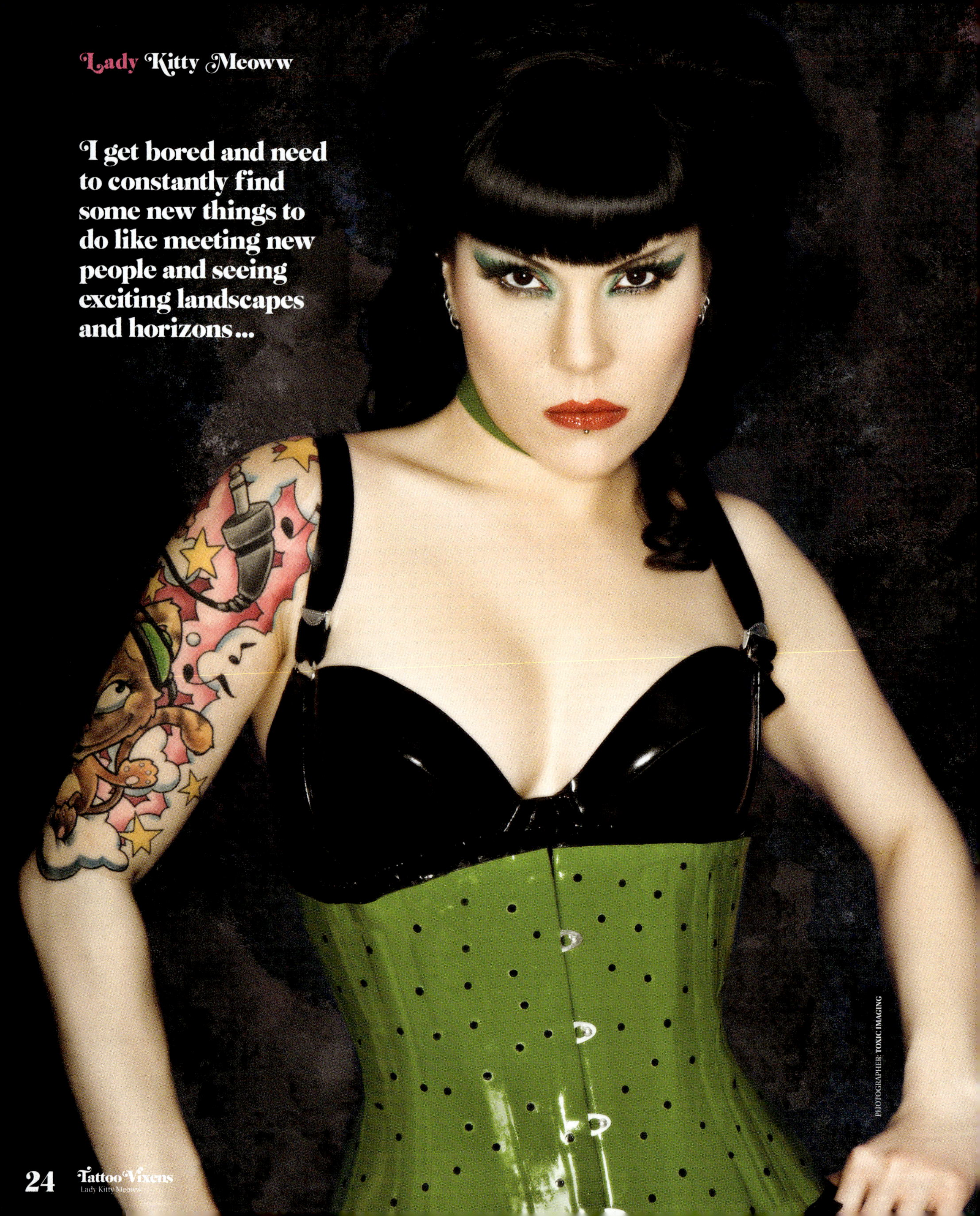

PHOTOGRAPHER: TOXIC IMAGING

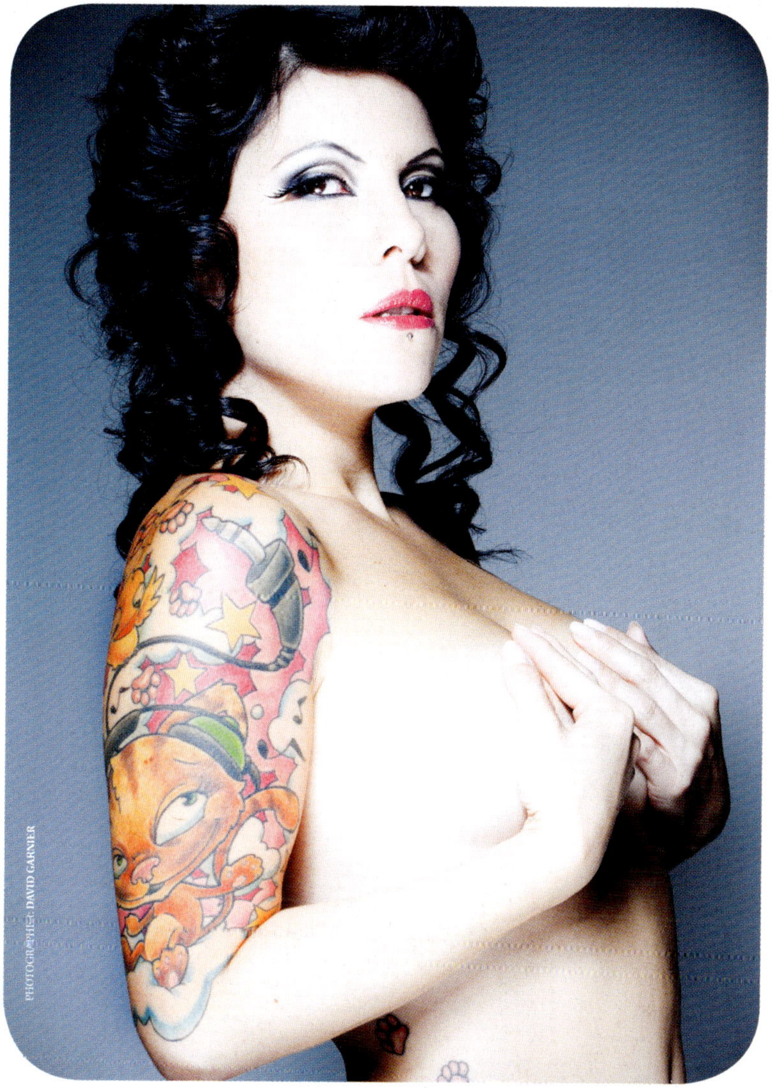
PHOTOGRAPHER: DAVID GARNIER

What's a typical day for you? Are you just starting out on this adventure and running a day job as well or is this a full time gig?

A typical day always starts with a cup of tea and some marmite on toast. I lived in England for almost 10 years and I got some bad habits! Then either I go for a shoot or to film and make some interviews for my boyfriend's web-tv Addict-tv which is now another one of my activities. Apart from that, I do have a part time job from time to time especially when I want to go on holidays. This summer I went to the US so I needed some extra shopping money. So I work on the side to be able to have more fun when I'm away!

... and what are your plans for the future? Is this the future or is there a different dream at the end of the rainbow?

I'm always in a dream, unfortunately I'm never really totally happy where I am. I get bored and need to constantly find some new things to do like meeting new people and seeing exciting landscapes and horizons so in the near future I think I might move away from Paris and get closer to the sunshine by moving to California. I'm in love with the place and I believe I'll have much more fun there than over here…

Some of our models in the book grew up around tattoos and it was only a matter of getting to be old enough to carry on the tradition – others came into it as a form of rebellion – which side of the fence do you sit on or do you have a different path?

As you can see I'm not as young as I seem! I've been around for a while, my tattoos have never been a form of rebellion for me, they have just grown on me with the years, they are just particular aspects of what I like in life. My tattoos are a part of me – they're not related to a gang, a religion, a political party or anything like this. They are simply all about what I am and what I want to be.

You have some unique French/Vietnamese genes – do you find that's a big advantage for you when it comes to finding certain kinds of work.

You're right, my father is Vietnamese and my mother was French – poor lady she doesn't belong to this world anymore – bless her! I don't think it's because of my genes but rather because of the way I look that people always say that I have an unusual look and face, by the way I don't really look Vietnamese – I just look

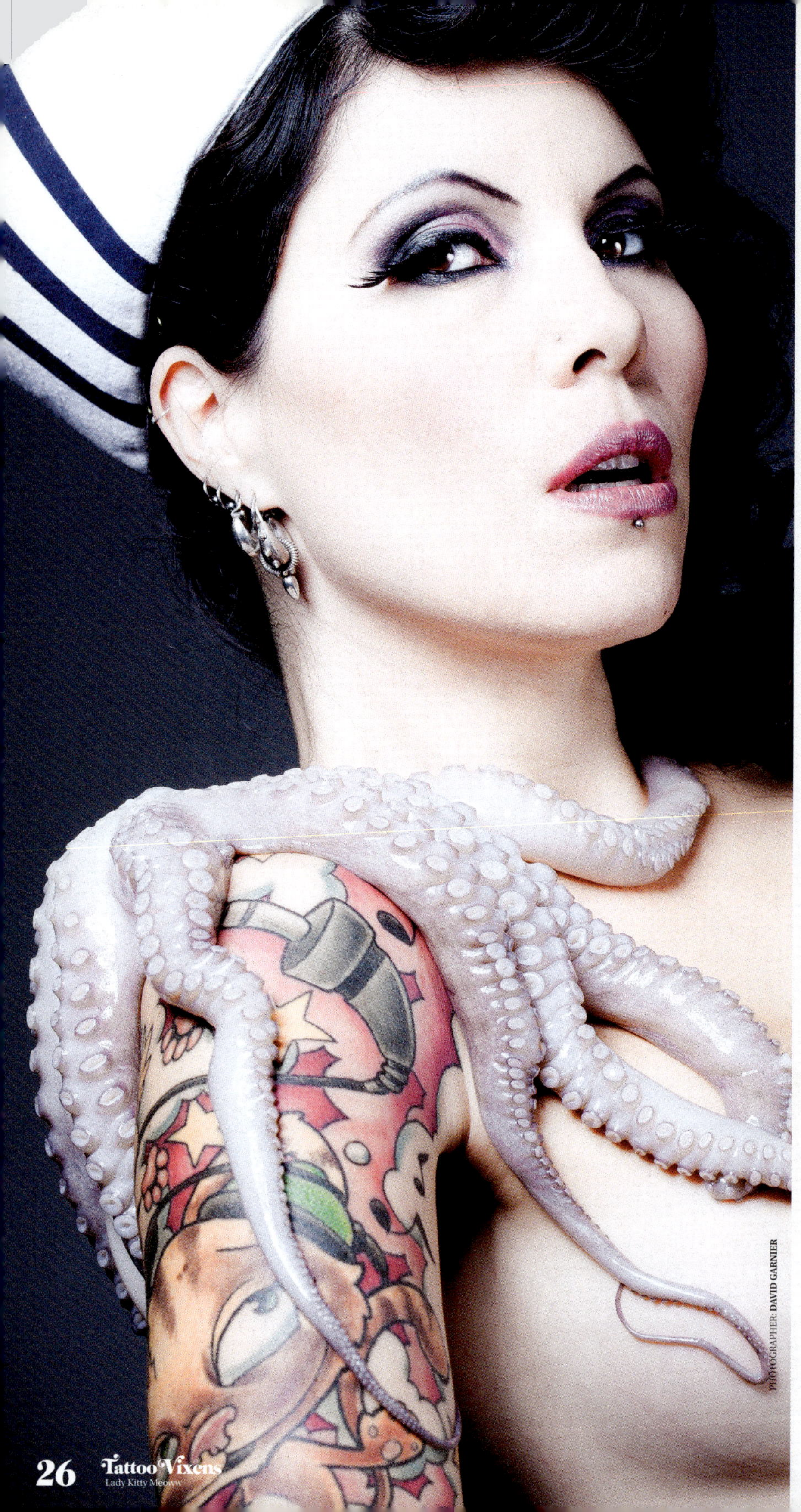

different and it's what looks good in photography, you don't need to be pretty and especially good looking to be a model but you need to be different, unusual… that's the reason I think photographers want to work with me because I have something different to give and not being a pretty face – it's something that all lovely girls can do, but not every woman can be a model!

Is that Chinese calligraphy down your spine? Can you tell us what that is or is it a big secret?

Yes it's a Mandarin calligraphy done by a Chinese man who I met briefly at a traditional Asian art exhibition. I wanted something done but I didn't want to go to the tattoo shop and ask for what I wanted because it was too complex and personal and too difficult to translate it. Only an older and wiser Chinese man could do this, so I went to see him and asked if he could write it on paper for me – because the language has many meanings for one idea, he had to go away for a couple of hours to think and to give me the best and closest meaning to what I wanted, he came back with it and I was so pleased and delighted to see what it looked like. I then went to a tattoo artist called David from David and Son and that's the story! The meaning? Well you have to understand the language to understand what it means and it's a big secret!

And finally, tell us something about you that nobody else knows.

Hmm, let me think… I hate pigeons and elevators, but some people know that already – I'm also ambidextrous! How's that?

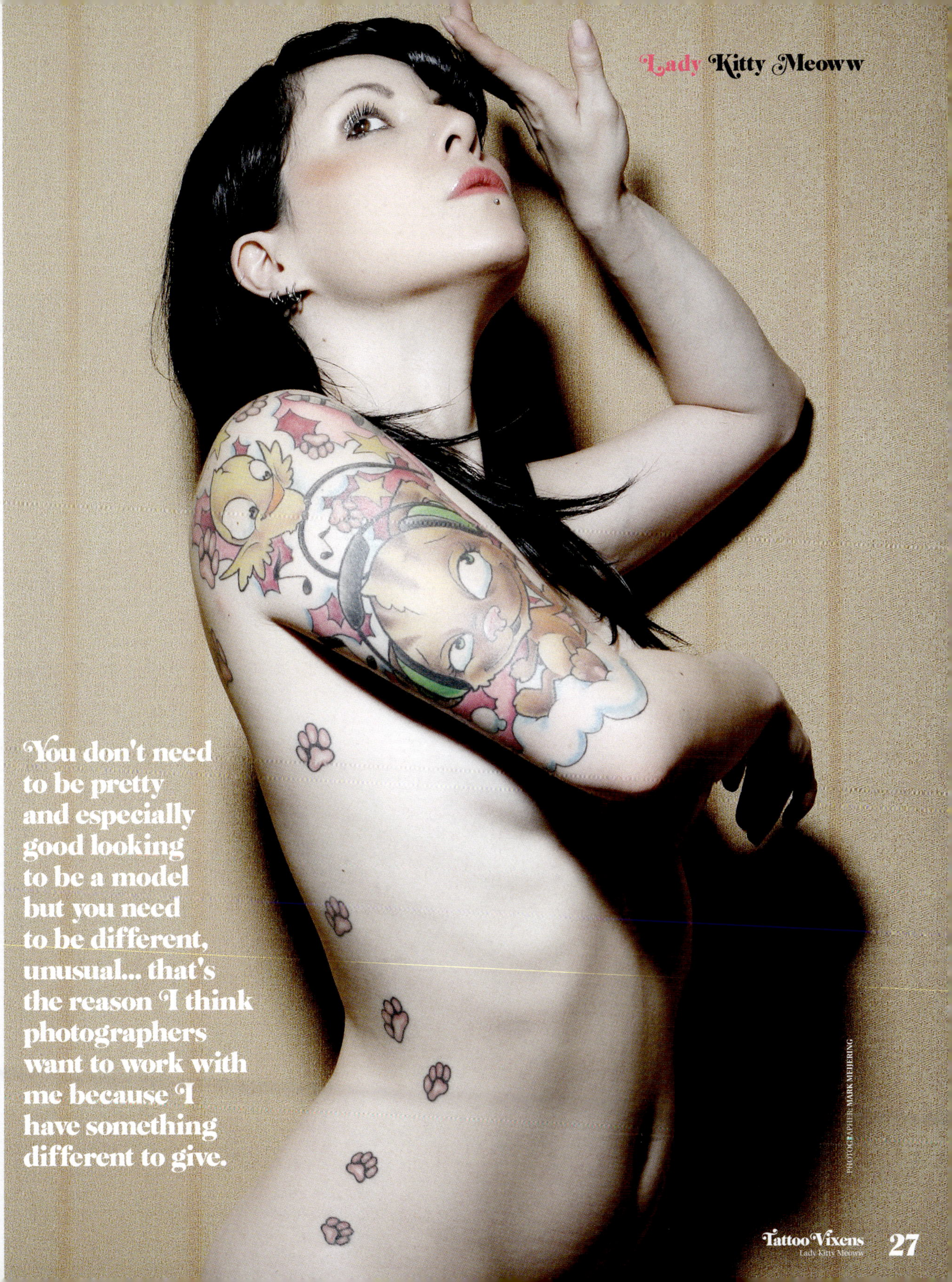

You don't need to be pretty and especially good looking to be a model but you need to be different, unusual... that's the reason I think photographers want to work with me because I have something different to give.

PHOTOGRAPHER: MARK MEIJERING

Kandy K

PHOTOGRAPHS: **ROBERT ALVARADO**

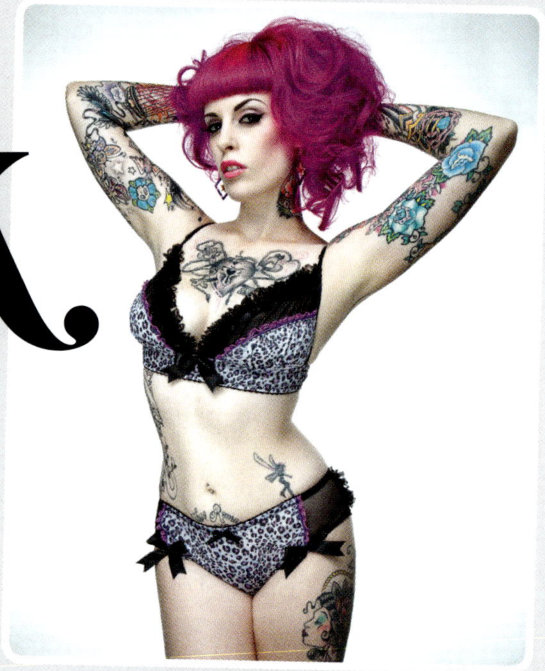

Model and mum, Kandy K, is a prime example of a tattooed woman who can (and does) have it all. Aside from British-style fish and chips... more's the pity.

What was it that made you fall in love with tattoos?

So many things: the feeling, the meaning, the way it brings people together. I love the idea of having artwork on my body that I will take to the grave, something that's personal to me and tells the story of my life. Each piece holds a memory, kinda like a photo. Hence modelling: photography, art and tattoos have so much in common to me. My granddad first introduced me to them, he served in the Royal Navy and has faded blue ink all up his arm; I always found them fascinating. Then growing up, I became friends with people in the industry who really inspired me. Tattoos have helped me through hard times, almost like a type of therapy, and have enabled me to meet and become friends with so many amazing people. I couldn't imagine not being tattooed. I look at myself in the mirror and they all just feel like a part of me, like I was born with them.

How do you balance your work and home life?

I'm lucky to have a very understanding husband, he helps as much as he can and really supports my career. Since having my son, work has become more complicated, but he comes to a lot of my shoots with me, and charms all the ladies. If you want something bad enough, then you find the time and put the work in, nothing in life comes for free. I appreciate having the opportunity to travel and work with amazing people, but I also love being home and getting to be a mother and wife to an amazing family. I couldn't ask for much more.

When did you leave England's shores for a life in the States?

I left about 3 years ago, I was pretty set up in the UK but after a few visits to the States, the place took my heart, and so did a certain boy. Since then I feel like I've achieved so much, both with my family and with my career. It was certainly scary leaving everything I knew but it was the best thing I ever did. Life's too short to just talk about our dreams - we need to take whatever steps we can to make it happen. Now I just have to figure out how to import all my friends and family!

Do you feel that tattooed women have it slightly easier now that heavily tattooed females are seen on TV and in magazines?

I wouldn't say we have it easier; tattooed women still tend to get a lot of bad press, especially with celebrity scandals and such. Some guy cheats on his wife, which is terrible, but if it's with a tattooed girl, well, the tattoos become the main part of the story, she has tattoos so

Name Kandy
Age 26
Occupation
Model Makeup Artist
Photographer
Robert Alvarado
Website www.kandyk.com
MUA KandyFace
Hair Amber Dexstress
Clothes
Purple leopard lingerie set www.purrfectpineapples.com
Corsets
www.waistedcouture.com

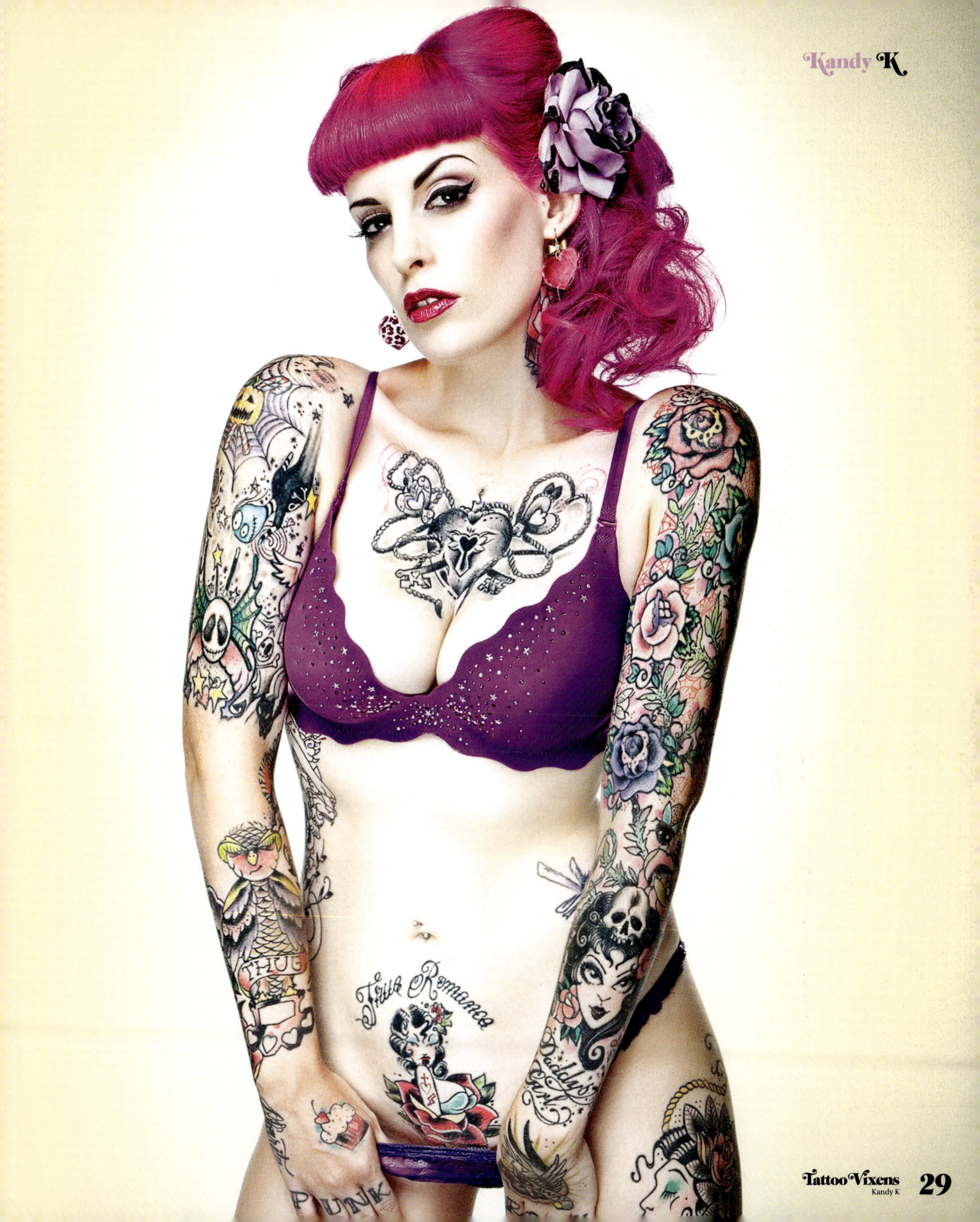
THUG
True Romance
Daddy's Girl
PUNK

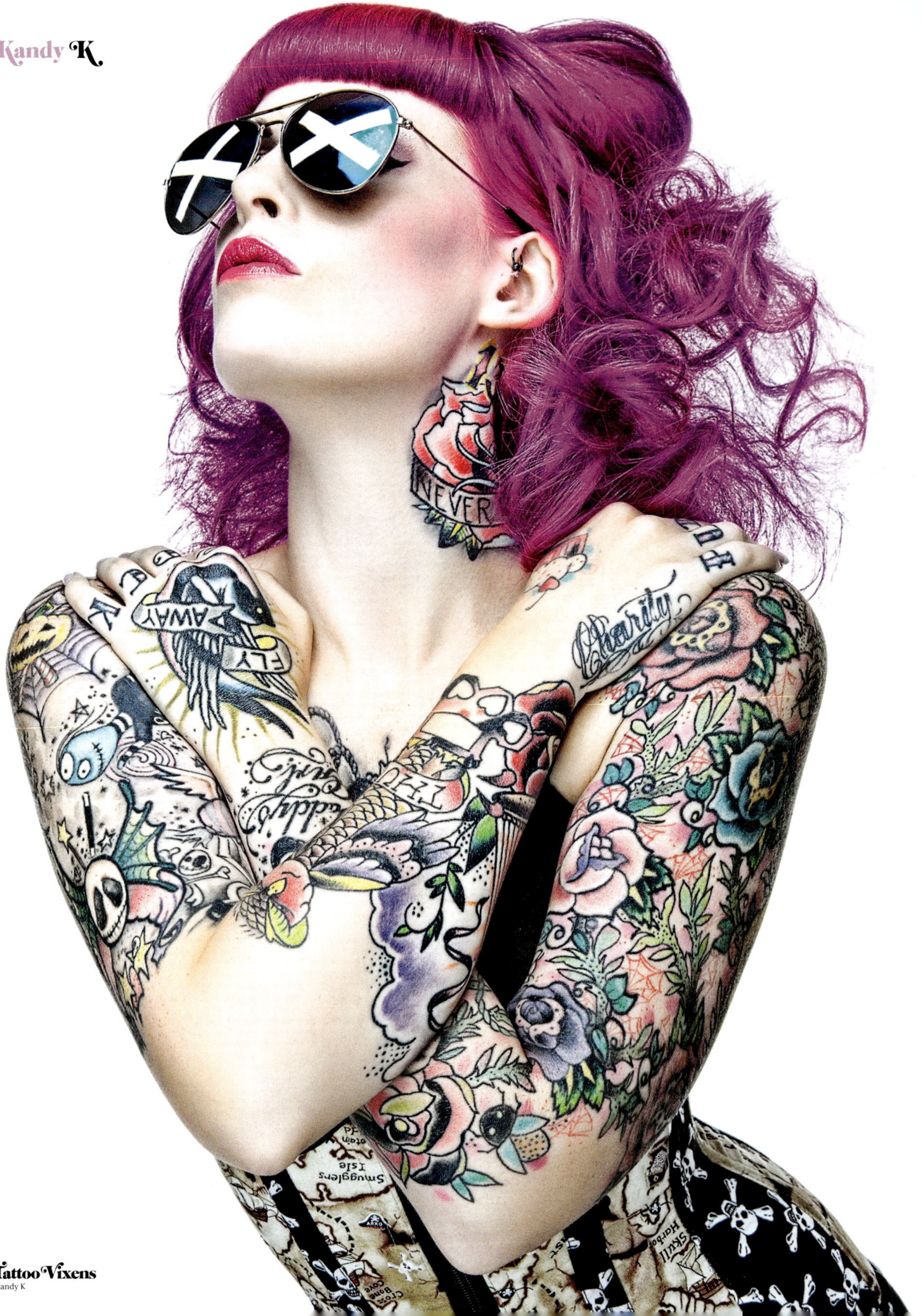
NEVER
FLY AWAY
Charity

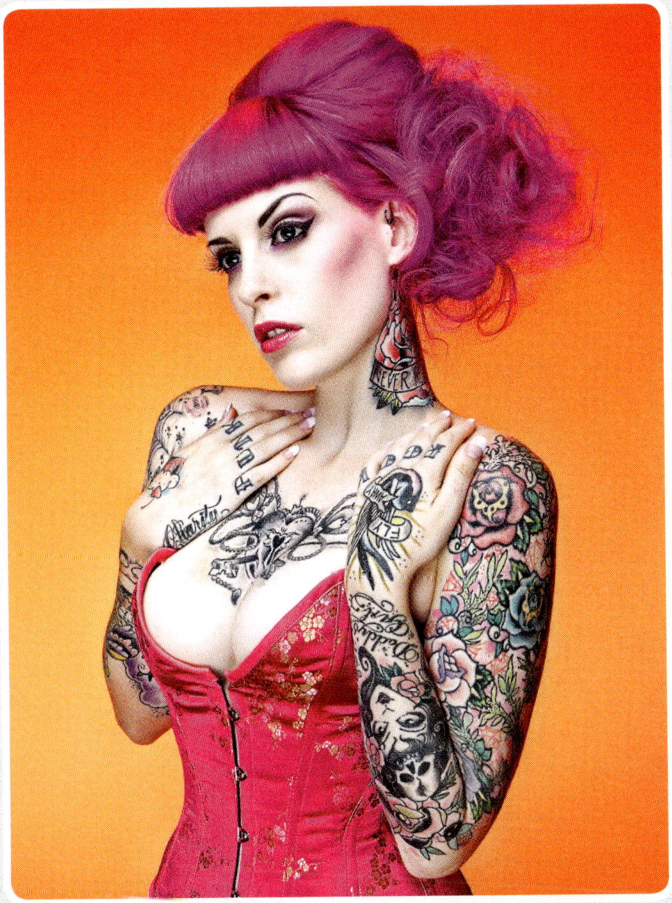

As tattoos are becoming accepted more for the art and less associated with criminals and junkies, a girl can be tattooed now and still hold down a good job and a 'normal' life.

she's obviously a crazy, junkie slut. I've lost count of how many times I've been asked if I slept with Jessie James. So stupid. We can take ten steps forward and then the smallest thing will drag us back again. I love that more heavily tattooed women are on TV making a positive change, Kat Von D is doing a great job of promoting the tattoo world and she's a fabulous businesswoman. But there will always be the taboo: I know people see me out with my baby and probably think I'm irresponsible and a bad parent - I've even been asked if I will tattoo my 1 yr old - but to hell with them, they know nothing. But I like to think I've brought a person in to the world that will grow up with an open mind and not judge, which makes the world a better place.

Have you noticed more women acquiring significant tattoo coverage in the past five years or so?

I would say so, but I tend to surround myself by women that share similar interests as me, so tattoos come with the territory. And as tattoos are becoming accepted more for the art and less associated with criminals and junkies, a girl can be tattooed now and still hold down a good job and a 'normal' life. I have plenty of tattooed girlfriends that work in the medical field, retail, business, and have families; it doesn't stop them from getting what they want in life. As far as I'm concerned, being heavily tattooed has really helped me.

Do any of your tattoos bear significance, or do you collect them purely for their aesthetic appeal?

Both. Some are dedications to people I miss or have lost. Some represent different parts of my personality. Some hold memories of certain times in my life, in fact, they all do. I can tell you a story that links to every piece I have ever got. Then there are some designs that I just wanted because I thought they were pretty, or I really loved the artist. I like travelling to conventions, so sometimes it's nice to get a little tattoo as a sort of souvenir of the trip. I have the Halloween half sleeve that was inspired by the art of Tim Burton and my favourite holiday. Many flowers because contrary to my mean look, I'm actually really girly. My back is a dedication to my mother, whom I miss terribly. I have a bird on my hand with a scroll saying 'Fly Away' because I flew from my home country to start a different life...and a bunch of other designs that all hold significance to me.

Are there any clothing or jewellery companies of which you're a fan?

Absolutely, part of my job is to work with some of the most awesome designers in this industry, I'm very lucky! In the past and currently I've been lucky enough to work with such companies as, Torture Couture, Clutterfly jewellery, Purrfect Pineapples lingerie, Boom Boom Baby Boutique, Rukus corsets, Mamasan, Lila Jo Accessories, Vanity Exposed clothing, Yardley December jewellery, Dickies, Toxico and many more. I have some really exciting collaborations coming up in the next couple of months and also started my own jewellery line called 'Gypsy Gold' which is tattoo and gypsy-inspired accessories. They can befound at www.etsy.com/shop/Kandyisbadass.

My back is a dedication to my mother, whom I miss terribly. I have a bird on my hand with a scroll saying 'Fly Away' because I flew from my home country to start a different life...

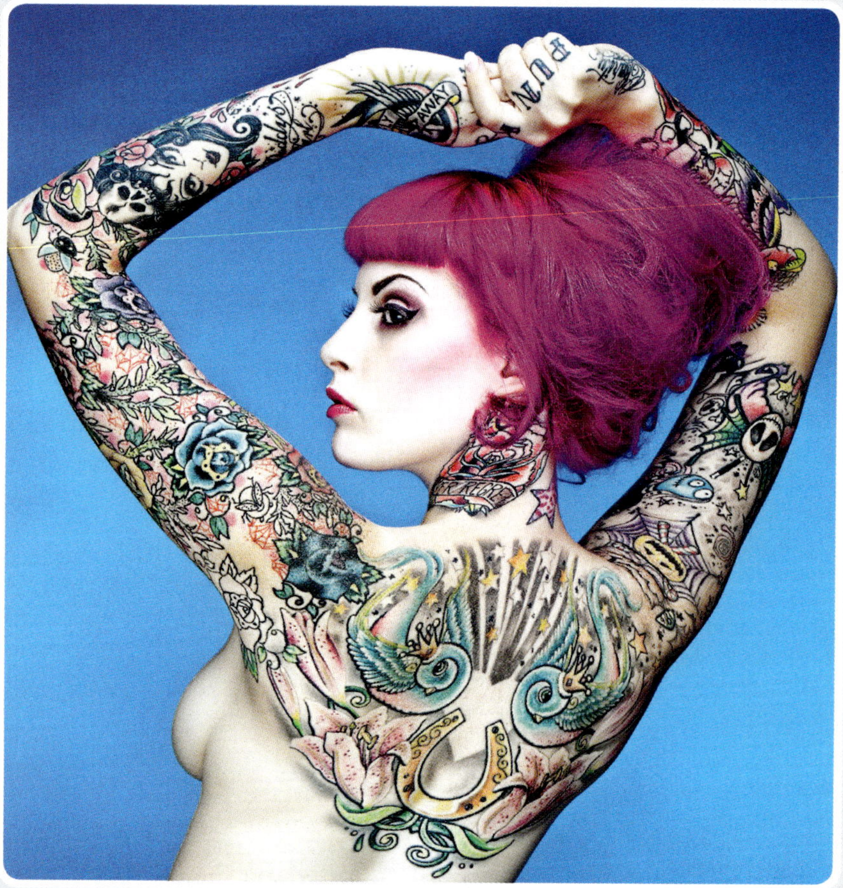

Are there any artists that you seek tattoos from in the near future?

I'm currently working on getting my ribs tattooed by an awesome local artist, Mikey Sarratt of High Noon Tattoo, Phoenix. I have a long list of artists I'd like to get tattooed by, and I'd also love to revisit the beautiful Dawnii at Painted Lady in the UK, who worked on my chest and leg back when I lived there - I really miss her. I love the work of Uncle Allen, Megan Massacre, Mo Coppoletta, Dan Smith, Nikki Hurtado, Angelique and a bunch more: someday it will happen!

Finally, the most important question I've asked yet: as an expat, do you prefer British chippie chips or American-style fries?

Nothing compares to a traditional bag of British Chips wrapped in newspaper! I've thought many times, why doesn't someone open a chain of English chip shops out here? It would do so well! Maybe I should do it myself and become a millionaire, but I don't think I could live with the chip fat hair and I'd end up over 400lbs. And I really miss pickled eggs…oh my god, it's been too long!

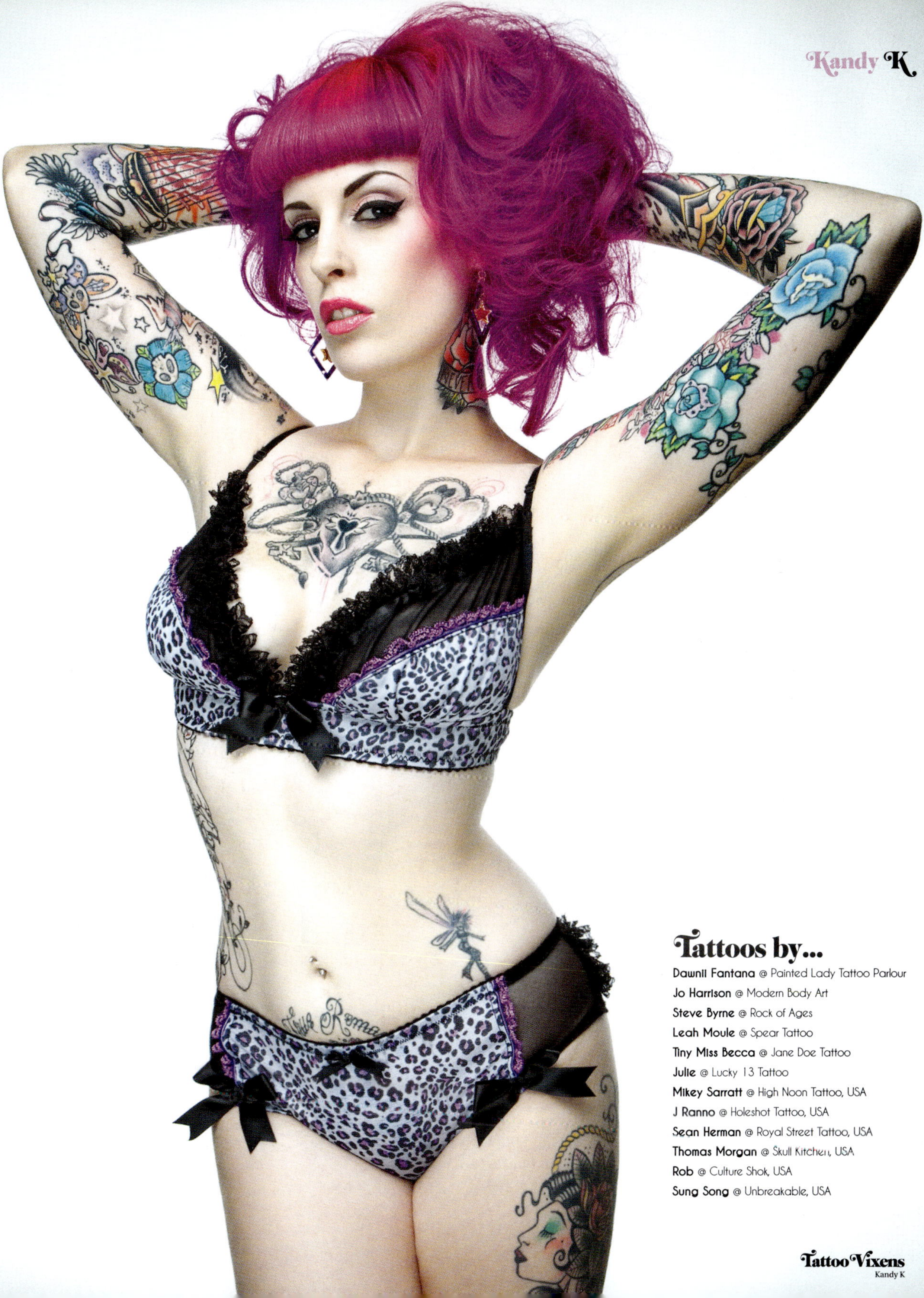

Tattoos by...

Dawnii Fantana @ Painted Lady Tattoo Parlour
Jo Harrison @ Modern Body Art
Steve Byrne @ Rock of Ages
Leah Moule @ Spear Tattoo
Tiny Miss Becca @ Jane Doe Tattoo
Julie @ Lucky 13 Tattoo
Mikey Sarratt @ High Noon Tattoo, USA
J Ranno @ Holeshot Tattoo, USA
Sean Herman @ Royal Street Tattoo, USA
Thomas Morgan @ Skull Kitchen, USA
Rob @ Culture Shok, USA
Sung Song @ Unbreakable, USA

Zoe

Zoe is one of the ever increasing legion of Suicide Girls and also one the most vocal when it comes to standing up and being counted on the side of real women across the world...

What drew you towards tattoos in the first place?

If I'm honest...I couldn't tell you why I started to get tattooed. I've always been very creative and have always been encouraged to be myself, not afraid to be different. I got my first tattoo when I was sixteen and it went from there, really.

How did you begin your modelling career?

It all started with Suicide Girls. When I was 18 I found out about them and loved what they stood for. I loved that you did not need to be stick-thin and really tall and was inspired by representing real women. I applied on my birthday and forgot about it: a few weeks later they emailed me advising that I'd been accepted and it all went from there.

Do you feel that alternative modelling represents women better than the more mainstream kind?

Definitely! Mainstream modelling encourages size zeros and eating disorders. It portrays that to be perceived as beautiful once again, you need to be stick-thin and super tall. Alternative modelling shows women for who they really are; I find I get a lot of interest because the way I look. I get a lot of emails from curvy women telling me that it's refreshing to see a curvy woman be confident and happy with her body and reassures them that they are normal and just because they have a set of hips and a sizeable rack, it doesn't make them any less beautiful.

Which of your tattoos has had the most impact in regard to how you are perceived by other people?

I think my neck tattoo has the most impact, purely because it's on my neck. But to be honest, everyone stared before I got my neck done too.

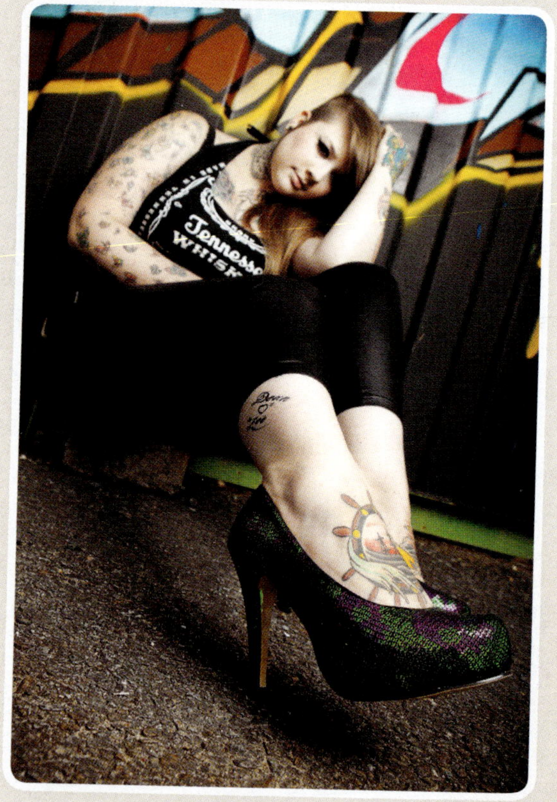

Name Zoe Age 23 Occupation Wouldnt you like to know? Favourite Book Chinese Cinderella Favourite Album Dark Side of the Moon Fast zombies or slow zombies If Im being chased then slow zombies, obviously. One interesting fact about you Im a fire breather.

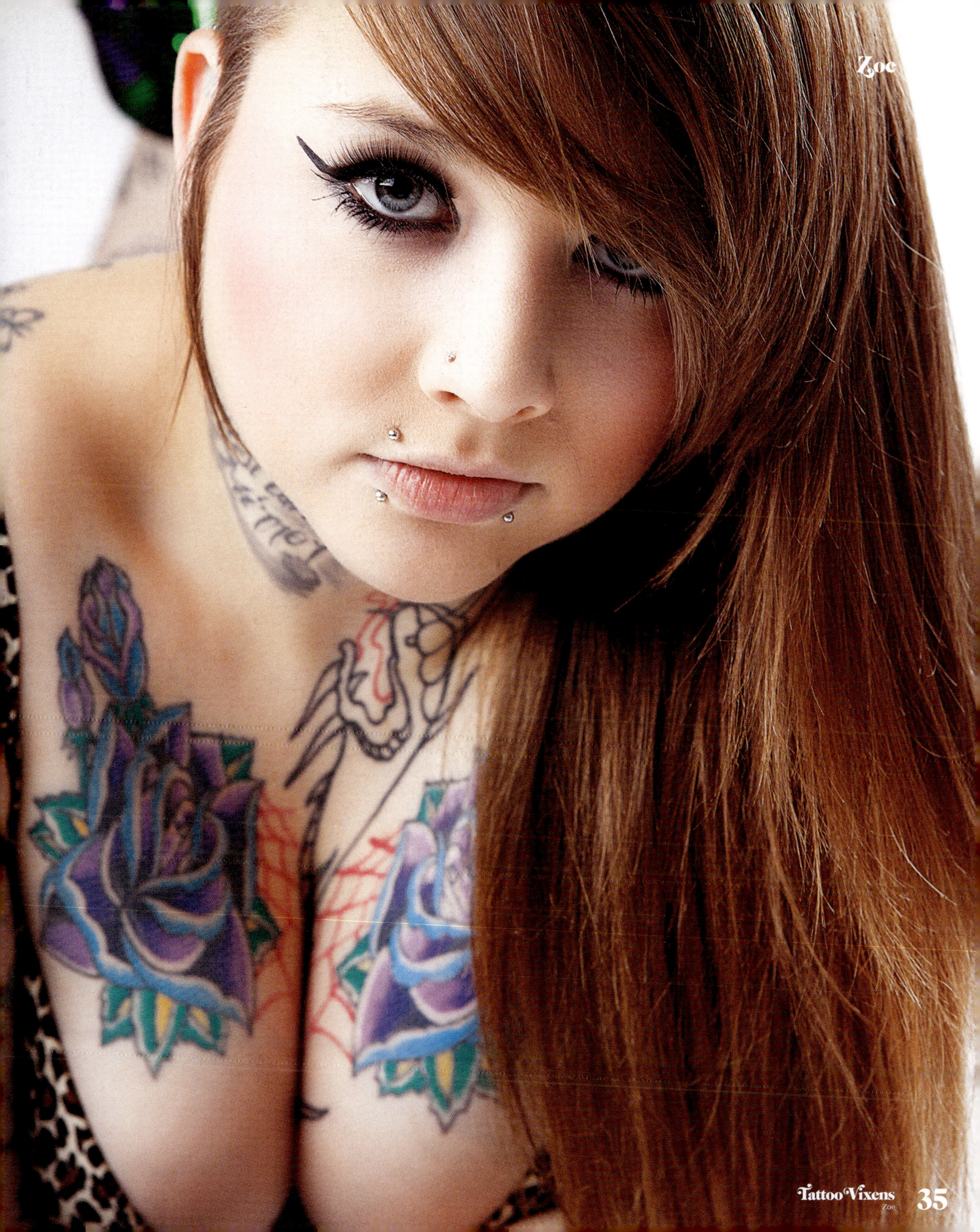

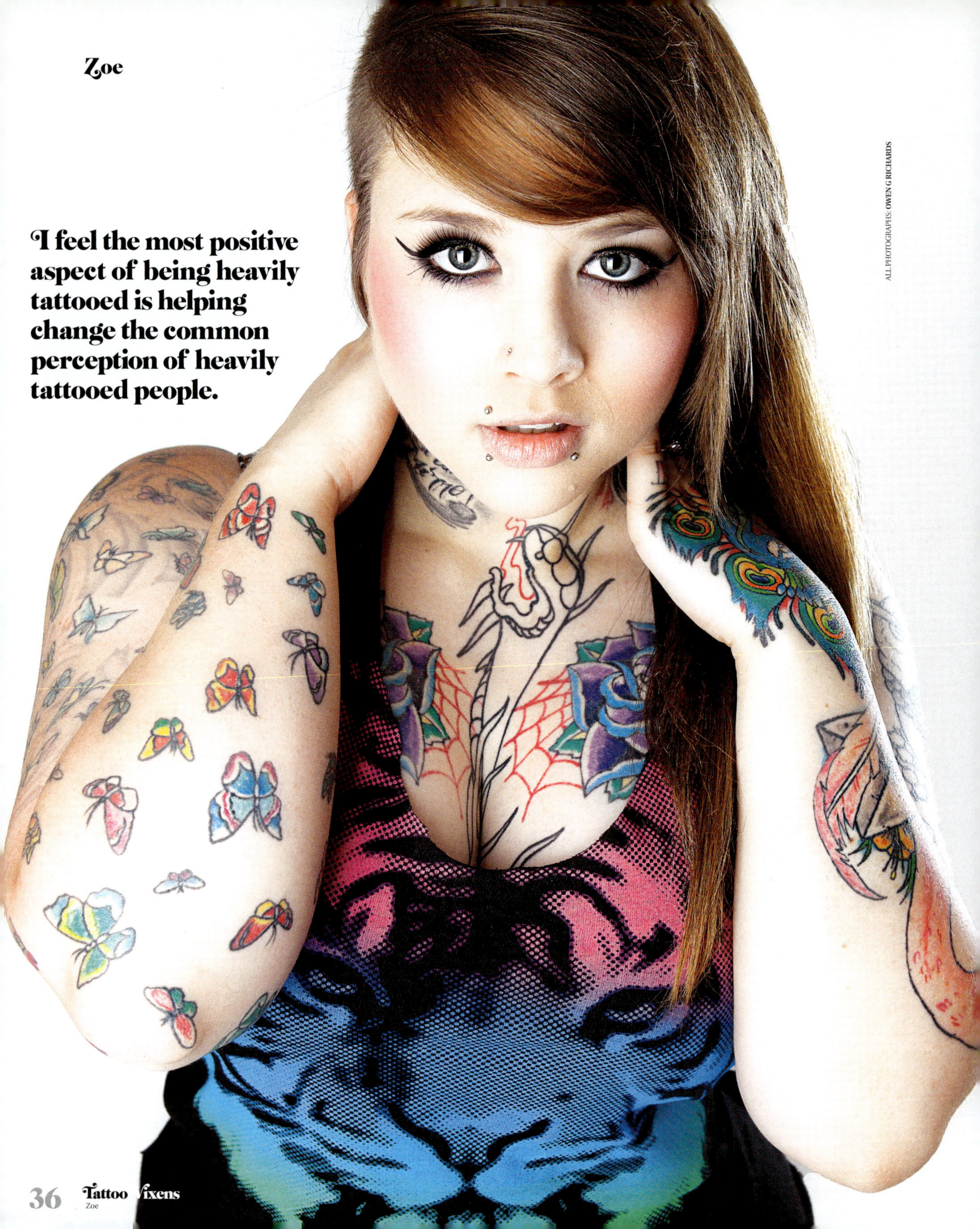

ALL PHOTOGRAPHS: **OWEN G RICHARDS**

'I feel the most positive aspect of being heavily tattooed is helping change the common perception of heavily tattooed people.

What would you say is the most positive aspect of being a heavily tattooed woman?

I feel the most positive aspect of being heavily tattooed is helping change the common perception of heavily tattooed people. I have my own house and car, I'm not in debt and I have a secure job, so not the usual down-and-out that I know people expect. I have been told on many occasions that I'm completely different to what they first thought, which in a way proves they judged me. However, I'm glad I was able to pleasantly surprise, ha!. I'd like to think that I encourage people to be themselves and dare to be different.

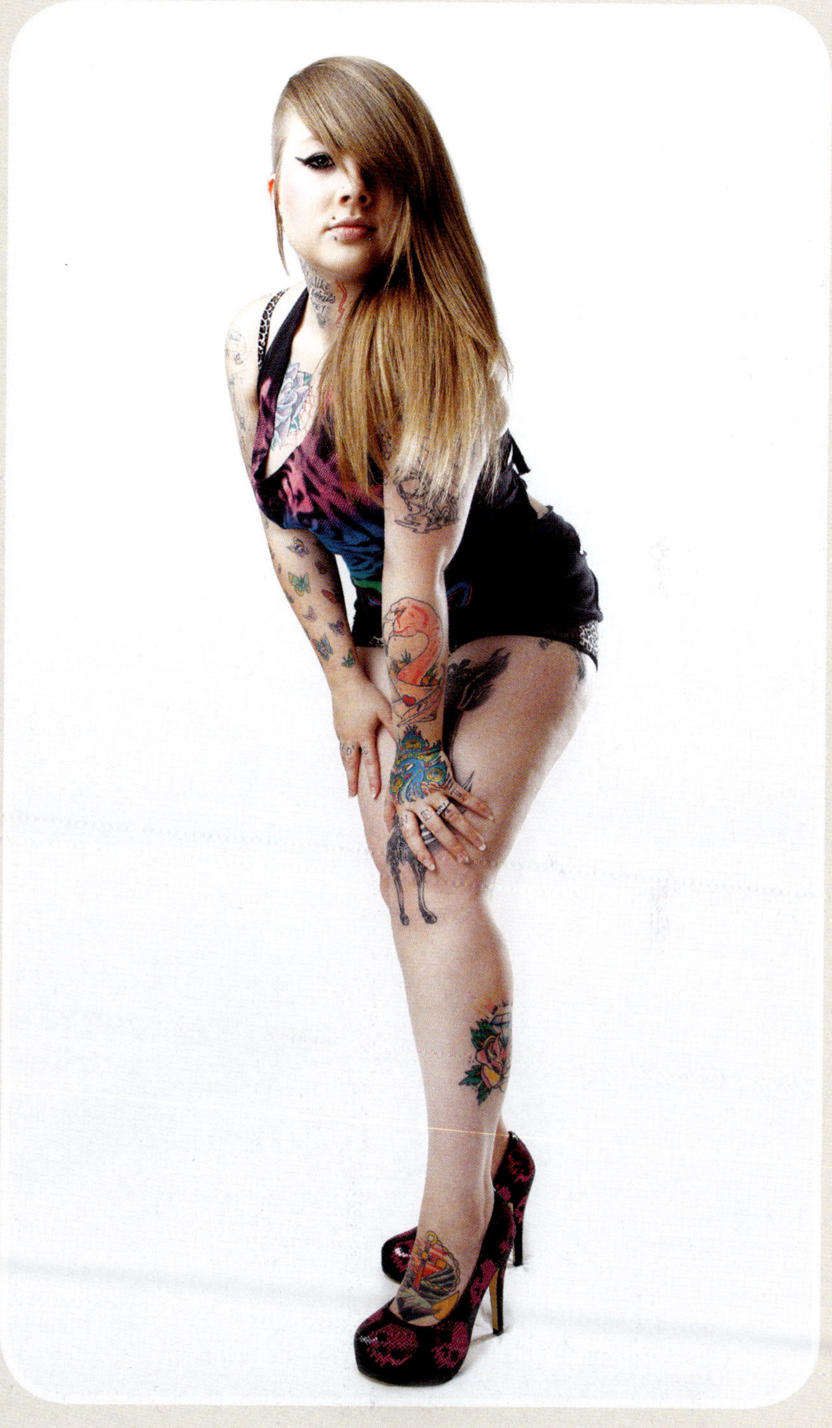

Do your tattoos have any particular significance, or do you collect them purely because of their aesthetics?

Some of my tattoos have significance and others are collector pieces. The most significant tattoos I have are my memorial tattoos: my left rib piece and my owl on my left arm, both in memory of the same person.

What advice would you offer to younger women who are considering tattoos on public skin before they've worn much coverage elsewhere?

Just be prepared for the stares that follow. I would recommend getting more coverage before considering your hands or your neck, for instance. I'm going to sound like an old woman now but if you have a changing personality and you're pretty impulsive, chances are you may end up regretting it, if not for anything else but job safety. I've been getting tattooed now for 7

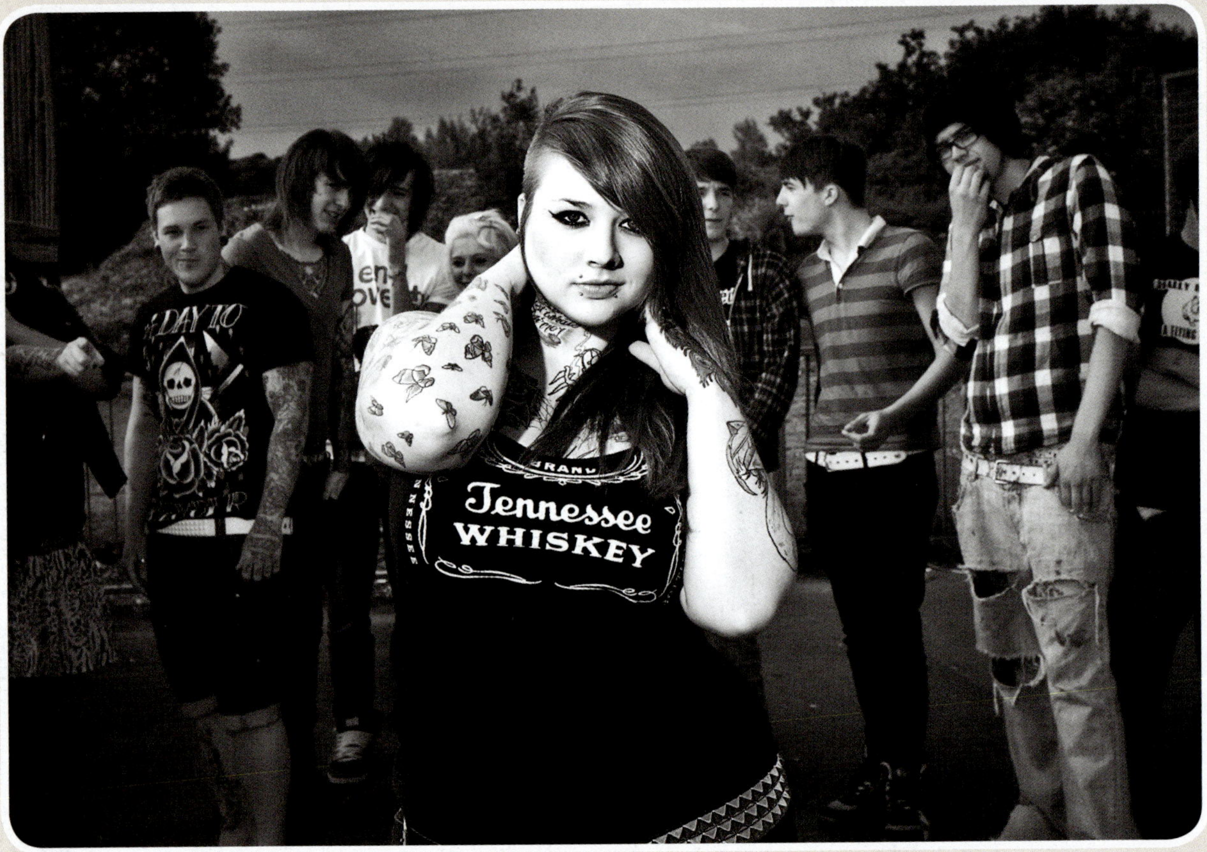

years and only in the past 2 have I got tattooed on very public skin. My job is pretty secure; I'm lucky enough to be in a job where I am not judged on the way I look and am still taken seriously even though I'm very heavily tattooed. Like it or not; if someone hasn't met you before, you are going to be judged on the way you look - it's human nature and it's the first thing people see. If the person who is interviewing you doesn't like tattoos then unfortunately thet may be all the concentrate on (they are pretty distracting, after all). If you are considering getting tattooed on public skin just make sure you're fully happy with the design and you've researched your artist to make sure he's the right guy for the job.

If just one person could tattoo you, who would it be?

Brandon Bond.

Finally, who would win in a fight between a sabre-tooth tiger and an angry rhinoceros?

Oh gosh… If we're speaking logically then seeing how a sabre-tooth tiger is extinct then quite obviously the rhinoceros - he would look a bit stupid if he lost to a dead animal. In fact, he'd look a bit stupid tossing about a dead animal in the first place. If we're speaking theoretically however then I think I'm going to have to say sabre-tooth tiger; they are more agile with epic gnashers, have prehistoric-scale primal instinct and attack capabilities. Rhino - fat with a horn.

Make sure you're fully happy with the design and you've researched your artist to make sure he's the right guy for the job.

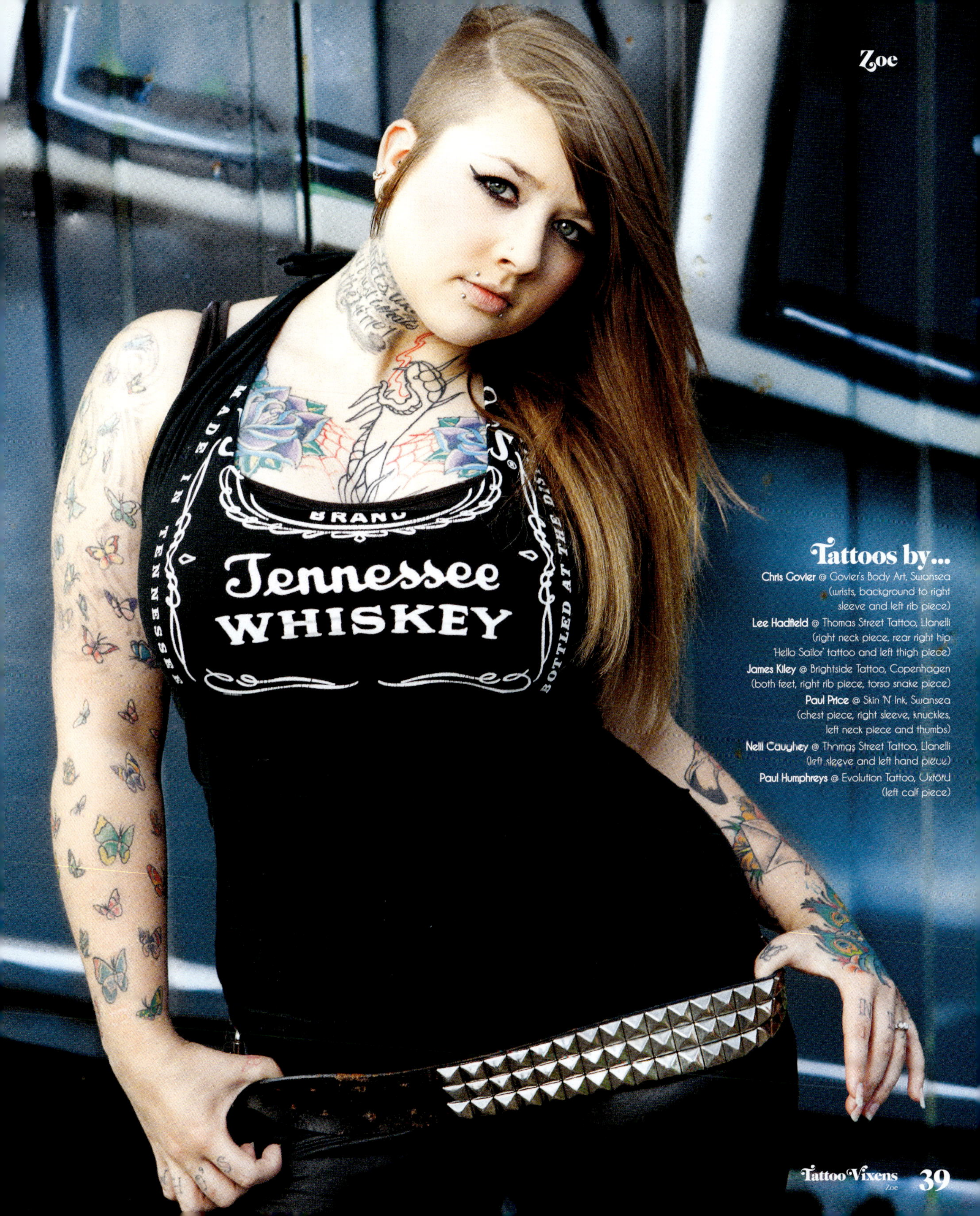

Tattoos by...

Chris Govier @ Govier's Body Art, Swansea (wrists, background to right sleeve and left rib piece)

Lee Hadfield @ Thomas Street Tattoo, Llanelli (right neck piece, rear right hip 'Hello Sailor' tattoo and left thigh piece)

James Kiley @ Brightside Tattoo, Copenhagen (both feet, right rib piece, torso snake piece)

Paul Price @ Skin 'N' Ink, Swansea (chest piece, right sleeve, knuckles, left neck piece and thumbs)

Neill Caughey @ Thomas Street Tattoo, Llanelli (left sleeve and left hand piece)

Paul Humphreys @ Evolution Tattoo, Oxford (left calf piece)

Full Name China Oliver "Chi Chi Revolver"
Age Very very nearly 27
Occupation Circus Girl

Chi Chi Revolver

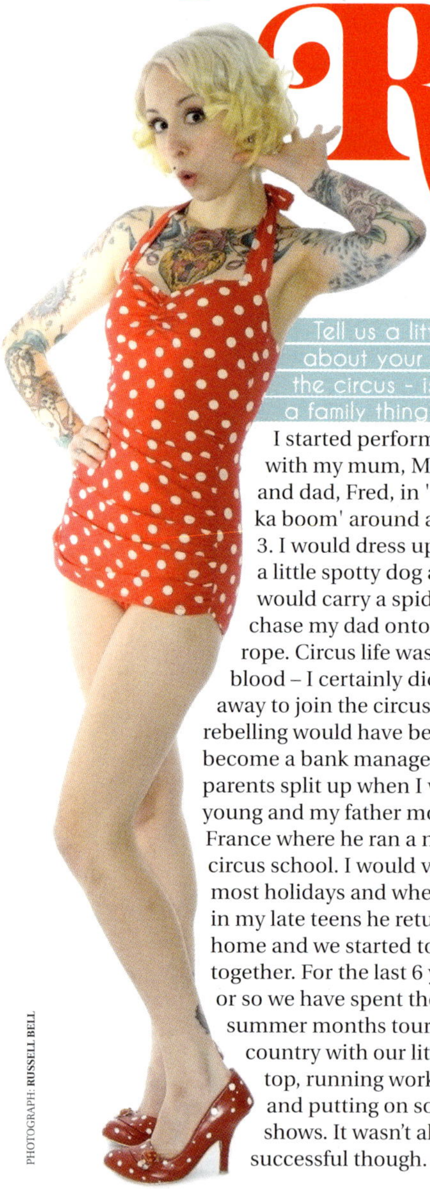

PHOTOGRAPH: RUSSELL BELL

China "Chi Chi" Revolver might possibly hold the world record for being the world's most tattooed circus hula artist. Anybody disagreeing?

Tell us a little bit about your life in the circus - is that a family thing?

I started performing with my mum, Mim, and dad, Fred, in 'ziz ziz ka boom' around aged 3. I would dress up as a little spotty dog and I would carry a spider and chase my dad onto a slack rope. Circus life was in my blood – I certainly didn't run away to join the circus. Me rebelling would have been to become a bank manager! My parents split up when I was young and my father moved to France where he ran a national circus school. I would visit him most holidays and when I was in my late teens he returned home and we started to work together. For the last 6 years or so we have spent the summer months touring the country with our little big top, running workshops and putting on sold out shows. It wasn't always so successful though. When we first started working together we would hire little village halls and put on shows there, we would spend ages putting up posters etc and we would be lucky to have more than 8 people in the audience! It was hard work! But it was a great time for us to get a great show together.

Four years ago my husband, Sam, joined us as a clown. He had never performed in his life before he met me, he worked for Harley Davidson, but he became a wonderful natural clown. He now works for a large circus company making amazing circus props - great for me when he comes home with new hula hoops for me to try out!

Ever had a nasty accident with those fire-hoops?

Not yet with the fire hoops! However, I seem to bash my funny bone a lot with my fire hoop and I did fall from my husband's shoulders in the circus and seriously dislocate my elbow. That was the year all three of us ended up in hospital at one point! Sam nearly took his eye out with a sledge hammer and Fred had a funny turn in bed...

When did the tattoo aspect enter your life - was it simply something that grew organically for you or a "career enhancing" move?

I got my first tattoo for my 18th birthday. It certainly wasn't a career move, I just really wanted to get tattooed! Fred is also now very tattooed and people always think that he influenced me to get tattooed. That couldn't be further from the truth! I had all my tattoos ➤

When we first started working together we would hire little village halls and put on shows there, we would spend ages putting up posters.

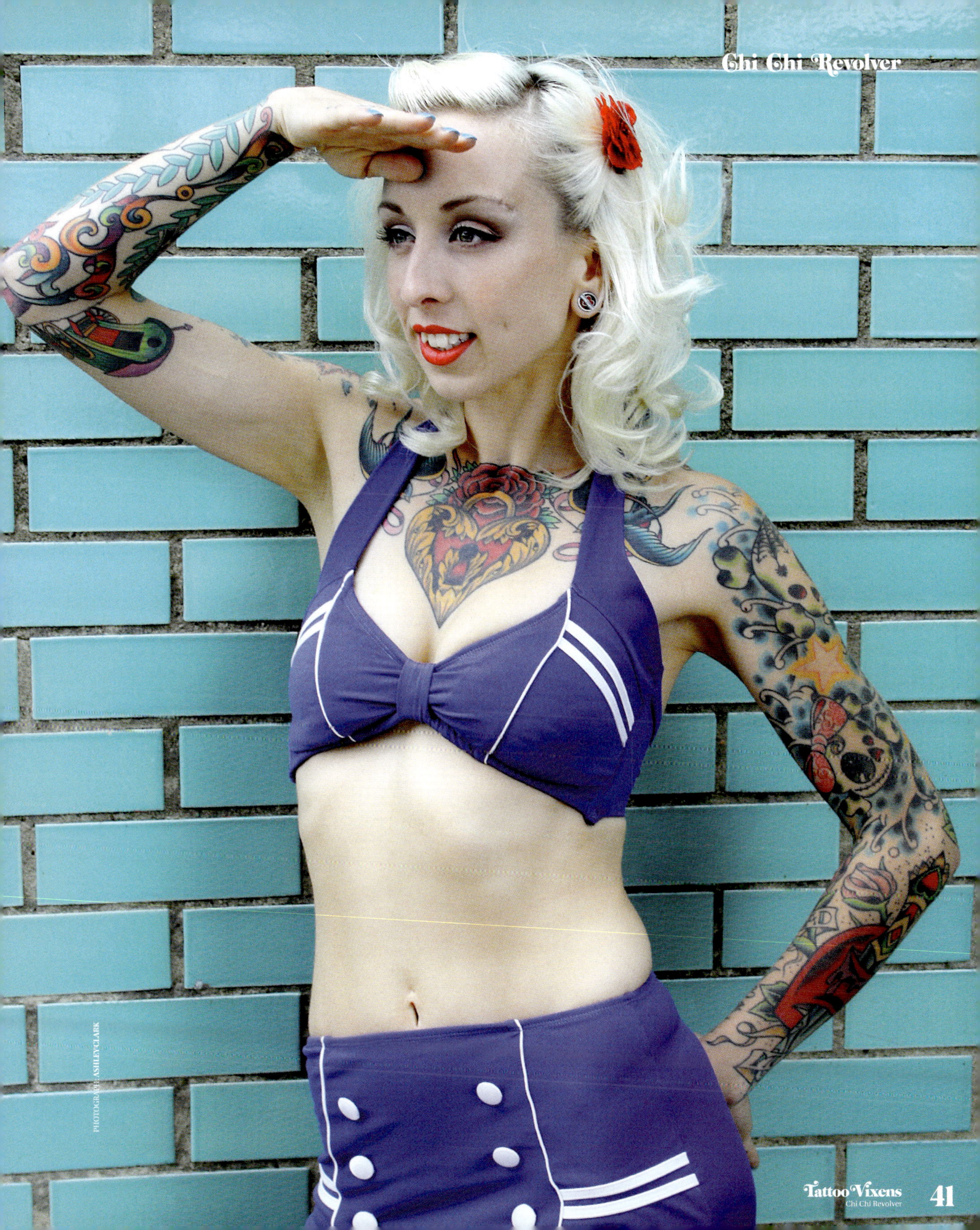

PHOTOGRAPH: ASHLEY CLARK

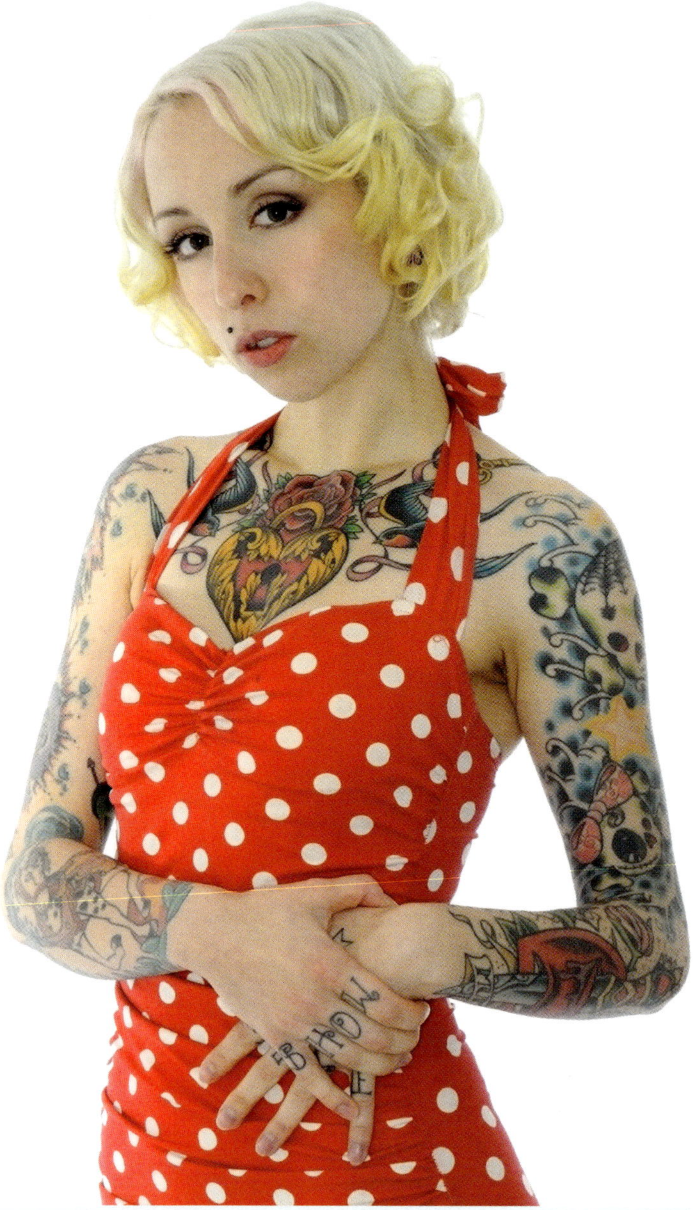

PHOTOGRAPH: RUSSELL BELL

years before he did - Fred had his first tattoo aged 47. So it was definitely me that led him astray. A lot of our work is in primary schools and the children love them. They always say - "I always thought tattooed people were scary and nasty, but now we have met you we know that's not true."

What does the future hold for you? Are you in the circus for life or do you have other plans as well.

I'll be a circus girl one way or another for my whole life, I know nothing else. I have started doing a lot of modeling and TV work too, but I'll always have my hoops, that's for sure!

My lower right arm is circus inspired with a circus horse, little circus tent and an old fashioned caravan.

I read somewhere that you've got a reputation as a serial quiz show contestant. You can't deny it - what's the deal with that? Looking to make a quick buck?

Ha ha! Yes, true very true - I have done The Weakest Link twice now. I was asked back to do a "best of the worst losers special"! Also a year ago, I went on 'Heads or Tails' with Justin Lee Collins and managed to win money to pay for my wedding. I love game shows – it's a mild addiction of mine.

Can you talk us through some of your art? Who did what and what you have planned for the future...

My next plan is to have giant mermaid across my lower right leg. My Mum thinks she is a bit of a mermaid, so it is to represent her. I'm very lucky to be very close to both my parents, I have Mum and Dad tattoos on my left arm. My lower right arm is circus inspired with a circus horse, little circus tent and an old fashioned caravan. My dad and I also both have 'show time' across our fingers.

As a whole then, is being heavily tattooed a positive thing in your life?

Yes it has been a very positive thing in my life, especially when I go on holiday. In Thailand in particular they love tattoos. I have a wonderful response to my tattoos there. I was chosen to be in the NDubz music video 'say its over' because of my tattoos - however when I got there they put me in a full body jumpsuit which hid them all – go figure, but I probably wouldn't have got the gig in the first place if I didn't have them!

I'll be a circus girl one way or another for my whole life, I know nothing else.

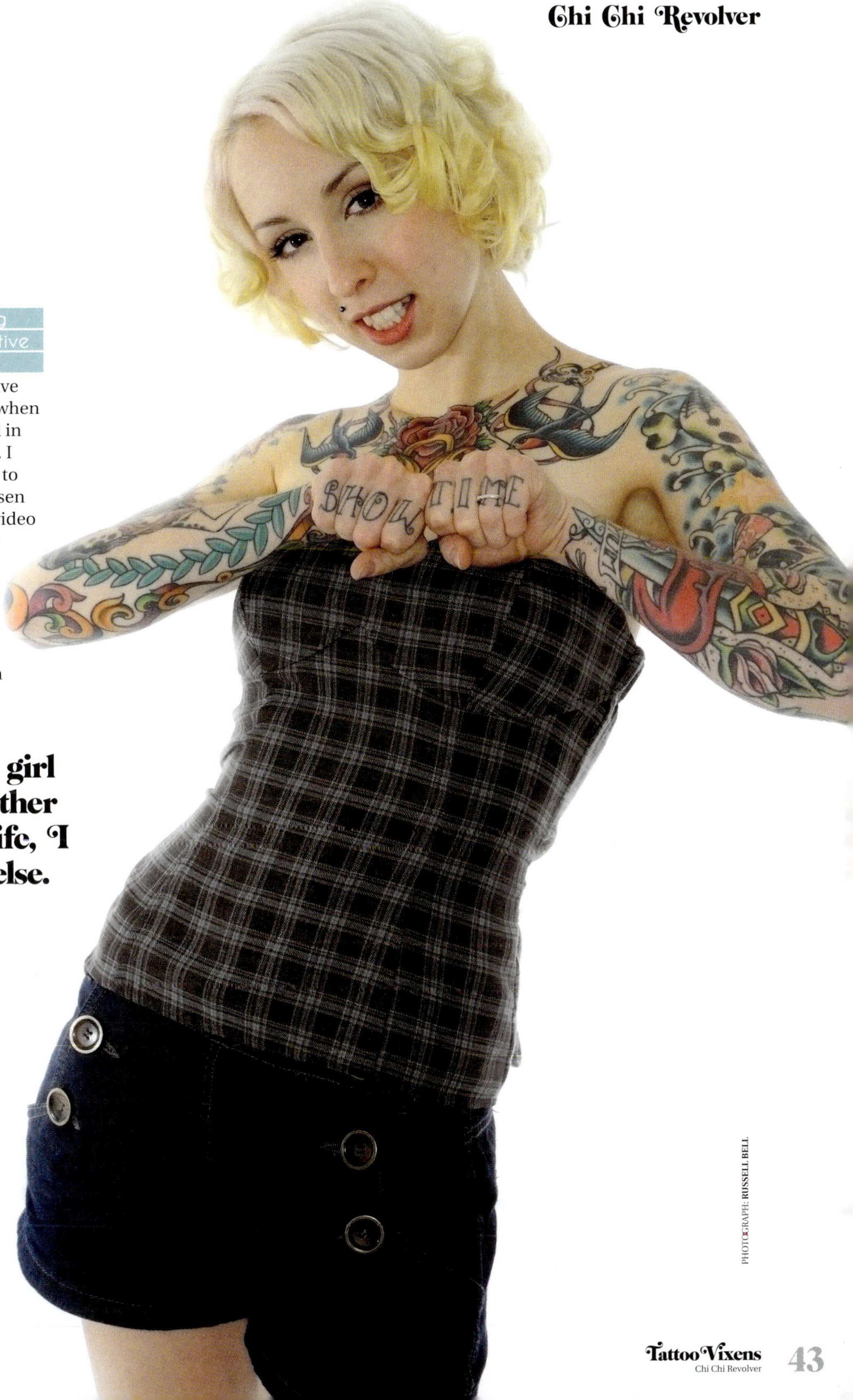

PHOTOGRAPH: RUSSELL BELL

Sophie Paranoid

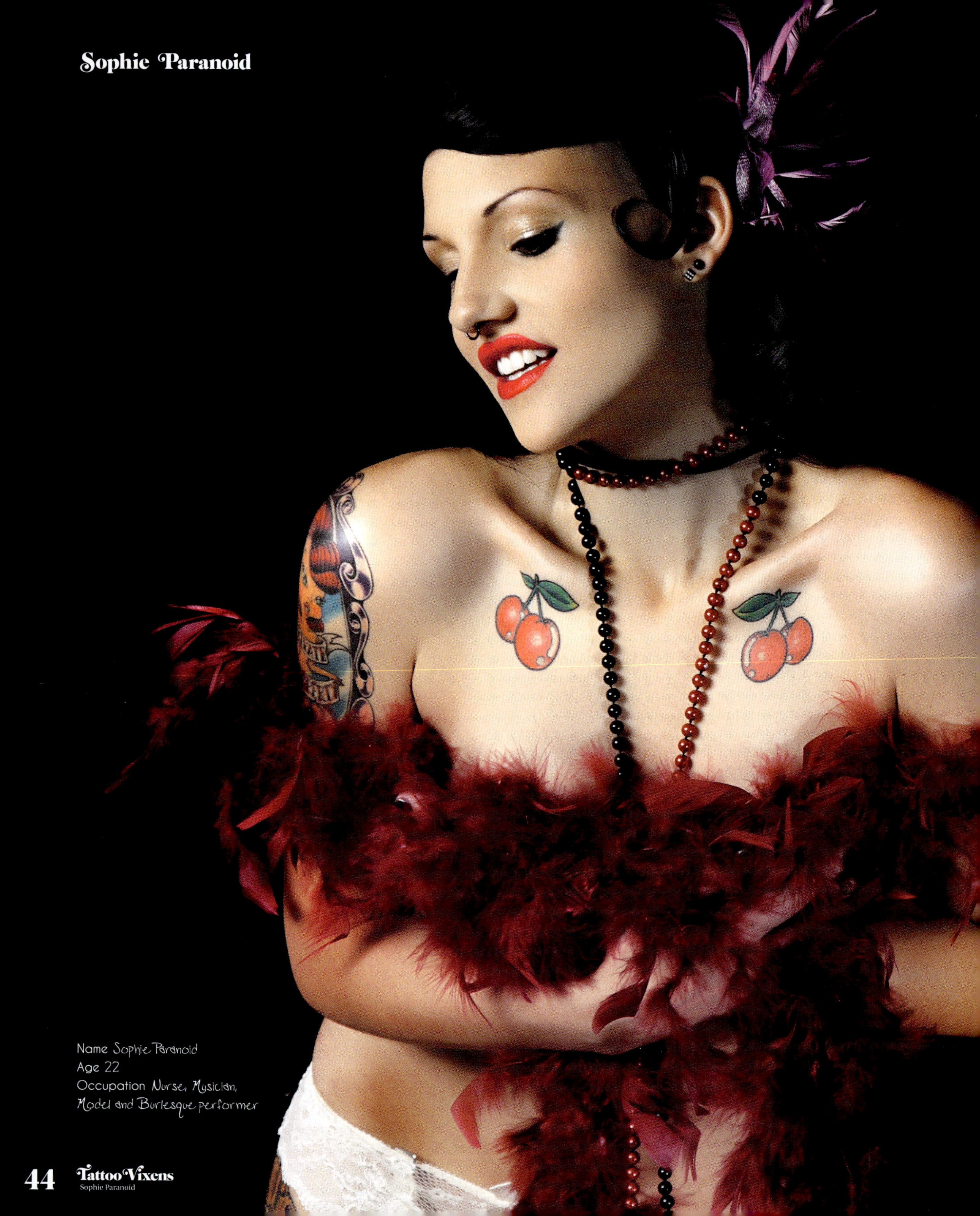

Name Sophie Paranoid
Age 22
Occupation Nurse, Musician, Model and Burlesque performer

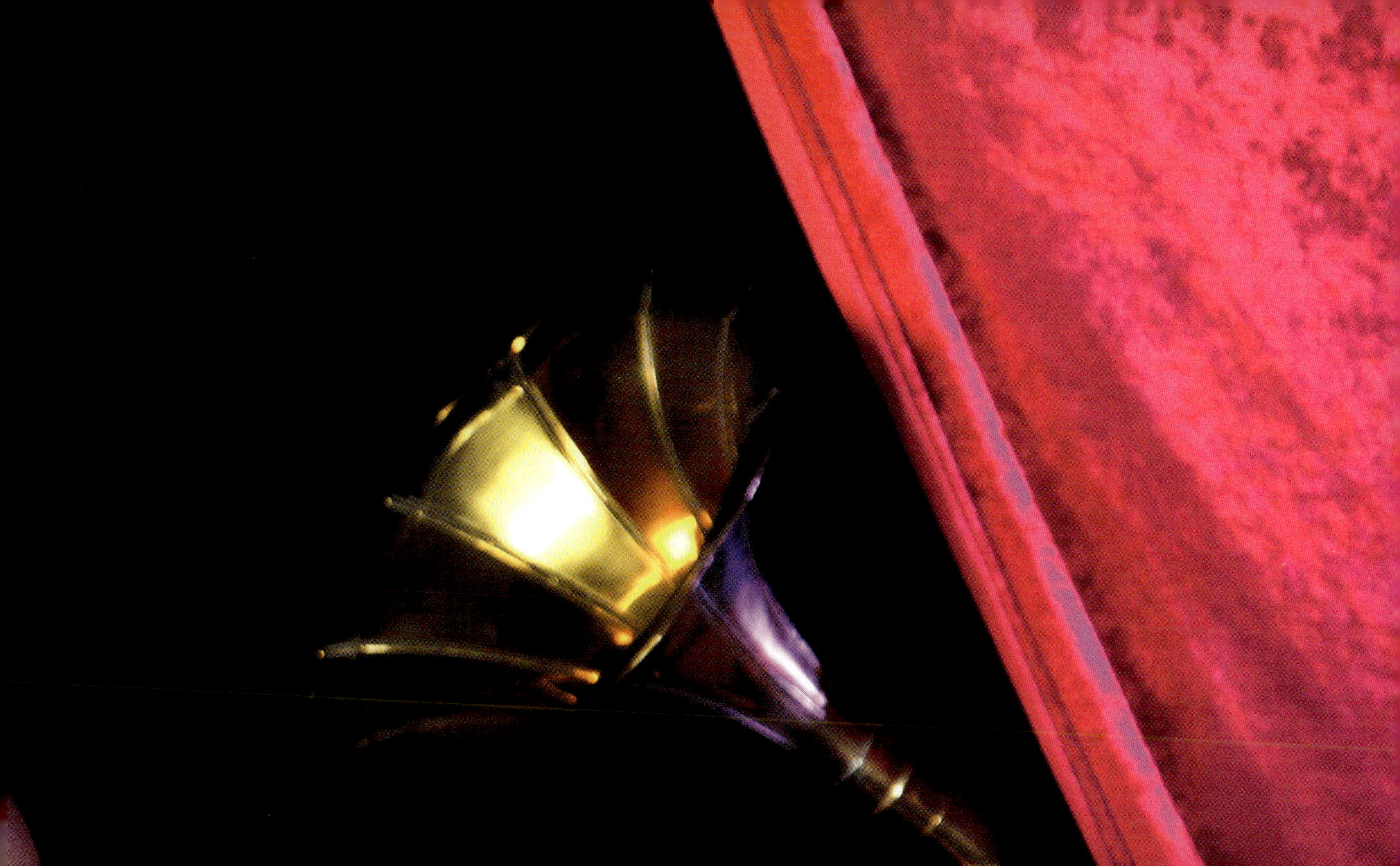

PHOTOGRAPHS: MARYA GARCIA

Sophie Paranoid

Not just a pretty face and a killer dancer with an amazing portfolio of images, we also discovered that by day, Sophie looks after children on a paediatric ward. Altogether… awww!

You have some really vibrant and beautiful work! Can you tell us the story - how did your tattoo adventure begin?
I always liked tattoo art, since I was a little girl. In fact, I love to make my own drawings, my arm tattoo is a sketch of mine. I recently bought my first machine and I hope I will tattoo in the future.

Where you brought up in a tattoo loving family or is this something you got interested in for yourself?
My family really hates tattoos! Even now they dislike my skin art. I don't think they even know about some of the tattoos I have. I think my mom would kill me if she could! My interest in tattoos is part of me and certainly not the influence of my social contacts.

Is there are story behind the two cherries on your chest?
I was in Salamanca with my band´s drummer, a small city 3 hours driving from Madrid. We were having a really good time and I decided to have my first tattoo - I had none at this

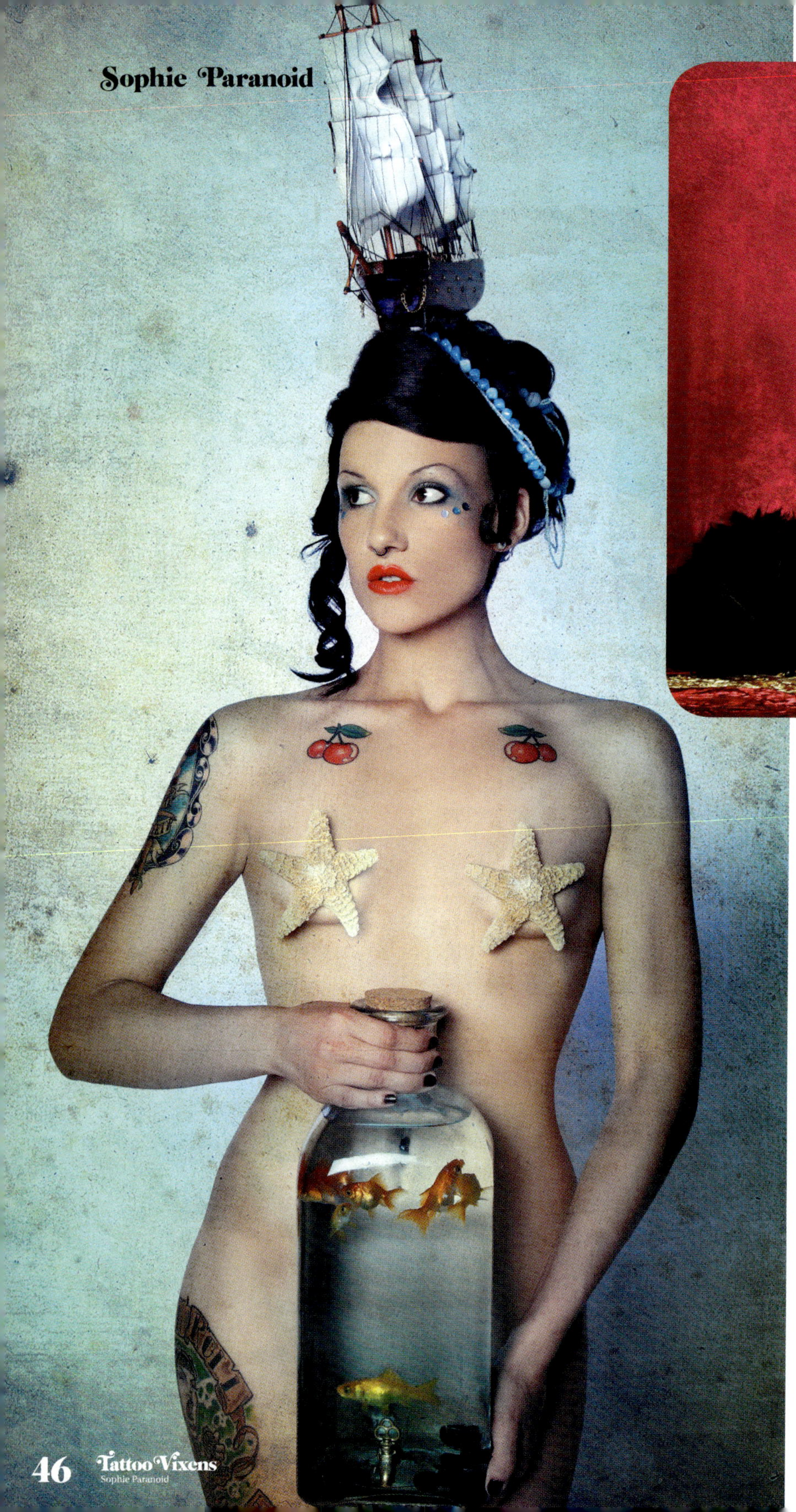

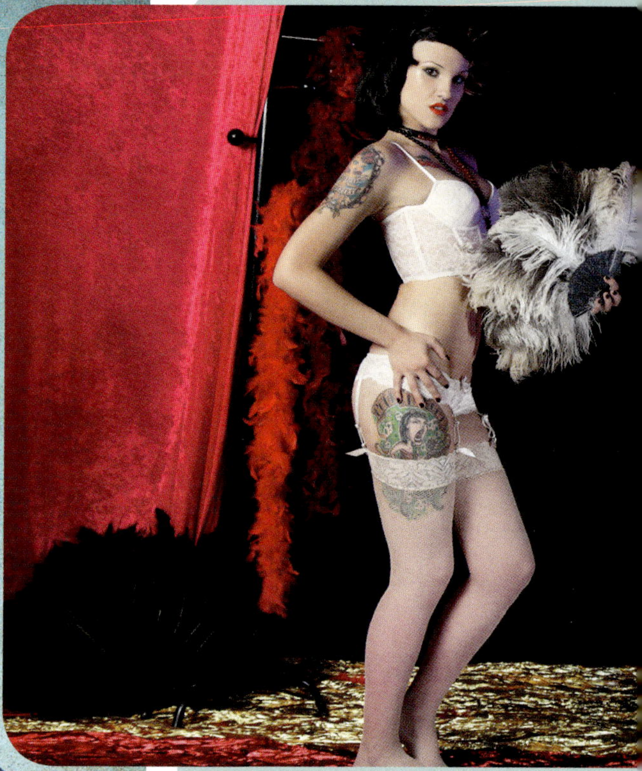

time - I loved cherries, they are so brilliant that they seem to say “eat me” and so I did.

I love what you have done in your shoots here - do you come up with your ideas yourself or is it something you like to work on with the photographer?

Thanks! It depends of the session and the photographer, sometimes the session is based on the model and sometimes they are based on the photographers idea and the model is just a part of that - like a toy in the scene. Anyway, in most sessions, I tend to have my own ideas and the photographers are willing to hear them, so it's easy to work with me!

What is the inspiration behind the photograph with the “Just Look Don't Touch” sign?

It tries to reflect the soul of Burlesque. This spirit is what we have in my Burlesque duo, The

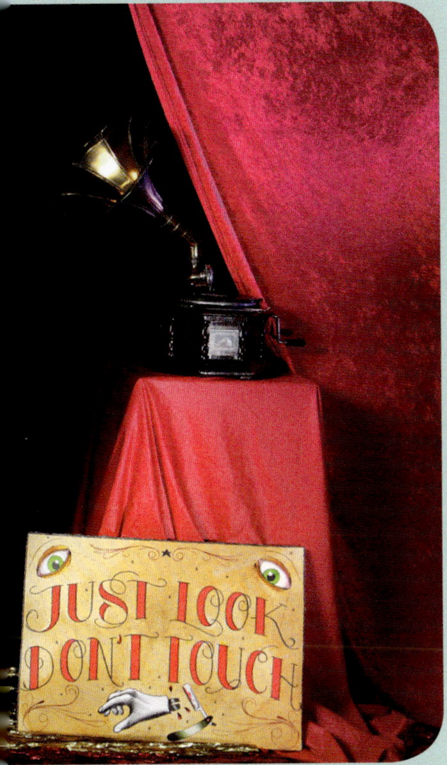

It's like watching old films, everything is black and white and you have to put the colour in yourself.

Shimmy Shakers -www.myspace.com/shimmyshakersmadrid - a kind of eroticism that you can see but not touch, something sexy but not nudity, something glamorous but not Playboy parties. It's like watching old films, everything is black and white and you have to put the colour in yourself with your own imagination!

And the one with the jar with the fish in it - is that your interpretation of a mermaid theme or just a bit of fun?

Inspiration for this tattoo was based on Angelique Houtcamp's work, one of her flashes was a woman with a ship in the hair,

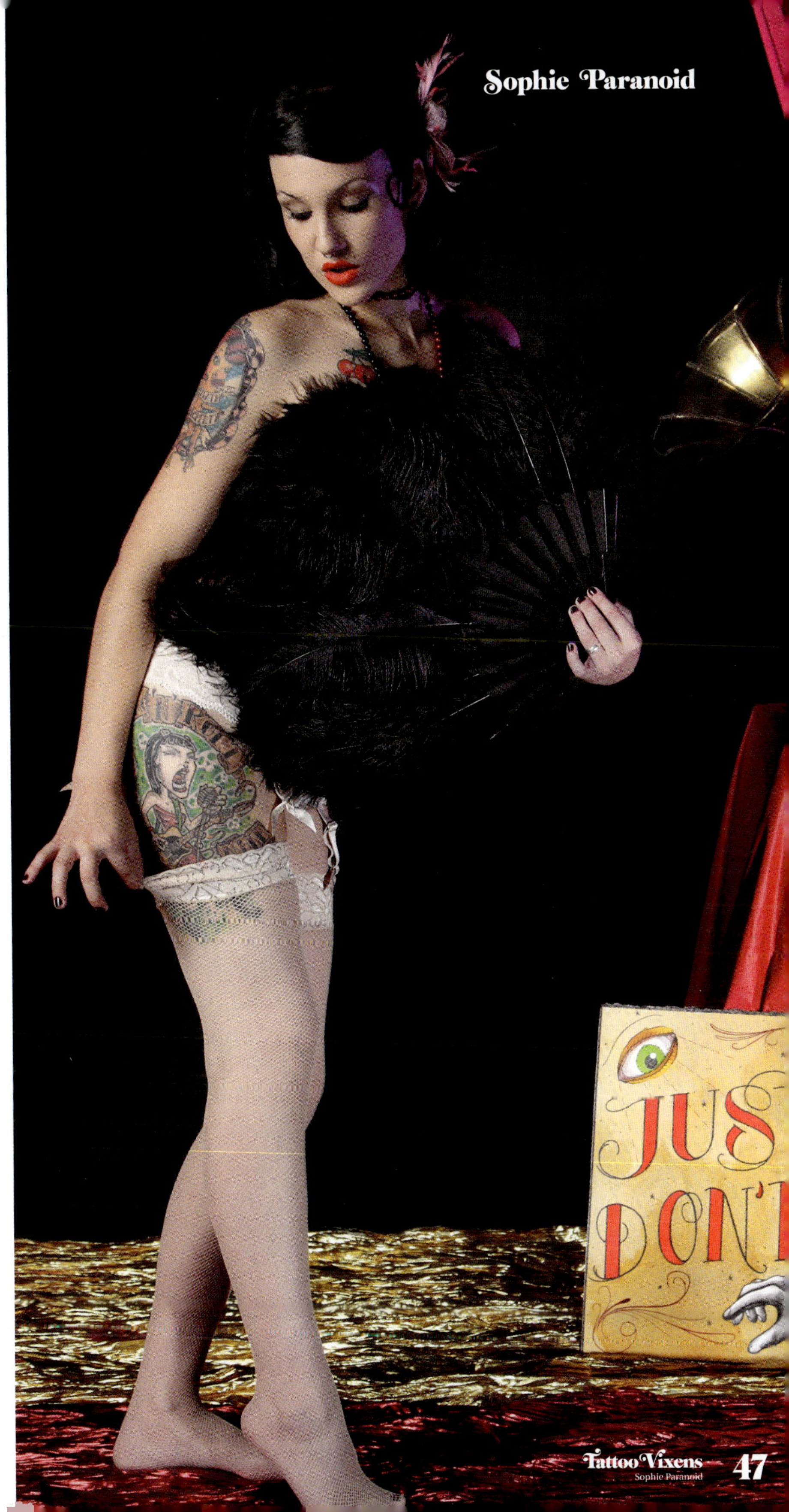

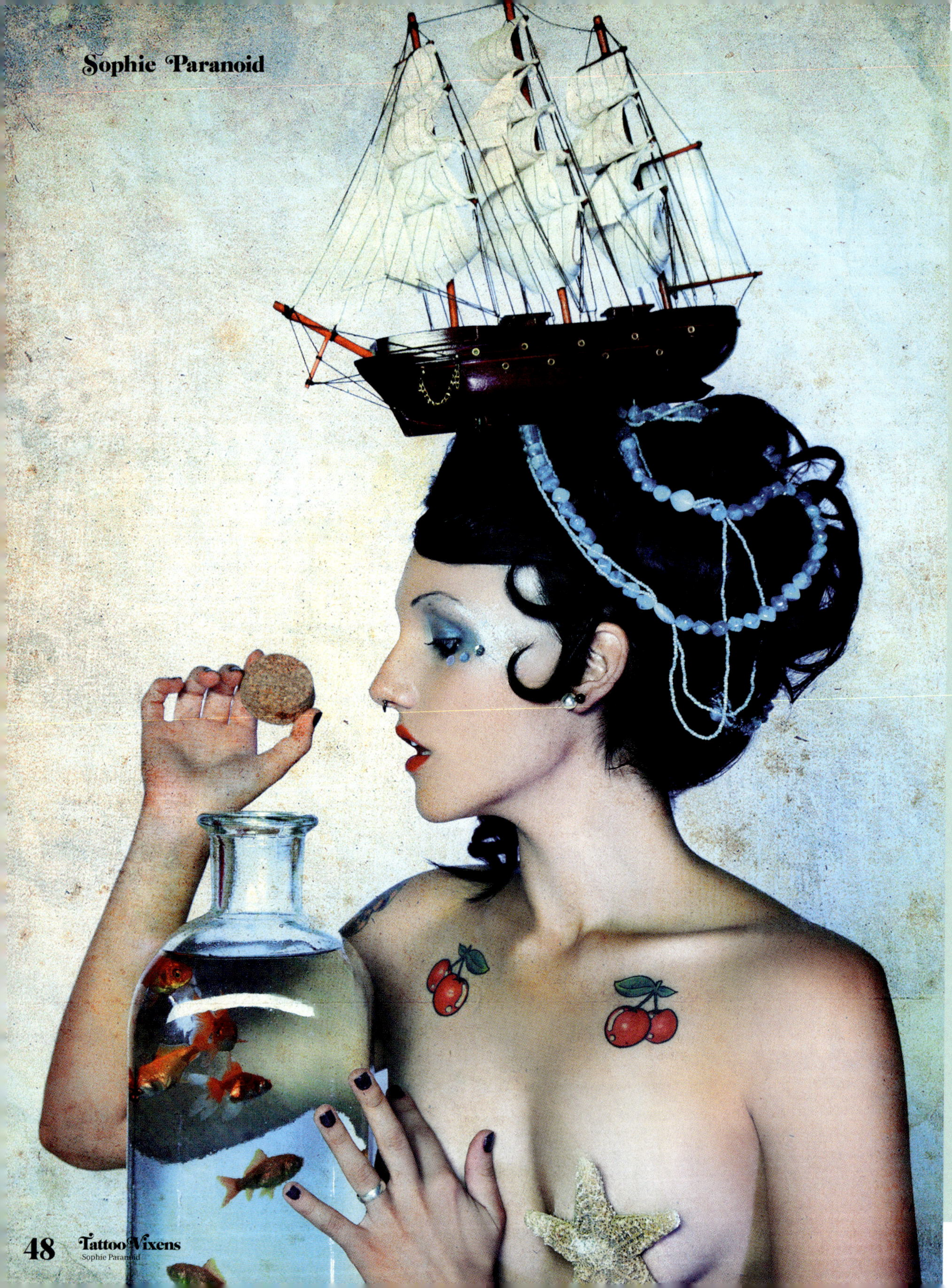

like navigating or sinking in a sea of dreams. After this idea we did our interpretation - basically, a jar and starfishes to hide my nudity! Maria wanted a tribute to Angelique and I think the result was great. It's without doubt one of my favourite sessions, I'm really proud of it.

What did you want to be when you were a little girl? Surely not a tattooed model?
You´re right, I didnt want to be a tattooed model, I wanted to be a tattooed rockstar! Modelling is funny, but playing rock and roll is even funnier, it's my absolute passion, but at this moment I'm a tattooed nurse - and I have no complaints from any of my patients!

I don't have a close up of the tattoo on your thigh - what is it?
That's my best work, it's a new school/cartoon of myself playing my guitar and singing in a band about my way of life - "Rock and Roll All Nite" - like the KISS song, which is really important to me. It was designed and tattooed by one of the best artists in this country, Juanma Matarradona from Tsunami Tattoo, Tarragona. I have more ideas to work with him!

What kind of work do you normally do - you have quite a unique look?
No, I don't have a unique look when I'm modeling, but I always have my look in my real life! In photography I do fetish, pin up, punk scenes - always "alternative modelling ".

You also have a very unique name - what made you choose that? Are you really paranoid?!
Paranoid is my husband's surname, when we met he used to call himself this, but I decided to use it for me! He's the Paranoid, I'm just crazy! Anyway, it's a cool name!

Do you keep your tattoos hidden during the day? Have you purposely not had too much work done in the more visible areas of your body for this reason - or are you building up to it?
I do not hide my tattoos, I like them and I like to show them. I don't have too much work because to be tattooed is not a game. It's cool to have a complete arm in a few months, but what does it mean? I try to have tattoos with a real meaning and not just pretty ones. When you work with children people tend to judge - you know, you have to be blonde, pale skin, mother's smile - but I realised that is better to be yourself and to do good work. Besides, on pediatrics, children love my tattoos! They want to get one too!

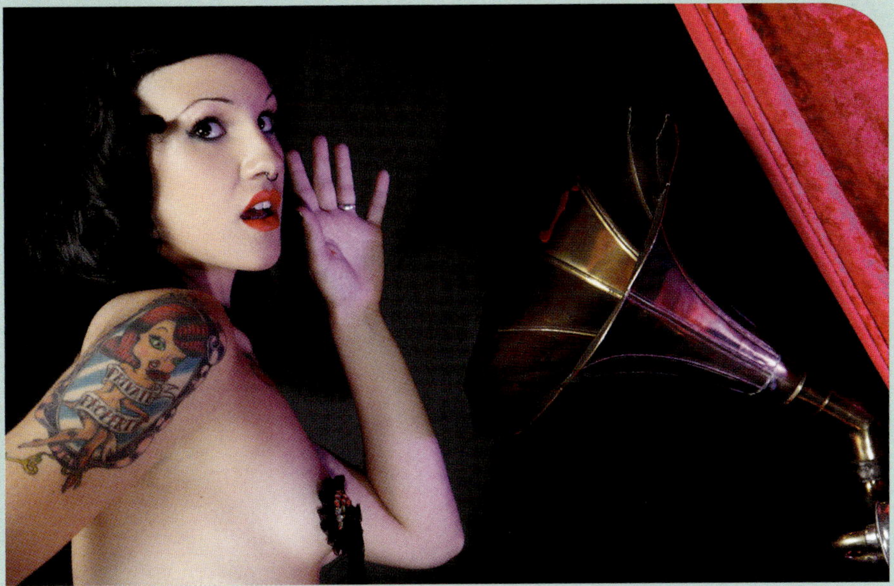

Modelling is funny, but playing rock and roll is even funnier, it's my absolute passion, but at this moment I'm a tattooed nurse - and I have no complaints from any of my patients!

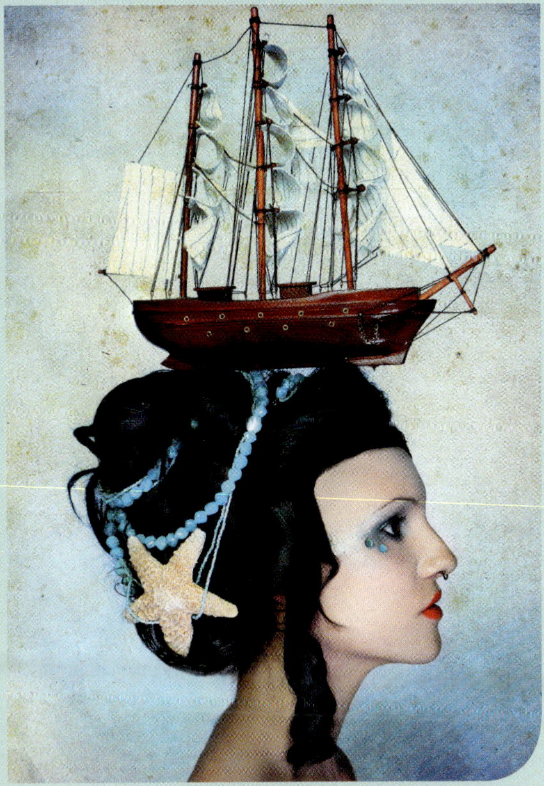

Name Femke Fatale (real name Femke Verstraete)
Age 27

Femke Fatale

ALL PHOTOGRAPHS: **IHSAN KEMAL**

The next-time you're shopping in a major high street retail store, have a quick check behind the counter - if you're lucky, you might find Femke sporting her ink - why not stop and say hi.

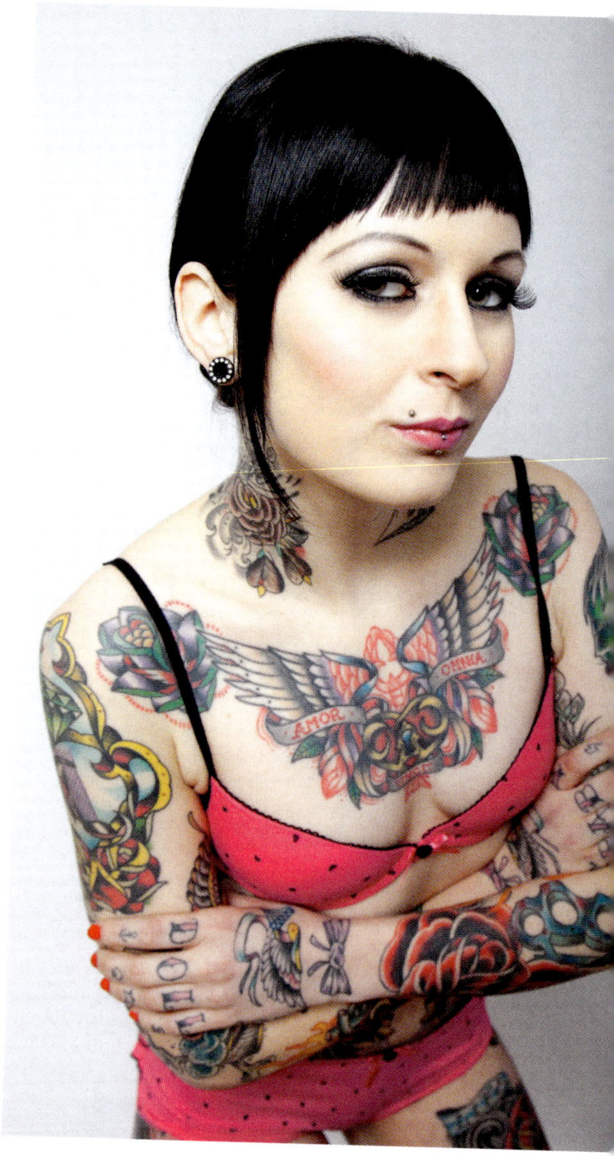

How does your modelling fit in with your ambitions?

I work part time as a sales advisor at H&M right now and I also am a tattoo model for clothing lines, tattoo magazines and calendars. I love it! It is a dream come true! I wish I could do it as a full-time job but you never know what will happen in the future...

Have you always wanted tattoos and what inspired you?

I wanted tattoos ever since I was a little kid - tattoos fascinated me, and I loved people with colours on their body, it made them unique for me. I grew up in a middle class family, full of artists, so it has always been good to be different at home. No one in my family has ink though, only me.

Tattooed people just inspired me because they dare to be different and they do not care! It takes courage to do that. People make bad judgements about tattooed people; they think we are trash and criminals. Thankfully that has changed a bit, but still, it is hard to be a tattooed woman. People often stare and criticise; you need to be a strong person to deal with all of these things. But for me, it is not to show off or to be cool, I got inked for myself.

What would you say is the most positive aspect of being a heavily tattooed woman?

I get a lot of opportunities I would not have without ink, such as being a tattoo model even though I am not the right size. I also meet people easily because they all want to talk to me about my ink or want a picture taken with me. Sometimes they make me feel like a freak show though! I went to a fun park once and so many people stopped me to talk or take a picture that I felt like one of the attractions there. But then again it is a good thing that people get used to seeing heavily inked ladies because tattooed girls rule!

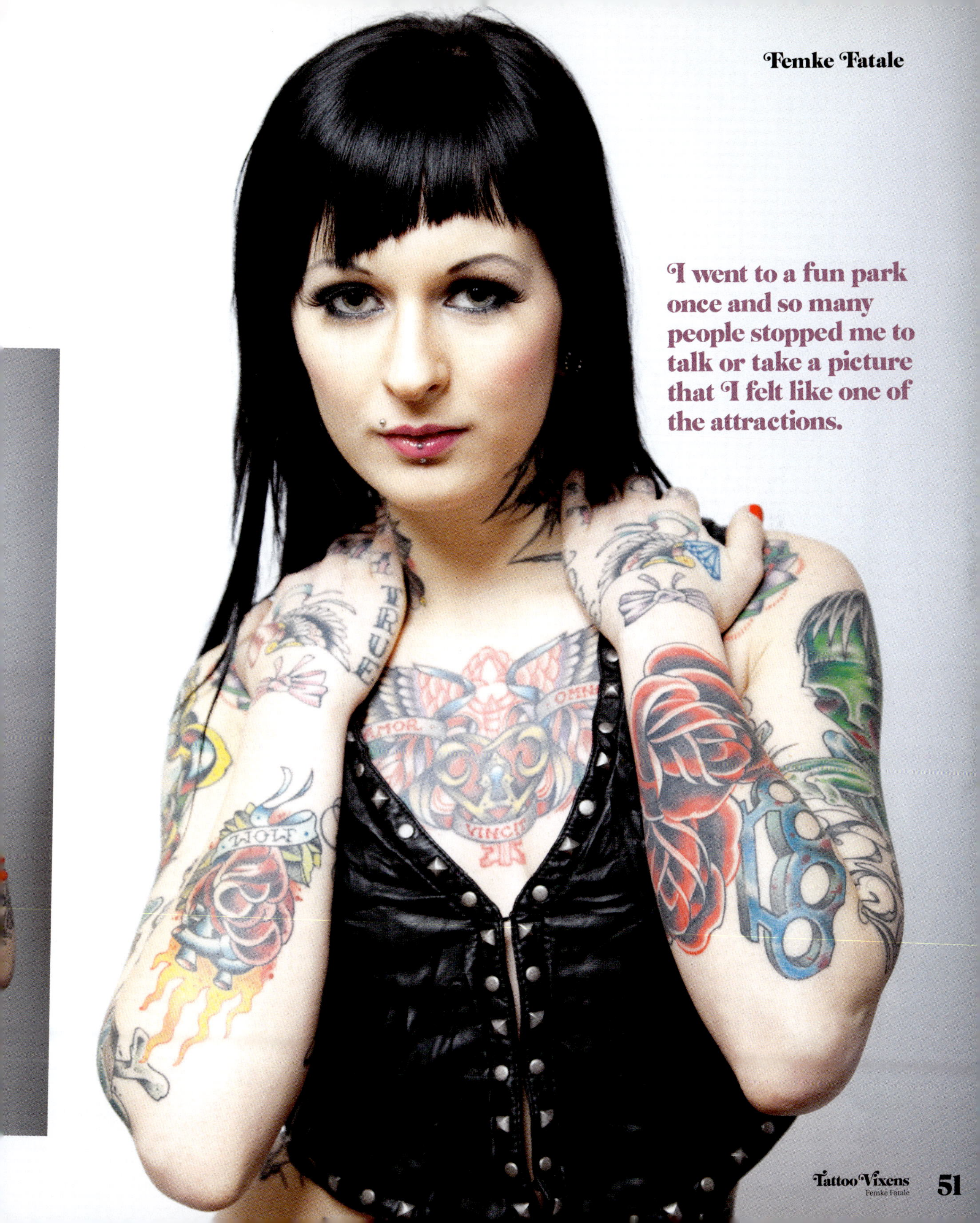

I went to a fun park once and so many people stopped me to talk or take a picture that I felt like one of the attractions.

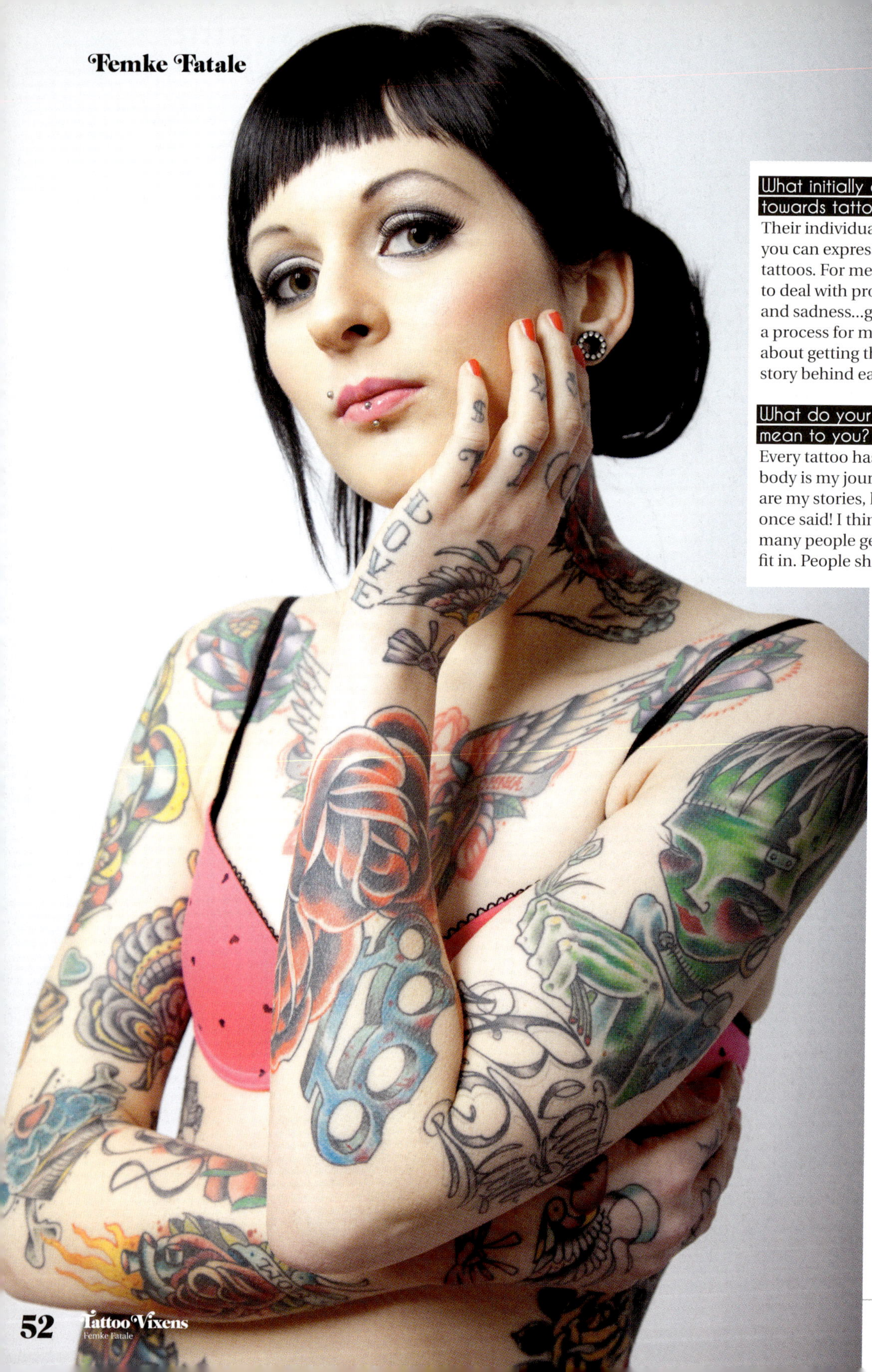

What initially attracted you towards tattoos?

Their individuality, the way you can express yourself with tattoos. For me it is also a way to deal with problems, joy, and sadness...getting inked is a process for me. It is not only about getting the ink; there is a story behind each tattoo.

What do your tattoos mean to you?

Every tattoo has its meaning, my body is my journal and tattoos are my stories, like Johnny Depp once said! I think it is sad that so many people get tattooed just to fit in. People should accept each

MUA: **BELLA SIMONSEN USING MAC PRO COSMETICS**
MUA: **JESSIE DEOL**
HAIR STYLIST: **CAMERON RAINS AND DAVE DIRT WEAVER AT PIMPS AND PINUPS LONDON**

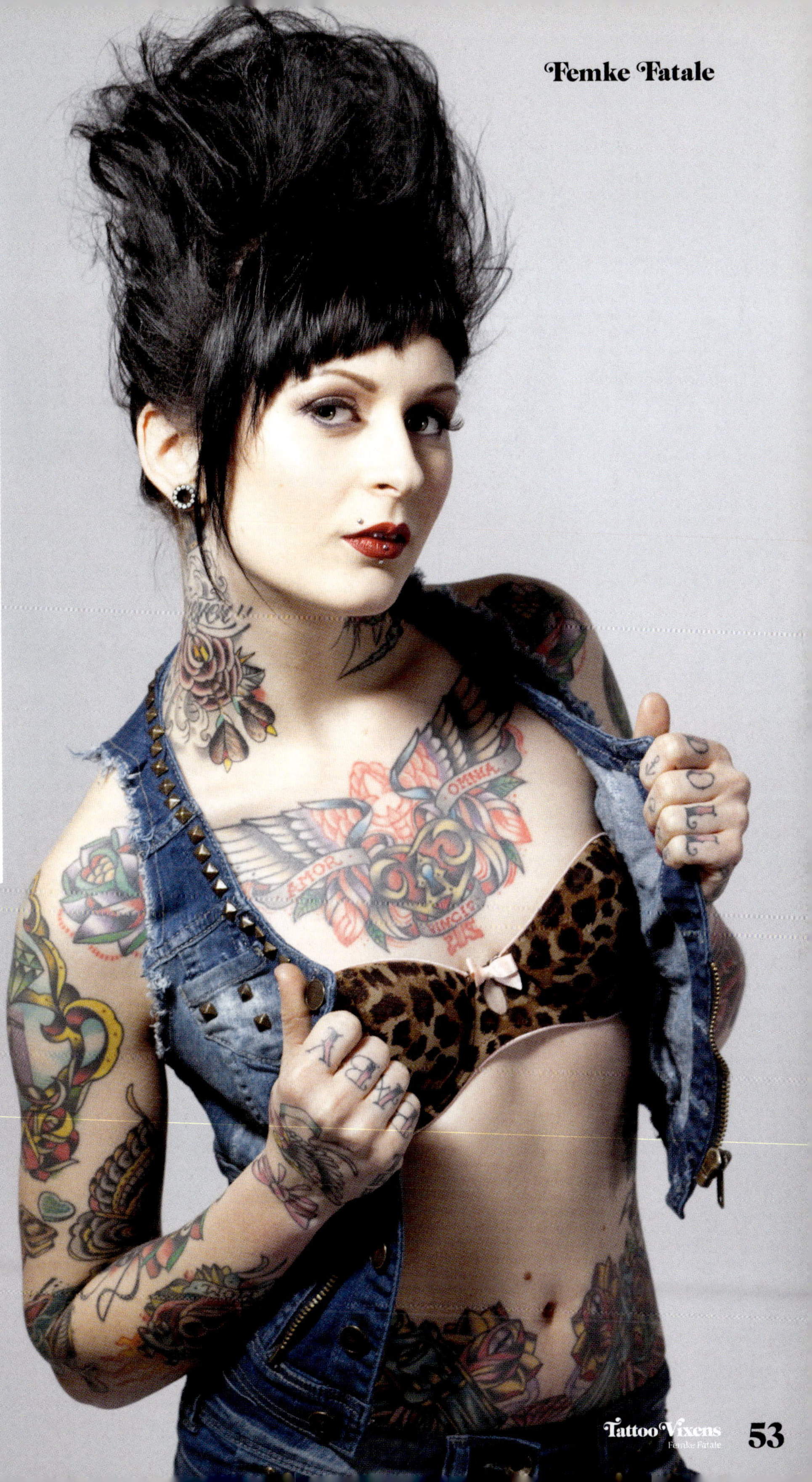

If I were to start collecting from scratch again, I'd definitely have the same ones done.

other as they are and stay true to their selves. So all my tattoos are very significant and if I were to start collecting from scratch again, I'd definitely have the same ones done.

If just one person could tattoo you, who would it be?
They have already tattooed me! I love my artists! Alexandre Wuillot, Jay Jay Blood Brothers, Jean Harai, Rinus Vanity Tattoo, Candy Cane and Uncle Allan! All amazing artists. They made me the piece of art I am today, for which I am very very thankful. Maybe someday I'll discover someone else I want to get tattooed by but at the moment I'm happy with my guys.

Miss Mischief

Ah - the delectable Miss Mischief! The lady that starts every single day of her life with a photo shoot. Be it professional or just with her friends, that's commitment for you!

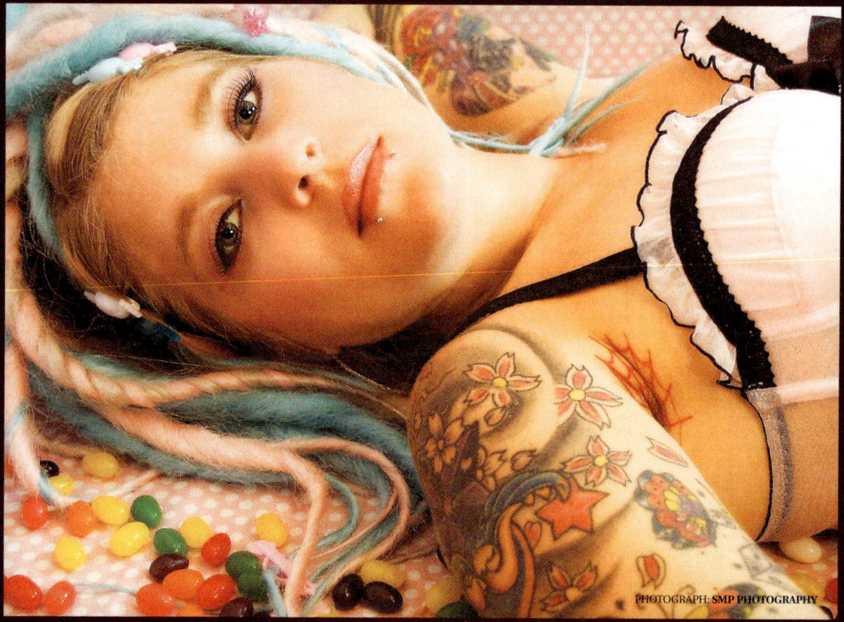

PHOTOGRAPH: SMP PHOTOGRAPHY

What's the most empowering thing about being a tattooed woman?

I wouldn't necessarily say I'm empowered. I'm just a chick with some rawking tattoos, some attitude and little bit of crazy!

Do any of your tattoos bear significance, or do you collect them purely for their aesthetic appeal?

I have a few that have specific meaning, but most of them are just because I thought they were

PHOTOGRAPH: FRANK BRADFORD PHOTOGRAPHY

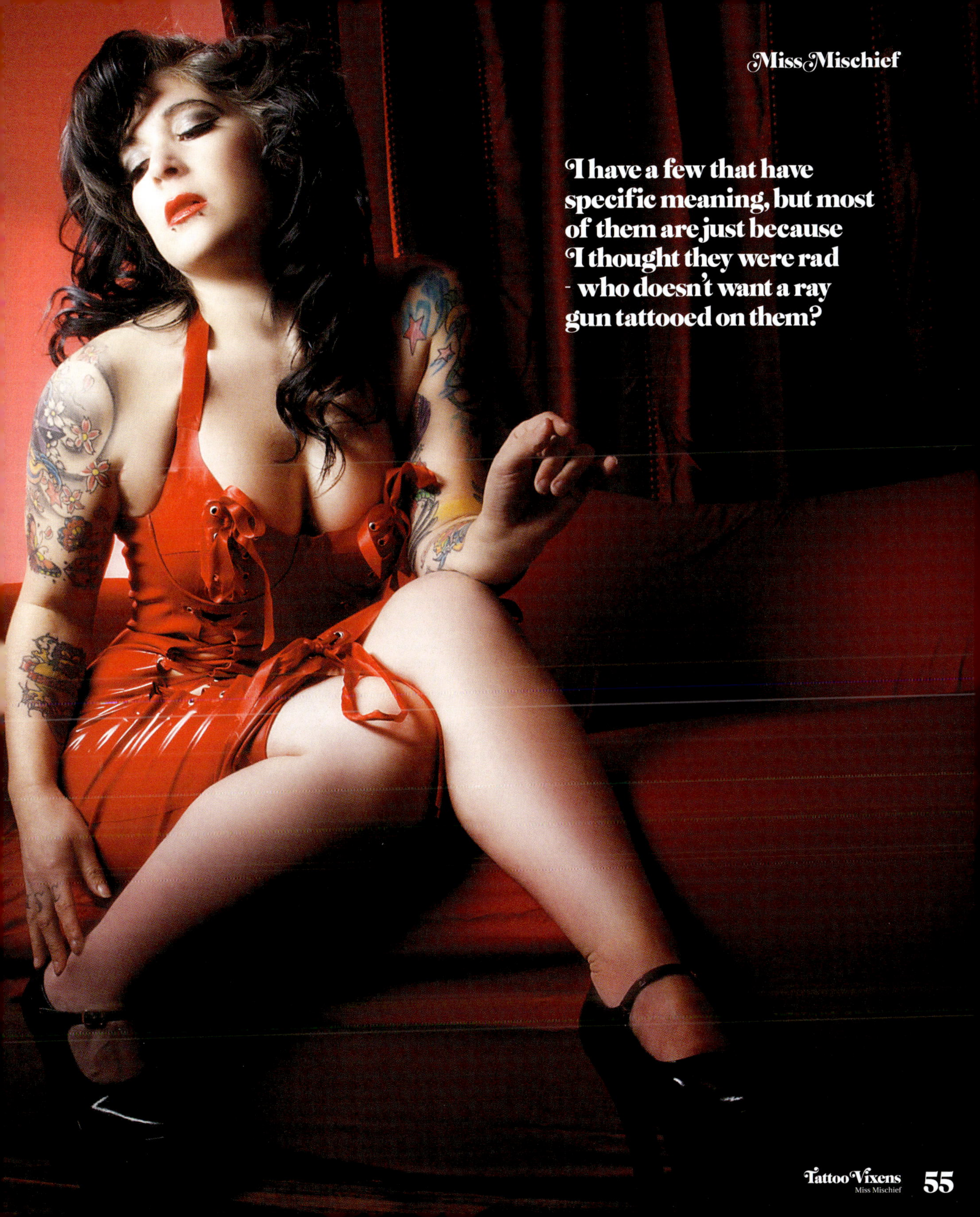

I have a few that have specific meaning, but most of them are just because I thought they were rad - who doesn't want a ray gun tattooed on them?

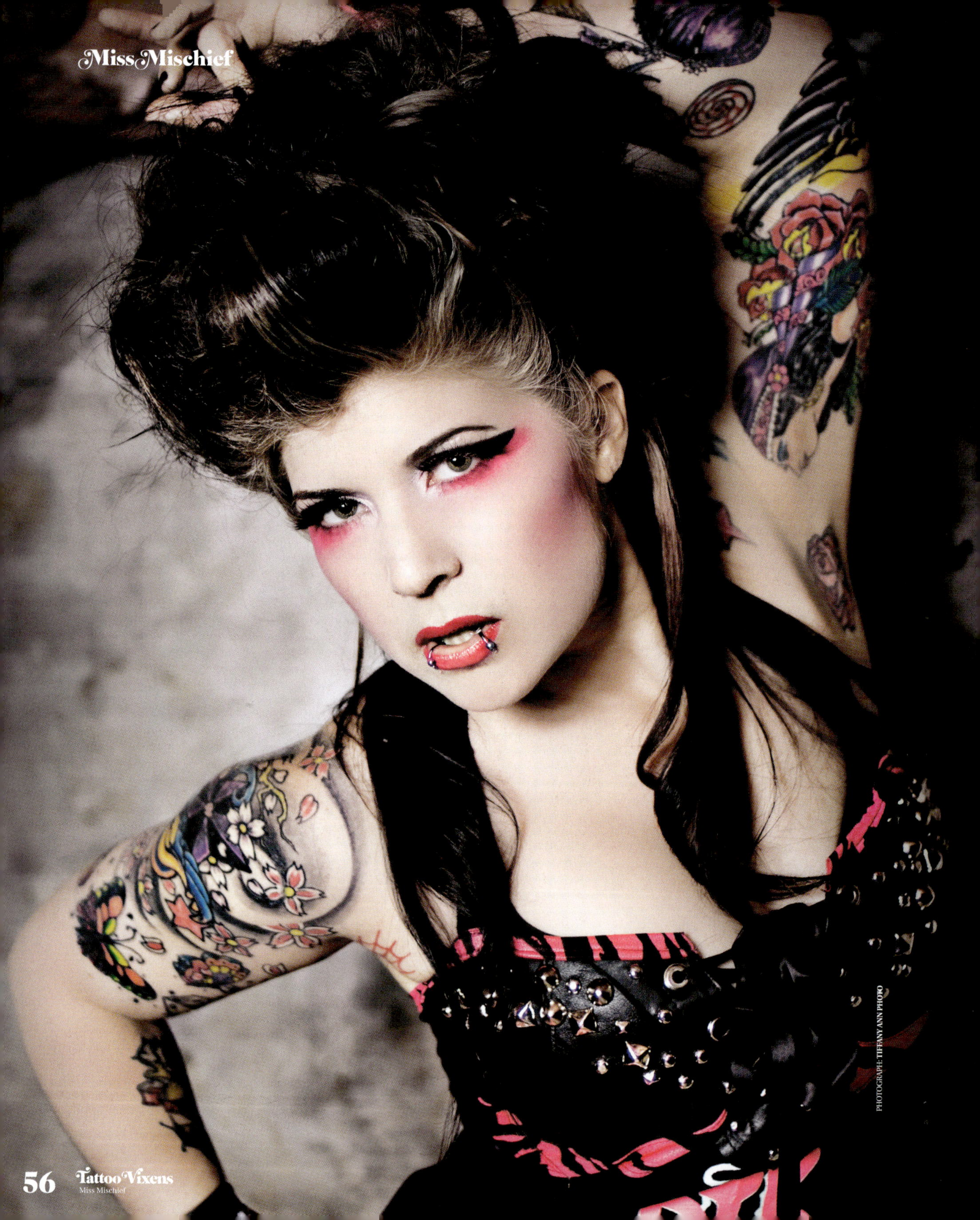

PHOTOGRAPH: TIFFANY ANN PHOTO

rad - who doesn't want a ray gun tattooed on them?

Whom do you particularly admire in the tattoo world (tattooists/artists/models etc)?

My favourite tattooist is Fred from Sinners & Saints and I love the artwork of Jeral Tidwell.

In your opinion, do women now have more of a level playing field in the tattoo world?

Absolutely! I don't think that tattooed women are treated any different to wonderfully tattooed men.

Have you noticed more women acquiring significant tattoo coverage in the past five years or so? If so, why do think that is?

I have. I think for some it's become more of a novelty instead of a form of artistic expression. I see a lot of Barbies with sleeves now.

What's on your iPod?

New Ditty, MSI, Otep, Pantera, As I Lay Dying, Etta James, Buddy Guy, Dresden Dolls, Nina Simone, Celldweller, All that Remains.

I think for some it's become more of a novelty instead of a form of artistic expression. I see a lot of Barbies with sleeves now.

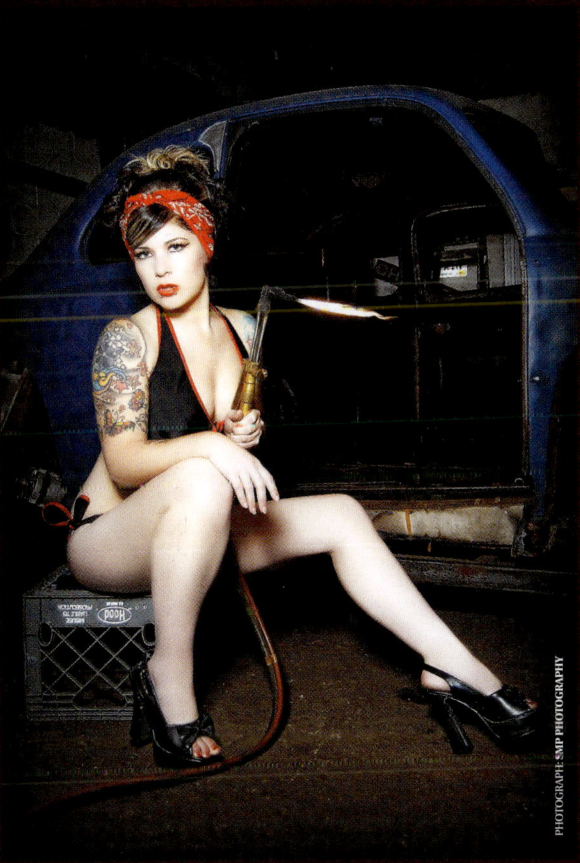

PHOTOGRAPH: SMP PHOTOGRAPHY

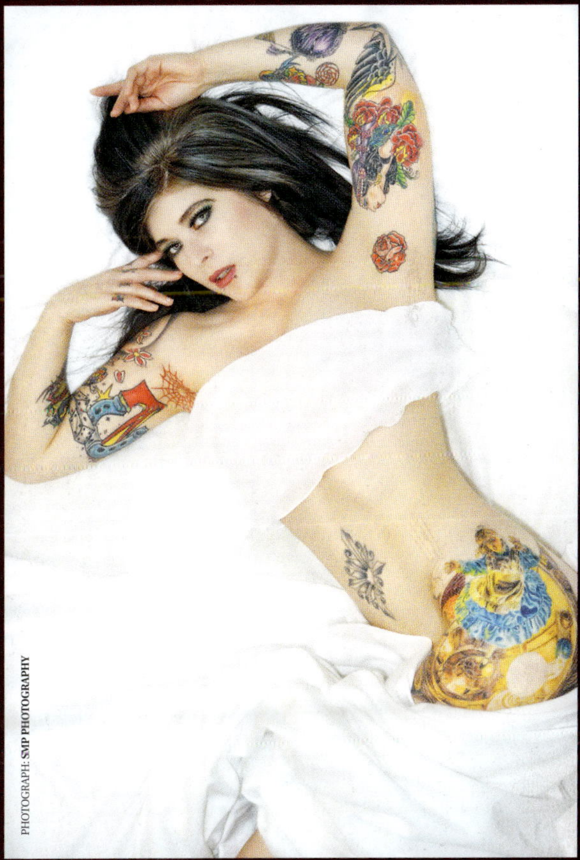

PHOTOGRAPH: SMP PHOTOGRAPHY

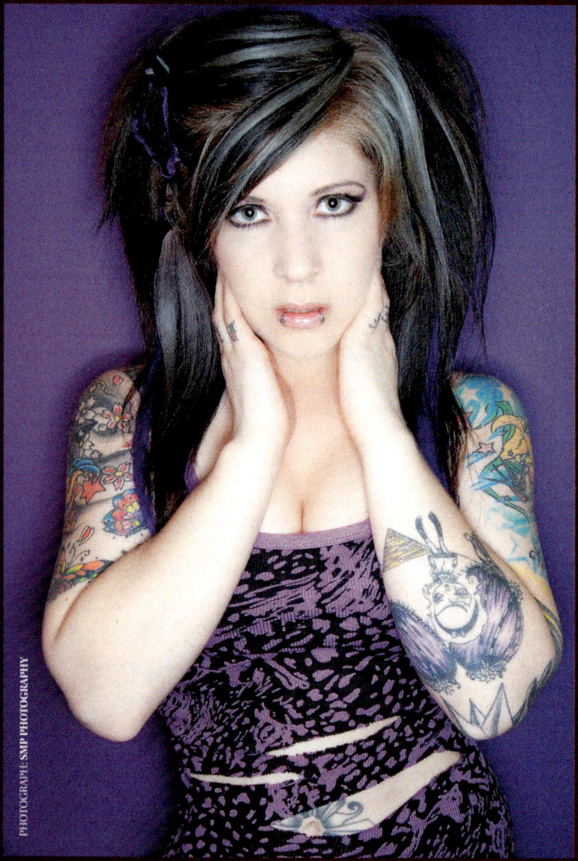
PHOTOGRAPH: SMP PHOTOGRAPHY

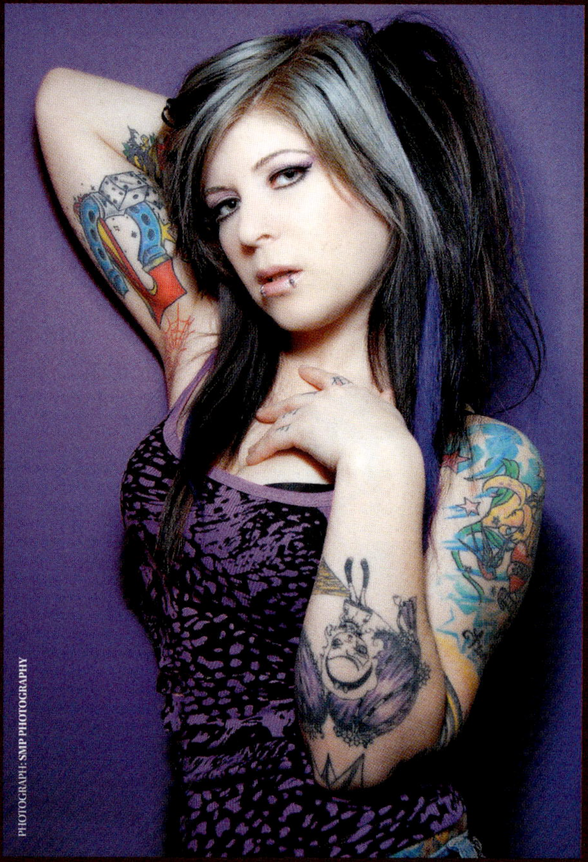
PHOTOGRAPH: SMP PHOTOGRAPHY

I like to jump on skateboards with heels, breathe fire in my front yard, shoot my 9mm at aerosol cans.

How much mischief can somebody with a name like yours really get up to?

Plenty!! I like to jump on skateboards with heels, breathe fire in my front yard, shoot my 9mm at aerosol cans and leave my neighbors presents after partying. And that's just during the day.

You currently work at a recycling plant (did I remember that right) - are you the most tattooed person there? What do the guys make of you?

I am the most tattooed person here. A lot of the guys were afraid to talk to me when I first started working here. I think I still scare some of them! The truck drivers I deal with on a regular basis know me now and can goof with me - sometimes scaring the guys off isn't such a bad thing!

What did you want to do when you were a little girl - is this what you imagined your future would hold?

When I was little I wanted to be an archeologist. I didn't exactly end up doing that. I'm still fascinated by archeology now. It's definitely not how I imagined my life, but I'm super stoked that my life is what it is!

Plans for the future?

I hope to continue working with awesome clothing designers and photographers. I hope to get to more conventions in the next year, other events and gigs and maybe score a few more mags - and of course, continue to get tattooed!

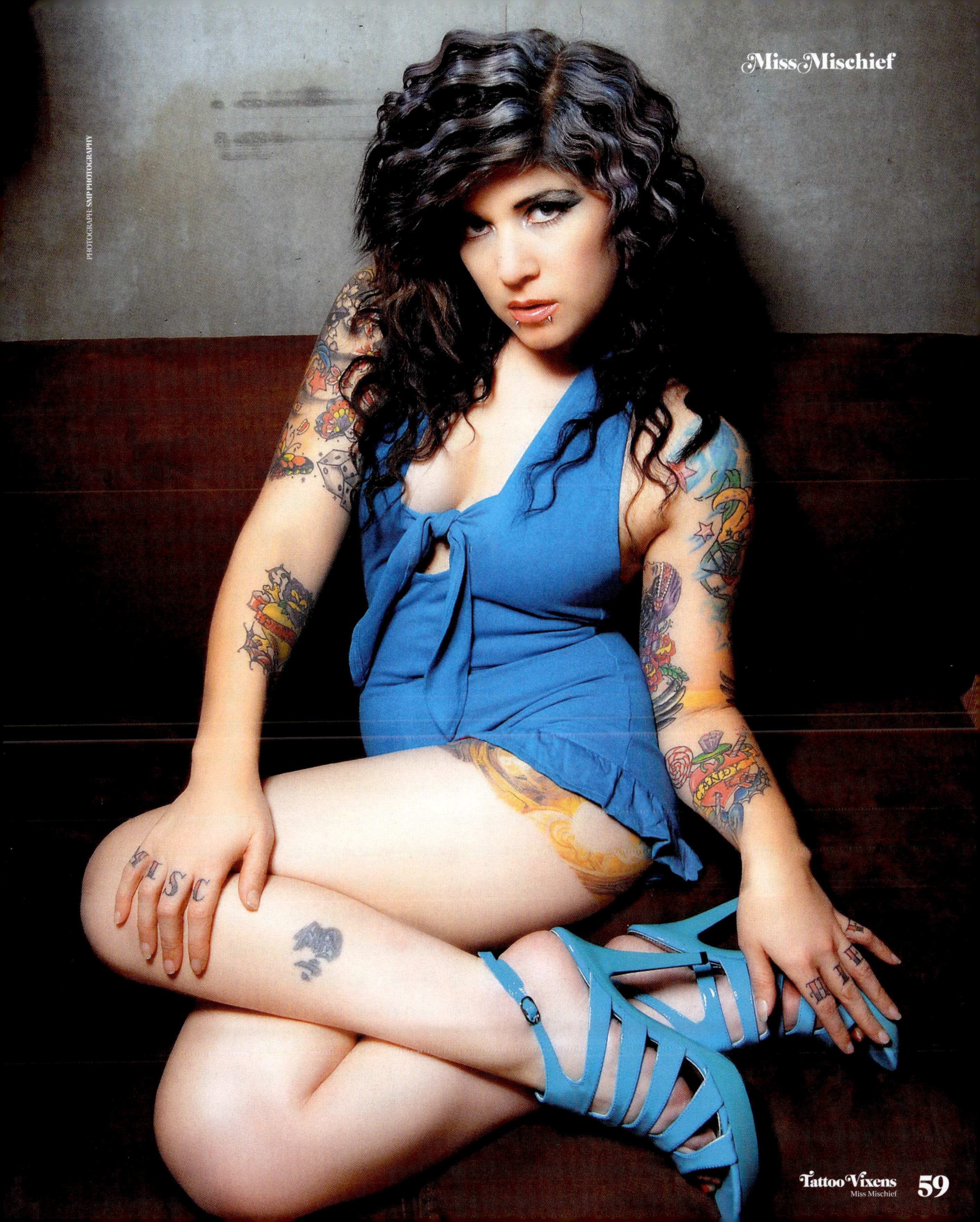

PHOTOGRAPH: SMP PHOTOGRAPHY

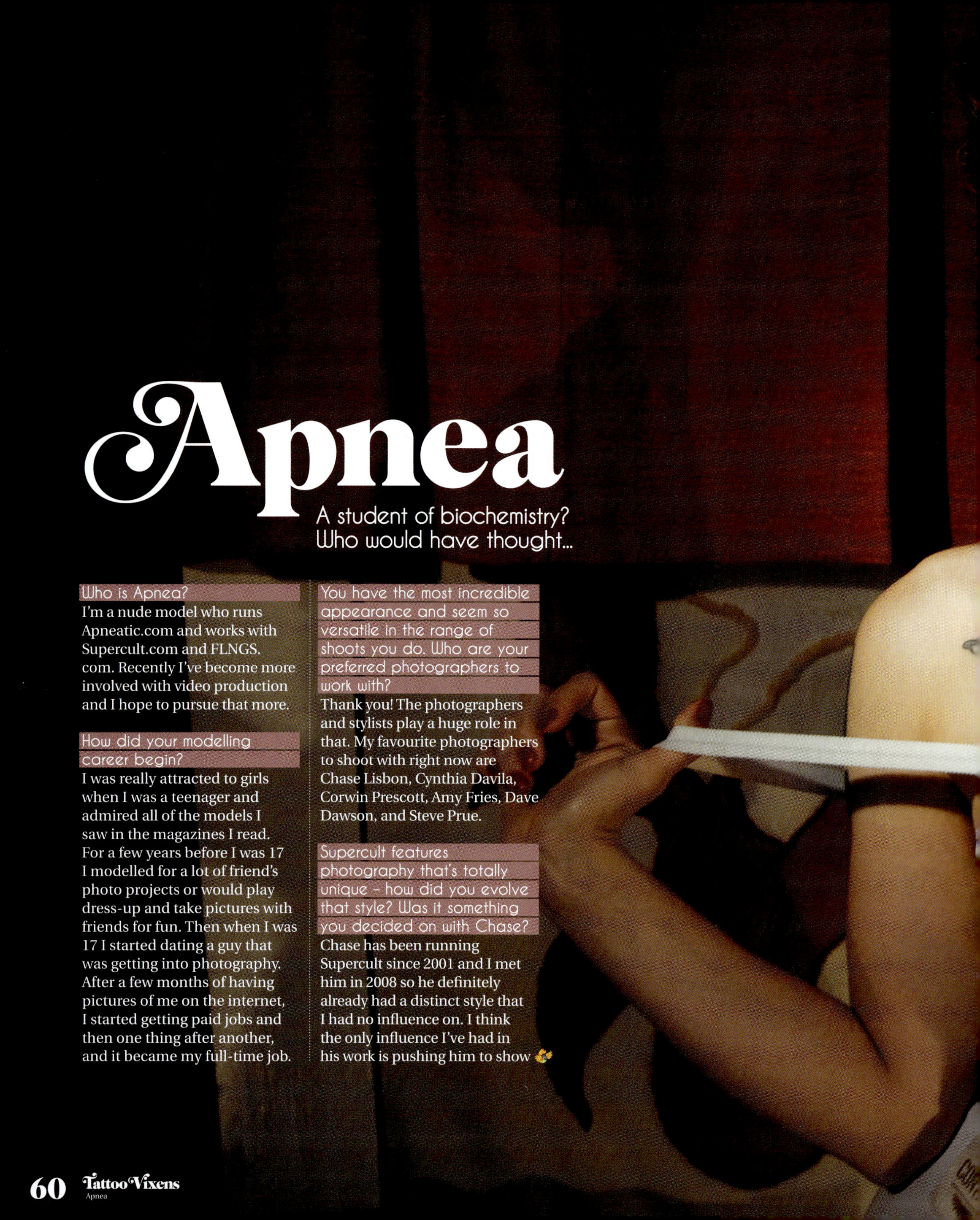

Apnea

A student of biochemistry?
Who would have thought...

Who is Apnea?
I'm a nude model who runs Apneatic.com and works with Supercult.com and FLNGS.com. Recently I've become more involved with video production and I hope to pursue that more.

How did your modelling career begin?
I was really attracted to girls when I was a teenager and admired all of the models I saw in the magazines I read. For a few years before I was 17 I modelled for a lot of friend's photo projects or would play dress-up and take pictures with friends for fun. Then when I was 17 I started dating a guy that was getting into photography. After a few months of having pictures of me on the internet, I started getting paid jobs and then one thing after another, and it became my full-time job.

You have the most incredible appearance and seem so versatile in the range of shoots you do. Who are your preferred photographers to work with?
Thank you! The photographers and stylists play a huge role in that. My favourite photographers to shoot with right now are Chase Lisbon, Cynthia Davila, Corwin Prescott, Amy Fries, Dave Dawson, and Steve Prue.

Supercult features photography that's totally unique – how did you evolve that style? Was it something you decided on with Chase?
Chase has been running Supercult since 2001 and I met him in 2008 so he definitely already had a distinct style that I had no influence on. I think the only influence I've had in his work is pushing him to show

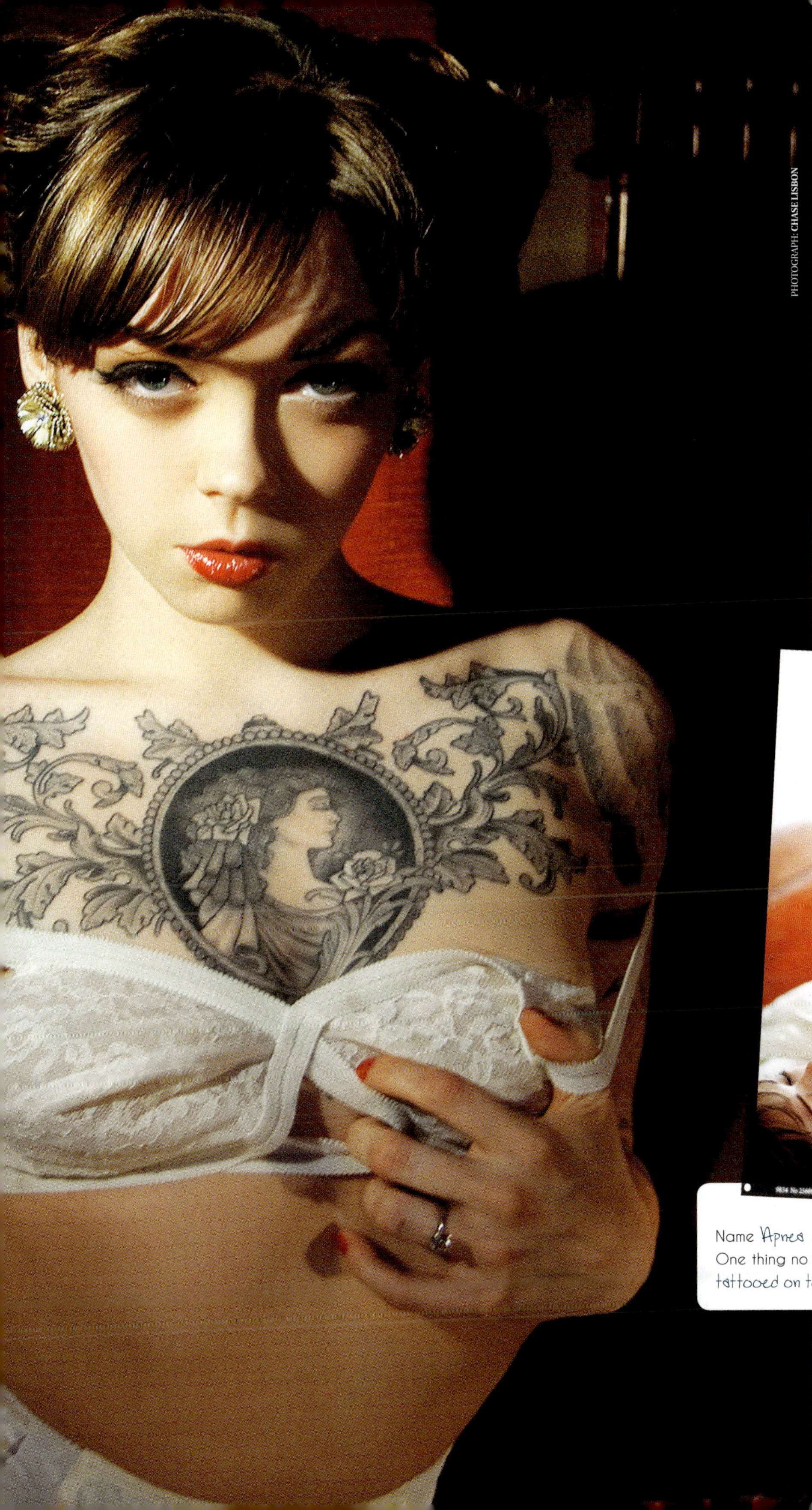

PHOTOGRAPH: CHASE LISBON

After a few months of having pictures of me on the internet, I started getting paid jobs and then one thing after another, and it became my full-time job.

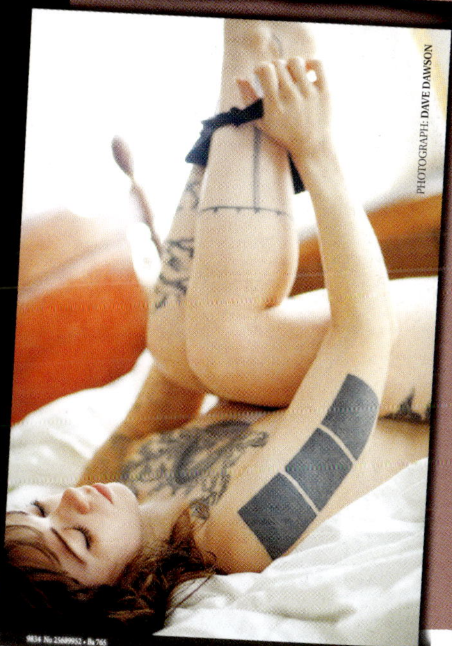

PHOTOGRAPH: DAVE DAWSON

Name Apnea Age 25 Occupation Nude model webmaster
One thing no one knows about you I have some lines tattooed on top of my head. Only hairdressers see it.

By the time I was 14 I knew I wanted to eventually be covered in them and I already tried to start planning everything I wanted.

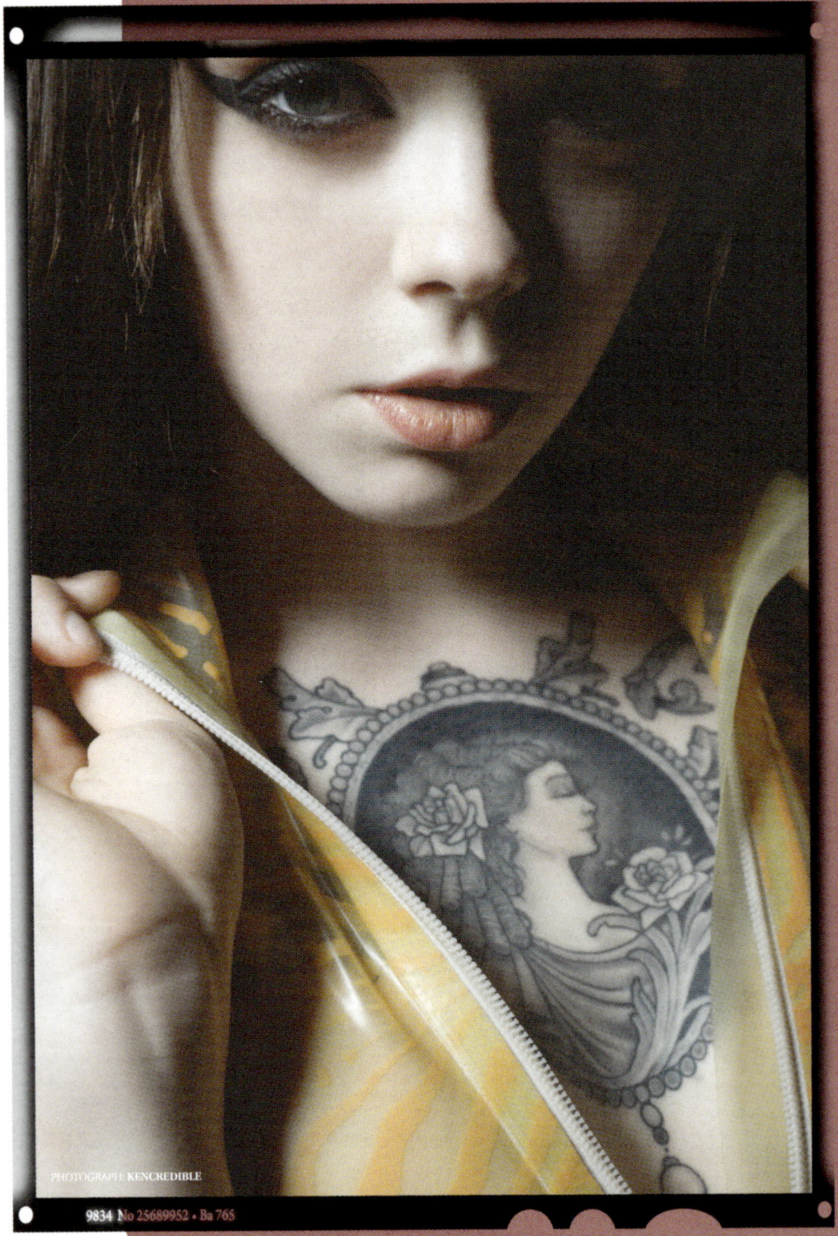

PHOTOGRAPH: KENCREDIBLE

his pictures bigger online and to start printing them so people could begin to collect his work. When I can, I try to get his models in higher heels, but that's just because I really like high heels.

Your blog is regularly updated, which is a refreshing thing to see! Tell us a little about it…

My blog's main purpose was to promote my website *Apneatic.com* but I ended up using it more like a real blog in the last two years. For the first two years of its existence I updated it every day and that made it one of the most boring things to read! It's all garbage. It mainly looks like a food log and pictures of my cat. But then in 2008 when I met Chase and he was a photo blogger for Nerve I enjoyed his blogs so much it inspired me to put more effort into my posts so I've been trying to make it more interesting since then without exposing myself too much.

When did you begin collecting tattoos?

I grew up around my step-dad and he has tattoos on his arms and chest from when he was in the Navy. Then my older sister started getting tattooed when I was 11 or 12 and I think seeing my family with them had a lot of influence on me. By the time I was 14 I knew I wanted to eventually be covered in them and I already tried to start planning everything I wanted. My first real tattoo was on my 18th birthday and then I kept holding back from getting

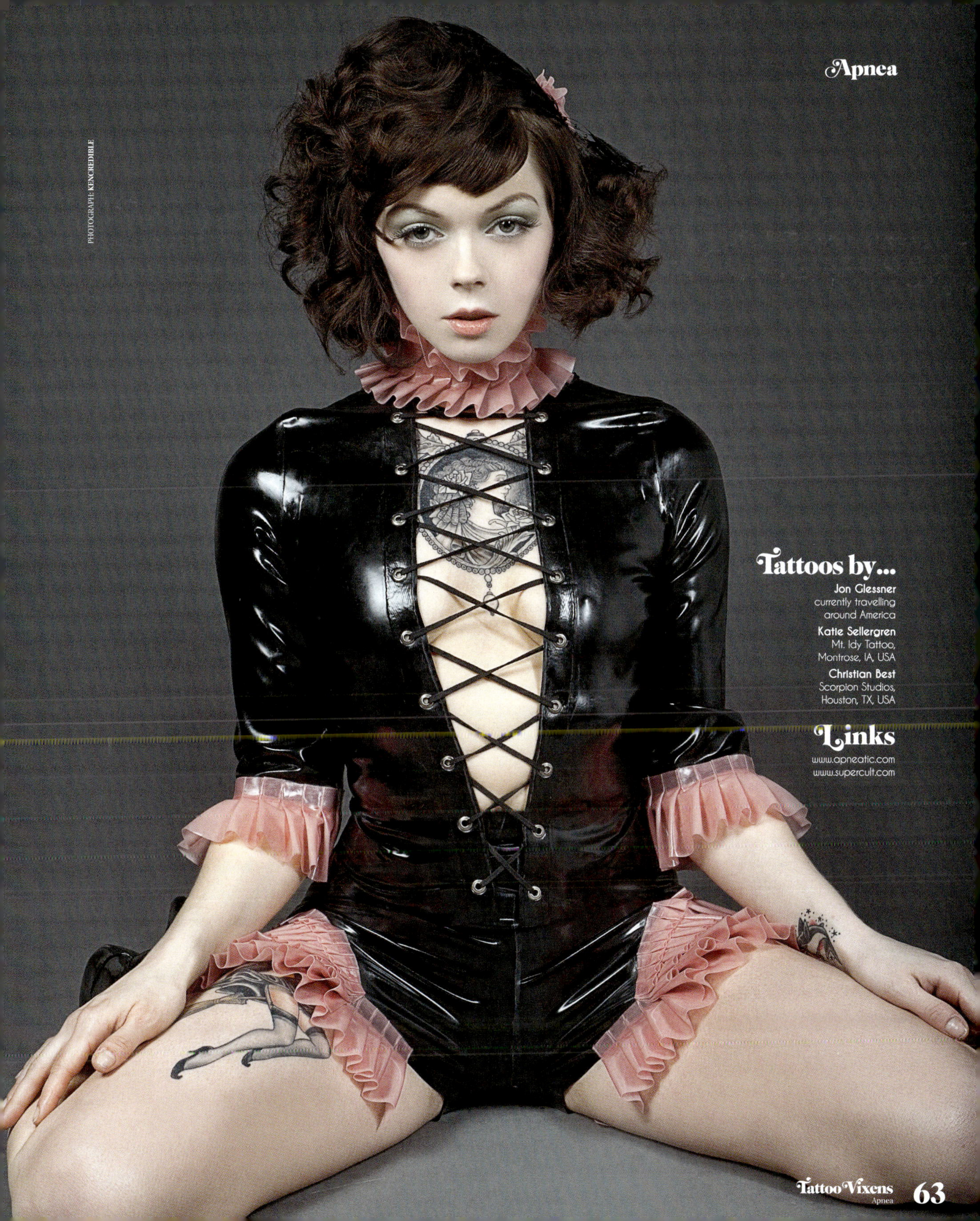

PHOTOGRAPH: KENCREDIBLE

Tattoos by...

Jon Glessner
currently travelling around America

Katie Sellergren
Mt. Idy Tattoo, Montrose, IA, USA

Christian Best
Scorpion Studios, Houston, TX, USA

Links

www.apneatic.com
www.supercult.com

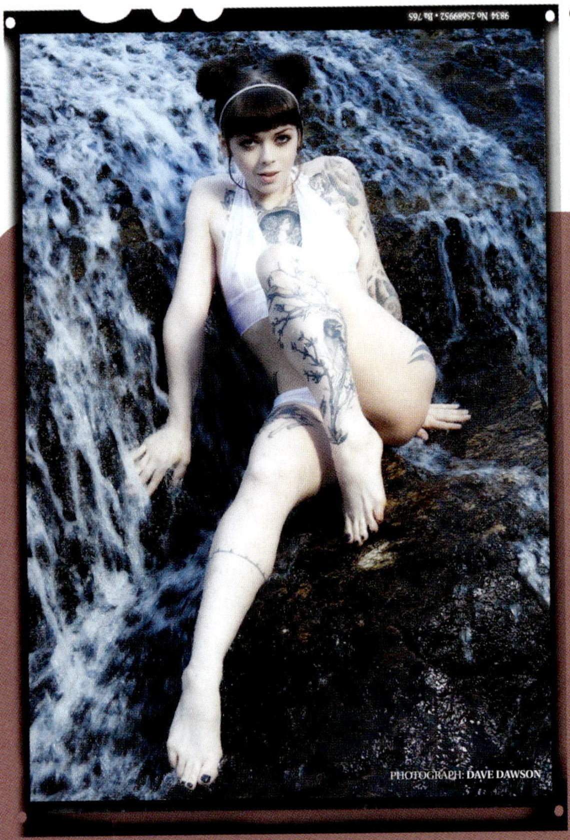
PHOTOGRAPH: DAVE DAWSON

I got a few bad tattoos that I wish I didn't have now. I'm in the process of getting a three quarter sleeve lasered so I can start over on my left arm.

them because of my modelling. I eventually got to the point where I didn't care anymore if I lost jobs over it. I went through a period of taking my life back and making decisions based on what I wanted to do and not what the people around me were telling me was best for me. The timing of it all worked out though. Before I met the friends that taught me the difference between a good tattoo and a bad one I got a few bad tattoos that I wish I didn't have now. I'm in the process of getting a three quarter sleeve lasered so I can start over on my left arm.

What's the most empowering thing about being a tattooed woman?

It will always be empowering to some people, but to others it's something fashionable like a handbag. So it depends on the girl's motivation. Some people seem to be into it for scene points. I meet a lot of people through work that just have them to be different even though it's becoming so commonplace and I feel like a lot of people are starting to develop stereotypes when they see someone my age with my job that looks like me. I just have to make sure that I put a lot of thought into what I get and choose the best artists I can so I make sure that I stay happy with the work I get. Having three quarters of my arm lasered is enough for one lifetime.

Do any of your tattoos bear significance, or do you collect them purely for their aesthetic appeal?

It's really both. There's a story behind all of them but it's mostly the aesthetic appeal. The stories don't hold any deep meaning or any key to understanding my

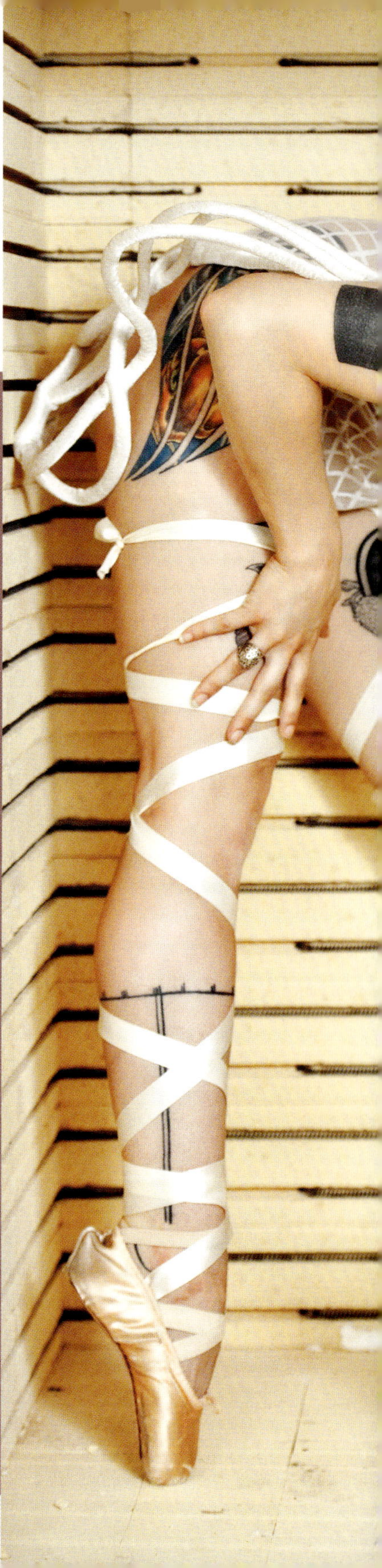

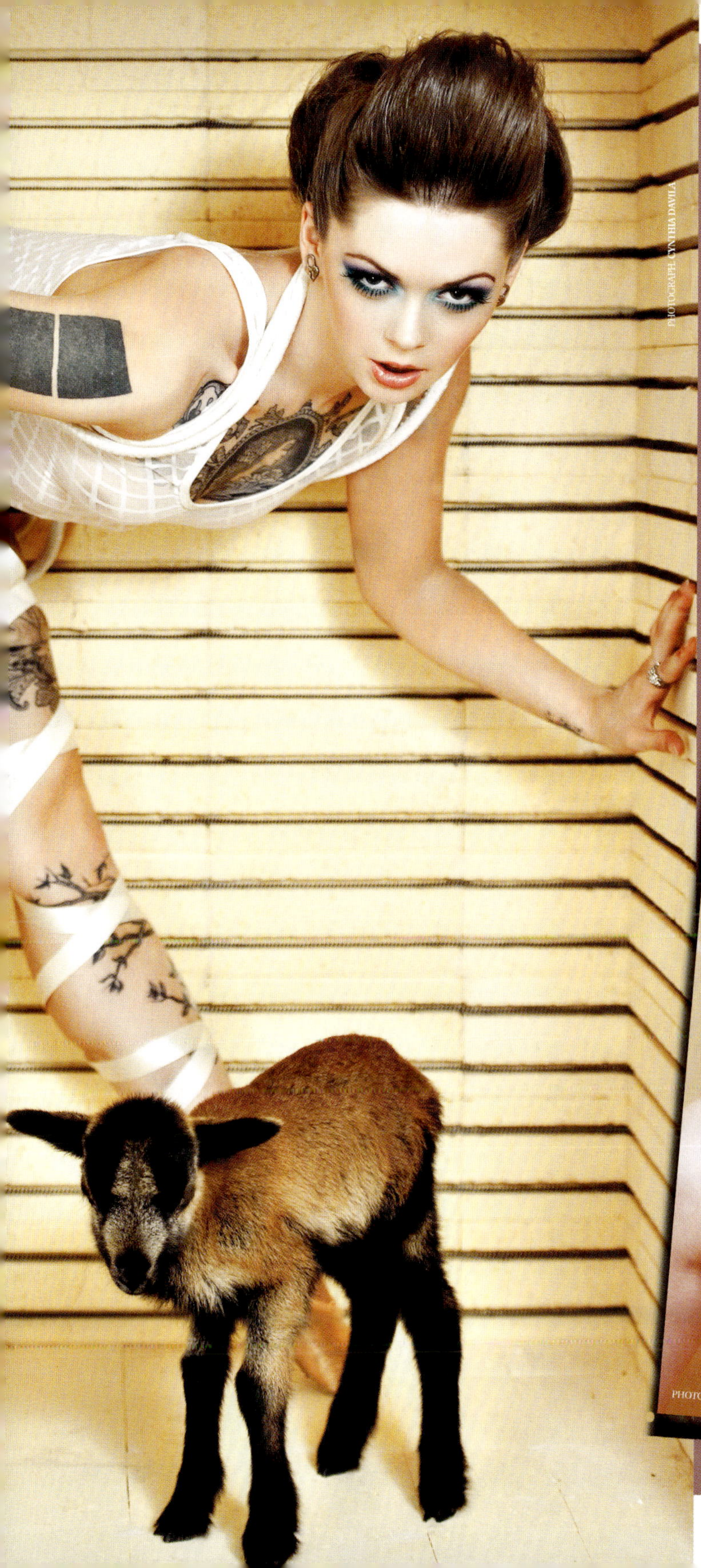

PHOTOGRAPH: CYNTHIA DAVILA

psyche. It's things like, I collect cameos, or it was shark week… that sort of thing.

What's next for you?

Keep an eye out for Chase Lisbon's next full-length movie. It's the first move where I've ever played a leading role so I'm very excited about it!

The stories don't hold any deep meaning or any key to understanding my psyche. It's things like, I collect cameos, or it was shark week...that sort of thing.

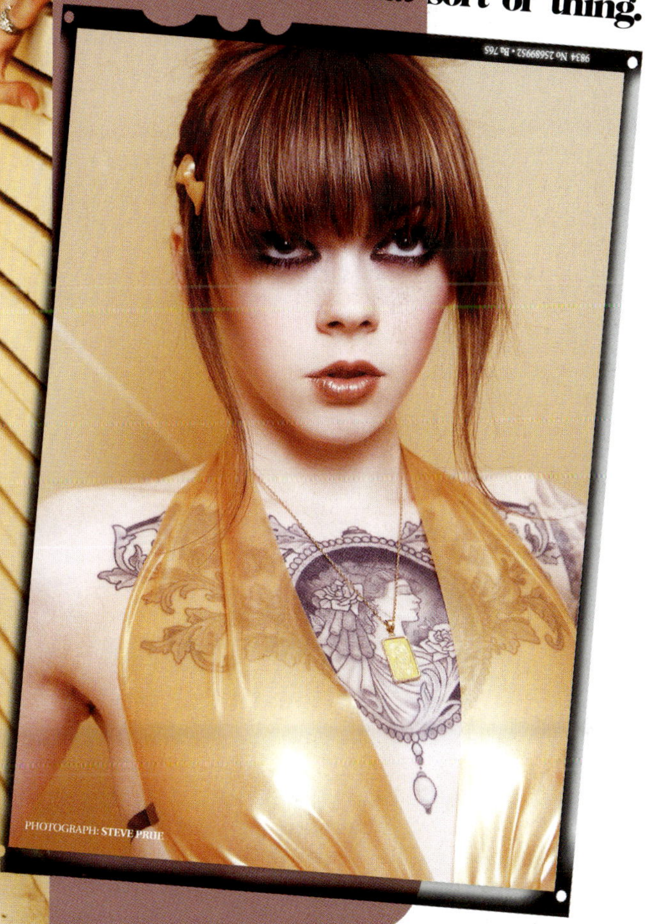

PHOTOGRAPH: STEVE PRUE

Laura

ALL PHOTOGRAPHS: **IHSAN KEMAL**

Since her first feature in Skin Deep back in June 2009, Laura has really been kicking out the jams!

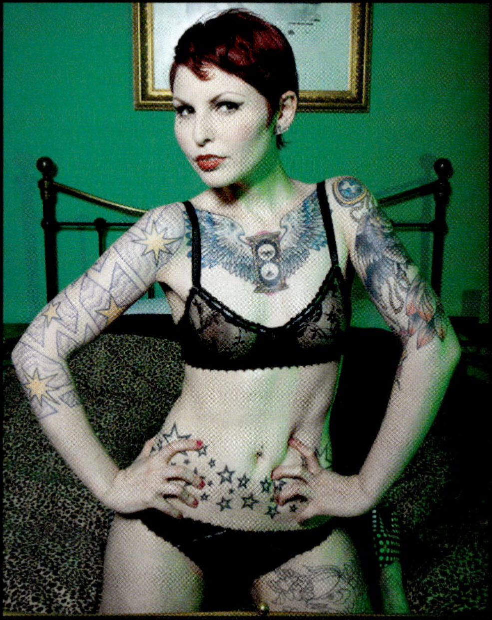

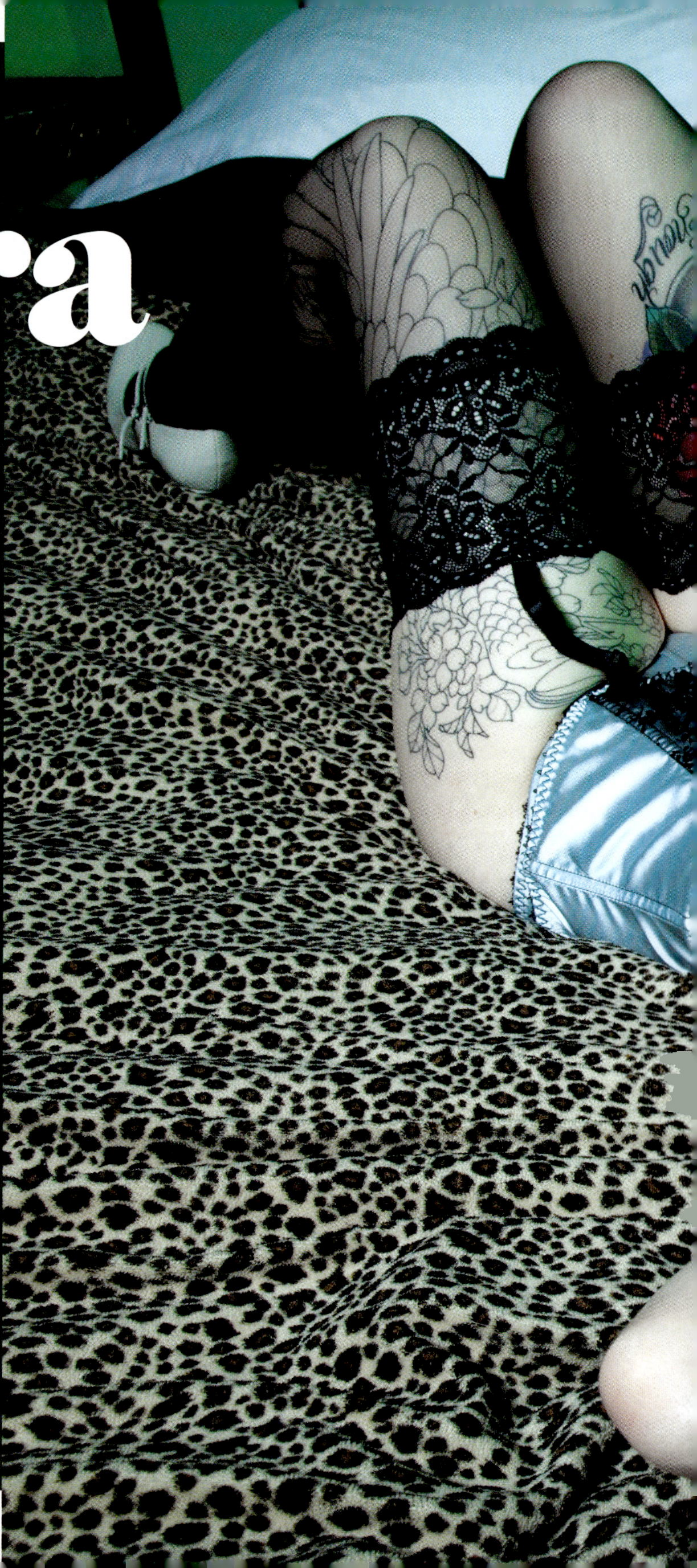

Name Laura
Age 24

How did you get into modelling and is it your full-time job?

I am already working in my dream career in London. I have a very 'normal' job and I am fortunate to have a very understanding employer, who lets me show off my tattoos. Since being in Skin Deep Magazine in June 2009, my modelling has really taken off.

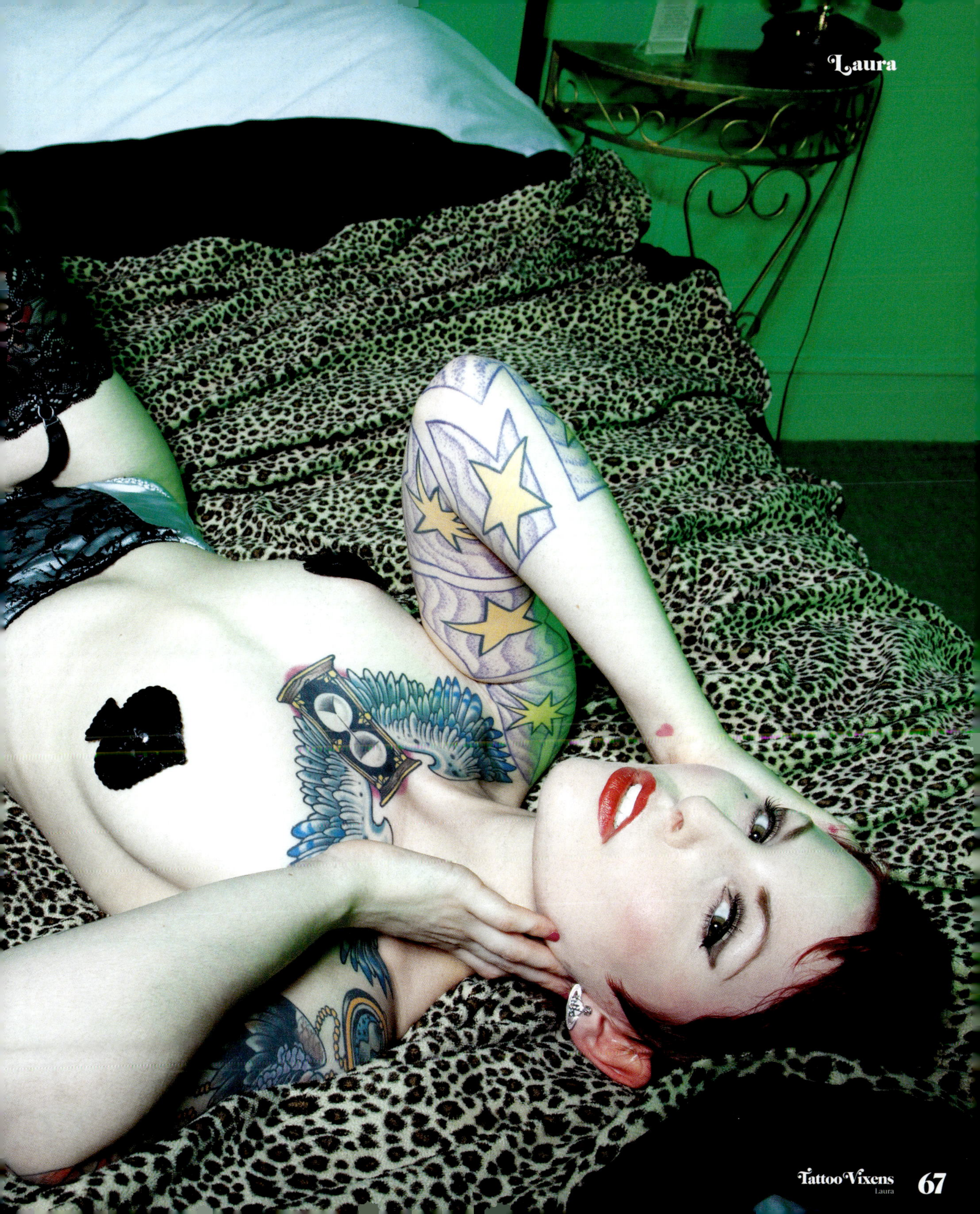

I try to arrange a shoot once a month and I have been lucky enough to have worked with some amazing photographers.

As for modelling full-time, I don't think anyone as tattooed and curvy as me can make a living out of it.

As for modelling full-time, I don't think anyone as tattooed and curvy as me can make a living out of it.

Tell us an interesting fact about you.
I ran away to LA when I was 19 and worked organising a burlesque tour for the Suicide Girls.

What appeal do tattoos hold for you?
I love the way they immediately

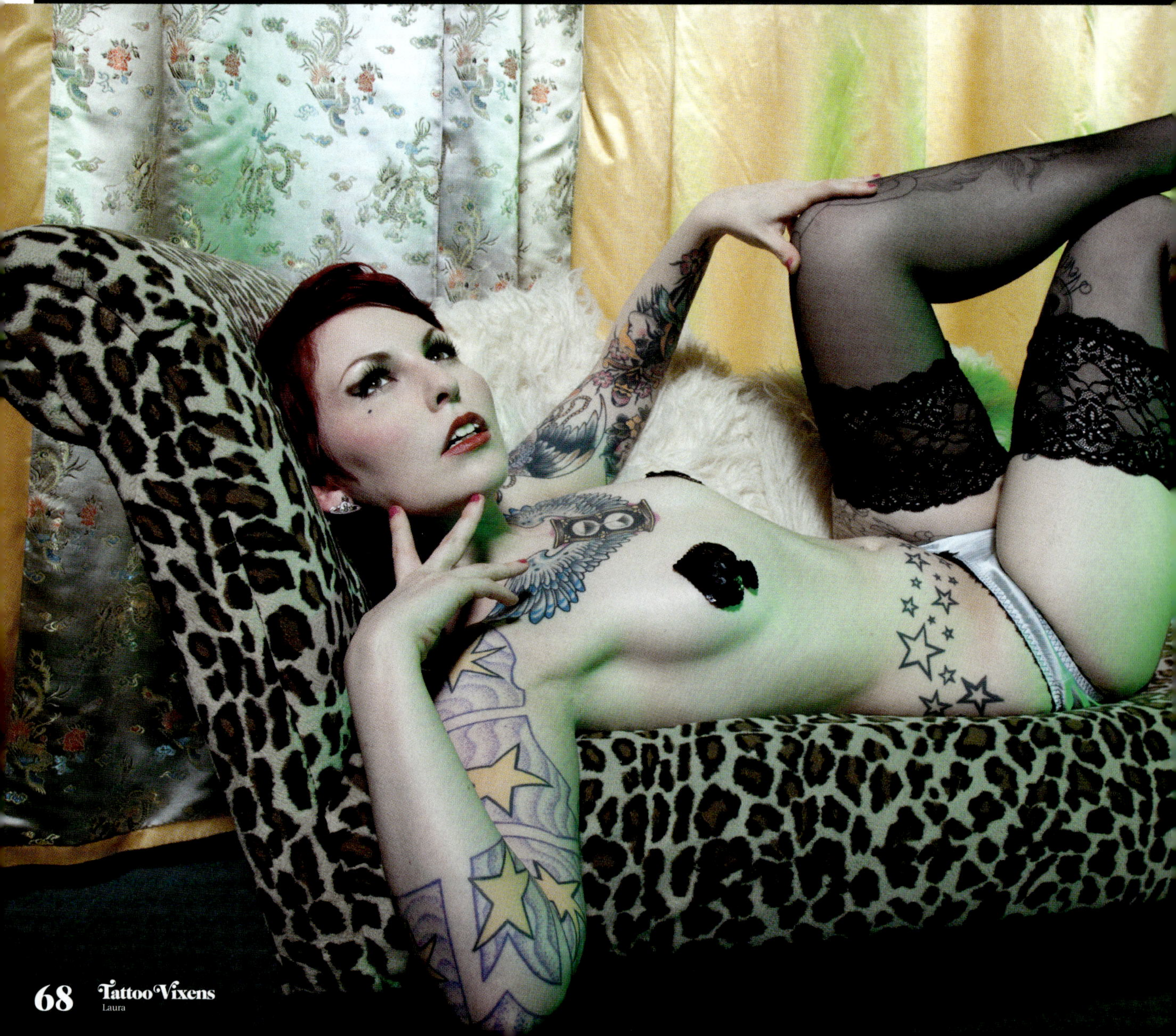

draw your attention to a person and make someone a walking piece of art. I knew from a young age I wanted sleeves and maybe some torso work. But as I have got older and was lucky enough to have friends in the industry, I have been influenced to get more pieces.

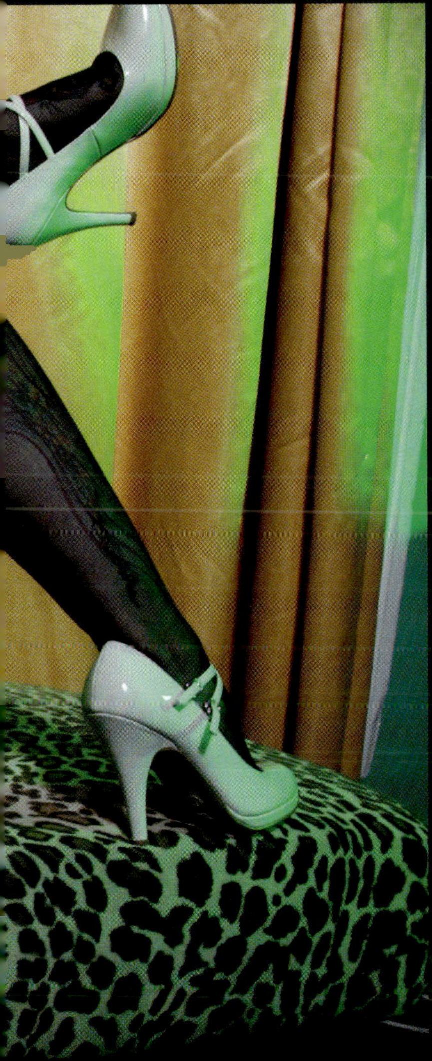

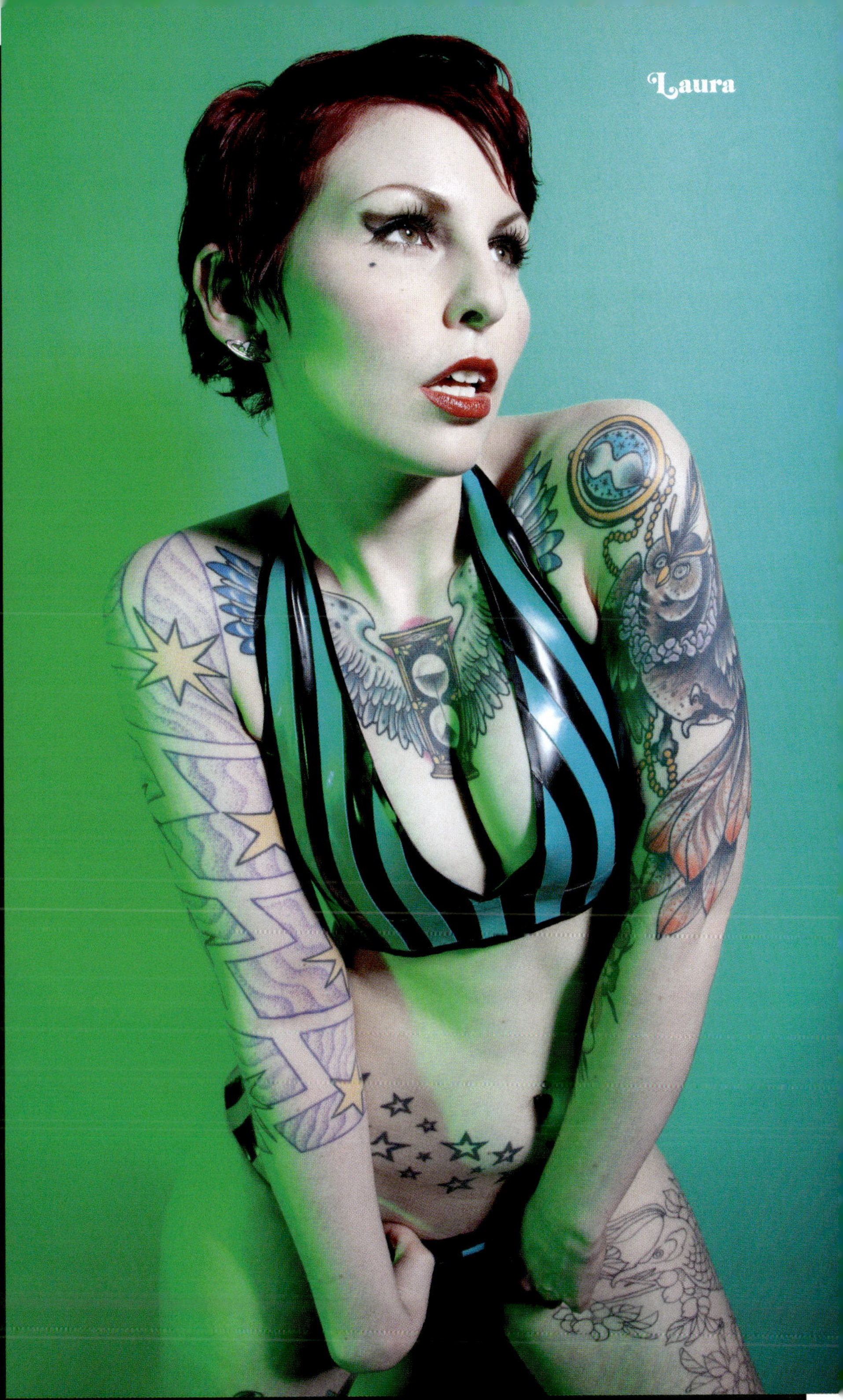

Laura

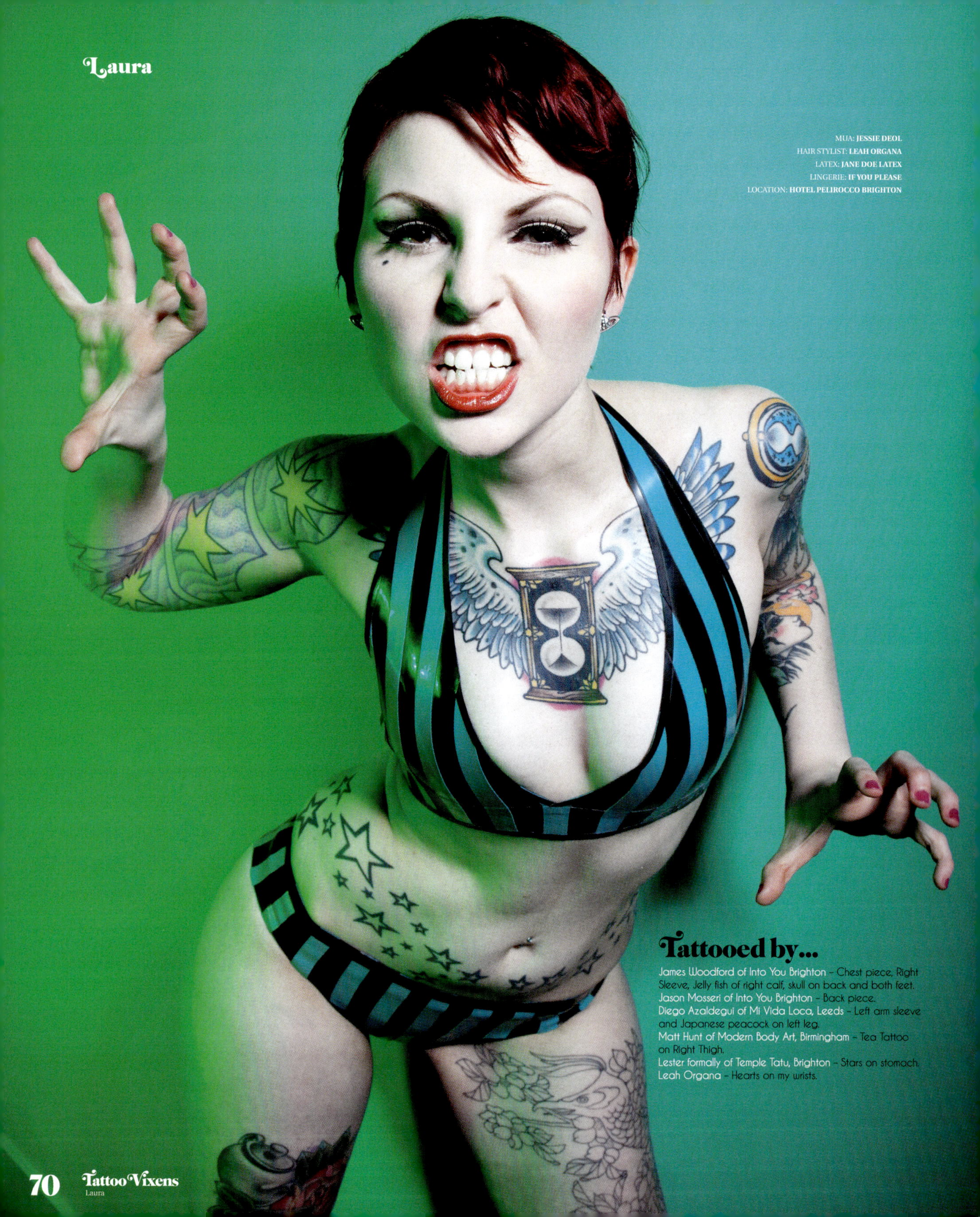

MUA: **JESSIE DEOL**
HAIR STYLIST: **LEAH ORGANA**
LATEX: **JANE DOE LATEX**
LINGERIE: **IF YOU PLEASE**
LOCATION: **HOTEL PELIROCCO BRIGHTON**

Tattooed by...

James Woodford of Into You Brighton - Chest piece, Right Sleeve, Jelly fish of right calf, skull on back and both feet.
Jason Mosseri of Into You Brighton - Back piece.
Diego Azaldegui of Mi Vida Loca, Leeds - Left arm sleeve and Japanese peacock on left leg.
Matt Hunt of Modern Body Art, Birmingham - Tea Tattoo on Right Thigh.
Lester formally of Temple Tatu, Brighton - Stars on stomach.
Leah Organa - Hearts on my wrists.

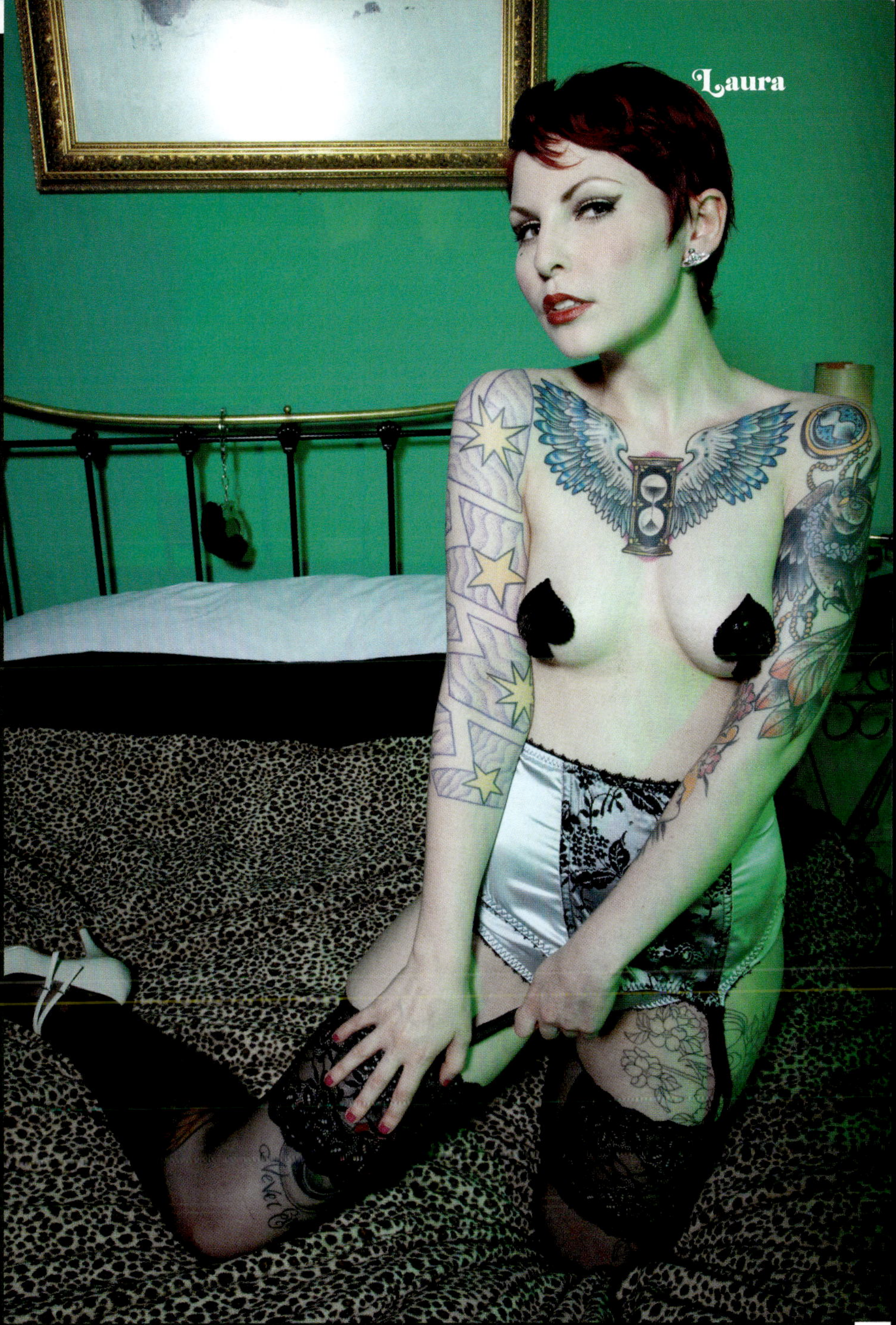

I try to have meaning and thought behind all my tattoos and always ponder on an idea for at least 4 months before jumping in and getting it done.

Which of your tattoos has has the most impact on people in the street?

Most of my tattoos are on show, so people always stare. But 99% of the time I never get any bad feedback and if anything people say how beautiful and flattering my tattoos are. My friends at work joke how different I look, but then I act in a completely professional manner, so people warm to me very quickly.

Do your tattoos have any particular significance, or do you collect them purely because of their aesthetics?

I would say 80% of my pieces have significance and others I have got as I felt the image would fit nicely into the area. I try to have meaning and thought behind all my tattoos and always ponder on an idea for at least 4 months before jumping in and getting it done.

What advice would you offer to people who are considering tattoos on public skin before they've worn much coverage elsewhere?

I would recommend them to talk to people who are already tattooed and see what sort of reaction they get from their friends, family and their workplace. I would also encourage them to research a number of reputable artists and pick someone they feel comfortable with, who can produce something unique and timeless.

Akasha D'Eville

Akasha is a former model turned photographer with a fiendish twist, proving that there is always life on the other side of the lens...

Name
Akasha D'Eville
Occupation
photographer (and former model). Deville Photography

What was it that got you started as a photographer?

I've always been passionate about photography, since high school, where I was a member of the Photography Club and learned the principles of photography and how to develop in the dark room. A few years later digital arrived and I bought my first digital camera and started shooting live shows and alternative models. There weren't many sexy tattooed girls back then and Suicide Girls were my main inspiration. I guess you can say that SG are the main reason why I love taking pictures of bad ass girls.

Tell us about your business and what led you down that road instead of more traditional photography.

When I moved to London, I bought a Nikon, still continued doing my modelling on the side, but I really loved being on the other side of the lens! I took a course on "Casualty and Special-Effects", so I'm a certified make-up artist specialized in horror and gore. I consider myself as being a strong and independent woman

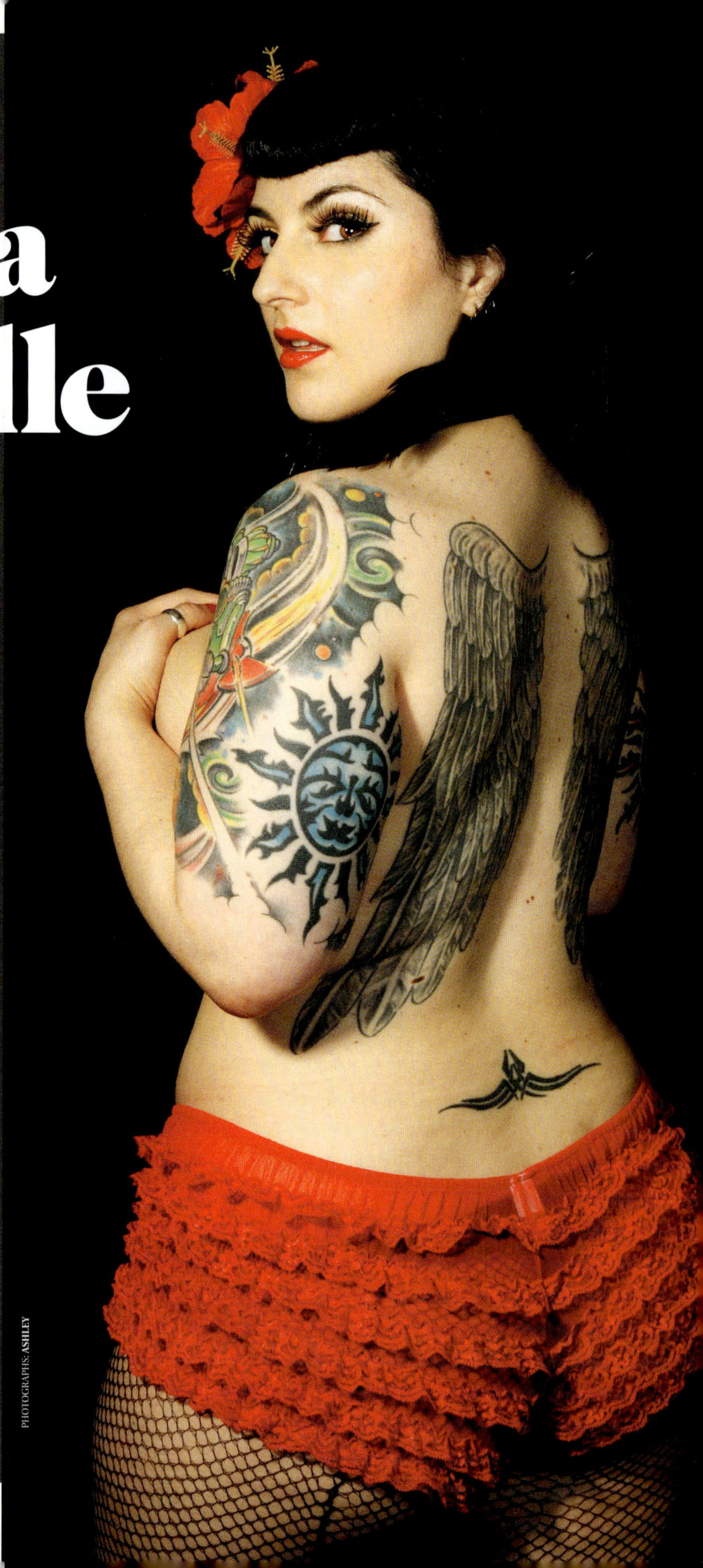

PHOTOGRAPHS: ASHLEY

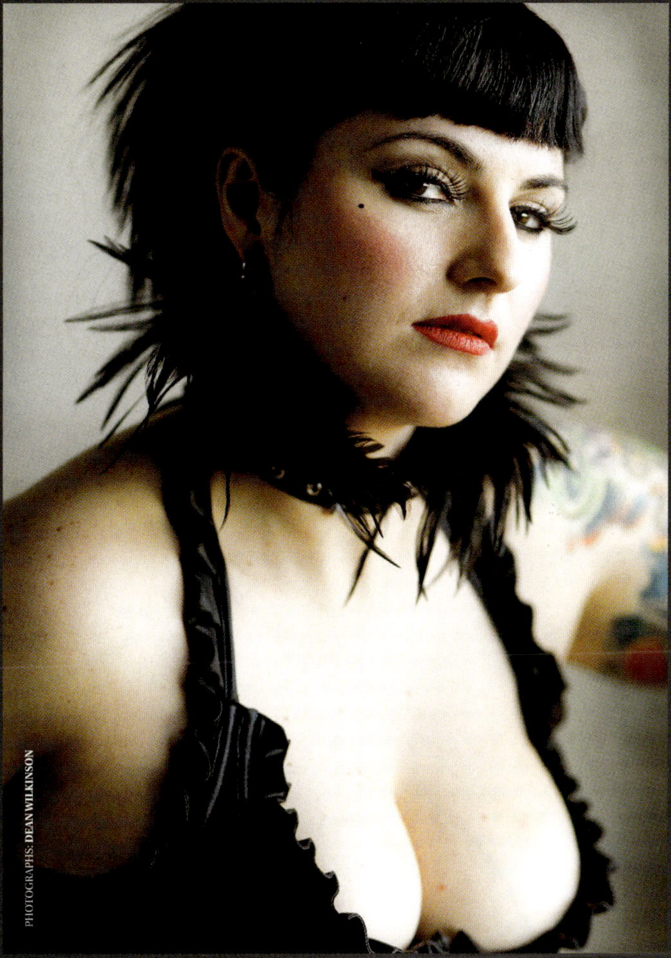

PHOTOGRAPHS: DEAN WILKINSON

with a taste for the macabre. My love for horror has manifested itself through my photography and allows me to create my own vision of modern horror and macabre. I think the purpose of art is to evoke emotion and my photos surely do that.

Your work takes you down a road that isn't walked too often these days and that is seeing the humour in horror - is that a fair assessment of where your head is at?

Most of my ideas are dreams (or nightmares) put into practice. You can't take life too seriously, so I try to put a smile on people's face with my horror photos. I get inspiration for my horror photoshoots from B-Horror movies (that everyone thinks are disgusting), macabre

You can't take life too seriously, so I try to put a smile on people's face with my horror photos.

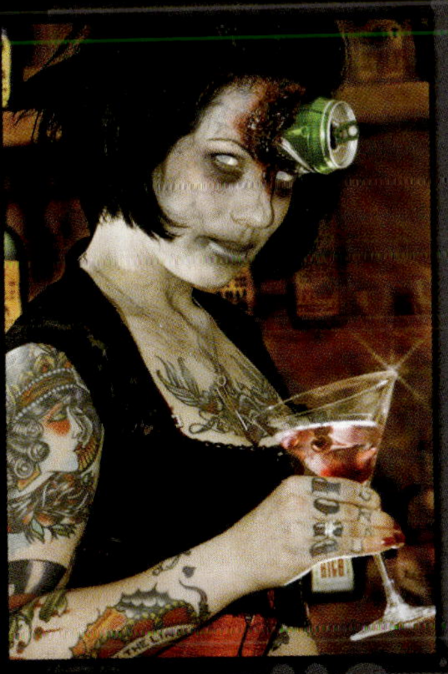

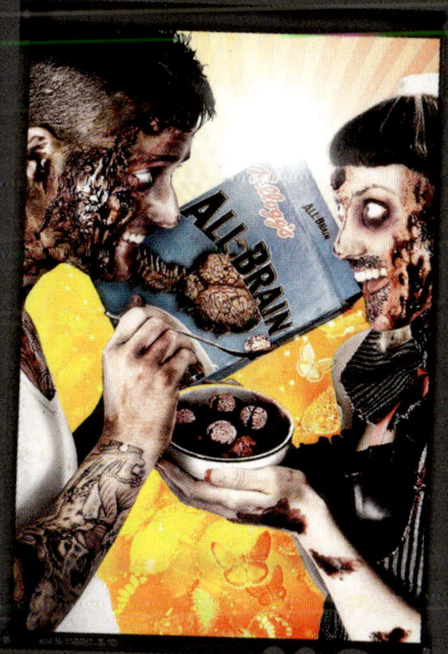

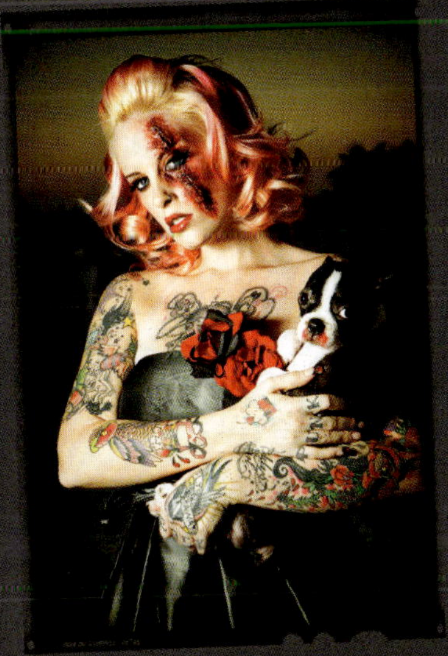

Deville Photography can be found over at www.akashadeville.com where you can marvel at her great horror and special fx shoots.

Asian horror, Romero's old school zombie flicks and Dario Argento's bizarre and gore-filled death scenes. My photography style has developed towards the "ugly beautiful" side of life - beautiful pin-up girls all gored up, extreme mod and heavily tattooed people, fetish and macabre styles allow me to play with the juxtaposition of humour and horror.

Beautiful pin-up girls all gored up, extreme mod and heavily tattooed people, fetish and macabre styles allow me to play with the juxtaposition of humour and horror.

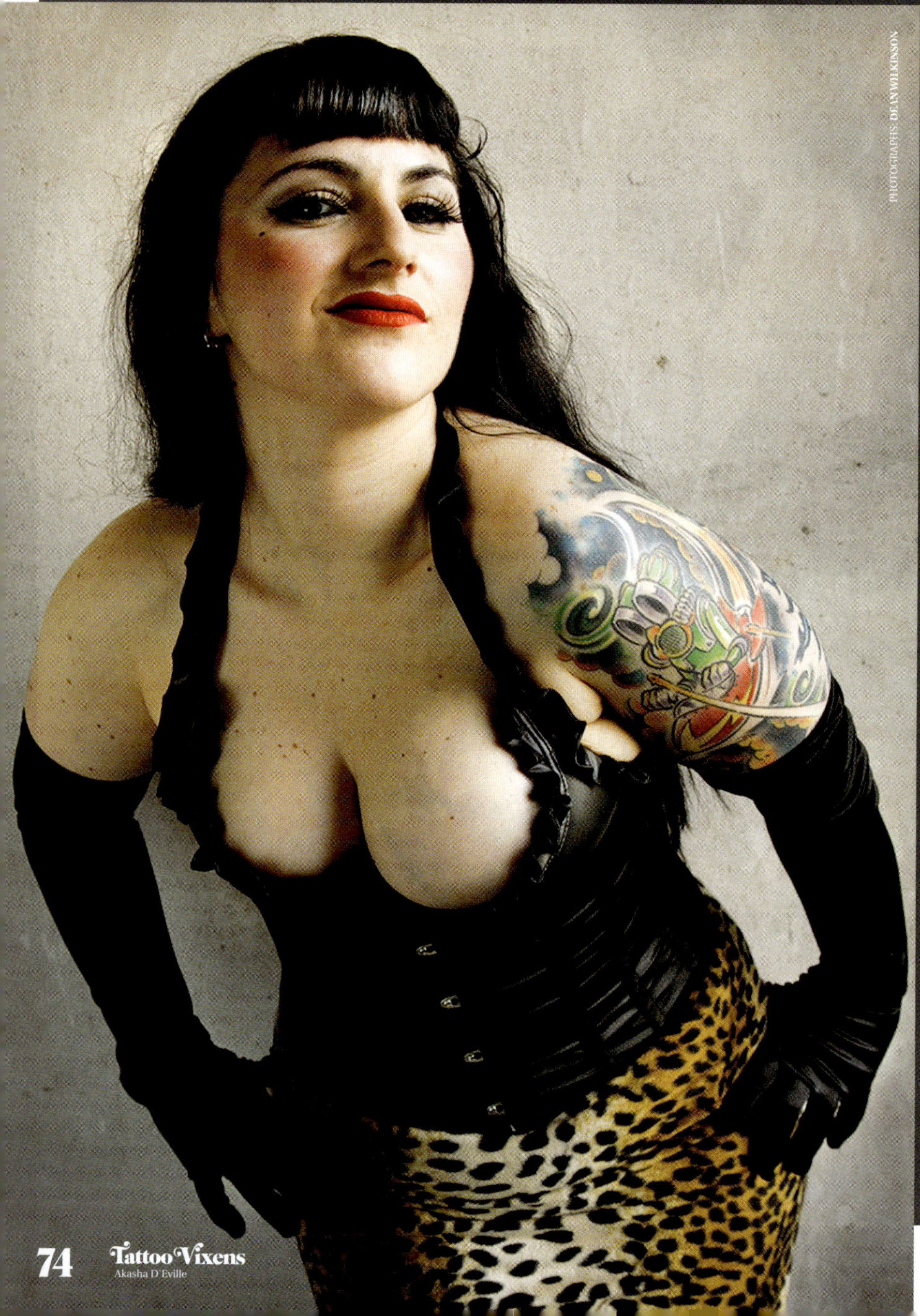

PHOTOGRAPHS: DEAN WILKINSON

When you were a kid - what did you think you were going to be when you grew up?
While I was growing up (in Lisbon, Portugal) I was known to my neighbours as being an animal lover, I used to spend most of my time chasing after stray cats and feeding them. I always wanted to be a vet. Unfortunately I'm no good at maths and I failed the exam.

As a heavily tattooed woman yourself and working in the field, do you think it's becoming more popular than ever? The UK and the US seem to be at the forefront of this - but do you see it gaining ground in other countries as well?
It's hard to say, there are certainly a lot of great tattoo artists from Europe, which would suggest that things may also be gaining momentum on the Continent. I can only hope that as the world becomes a more understanding place it results in a more colourful and tattooed planet.

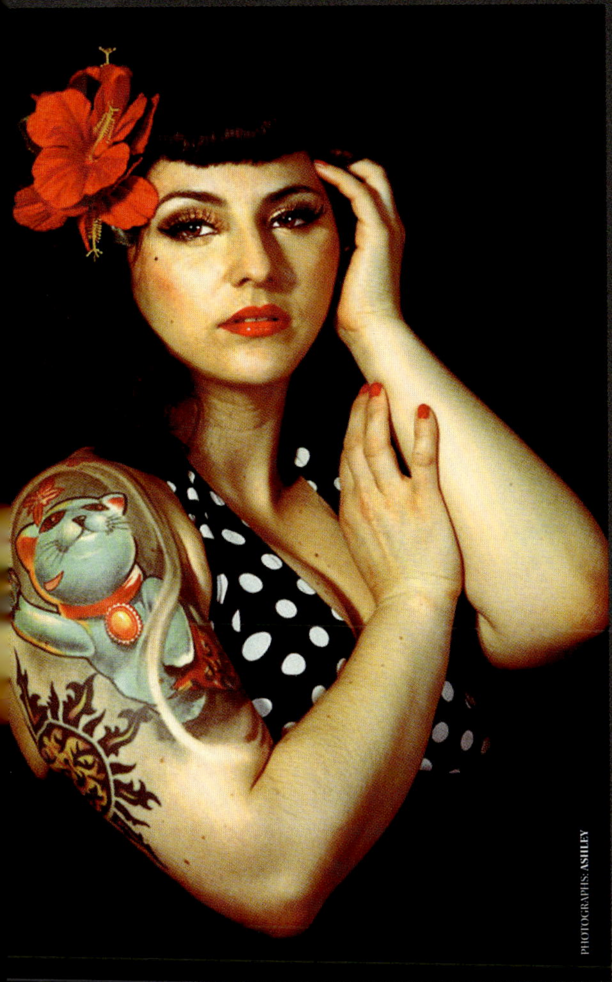

PHOTOGRAPHS: ASHLEY

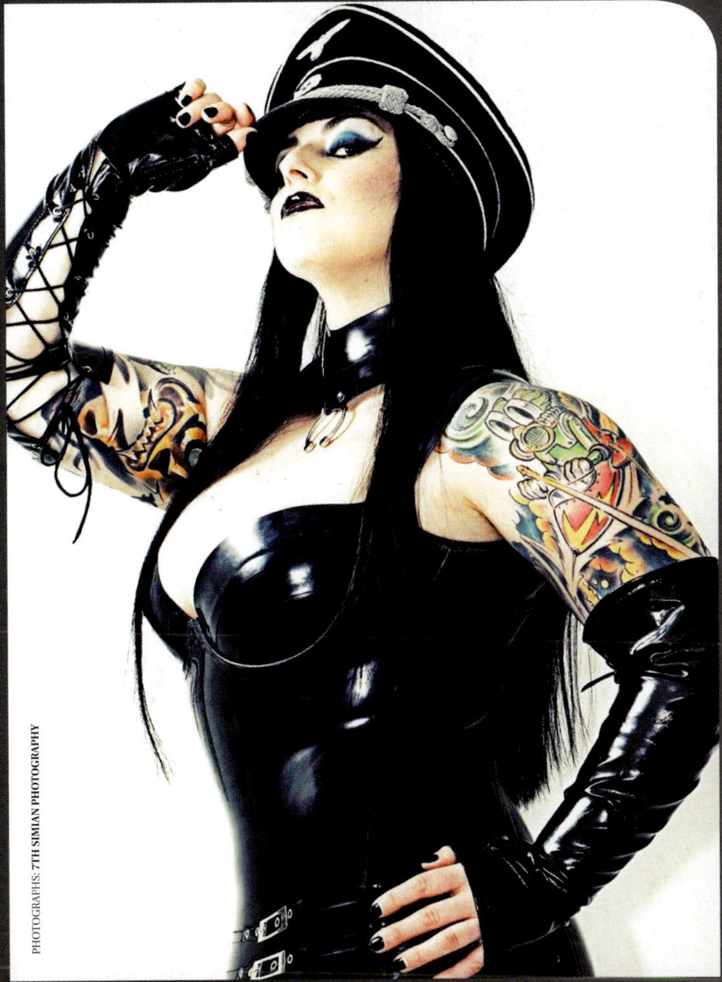

PHOTOGRAPHS: 7TH SIMIAN PHOTOGRAPHY

Tell us a little about your own work - what got you started, who the artists were and what your plans are for future ink if you have any.

I've had most of my tattoos done at Atomic Tattoo Studio in Lisbon, Portugal. I've known Francisco for many years and we are good friends. He's very talented and one of the best in Portugal.

I have tribal coloured suns on each arm, one is red because it symbolizes fire, the other is blue because it symbolizes water. These are some Earth elements we cannot live without. My angel wings - I'm an Aries and in Chinese culture I'm a horse of fire which is symbolized by an angel. The leopard stars on my feet are just because I love stars and leopard print and I've never seen any tattoo like the one on my feet. I like to be original when it comes to tattoos. The half sleeve on my left arm is inspired by a full sleeve that Tim Kern made some years ago. The alien has a gas mask because I just love gas masks - there's something really twisted about them!

The half sleeve on my right arm is by Kamil Mocet, from London. The main design is a Maneki Neko (Japanese lucky and fortune cat) in memory of my 17 year-old cat that passed away. The inner arm has a Tiki mask of Ku, the Hawaiian god of war. His mouth is rendered open as if to suggest the devouring of enemies. Human sacrifices were often made to statues of Ku and I'm intrigued by cannibalism. Future ink? It's a secret! I have most of my body meticulously planned but now I just need the money for it...

The inner arm has a Tiki mask of Ku, the Hawaiian god of war. His mouth is rendered open as if to suggest the devouring of enemies.

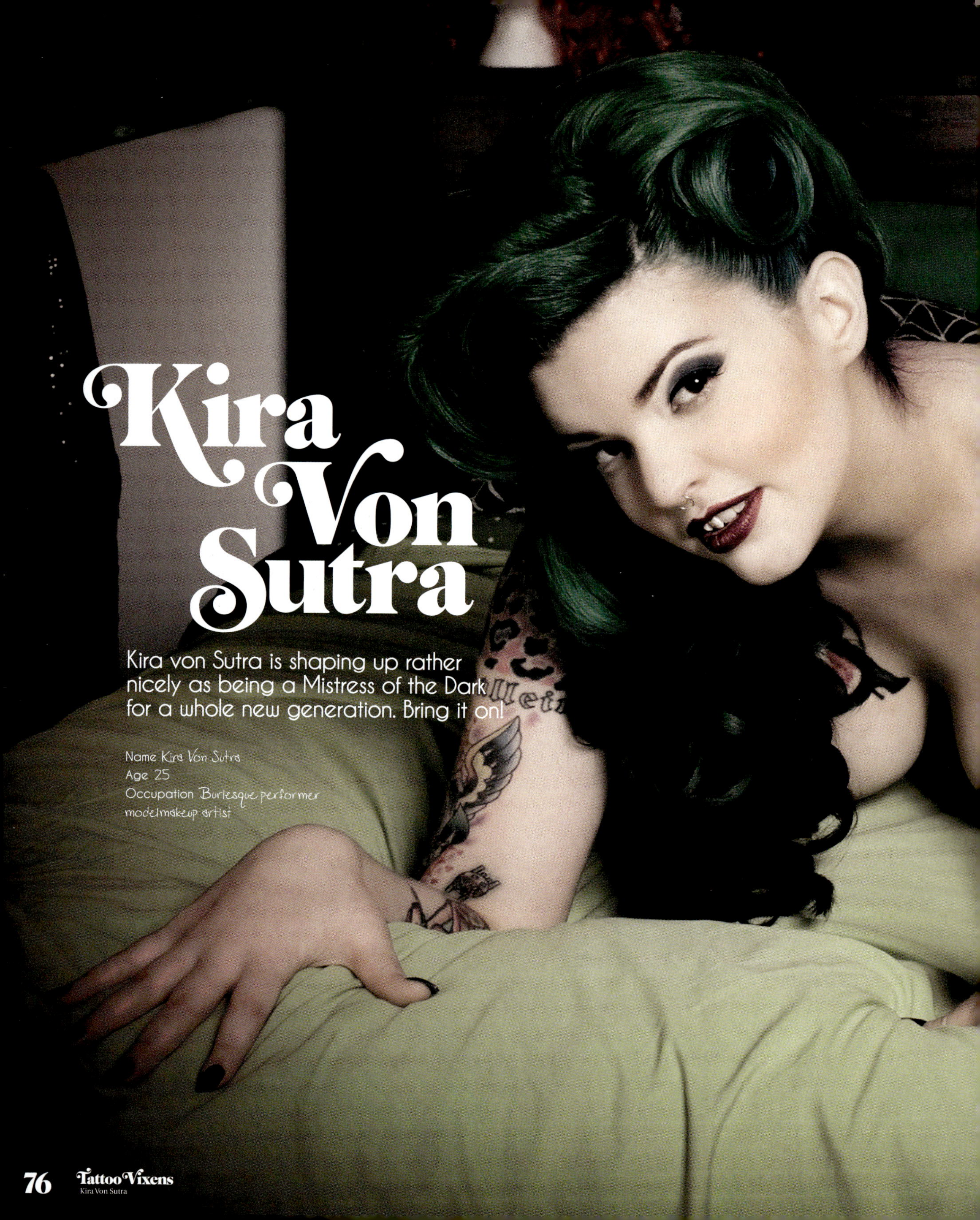

Kira Von Sutra

Kira von Sutra is shaping up rather nicely as being a Mistress of the Dark for a whole new generation. Bring it on!

Name Kira Von Sutra
Age 25
Occupation Burlesque performer model/makeup artist

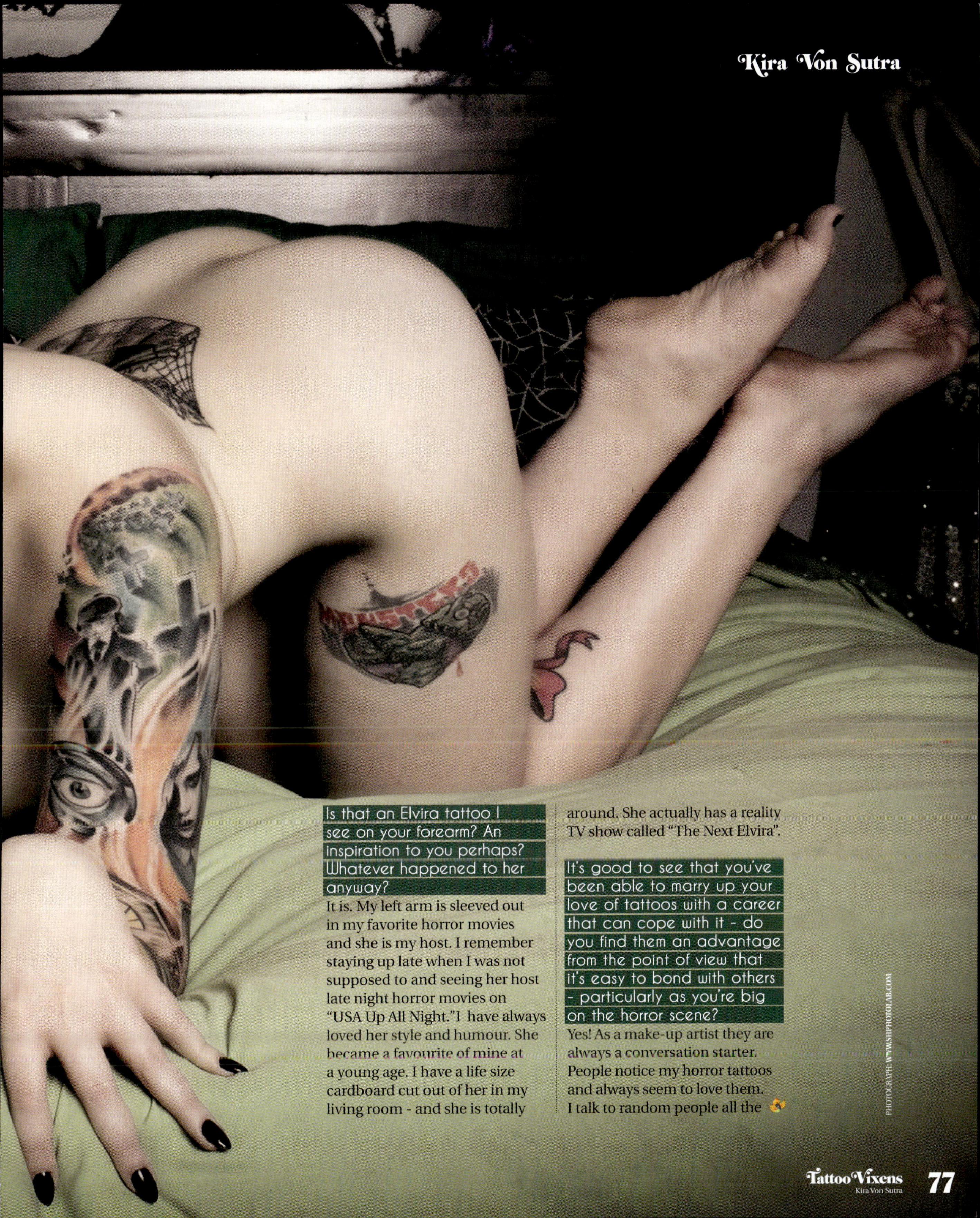

PHOTOGRAPH: WWW.SHPHOTOLAB.COM

Is that an Elvira tattoo I see on your forearm? An inspiration to you perhaps? Whatever happened to her anyway?

It is. My left arm is sleeved out in my favorite horror movies and she is my host. I remember staying up late when I was not supposed to and seeing her host late night horror movies on "USA Up All Night." I have always loved her style and humour. She became a favourite of mine at a young age. I have a life size cardboard cut out of her in my living room - and she is totally around. She actually has a reality TV show called "The Next Elvira".

It's good to see that you've been able to marry up your love of tattoos with a career that can cope with it - do you find them an advantage from the point of view that it's easy to bond with others - particularly as you're big on the horror scene?

Yes! As a make-up artist they are always a conversation starter. People notice my horror tattoos and always seem to love them. I talk to random people all the

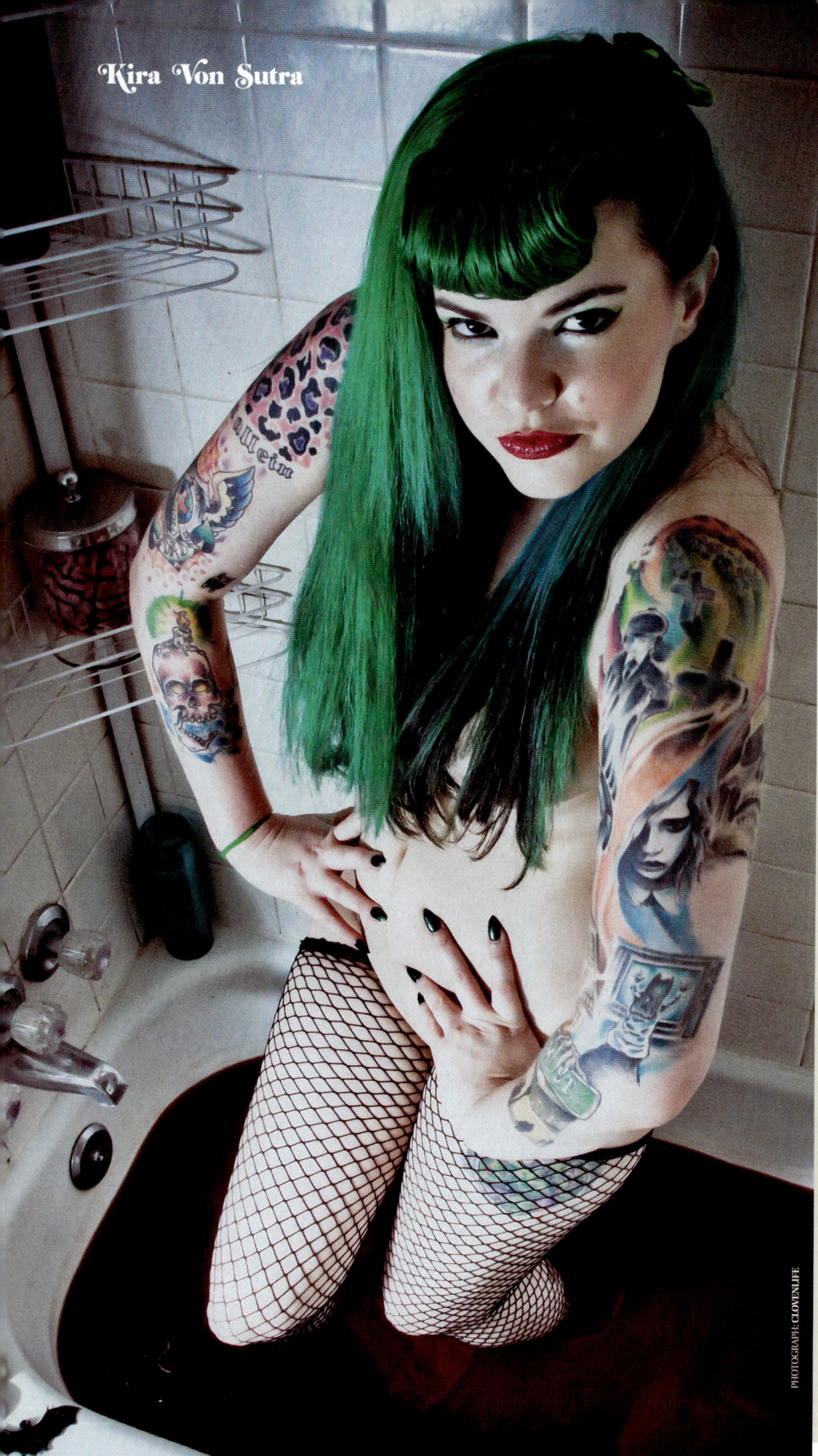

PHOTOGRAPH: CLOVENLIFE

time that happen to be in the industry just by them seeing my tattoos in passing. It is cool. It's like advertising by accident.

Do you have any plans to move into acting in this field? There's been some great scream queens over the years - Linnea Quigley was always a favourite of mine in the 80s - she could have used some skin art!

I actually have considered this. I wouldn't mind but I am not trained in acting. So I get a little scared about it. I guess that doesn't really matter in B-rated horror movies though!

Give us your top five horror movies:

The Exorcist.
The Omen.
A Nightmare on Elm St.
Amityville Horror
Poltergeist

...and what was the last truly great horror movie you saw? I've become a little desensitised to them!

Oh, me too! Hollywood has really messed everything up. It is so watered down! I really love the remake of Dawn of the Dead though.

Was the tattooing an act of rebellion or a love of the art - or both. For a lot of people I've spoken to who love rock music, it's seems like a really natural thing to do so - myself included.

It was both I think. But really, when I was a teen in school I used to draw all over myself anyways. I did it before I even thought of getting tattoos. I used to be an art major. It was really the only thing I was good at in school. I am dyslexic so art was the only subject I always

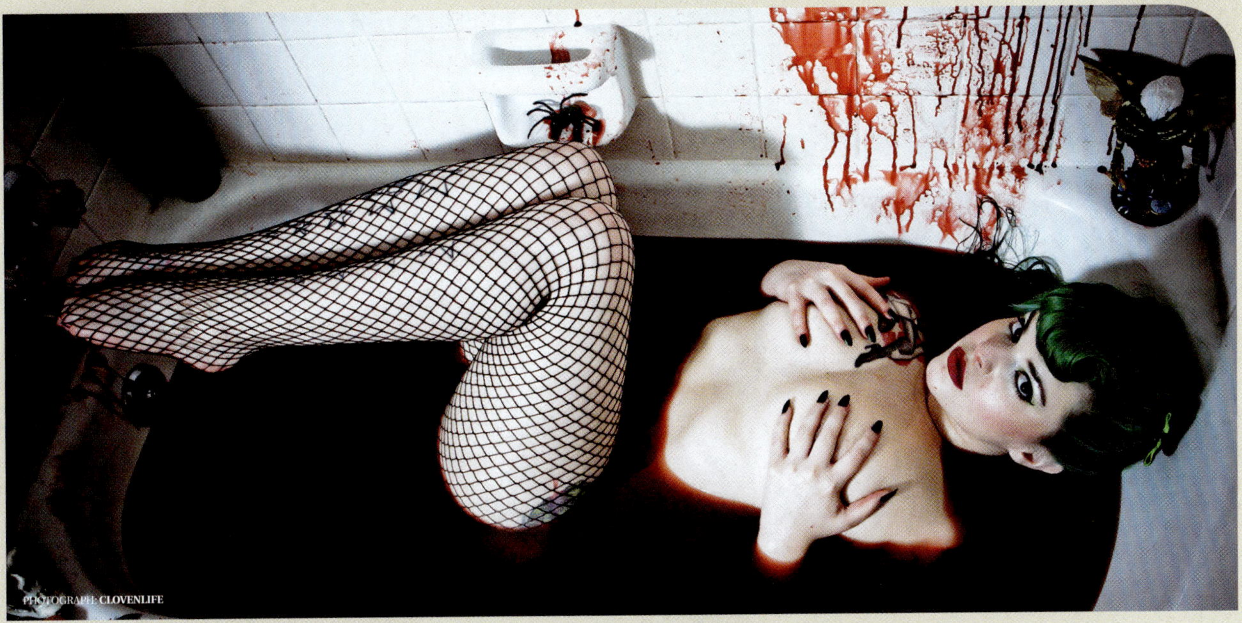

made top grades in. Sometimes when I came home from school, my mother would yell at me and tell me I was going to get ink poisoning from all the pen drawings on my arms – and now I have sleeves. Go figure.

What sort of things do you work on out there in Hollywood? Your beloved horror movies or something a little more mundane?

I never live my life mundane! I do many things. Make-up on films, create and shoot insane photo shoots from the depths of my horror obsessed mind and I perform all over - including Europe now. I even sell the rhinestone pasties I make on ebay or my lingerie that I have modelled in and no longer need.

You're a Burlesque performer too… sounds to me like you're too busy to do this very much! True? Or do you make the time!?

I am the type of person that needs to go a billions miles a minute. I'll do a photo shoot during the day, then perform at night. I haven't done more than one show in a night but I wouldn't put it past me. I can't just sit around.

I came home from school, my mother would yell at me and tell me I was going to get ink poisoning from all the pen drawings on my arms

Finally - what's the tattoo on your leg? That looks like a really nice piece of old school work.

It is actually an amazing traditional piece by my good friend and amazing artist Matt Kolling based out of Minneapolis at Twilight Tattoo. She is my Burlesque fan dancer. I simply asked for a Burlesque fan dancer pin-up. I was only in Minneapolis for a few days. I walked into his shop and he showed me this huge drawing and told me to sit and stay because we have one shot at this tattoo to get it all finished. He was right because I have not made it back since. Everyone should look him up. He is truly an amazing artist and top in the country in my opinion. I have worked in several tattoo shops and all my artists were drooling over my leg piece by him.

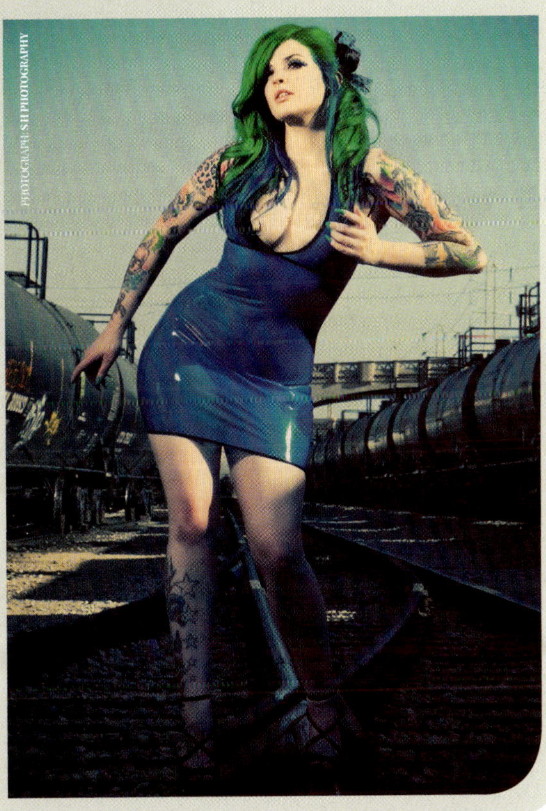

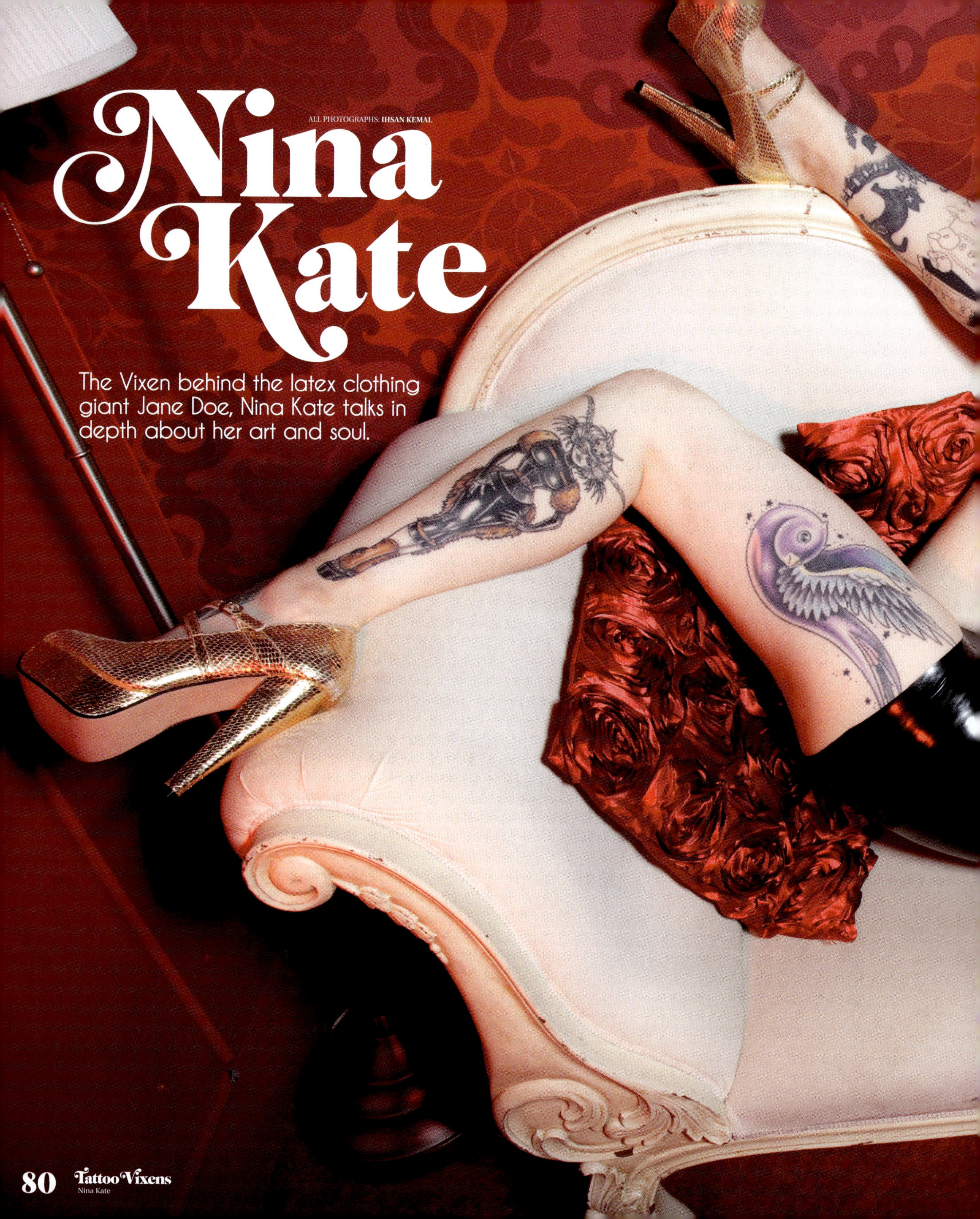

Nina Kate

ALL PHOTOGRAPHS: **IHSAN KEMAL**

The Vixen behind the latex clothing giant Jane Doe, Nina Kate talks in depth about her art and soul.

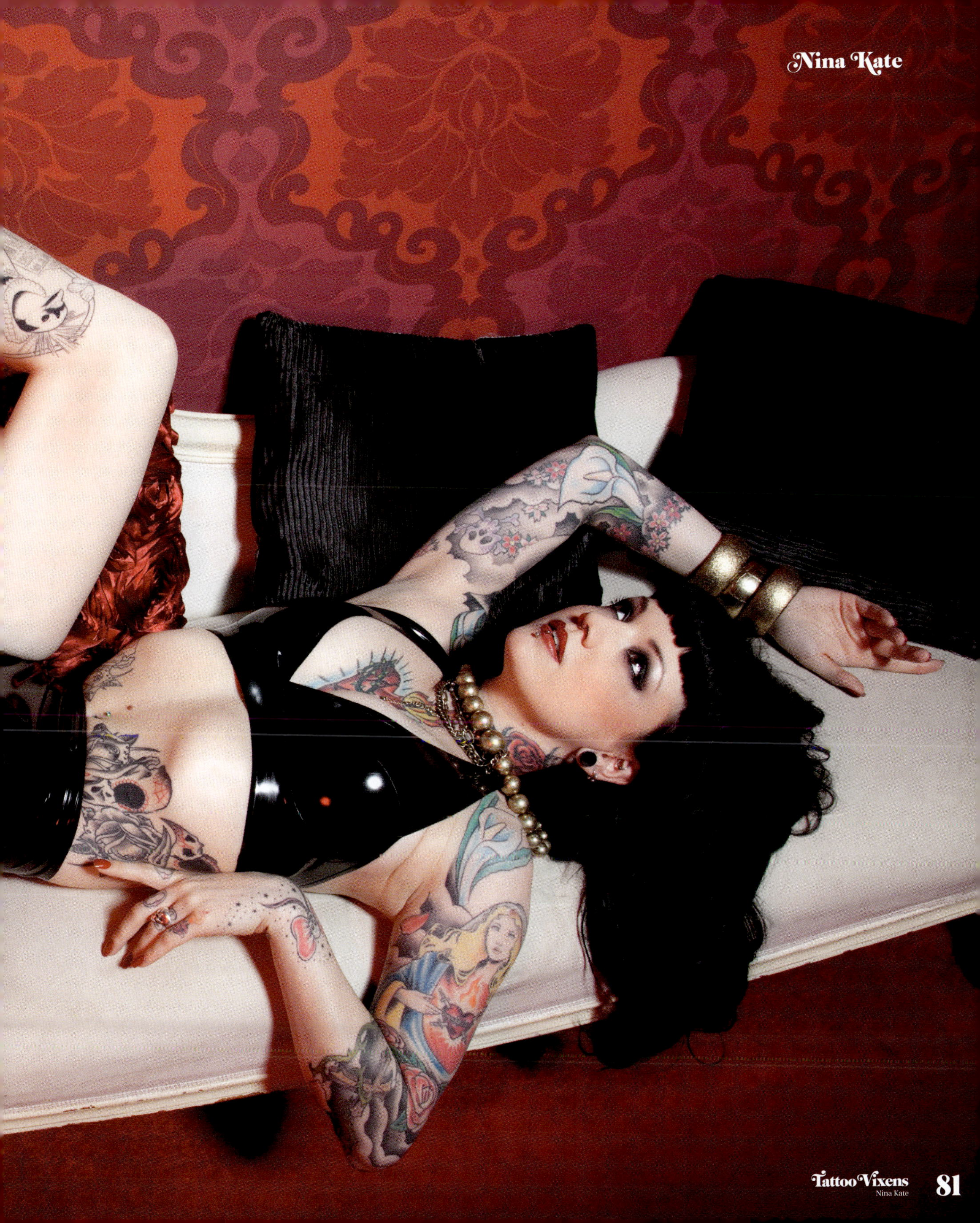

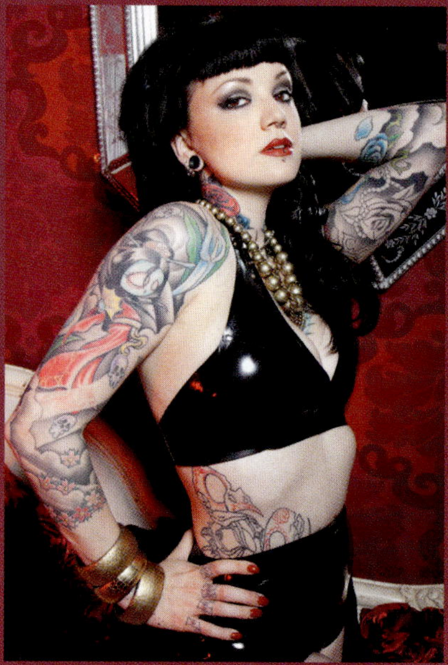

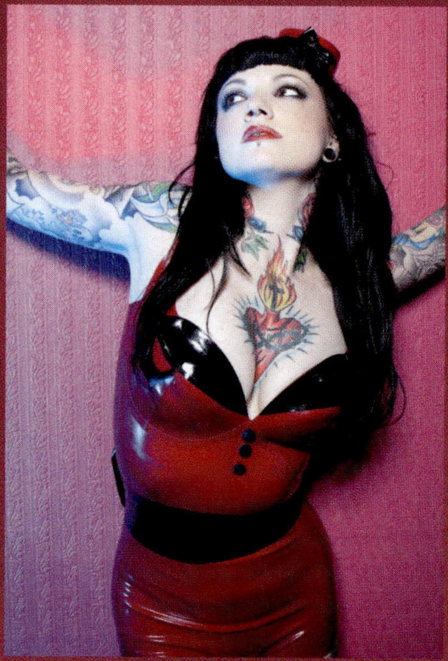

When I hit 17 I started going to places like the Torture Garden, which really opened my eyes to the potential of latex clothing and doing fun stuff like that.

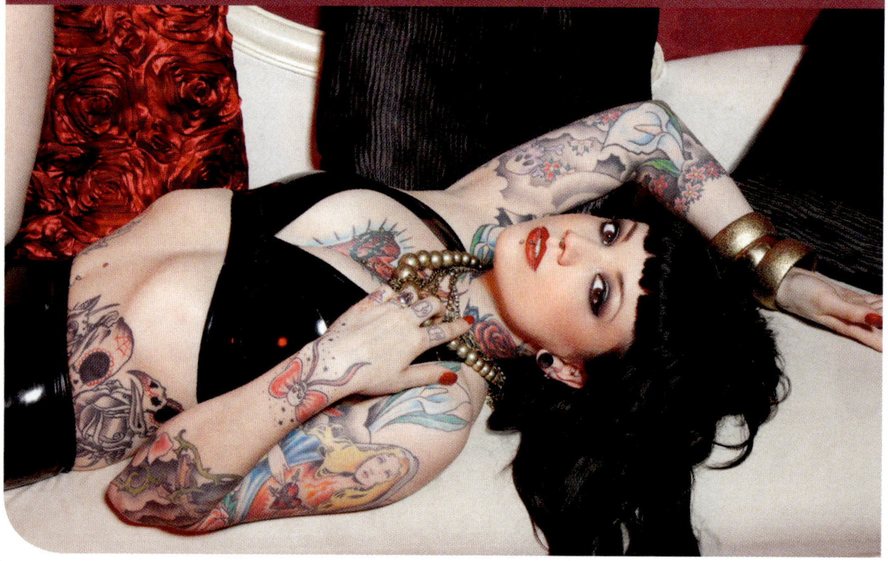

What are you currently doing career wise or what do you aspire to be?

For the last 5 years I've been running my latex clothing company, Jane Doe. I still have a lot of goals though! At the moment working on my latex clothing and modeling and acting are about 5.

Tell us something about your childhood, what ambitions you had, where did you grow up and what has inspired you?

I grew up in Camden, but moved to Cambridge at about 13, then back to London at 18 to start a latex clothing apprenticeship. As a child we travelled around a lot due to my dad's job as a pyro-technician. When I hit 17 I started going to places like the Torture Garden, which really opened my eyes to the potential of latex clothing and doing fun stuff like that. It was around then too that I started doing a few modeling jobs.

What initially attracted you towards tattoos?

I knew I always wanted them, growing up in Camden I saw a lot of them! I started planning for my first one at 14 and finally got it done at 16, it was a birthday present from my mum.

I started off getting small things really as I didn't know much about where to go to find good artists but once I hit 18 I started getting more significant pieces. At first I didn't have much of an ambitious plan but now I definitely want to be covered, and that's mostly because I know so many amazing artists that I'm almost running out of places since I've pretty much designated them all now!

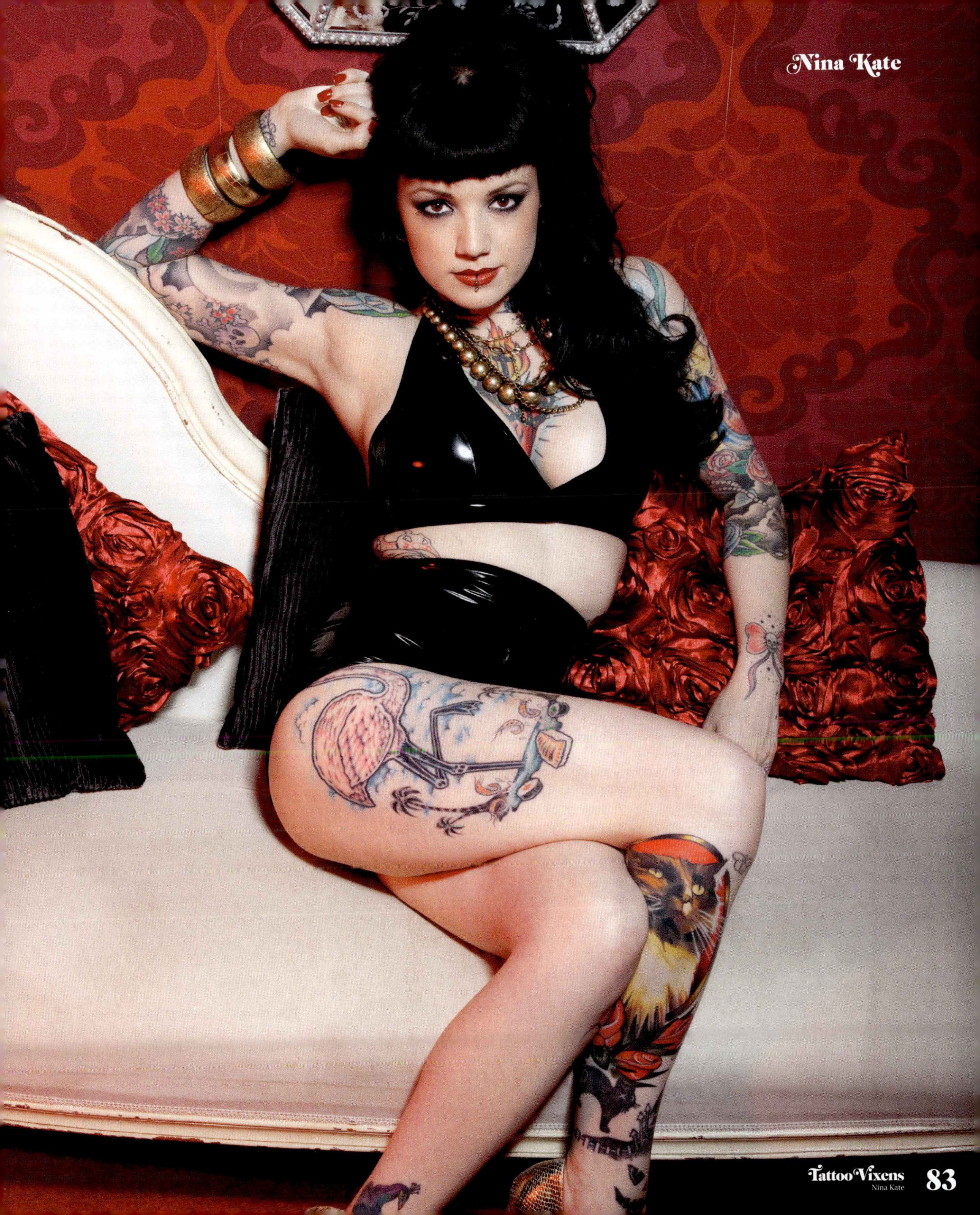

Nina Kate

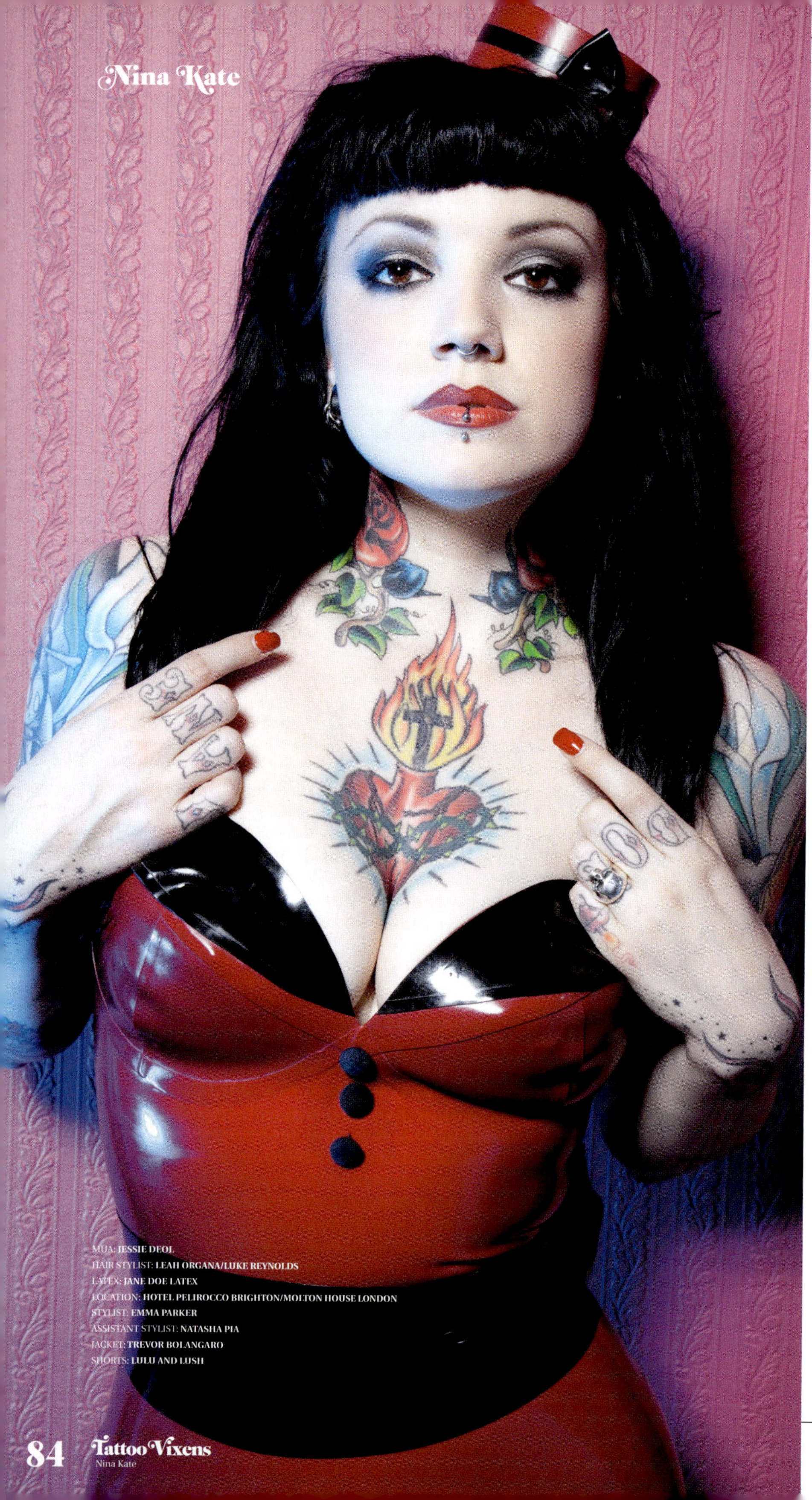

MUA: JESSIE DEOL
HAIR STYLIST: LEAH ORGANA/LUKE REYNOLDS
LATEX: JANE DOE LATEX
LOCATION: HOTEL PELIROCCO BRIGHTON/MOLTON HOUSE LONDON
STYLIST: EMMA PARKER
ASSISTANT STYLIST: NATASHA PIA
JACKET: TREVOR BOLANGARO
SHORTS: LULU AND LUSH

I'm definitely a believer in working your way up to getting things like necks, hands and chests done. It seems crazy to me that someone who is 18 would go get their neck done first!

Which of your tattoos has had the most impact, in regard to how you are perceived by other people?

I suppose the ones on my fingers and neck as they are the most visible, but I think all of them as a whole tend to get peoples' attention, which I have to say I really hate! If there was a way to be covered in tattoos and not stared at on the street I wish I knew.

What would you say is the most positive aspect of being a heavily tattooed woman?

Well it makes me happy to look at them and I know I'm doing exactly what I want to do with myself. I know that I won't get older and feel like I missed out on anything. I also get a lot of commercial work due to my coverage, so in a way they pay for themselves!

Do they have any particular significance, or do you collect them purely because of their aesthetics?

Not really, I mostly get them

because they are pretty! Sure some have significance, like the 'Till Death' I have on my wrists - my husband and I got them done together on our honeymoon. I also have a portrait of my cat, Maurice on my calf.

Would you care to farm out advice on mass coverage?

I'm definitely a believer in working your way up to getting things like necks, hands and chests done. It seems crazy to me that someone who is 18 would go get their neck done first! I think you really have to be sure of what you want to do with your life before jumping into something that'll really affect your ability to get 'normal' jobs. I'm lucky in that I work for myself so I don't have to worry about that so much.

If just one person could tattoo you, who would it be?

Oh I couldn't pick just one! I'm hoping to get a piece started soon by Hannah Aitchison though.

One interesting fact about you:

I have freaky kidneys!

Tattooed by...

Matt Difa @ Jolie rouge did my sleeves; neck, left thigh, fingers and back

Allan Graves @ Haunted did my wrists (the skull bows & stars) and my giant flamingo on my right thigh

Inma @ Haunted did my Maurice portrait and the piece I just started on the inside of the same calf

Rachael Huntington @ Rampant Ink did my pin up girl on the other calf

Nikole Lowe did the peacock on my foot

Andras Zelena @ Haunted did the skulls on my stomach/ribs

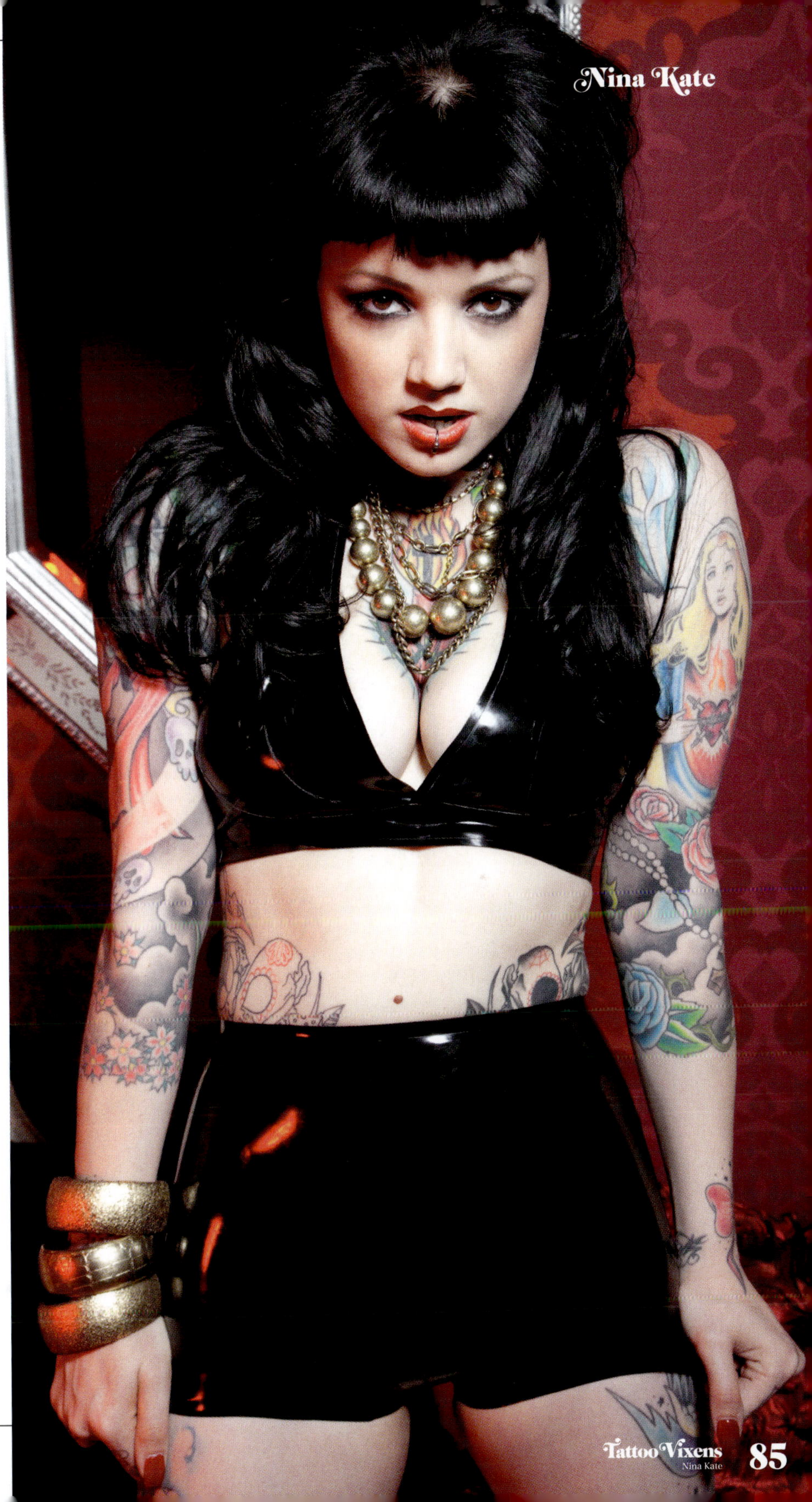

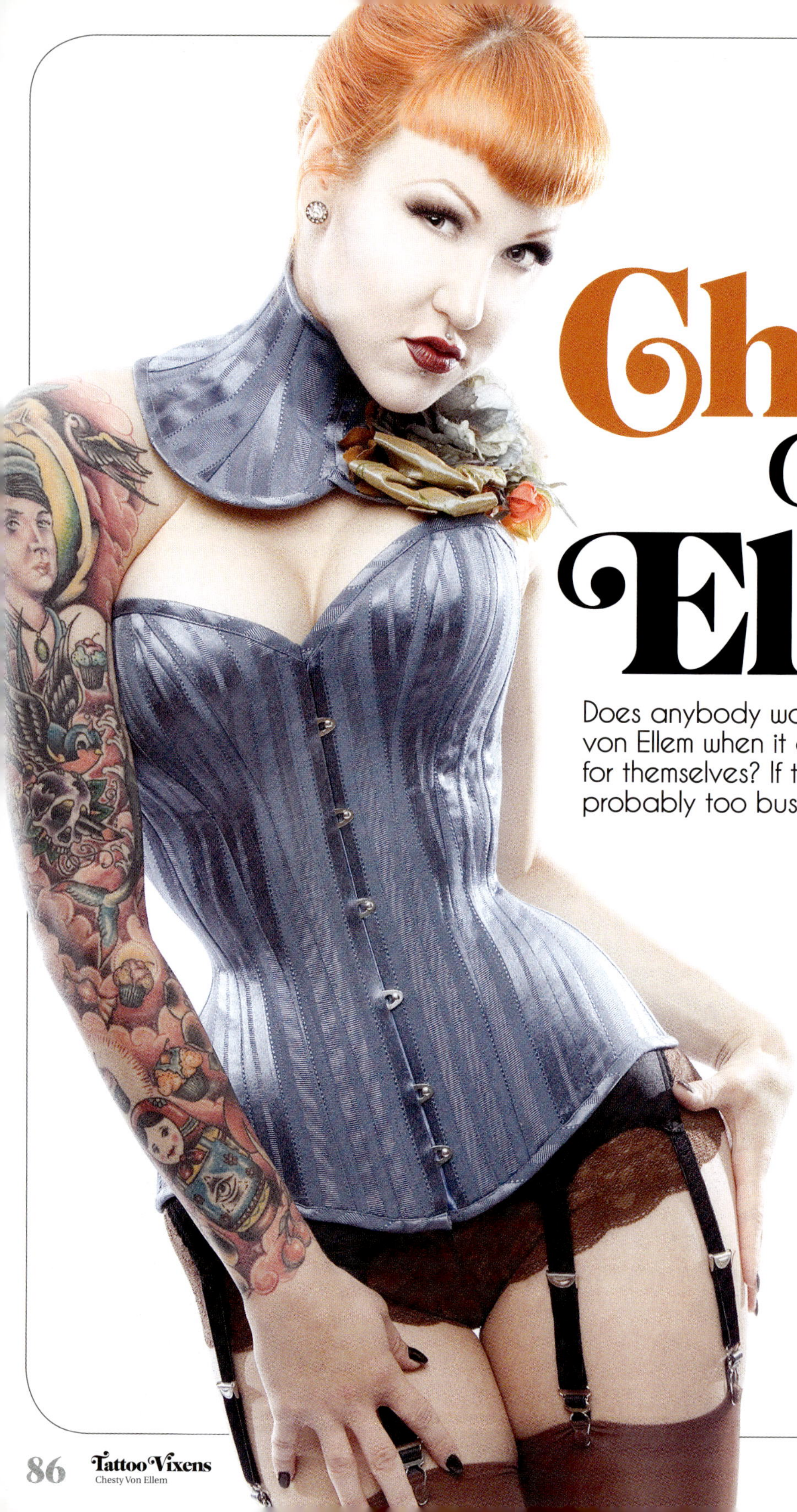

ALL PHOTOGRAPHS: **AMA LEA**

Chesty Von Ellem

Does anybody work harder than Chesty von Ellem when it comes to making a name for themselves? If they're out there, they're probably too busy to talk to us!

You have quite a few strings to your bow! How did your tattooed adventure start – and how did all the other parts follow into it?

I'm a busy girl indeed. I don't know how to stop. If I want something, I go for it and there is a lot that I want in this world! When it comes to the tattoos, I got my first one as soon as I turned 18. Me and my ex-boyfriend got each others names in hearts with ugly-ass wings on the sides! I drew it all myself and was very proud – ha! I could smack that tattoo artist around for letting me get that as my very first tattoo at 18 years old, he didn't seem to care enough to even try to tell me I was being very stupid. It wasn't so much the name as that was easily covered, but the big ugly

> **I got my first one as soon as I turned 18. Me and my ex-boyfriend got each others names in hearts with ugly-ass wings on the sides! I drew it all myself and was very proud – ha!**

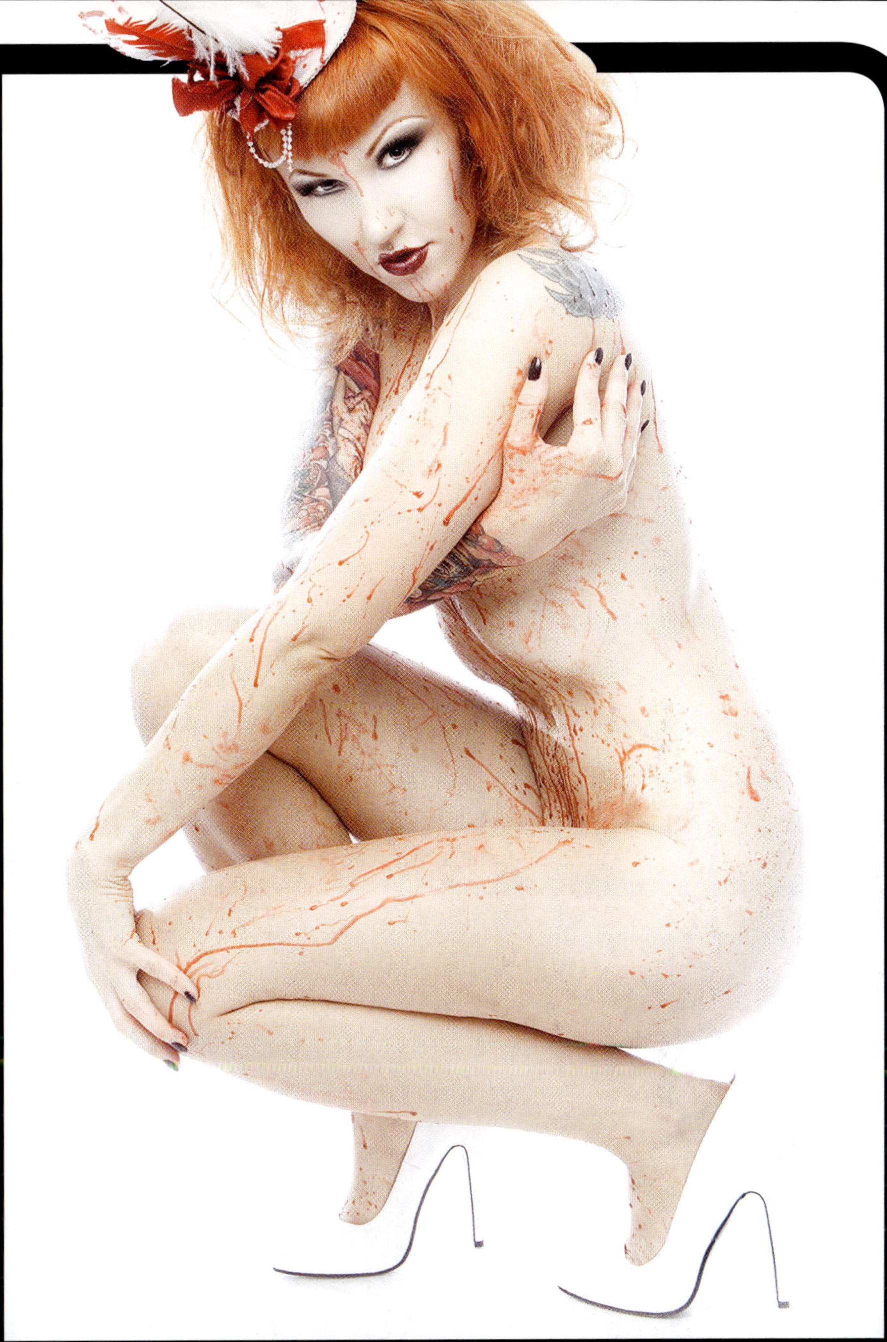

wings which thankfully are now covered up with nicer wings!

Anyway, after that first one I was hooked, as I had predicted I would be. I think the next one I got was a swallow/skull on my right arm and then a friend of mine started tattooing for fun, which ended up in me getting a star behind my ear, a text on my ribs in "elvish" and some other pretty silly ideas. I started tattooing a bit myself as well and did actually mess up some peoples' skin with my art there for a while, but I ended up never having time to practice and quit.

The first thing I did was the three bats on my own foot! When I moved to Stockholm I met Lenny at East Street tattoo through my ex, Lenny is an apprentice but a very talented one! He's done my sleeve. I also met Robin there who does laser and he's working on the heart - that ugly thing in my lower back that once was a anchor/skull and the text on my ribs. I'm going to laser everything well enough to be able to get decent cover-ups. I'm truly a work in progress, there's so much I want to get done when it comes to tattoos!

As far as the modelling goes, I started late. I was contacted by an agency and some photographers when I was around 17, but I had never thought of myself as a model and didn't have enough confidence to try. But the thought was born, and I did my first shoot when I was 20. I was so nervous and the pictures were bad, but I loved them! I put them up on a Swedish website expecting to maybe have one photographer contacting me. The next day, I checked my

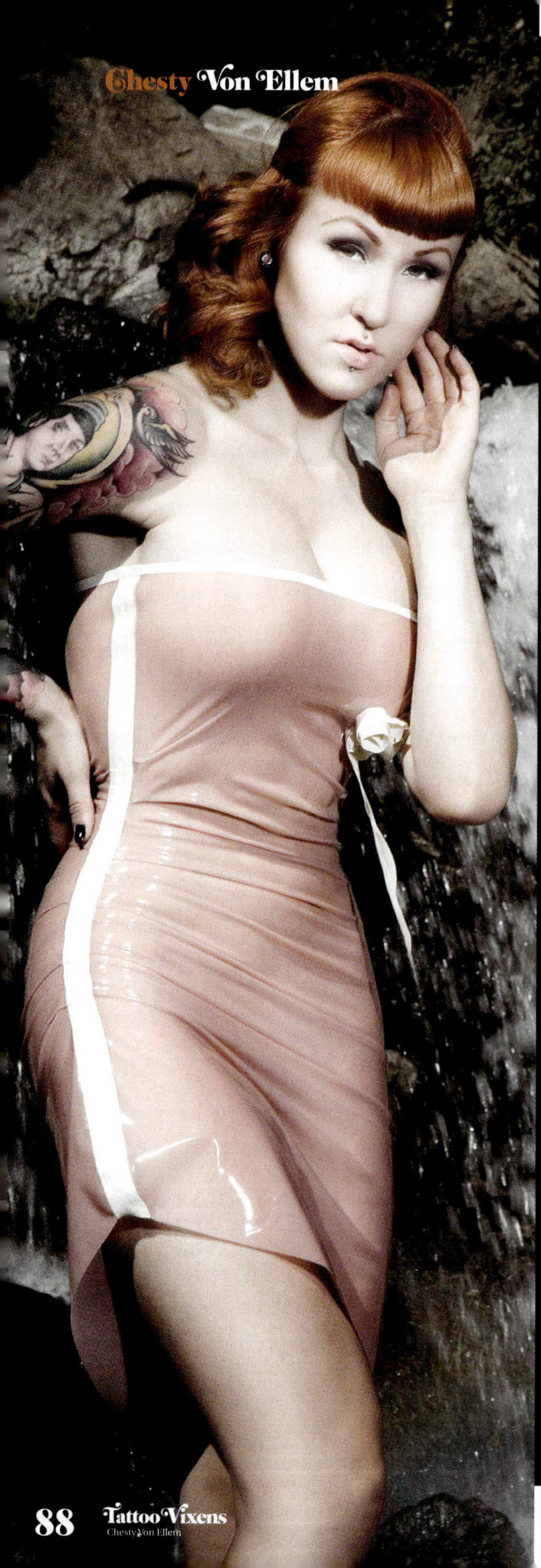

The agency I was represented by wanted to put together a burlesque show and since I had been talking about starting to perform with some of my friends, we took the chance and created routines for the show.

inbox and I had over 30 emails from people who wanted to work with me! I started with no knowledge of the business, worked with pretty much anyone who owned a studio and thought that meant they were successful photographers. Before I even started realizing that wasn't the case, my ex-husband stopped me. He got very jealous and I quit modeling for him for about 2 years until our divorce. I picked it up again right away and I have been doing it full speed since then.

I started performing about 15 years ago. It just sort of happened. The agency I was represented by wanted to put together a burlesque show and since I had been talking about starting to perform with some of my friends, we took the chance and created routines for the show. I think I did 4 performances in that one night, it was intense. I was extremely nervous but I loved every second of it!

In your burlesque routine, does being tattooed set you apart or do you find that you are in the majority now and that girls without tattoos are minority?

Well, in Sweden I'm definitely a minority being tattooed and performing. Everyone looks so naked when they get naked, I just want to run up and draw all over them! I know that there's a lot more tattooed beauties doing burlesque in the States. The burlesque scene in Sweden is just so small.

You've just been on tour - dancing or modelling - or as much of everything as you could do?

Modelling - I wanted to do some shows as well but there just wasn't enough time. I just got back last week - I've been traveling around the USA for almost three months doing shoots! I got to work with so many amazing talents and meet so many wonderful people. I wanted to go back right away as soon as I came home!

Have you got concrete career goals or are you just seeing where the road takes you?

Well, my goals keep getting bigger the more work I get, but I really love doing this for the creativity of it. If I wasn't modelling and performing I would be drawing, painting, sculpting all the time instead - this truly is a way for me to express myself. That said, I work very hard with my modelling and performing, I wouldn't be where I am today just relaxing and playing around, and I keep aiming higher. I want to work with amazing people, be published in amazing magazines and have a great time getting it done! Especially being from a small country with such a small

Chesty Von Ellem

alternative scene, it's hard to be a successful alternative model and performer unless you work very hard to promote yourself.

I would love to be able to work full-time with this and make a decent living out of it without having to do jobs that don't appeal to my personal taste of creativity, but for that to be possible I would probably have to move from Sweden, which I'm actually thinking of doing!

Do you think you'll be doing this - or something similar for the rest of your life or do you have other plans and dreams?

I hope so! I will do this for as long as it's fun and I feel that I'm getting something out of it. I probably won't be able to support myself with it for the rest of my life unless I stop ageing though! At least not the modelling. I will definitely always work with artistic things though. Art is what drives me, I love traveling and I love doing something different. I would probably feel very limited and bored with a normal job. I do however have another job as well – I'm a personal assistant for an awesome guy who needs assistance because he's paralysed. I also love animals (especially lizards), history, literature... who knows what I'll be doing in twenty years?

I would love to be able to work full-time with this and make a decent living out of it without having to do jobs that don't appeal to my personal taste of creativity.

Can you tell us something that you wish somebody had told you before you started - and is there anything you'd like to pass on to others who think what you do is easy?

I wish I would've known more about the industry before I started. I wish I could travel back in time and hit myself in the head for being stupid enough to let a guy stop me from doing anything I wanted to do. When it comes to people thinking this is easy, I would have to say that in many ways they're right! I love what I do, and for that reason it is easy for me to do it, but to be able to work as a model and performer you have to constantly promote yourself, improve, challenge and push yourself. If they spent a week with me they would realize how much work I really put into this.

I spend almost every day networking, finding new collaborations and jobs, promoting myself, updating my portfolios, answering tons and tons of emails etc. When I don't do that, I'm planning new shoots or shows, practice for them, getting wardrobe together (I make a lot of my own wardrobe for my performances), and then of course I also do shoots and shows on a regular basis.

So I guess I would advise anyone who wants to start to model and/or perform to do your homework, work hard and to never let anyone stand in your way, cliché but so true. You will not get anything for free, you have to make it happen, and once you've actually put hard work into it, things might start to come to you as well and your hard work will be rewarded.

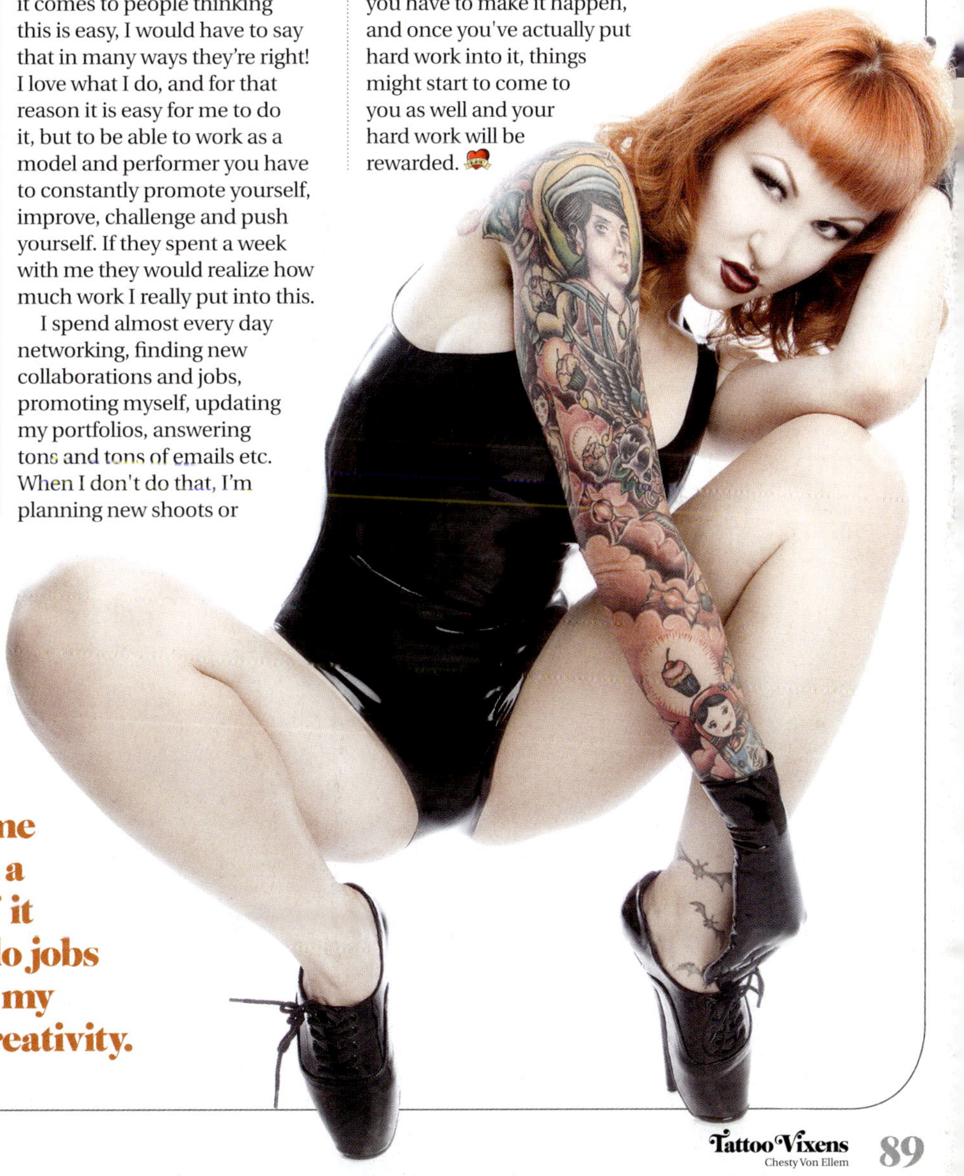

Miss Ivi

From the ice-capped mountains of Switzerland, we bring you the pin-up queen of the decade - Miss Ivi:

How long have you been doing pin-ups for now - and how did it all begin for you?
It all started about 3 years ago. At first I didn't plan a pin-up career. I just wanted some nice pictures of myself. My first shoot turned out to be a complete failure because the photographer was a joke to be honest. After that my husband gave me a professional shoot with a star photographer from Germany as a birthday gift. Two photos from this shoot turned into my first two magazine covers. I was totally surprised with how fast things can go.

You must have done more varied shoots than anybody I've ever seen - and show no sign of stopping soon. Do you get frustrated at not being able to do even more?
Frustrated? No why? I love what I do! Besides, frustration will not get a perfect picture – smile! In the meantime, I am in the very lucky position that I can choose what I would like to do and what not to do. Since I'm doing all the shoots in my spare time - of which I don't have a lot – I'm very picky, because I just want have fun on the shoot and good pictures to balance out from my busy job.

Two photos from this shoot turned into my first two magazine covers. I was totally surprised with how fast things can go.

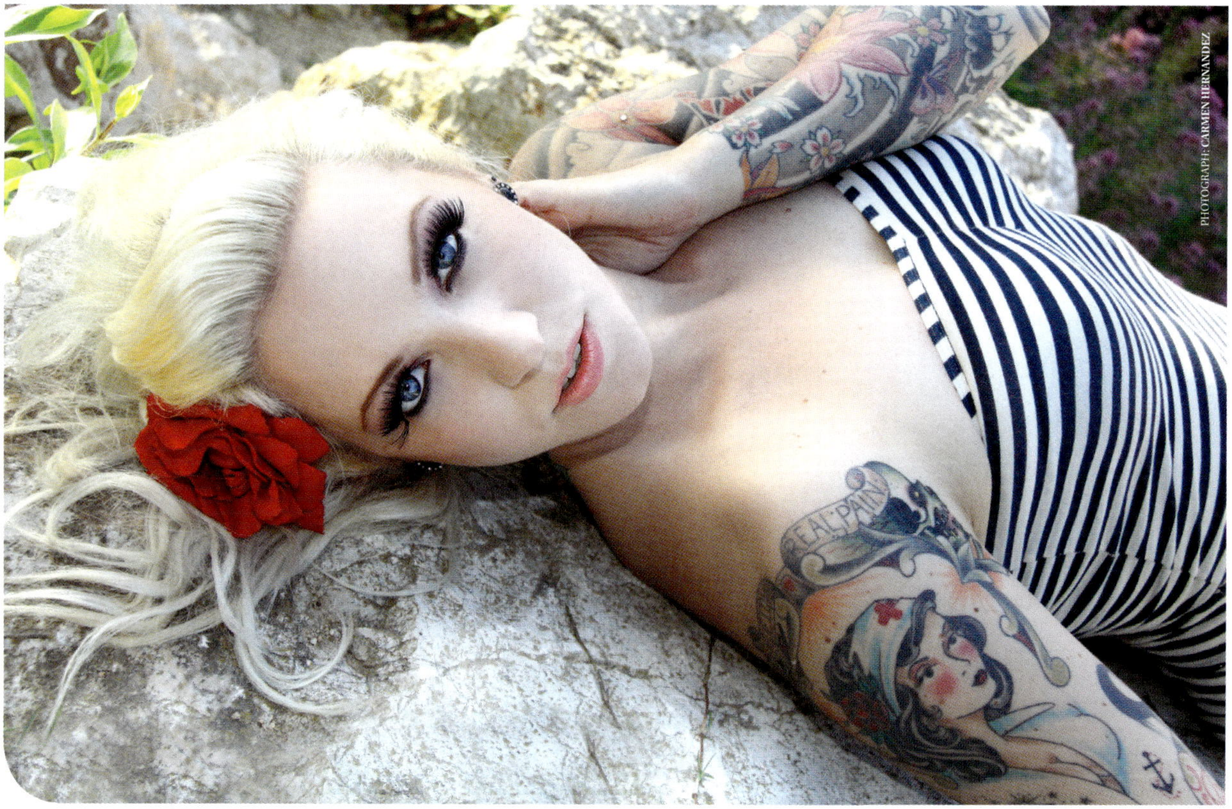

PHOTOGRAPH: CARMEN HERNANDEZ

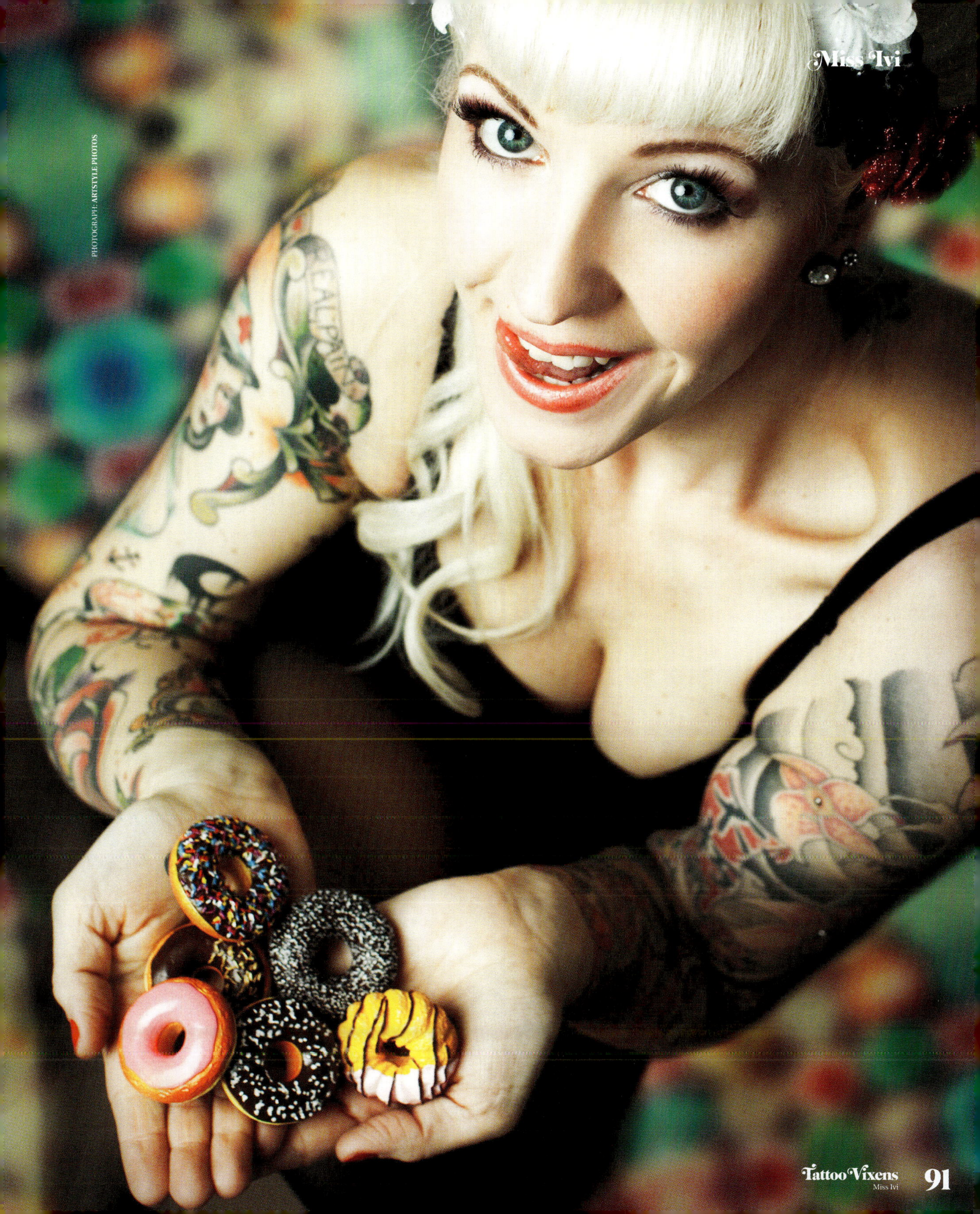

PHOTOGRAPH: ARTSTYLE PHOTOS

I know you put your own merchandise out - such as your calendar but where else can we find you in the world? What sort of things do you get asked to do?

Yes, my third calendar is coming out right now. I worked with great photographers again this year. Check it out. You can order your own Miss IVI calender 2011 here: www.missivi.com or www.tfd-tattoos.com

I also get asked to do lots of other stuff, poster model for tattoo conventions, flyers, internet shops, t-shirt motifs, jury for tattoo conventions, skateboard decks and so on. Also in our shop of course and we started a school charity project in Thailand.

You're a little different than a lot of the people we've interviewed for this book as you're based in Switzerland. Are you alone out there? Are you the only tattooed lady in town?

Different? Sounds good - thanks for the compliment! No - I am not alone out here, my husband's here, my dad, and my sweet pirate hamster Pip - and don't forget my friends! Seriously though - getting tattoos are not a male dominated area anymore. I would guess that at least 50-60% of our customers are female. So no, I'm not the only tattooed lady in town, but I am the most tattooed one!

I would guess that at least 50-60% of our customers are female. So no, I'm not the only tattooed lady in town, but I am the most tattooed one!

When you first started getting tattooed, was it something you thought long and hard about? Was it something you knew would set you apart from the others or did it start off small and soon snowball into what you have now?

I got my first (small) tattoo 13 years ago, and even back then I thought about it long and hard,

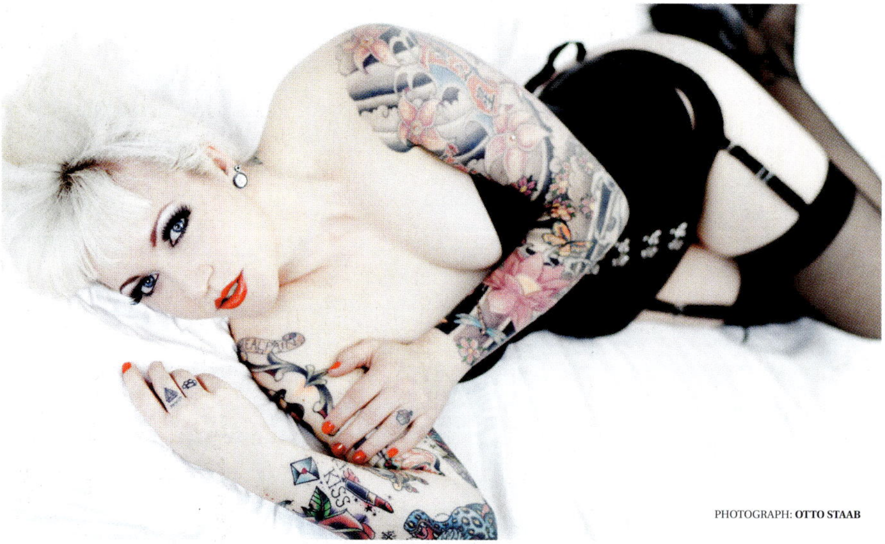

PHOTOGRAPH: **OTTO STAAB**

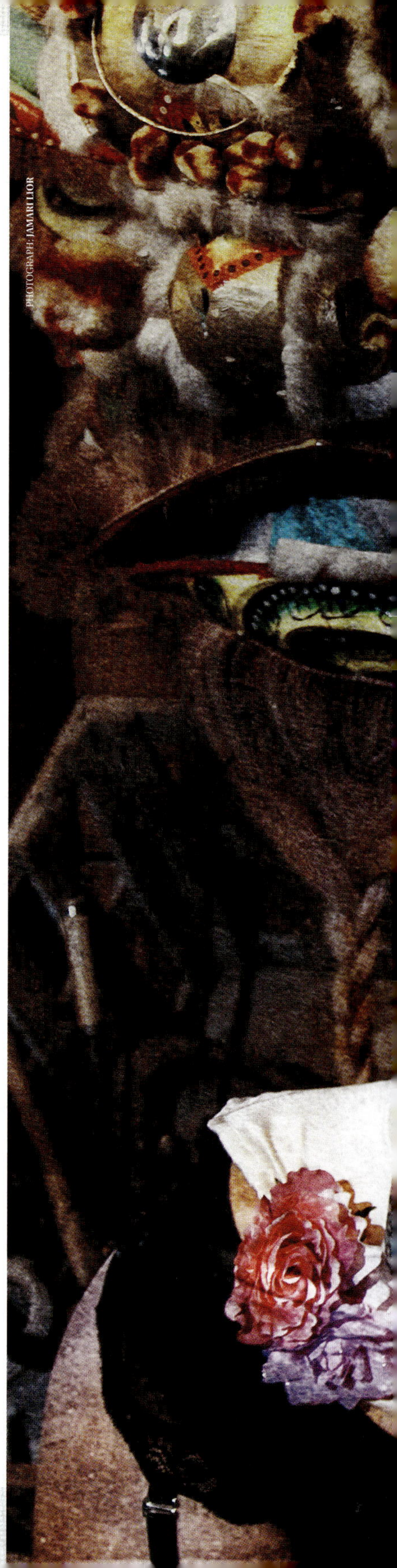

PHOTOGRAPH: JAMARI LIOR

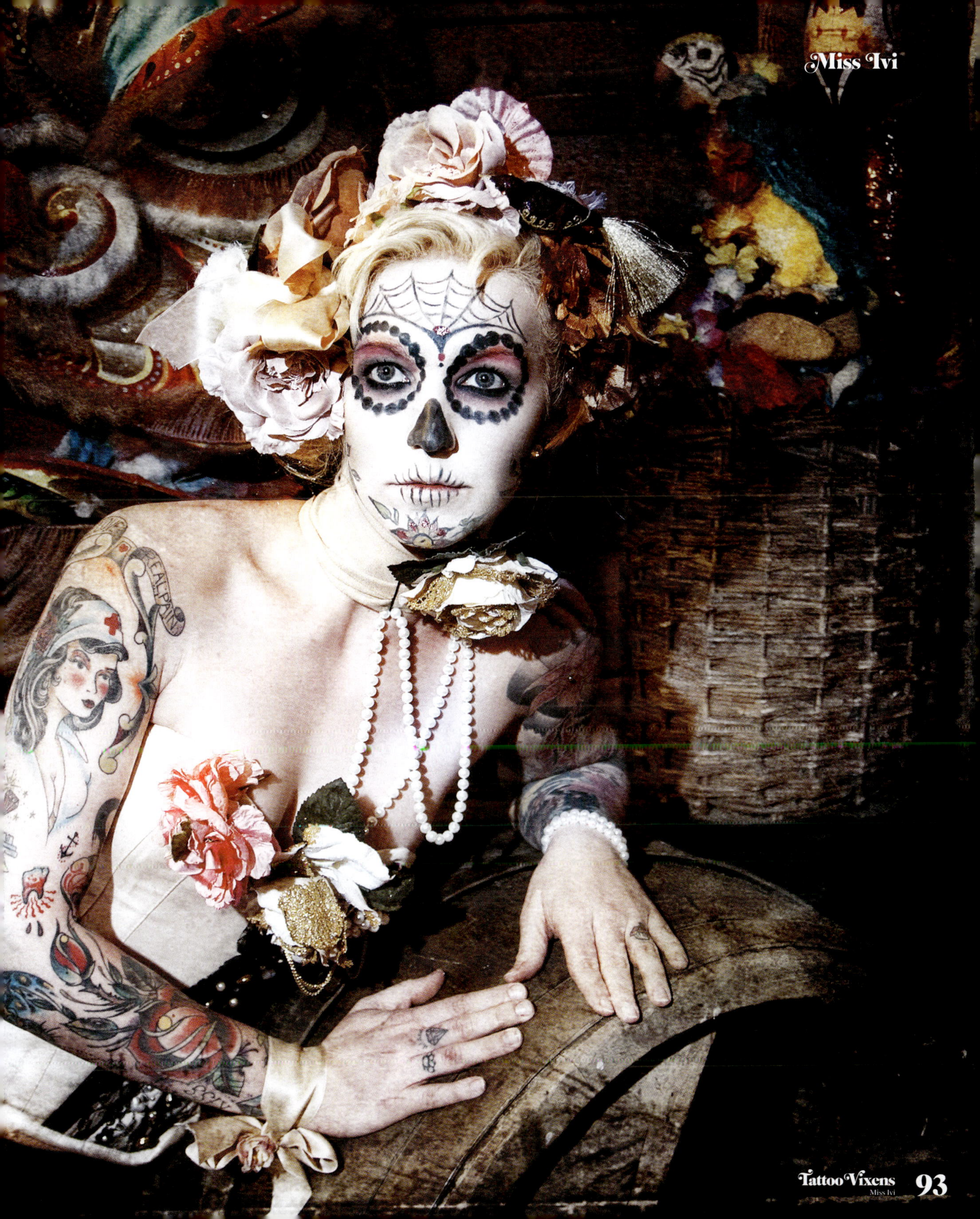

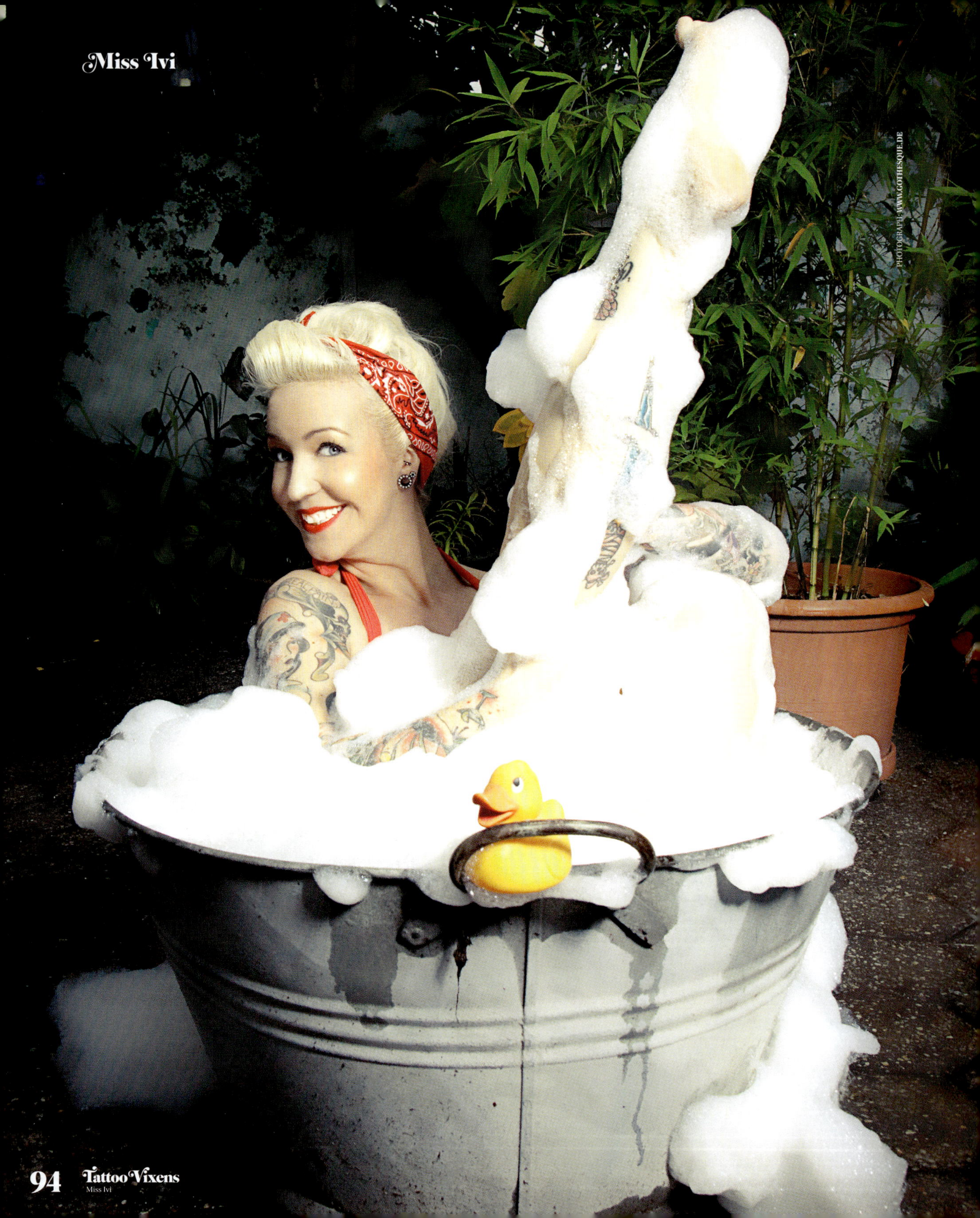

PHOTOGRAPH: WWW.GOTHESQUE.DE

as I still do today. Setting myself apart from the others wasn't on my mind so much. I just always liked tattoos and always wanted to have a lot of them. It was not until I met my now husband, (who was my tattoo artist before) that it all snowballed into what I have now. I'm such a lucky girl, that my whole life developed that way, because in my old job as a secretary it wouldn't have been possible.

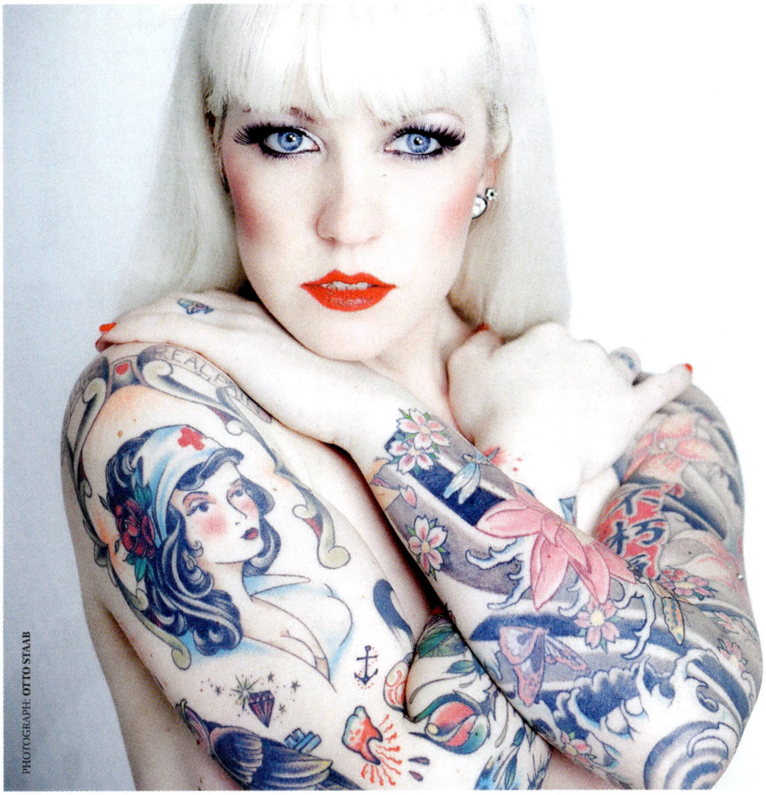

PHOTOGRAPH: OTTO STAAB

Where do we go from here with the genre? Do you think pin-ups have reached their peak or is there more creativity still left in the artform? Once upon a time, it used to be a real treat to see a pin-up calendar, but now it seems like everybody thinks they can do it. Can they?

Can they? Yes, they can try - but not every girl who tries, is also a real pin-up just because they are dressed up like one. There's a big difference between playing one and living it!

It's important to be your true self and to love yourself, to be confident in your own body… and to show it in front of the camera. A lot of girls seem to be jumping up on the pin-up train instead of living it passionately!

Do you think that being tattooed changed you at all? Did (or do) people react to you differently than they once did - even people who know you or have you found it a totally positive experience?

I think it may have changed me in some ways. I am feeling stronger and more self confident and more in touch with myself, but mainly I am still and will always be the same and crazy and happy girl as before.
Of course, there are always complete opposite reactions from other people.
Some good and positive - and other not so funny ones, but if people reduced me to my tattoos or put me in a box just by my appearance I just don't care.
I think tattooed people are the most flexible in the world. We don't care if the people we meet are tattooed or not, we treat them all the same and accept them as they are. I still find it strange that just because I have a few pictures on my skin some people treat us like dirt. Half of the time I don't notice my tattoos anymore, they are a part of me and what makes me unique.

Would you care to give advice to somebody wanting to become a pin-up?

I think there is only one thing to say. Be yourself! Don't play act or dress like a pin-up! Being a pin up is a passion and a lifestyle, not dressing up occasionally.

Finally - is there something you wish somebody would have told you before you started out?

Yes - spend a little bit more money on your first shoot and get a good professional photographer. It will definitely pay off!

> **"I think tattooed people are the most flexible in the world. We don't care if the people we meet are tattooed or not, we treat them all the same and accept them as they are.**

El Wood

ALL PHOTOGRAPHS: **IHSAN KEMAL**

With a diploma in specialist make-up and a day job in one of the most famous tattoo studios in London, it's only a matter of time until the name El Wood starts to drip off your tongue:

Name El Wood
Age 20

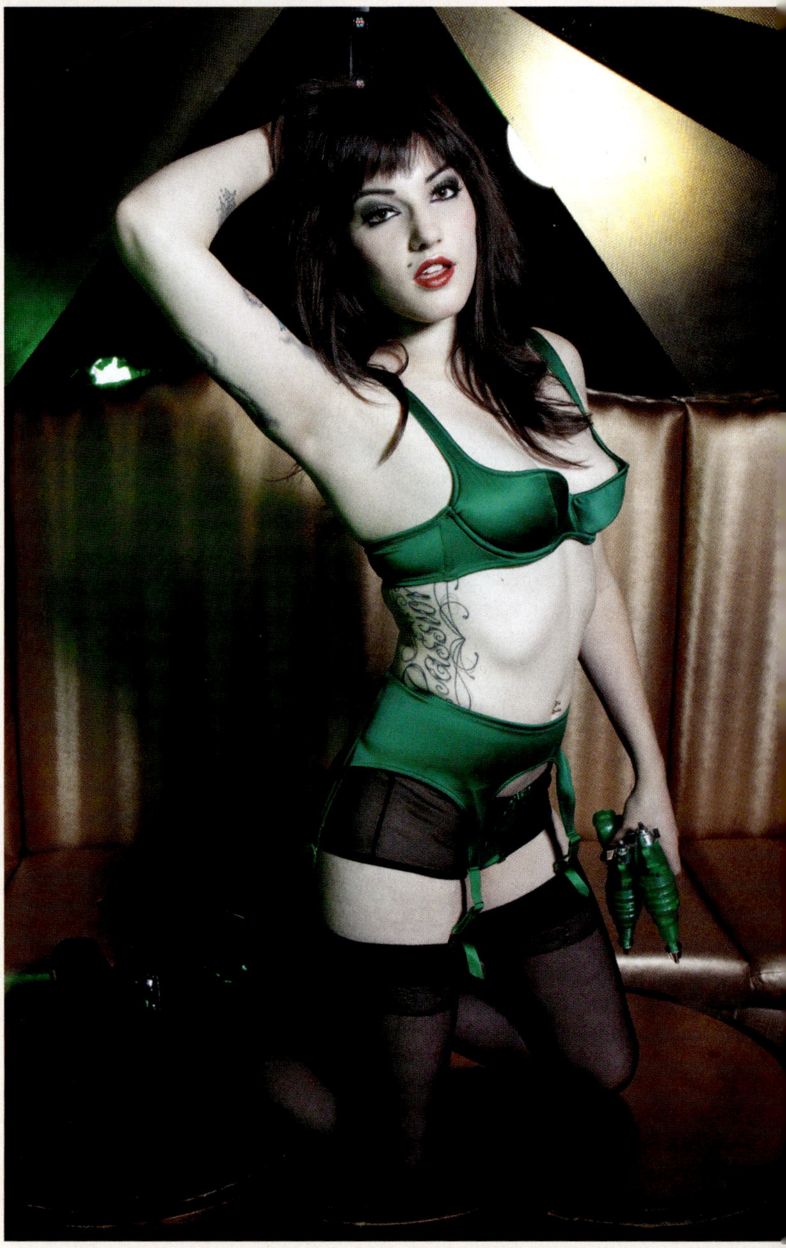

What are you currently doing career-wise and what do you aspire to be?
I just graduated with a higher national diploma as a specialist make-up artist but at the moment I am working at Frith Street Tattoos, Soho, helping at reception etc. I would love to do special effects make-up for horror movies but right now I am very happy working in the shop!

Have you ever considered becoming a full-time model?
I have always just done it for fun but saying that I have been very lucky. I have done it for the last year and a half and have been published numerous times in different magazines and been on covers too.

Tell us something about your childhood, what ambitions you had and what has inspired you?
I first wanted to be an astronaut, then after a trip to Universal Studios I wanted to be a stuntwoman! I'd done gymnastics since I was 4 but then in my teens came the discovery of rock 'n' roll. It was then that I got progressively nerdier the older I became and turned into a big art enthusiast. I find inspiration everywhere!

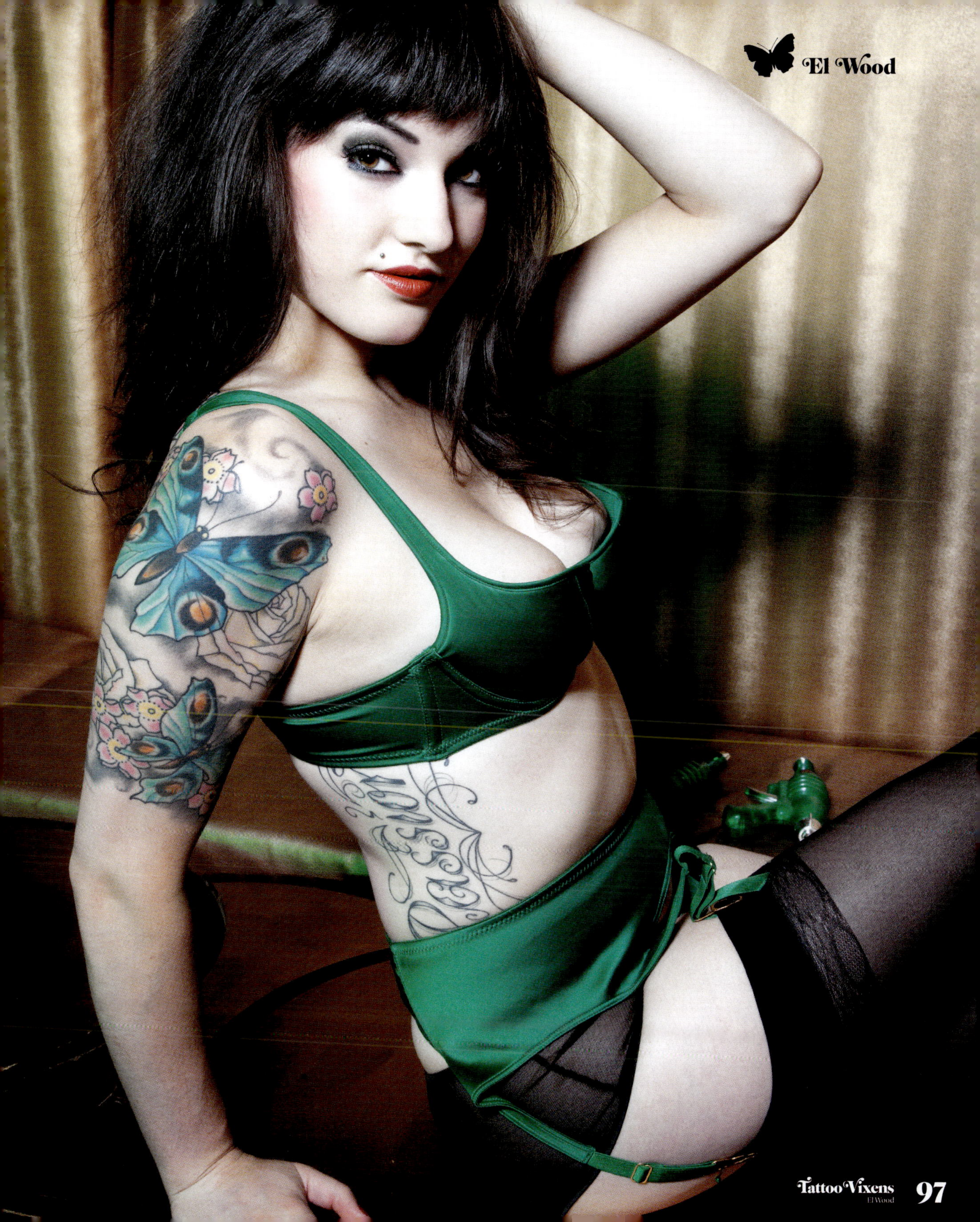

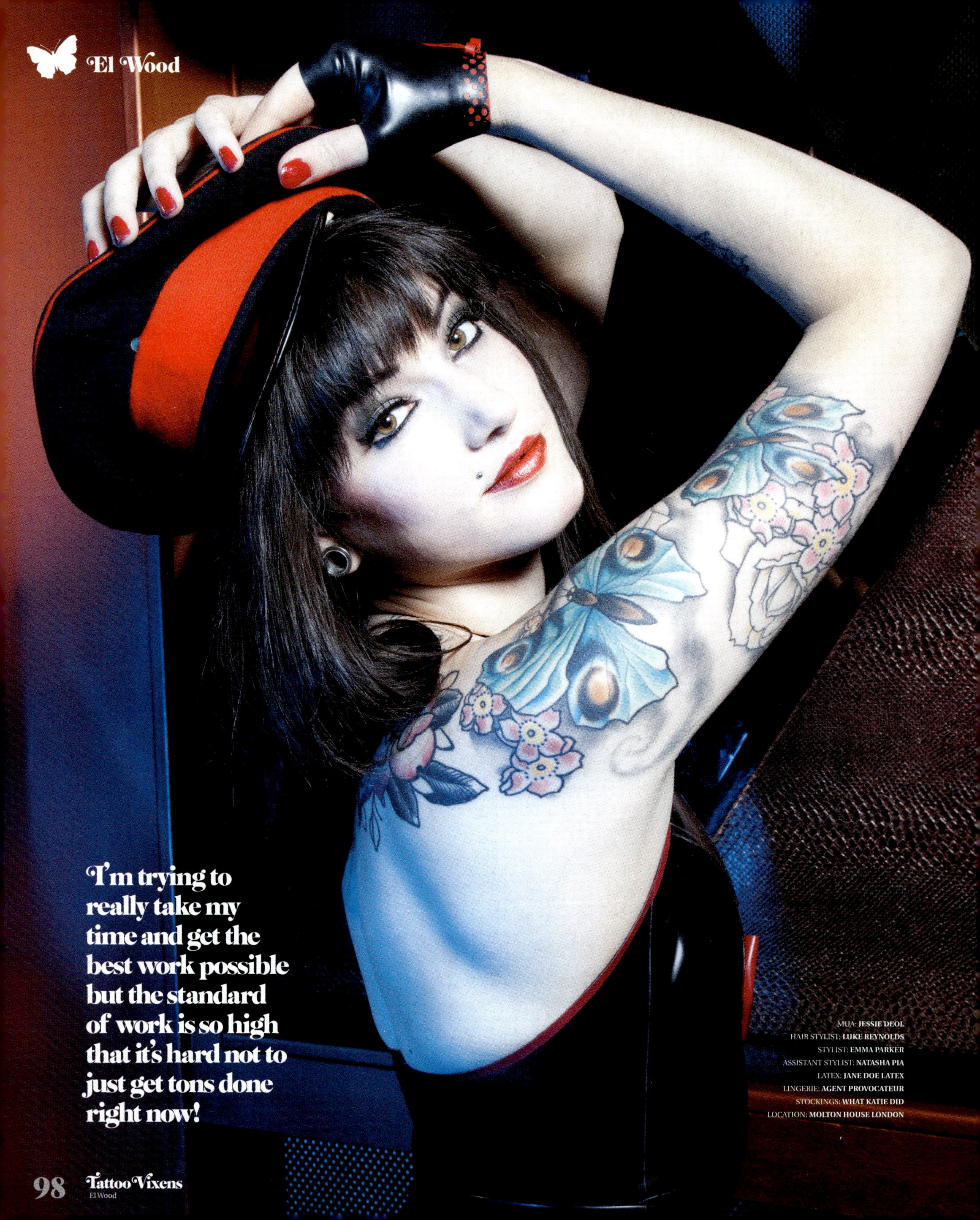

I'm trying to really take my time and get the best work possible but the standard of work is so high that it's hard not to just get tons done right now!

MUA: **JESSIE DEOL**
HAIR STYLIST: **LUKE REYNOLDS**
STYLIST: **EMMA PARKER**
ASSISTANT STYLIST: **NATASHA PIA**
LATEX: **JANE DOE LATEX**
LINGERIE: **AGENT PROVOCATEUR**
STOCKINGS: **WHAT KATIE DID**
LOCATION: **MOLTON HOUSE LONDON**

What initially attracted you towards tattoos?
My older brother had some and I really looked up to him. By the time I was 12 I knew I would have one. Also I grew up around arty people and in school I used to get asked by other kids to draw all over their arms in class. I remember my friend used to draw manga characters and I started to develop an interest in Japanese culture...maybe that's why my first tattoo was of Japanese influence.

Was acquiring significant tattoo coverage a conscious decision or a by-product of discovering the number of great tattoo artists available to you?
I see it like this...I have so many ideas and not enough skin. I'm trying to really take my time and get the best work possible but the standard of work is so high that it's hard not to just get tons done right now!

Do your tattoos have any particular significance, or do you collect them purely because of their aesthetics?
The only sentimental one I guess is my half sleeve. The butterflies are the same ones that flew around my garden as a kid but I changed the colours to symbolize change and growth of my life.

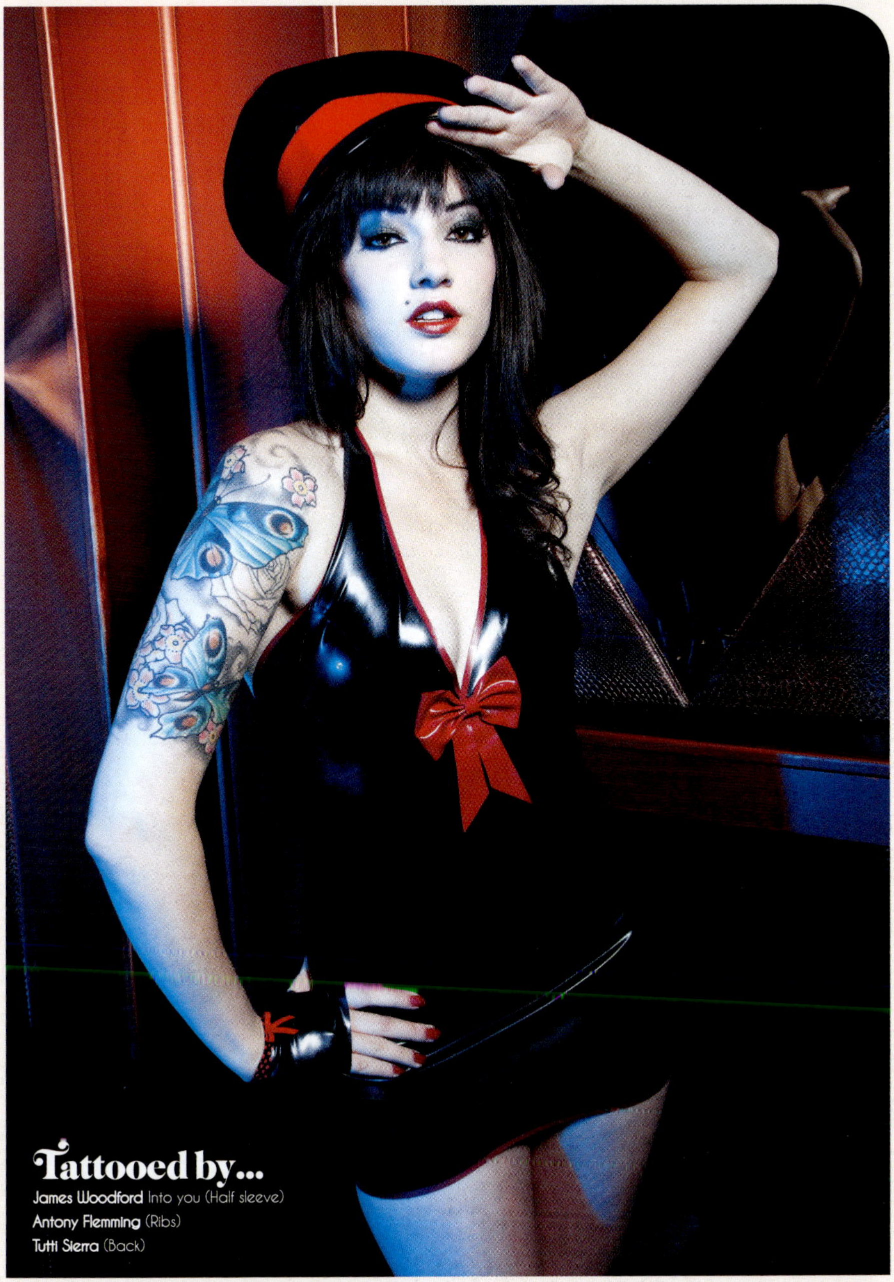

Tattooed by...
James Woodford Into you (Half sleeve)
Antony Flemming (Ribs)
Tutti Sierra (Back)

The only sentimental one I guess is my half sleeve. The butterflies are the same ones that flew around my garden as a kid.

What advice would you offer to people who are considering tattoos on public skin before they've worn much coverage elsewhere?
Think hard. There are always going to people who do not like what you have got... there will always be people who don't mind telling you that either! So make sure you love it and are proud to walk around with that work on you. It's a big commitment so think hard and research your artist well.

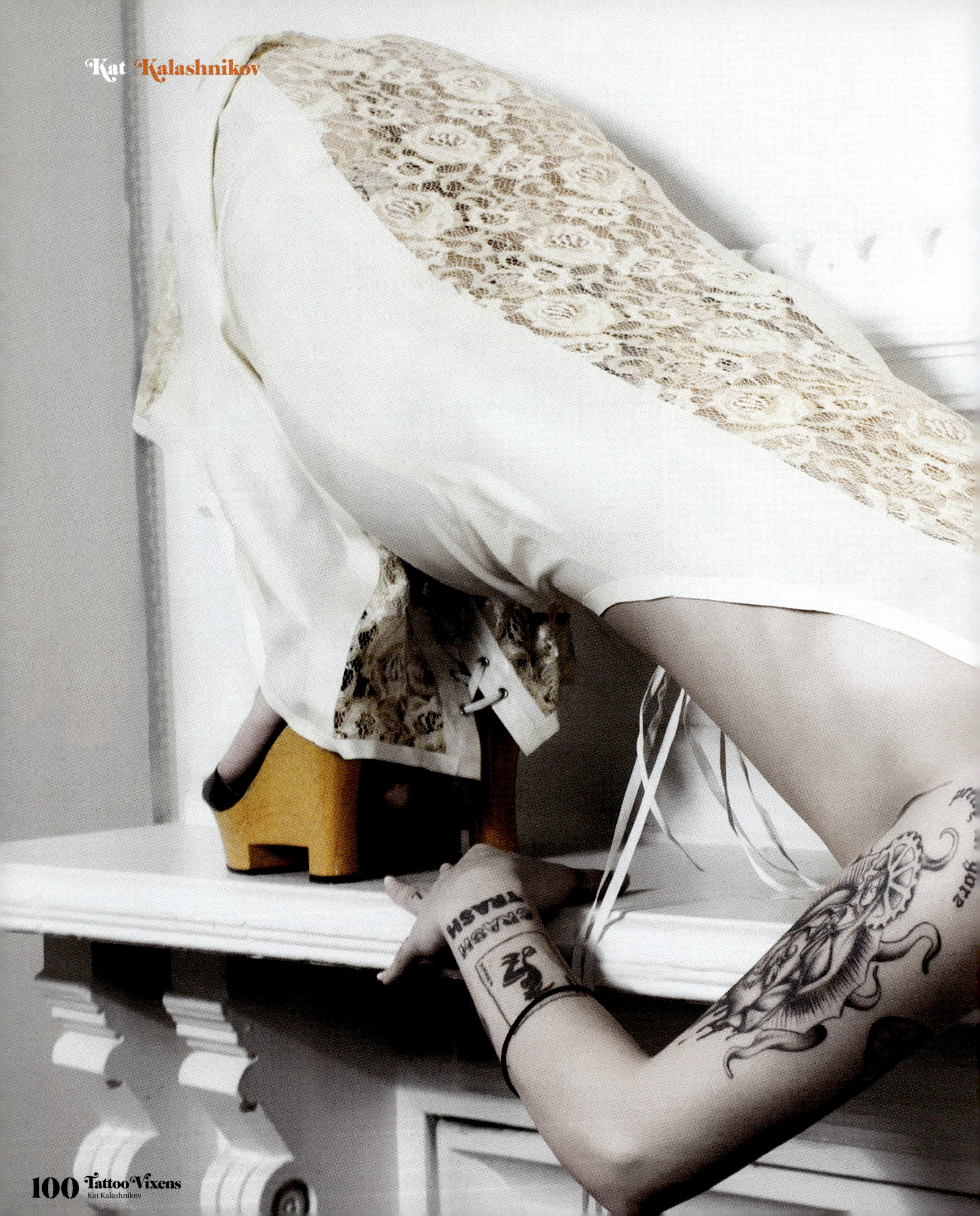

Kat Kalashnikov

ALL PHOTOGRAPHS: **CORRUPT IMAGE DATA**

Kat isn't one to let a little accident stand in the way of a good interview - even if she did have to submit it via some deft left-handed text messaging.

Where are you?

At the ER with a broken wrist. Playing too rough with my boyfriend. I actually made a cute video clip while waiting in the ER though.

From where I'm standing, I'd call you one of the new breed of tattooed models out there - brash and sassy but genuine too - would that be a fair statement to make? Have you found your niche?

I would say it's a fair statement,

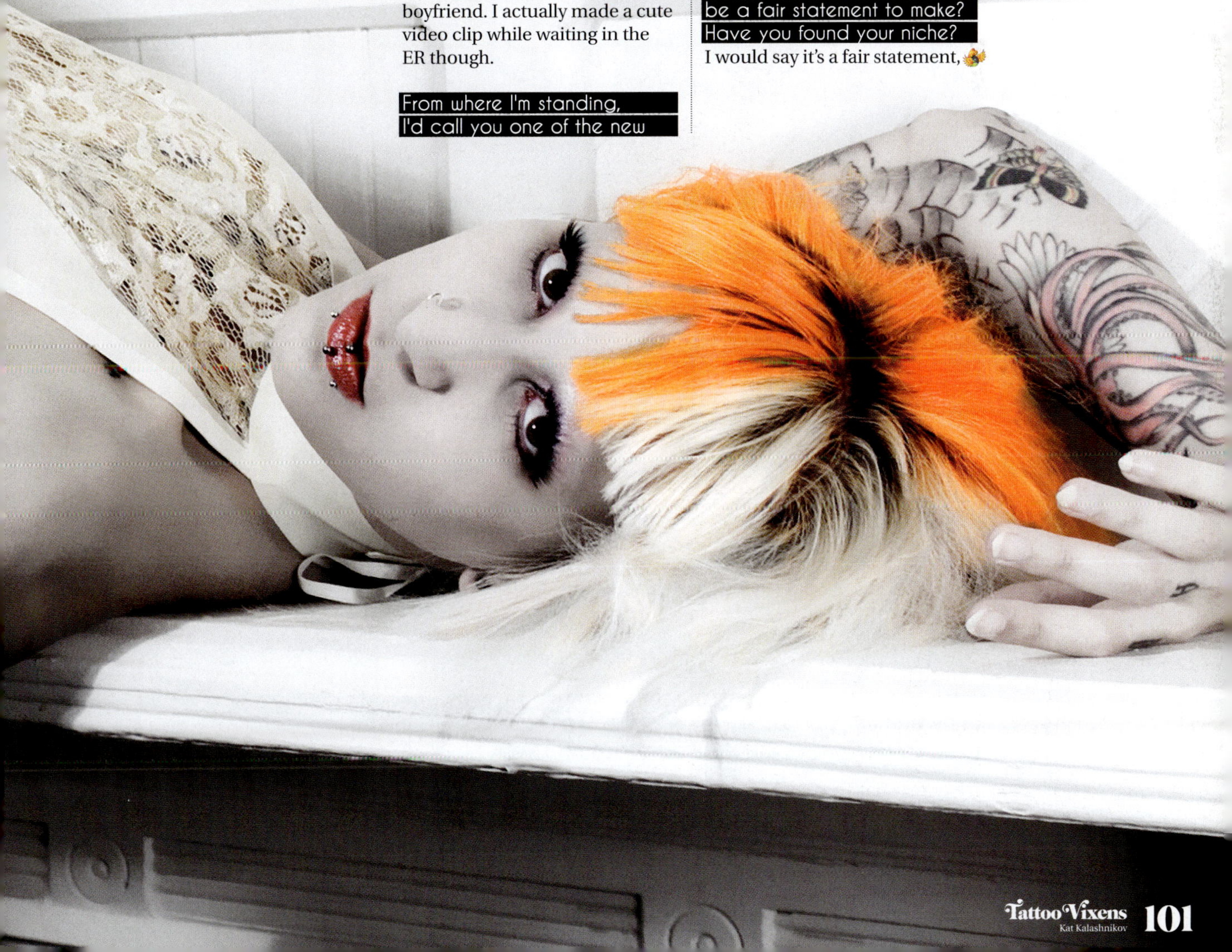

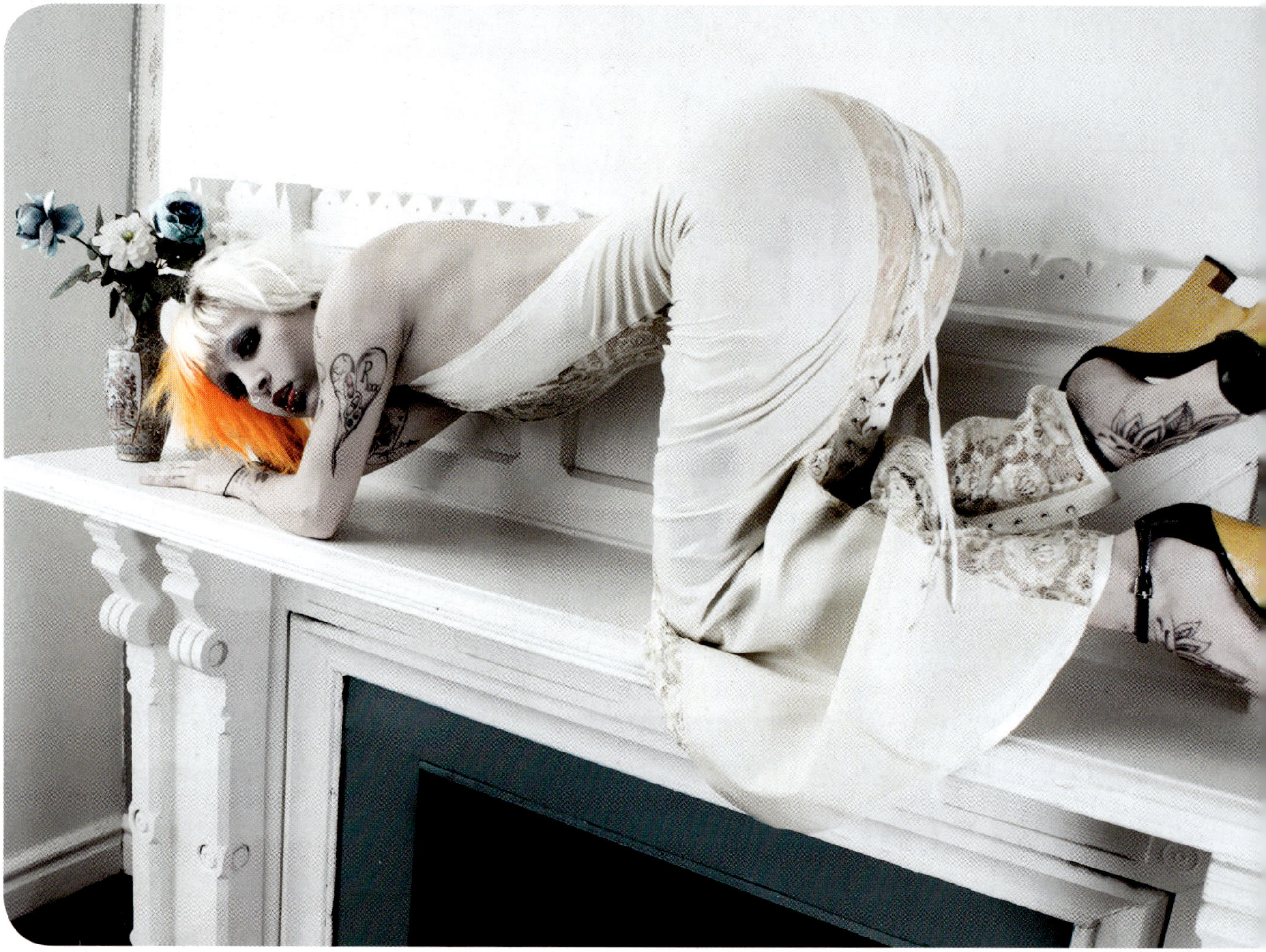

I'm not afraid to be alternative mainstream and do things other models might not find attractive or want to convey.

my niche is being an alternative and fetish model by definition. I'm not afraid to be alternative mainstream and do things other models might not find attractive or want to convey.

Now that you've committed to this level of tattooing, has it had a positive or negative effect on your day to day life or do you simply live life and not pay attention to the world outside?

I dont pay attention at all. Sometimes I forget and wonder why someone is staring at my arms or legs!

Can you talk me through some of your art - where it was done and who by - and what your plans are for the rest of your body in the future?

The majority of them were done by Jason Moore - he is currently at Hardwire Tattoo in Wilmington. I want to cover my legs and finish my arms. I have plans for a spine made out of guns and a pig skeleton.

Assuming that this wasn't what you wanted to do when you were a kid - what did you want to be when you grew up... and do you think you'll ever get around to doing it later?

I wanted to be a college professor for cultural anthropology - I think it's still possible.

Kat Kalashnikov

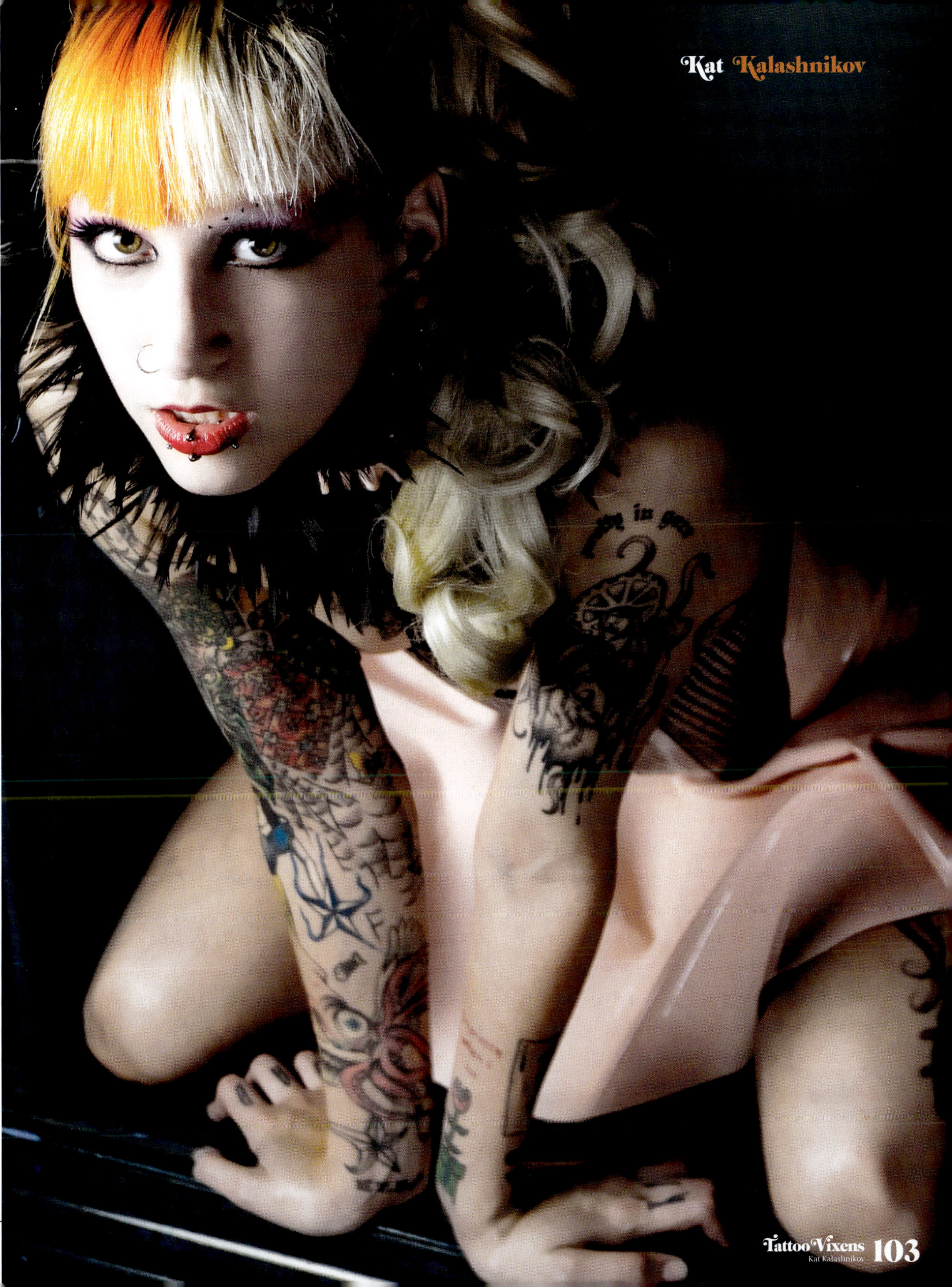

ALL PHOTOGRAPHS: JAY MCLAUGHLIN

Hollie

Nurse by day, insanely popular model at all other hours, Hollie Bryant is one of the names to watch out for in the future. If you're wondering why, you're reading the wrong book.

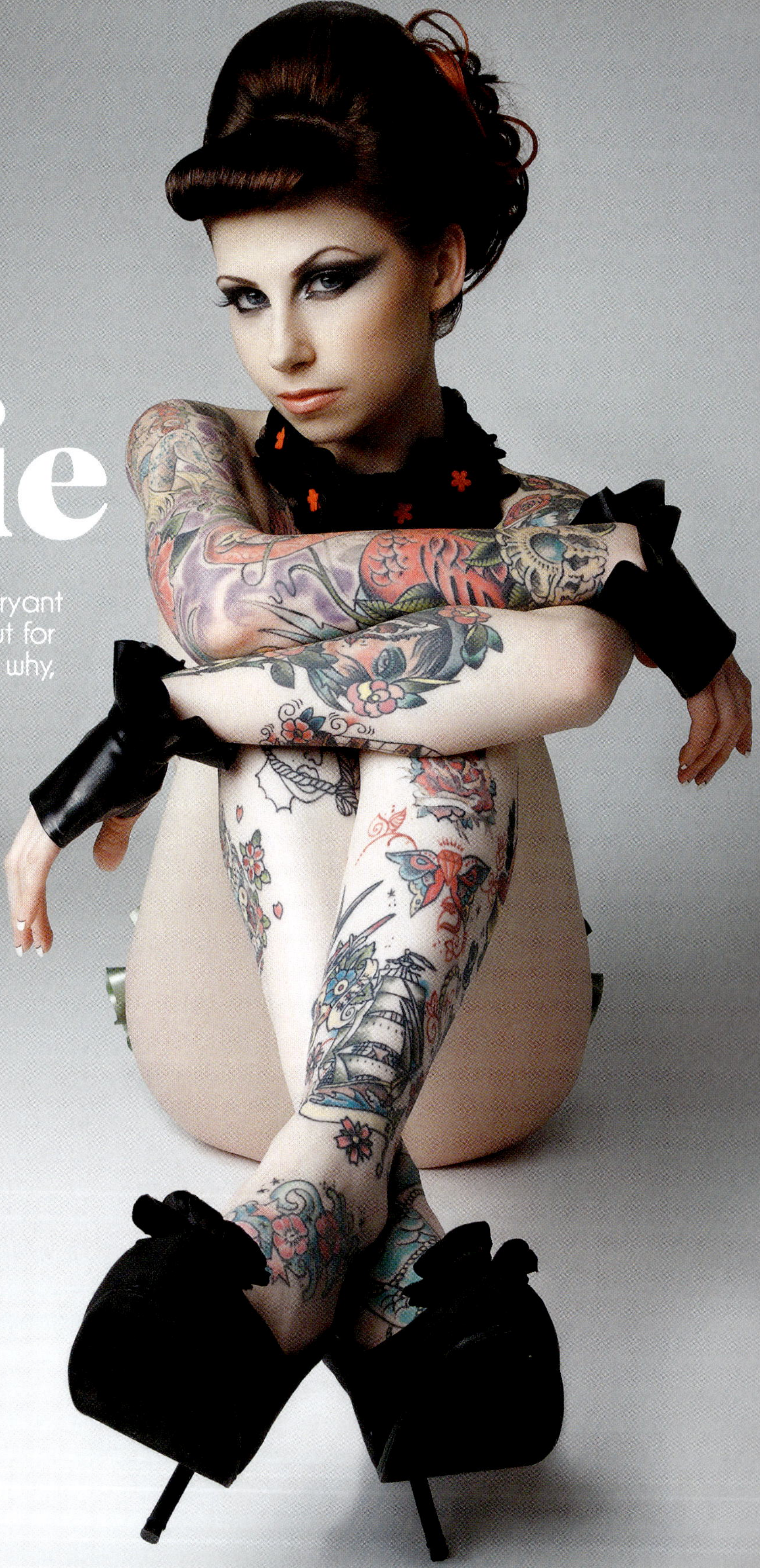

Have you ever considered becoming a full time model?

It's hard to get the time nowadays but I try to do a as much modelling in my spare time as I can fit in because I really enjoy it. Most of the shoots I work on are for alternative clothing companies and an alternative website and some magazines. I have considered becoming a full time model but unfortunately it doesn't pay the bills as well as my full time job and there isn't always guaranteed work so for now I will have to stay put. At the moment it is more of a hobby rather than a job.

Where did you get your tattoos done? What made you go to these particular artists over others?

Most of my tattoos have been done by Dawnii- painted lady Tattoo Parlor and Phil Kyle at Magnum Opus. The reason I went to Dawnii was because her work really stood out, I

"I have considered becoming a full time model but unfortunately it doesn't pay the bills as well as my full time job.

have been getting tattooed by her for around 4 years and each time I have been so happy with the results. Her work is so bright and colourful, I am never disappointed. I have loved Phil's work for ages after seeing some of his art on his MySpace Page. His work is so imaginative and I love his unique style. You can really see how he has influenced a lot of artists! He has been working on my left sleeve and I will definitely be going back for him to finish it off.

Do your tattoos have any particular meaning or symbolism behind them? What made you get them?

Some of my tattoos have meaning and some of them don't. Quite a lot of my tattoos have been inspired from things that I have a passion for such as old school imagery and animals, especially birds. I think I have about 5 big birds dotted around on my body and I'm due to get a peacock soon.

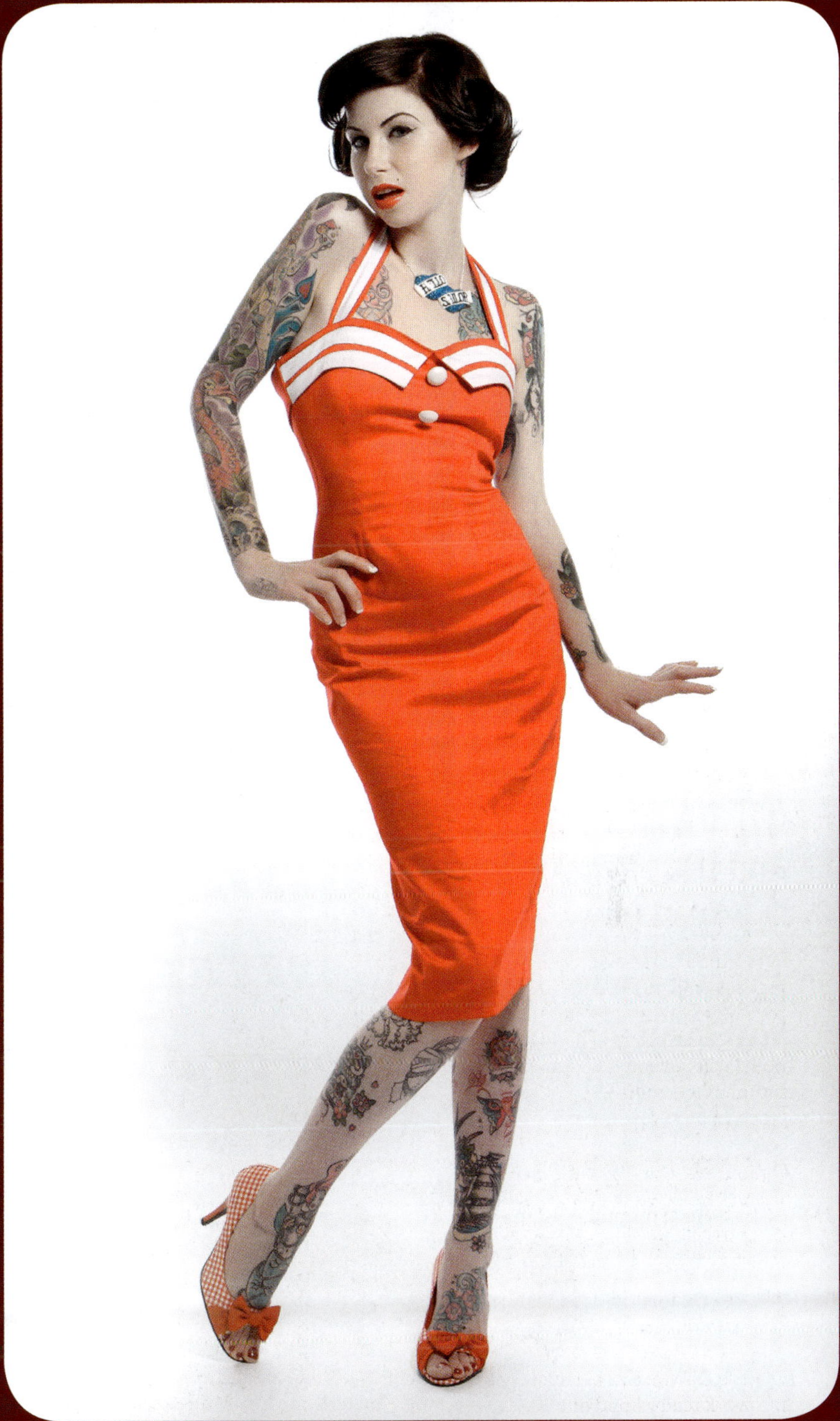

Have you had any negative reactions to your tattoos from your family or other people?
I get a mixed reaction to my tattoos from different people. My family are totally cool about them, even my Nan loves them. They know me and they know I love art and tattoos so they never really have anything negative to say which is really nice. People who don't know me do tend to stare and sometimes whisper, especially where I live as it's quite 'posh'. Despite this I also get a lot of positive attention from people I don't know. Lots of people want to touch them which is sometimes uncomfortable and I have spent many a time answering questions like where I got them done, how long they took. It can be annoying but in away I like doing this because I feel like I'm educating people and maybe giving them some information which will give them the courage to go and get their first tattoo.

My family are totally cool about them, even my Nan loves them. They know me and they know I love art and tattoos so they never really have anything negative to say which is really nice.

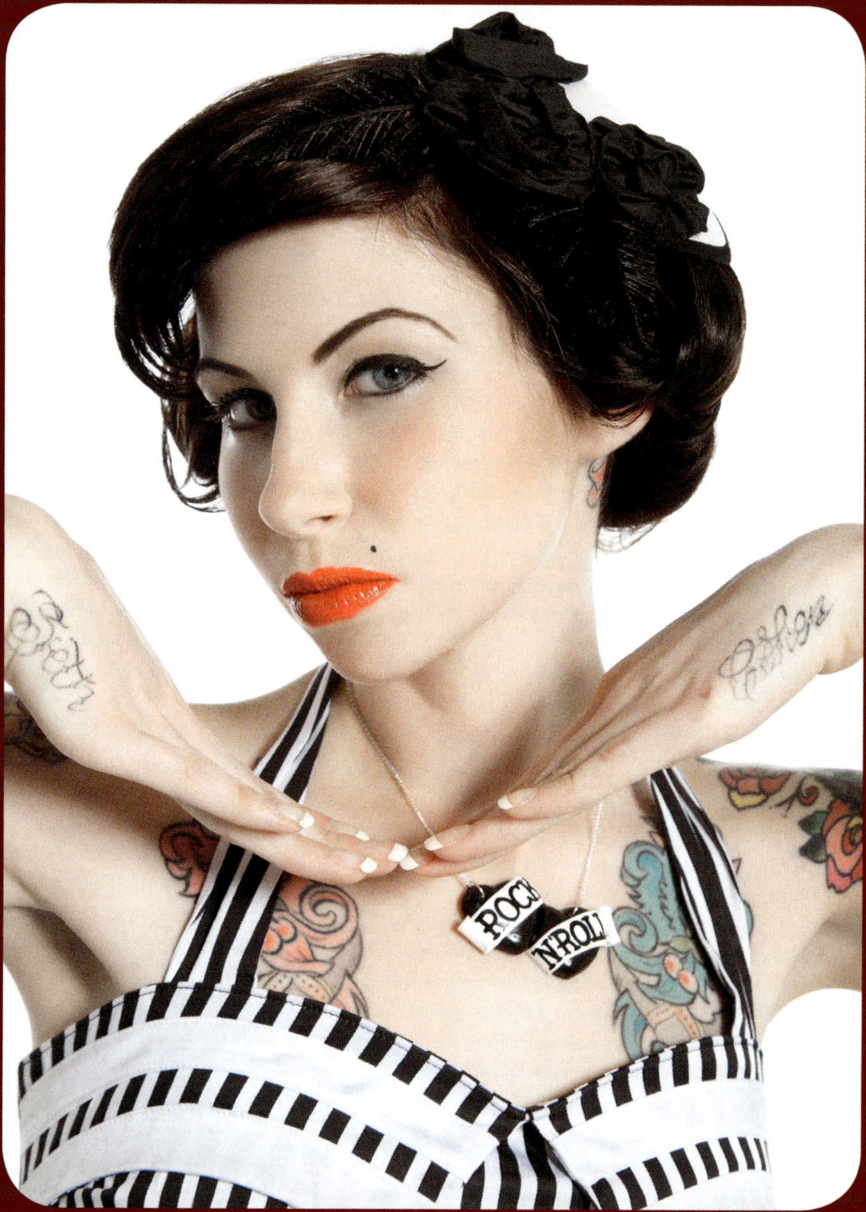

Do you have any future tattoos planned? What artists do you hope to have tattoo you?
I have quite a few bits and pieces planned. I would love to get some work by Jo Harrison at Modern Body Art and would also like some work by Uncle Allan and Amanda Toy. I really want some work by Bob Done at Magnum Opus. I have always loved his art work that he was producing while apprenticing and I would love to get some ink. I'm booked in With Dawnii as well in October so I'm looking forward to see what will come of that. We just sit there and chat then after six hours I look down and she has created something amazing.

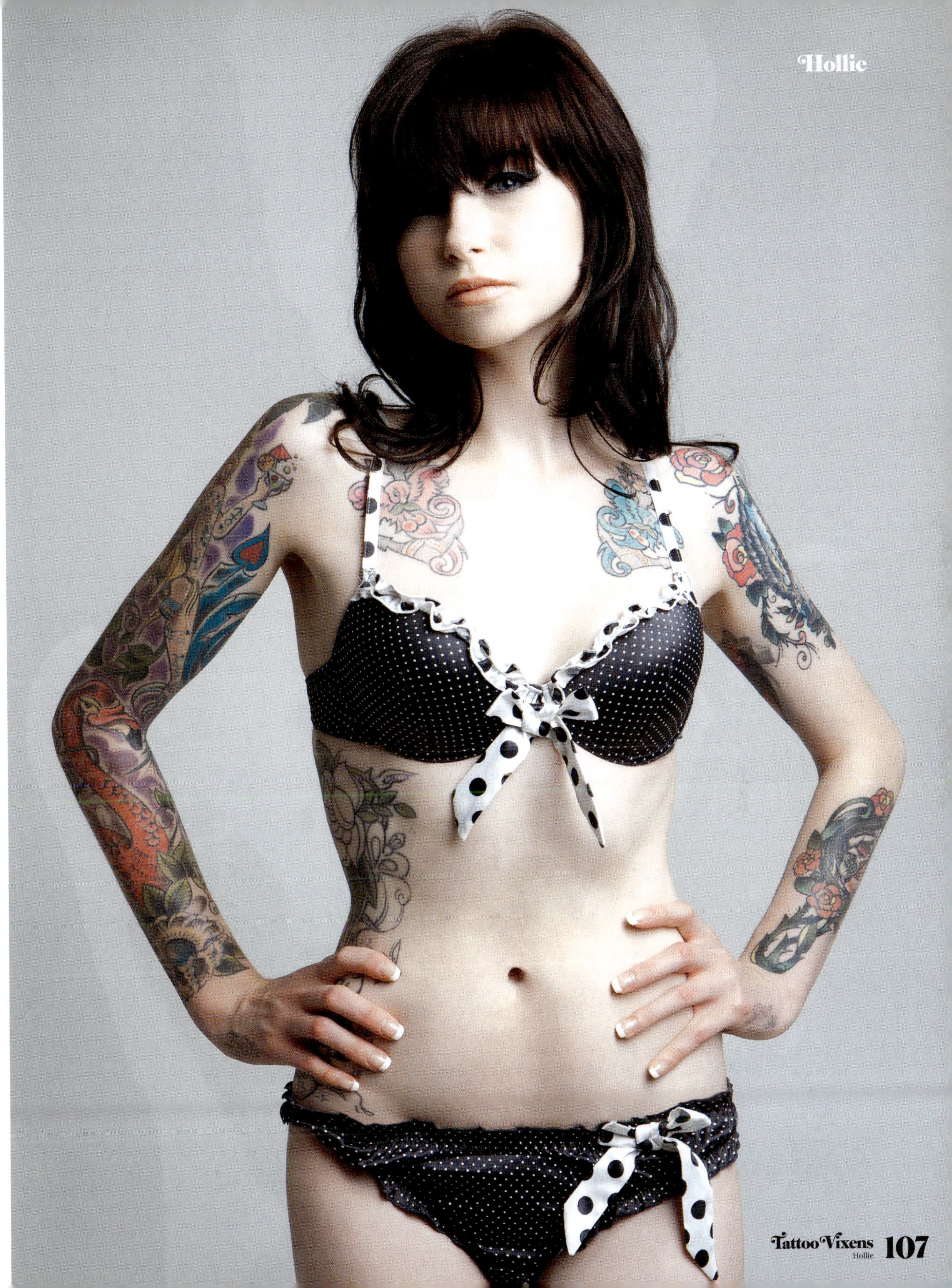

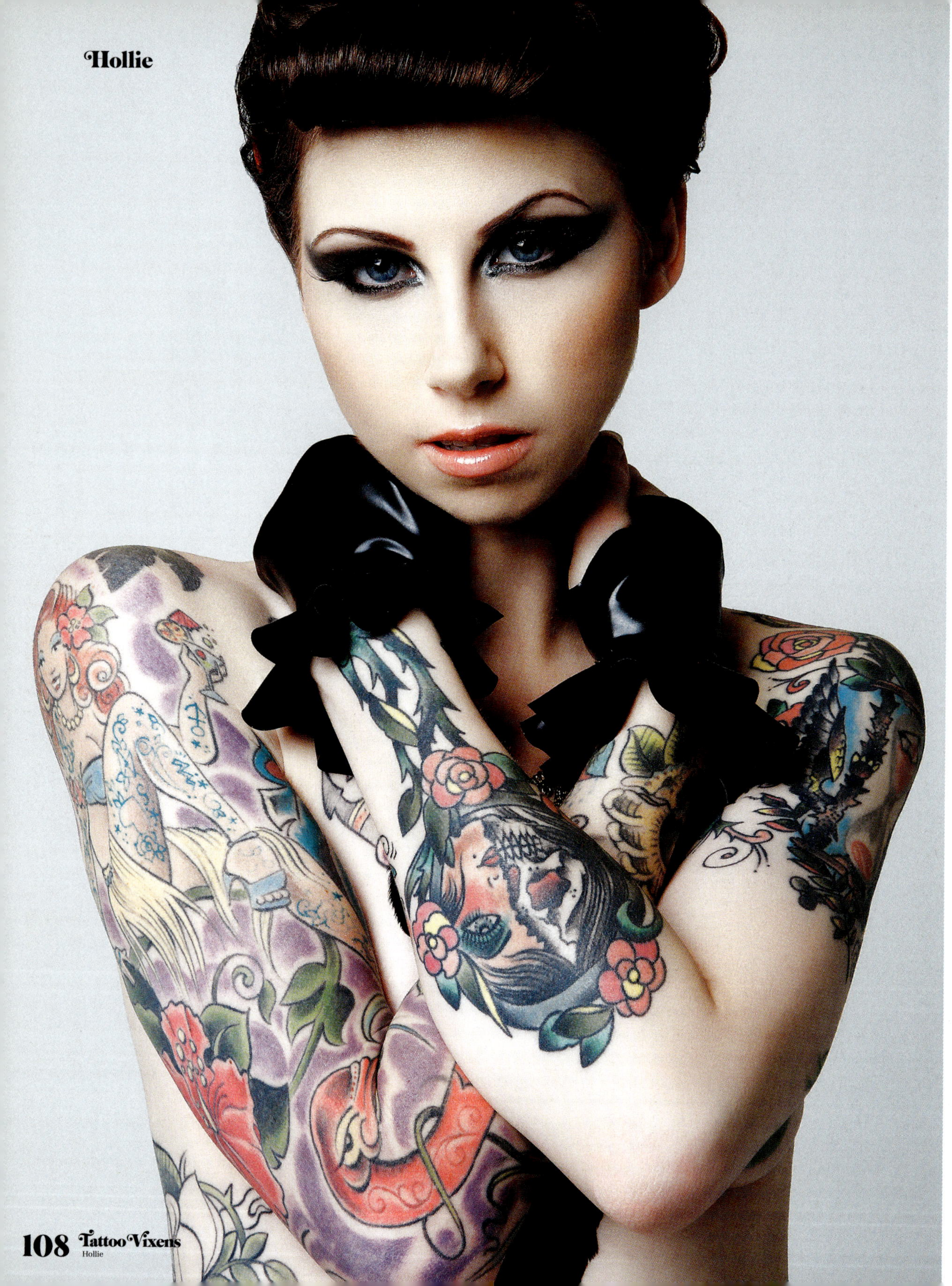

Are you worried about the amount of coverage you have at such a young age of 23?
Definitely not. I still have plenty of empty space. My tattoos just seem to be in places people can see them instead of hidden. Some people say my tattoos will affect my chances of getting a job in the future but I have graduated from uni and been in my profession for 3 years so I think my job is safe. I wouldn't want to do a job that judged me by the way I looked anyway so I don't think they will pose a problem.

I have graduated from uni and been in my profession for 3 years so I think my job is safe. I wouldn't want to do a job that judged me by the way I looked anyway.

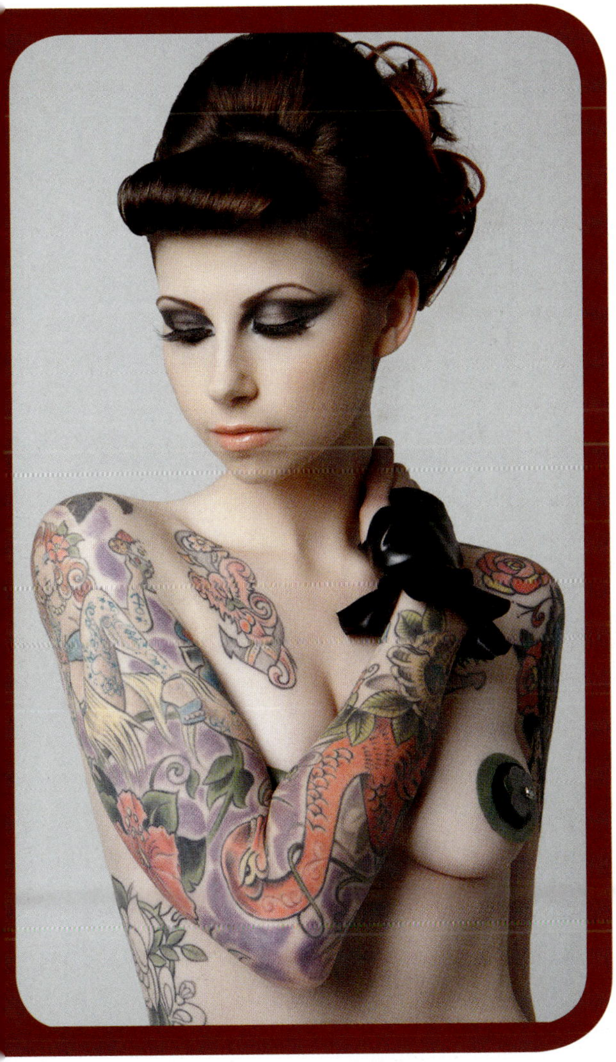

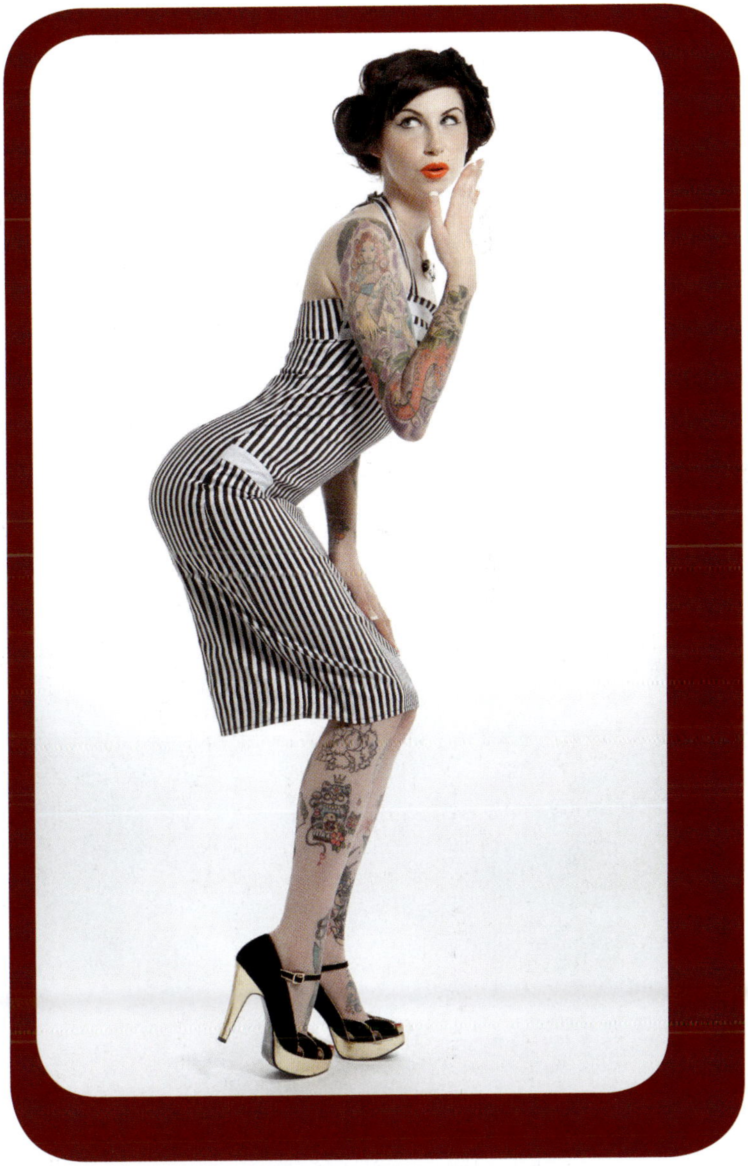

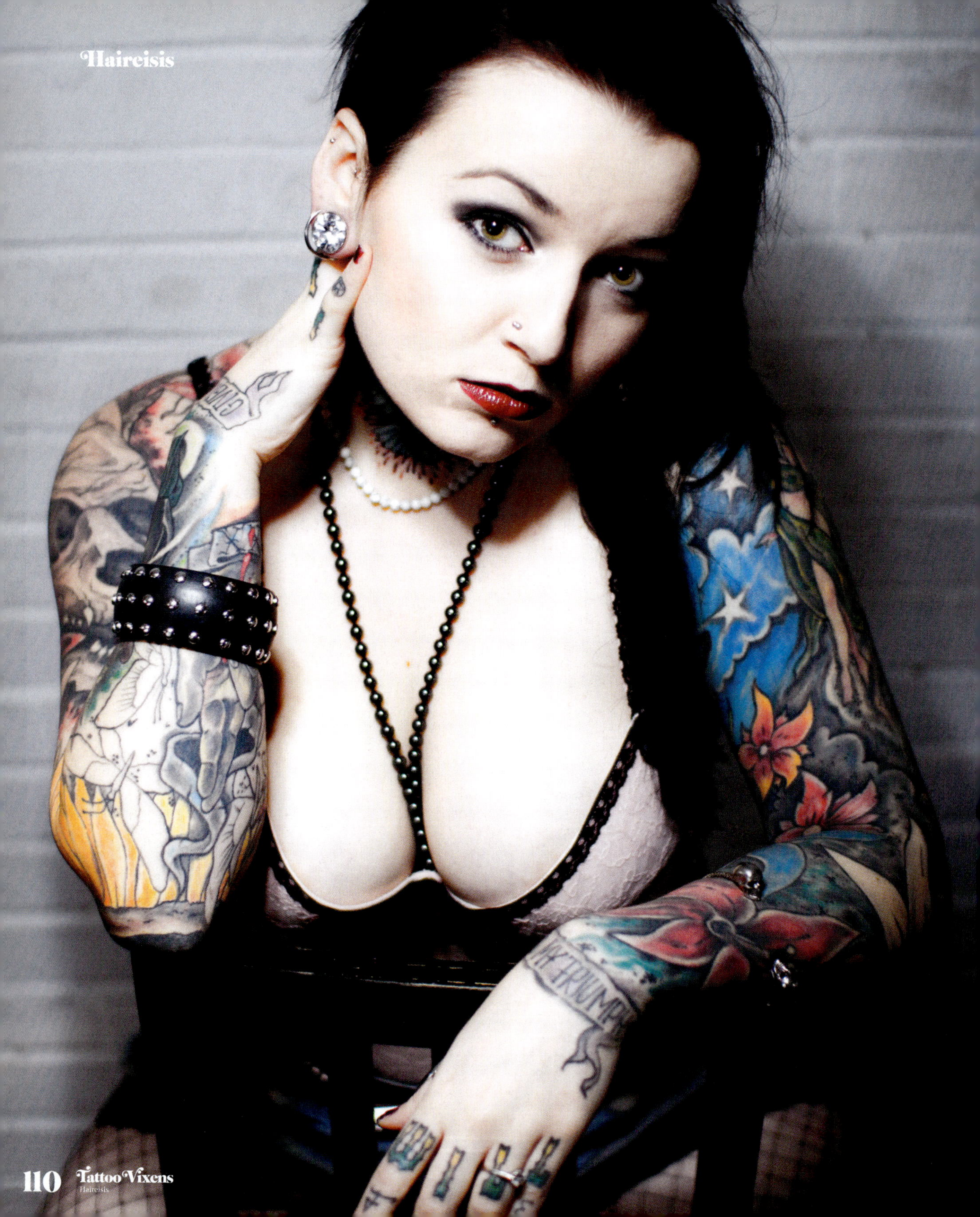

ALL PHOTOGRAPHS: XANDY EDGEX

Haireisis

A music and events photographer, Haireisis tells how being heavily tattooed can be of no small amount of assistance when it comes to getting close to the music.

What was it that got you started as a photographer?
I have pretty much been involved with the arts since I was a kid. I was playing keyboard, writing poems, singing in a hardcore/punk band. When I was about 9 years old, I joined a local theatre group, so acting has been my passion for over a decade. Soon after my 18th birthday I decided to move to England to start my adult life. Here I couldn't continue acting which made me very miserable for quite some time. I needed a replacement - something that would help me get through tough times and keep me active creatively and artistically.

I have always had a "thing" for photography – unfortunately I could never afford a camera before! Being a teenager, I had been working on borrowed zeniths and film compacts. I didn't get my first camera until I was 20! I started to photograph the bands on a 7mp point and shoot camera, soon upgraded to a DSLR. I did everything from street photography to landscapes, but my passion is event and music photography in all forms. I still have a regular full-time job outside of photography as well but my goal is to become a full time photographer in the near future.

You work mostly in music - do you think that being heavily tattooed helps you connect quickly with the bands you work with?
It definitely does! In most of the cases we are communicating with each other more on "buddy" level rather than official – photographer vs. customer. To be honest, most of the musicians I work with are quite heavily tattooed themselves so we have a lot in common - which is precious especially when it comes to longer projects like joining the band in the recording studio for example.

And on that same subject, does it ever have the opposite effect?
In music industry it doesn't so far... but I was once refused a job on a cruse ship as a junior photographer because the way I look.

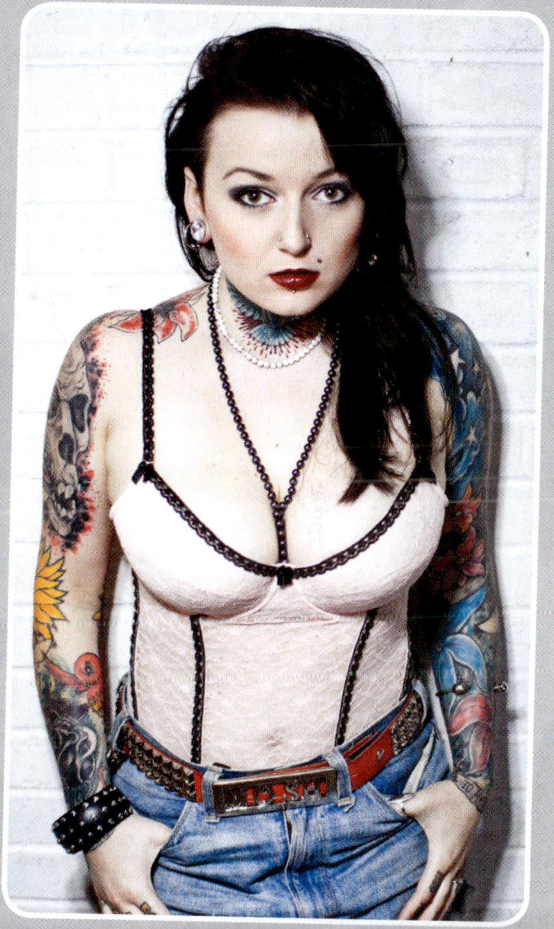

Name Haireisis
Age 24
Occupation Photographer (parttime) Quality Inspector (fulltime)

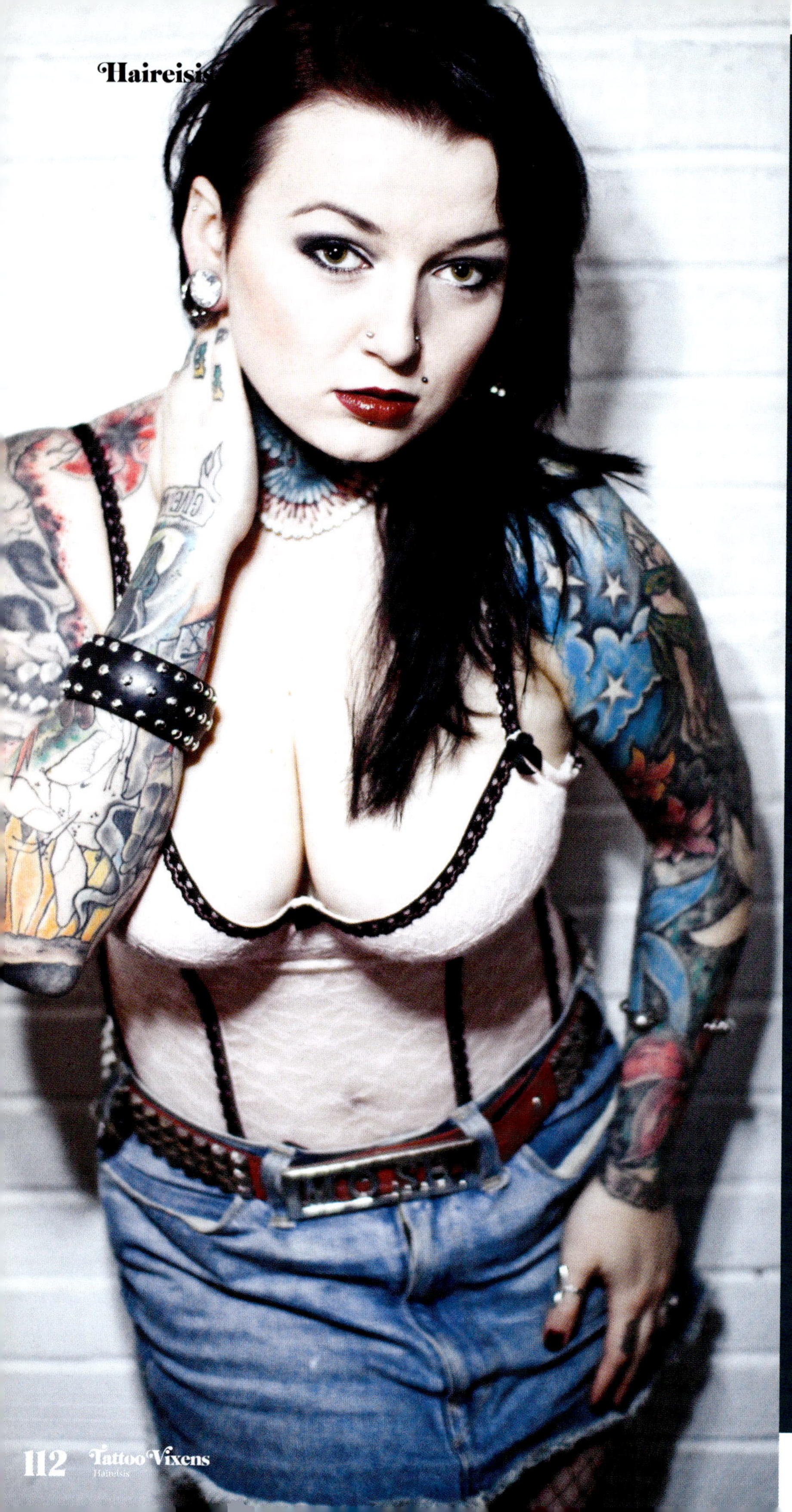

Over the years I have developed my personal "tattoo taste" and I was ready to take the next step in my carefully planned tattoo journey.

Have you stayed with the same artist for all your work?
All my tattoos apart from my throat were done by a great artist – Andy X Edge (Pulse, Northampton). My neck was done by world class artist - Tim Kern (Tribulation Tattoo, NYC).

Do you ever go back Poland? I'm interested in what you think the tattoo scene is like over there and whether tattooed women are as popular as in the UK/USA.
I travel there at least once a year. The Polish tattoo scene is getting impressively stronger and there's also a lot of going on festival wise – tattoo conventions in all major cities – Tattoofest in Krakow seems to be the most popular. There are quite a few amazing artists: Daveee, Tofi, Lenu, Gonzo and Mysków are definitely worth checking out.

Tattooed women aren't so popular in Poland outside an artistic environment - and you won't pass them by on the street as often as in the UK. I guess they are still misunderstood by society, especially in smaller towns. I experience that every time I'm visiting my hometown – rudeness of strangers, stares and comments are unfortunately quite common.

Let's talk about your neck piece for a moment - do you think that has the most impact on your life?

I don't think it does. It didn't affect me at all on a professional or private level. I've been very lucky to work with fantastic people who in spite of being tattoo-less, have this cool tattoo-friendly attitude. In public, people might stare a bit more but I'm not bothered because I've kind of gotten used to being watched.

Before I had my neck tattooed, I already had my sleeves, back, and fingers covered. Over the years I have developed my personal "tattoo taste" and I was ready to take the next step in my carefully planned tattoo journey. I need to mention here, having a dove on my throat was very well thought out – the whole idea was born in my head over 2 years before the actual making.

What advice would you offer to other women who are considering tattoos on public skin before they've worn much coverage elsewhere?

I would advise to give it a lot of thought as I said. Don't get them impulsively! To fashion followers: maybe consider henna tattoo instead – it will probably last longer than trends anyway! Maybe I'm a bit old-fashioned when it comes to tattoos but I believe they are supposed to be for life, so please take your time planning them. Tattoos on public skin are an extremely strong statement - make sure that you know who you are and where it is that you are going before you decide to get one -just to avoid future disappointment!

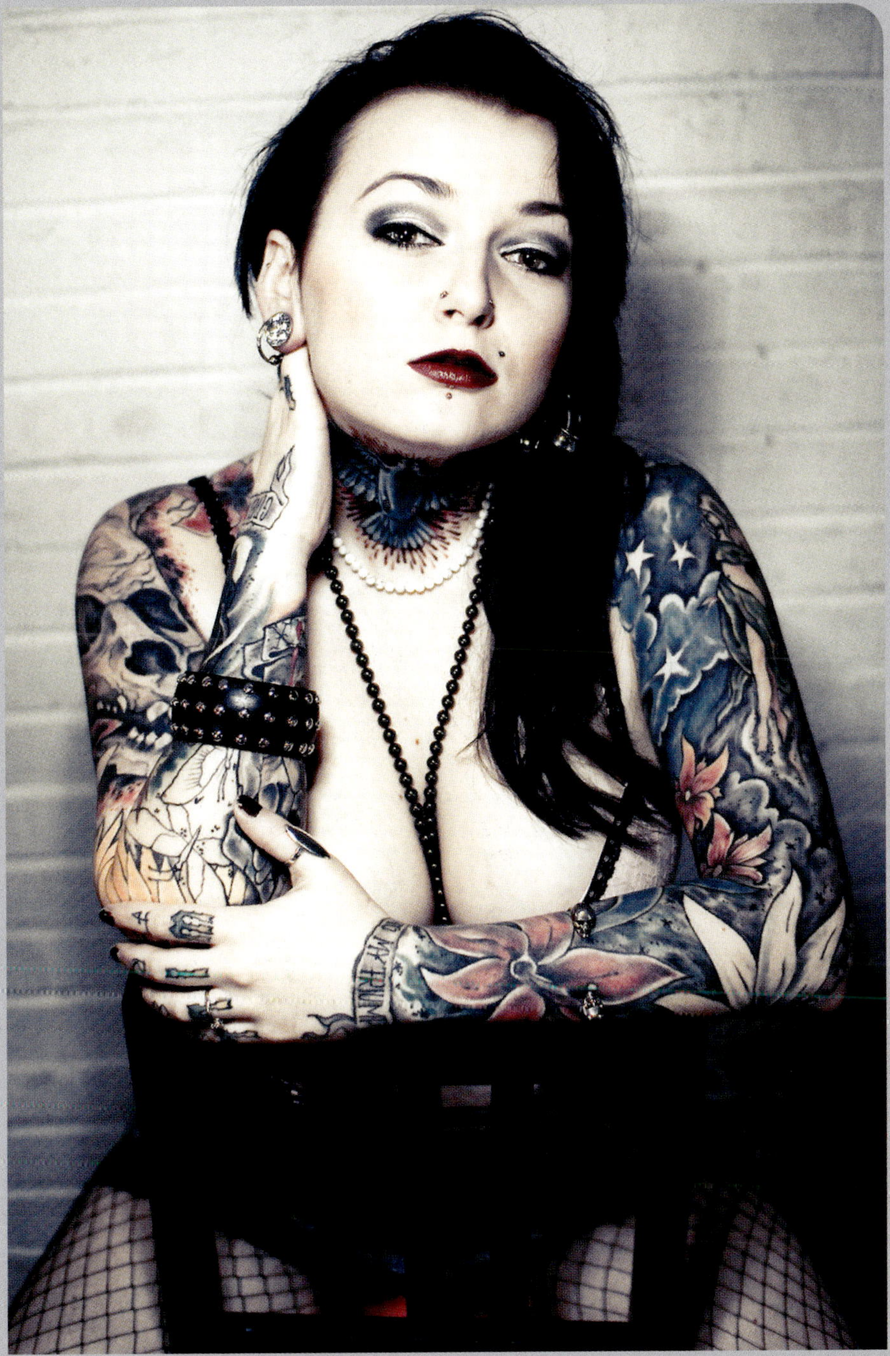

"I need to mention here, having a dove on my throat was very well thought out - the whole idea was born in my head over 2 years before the actual making.

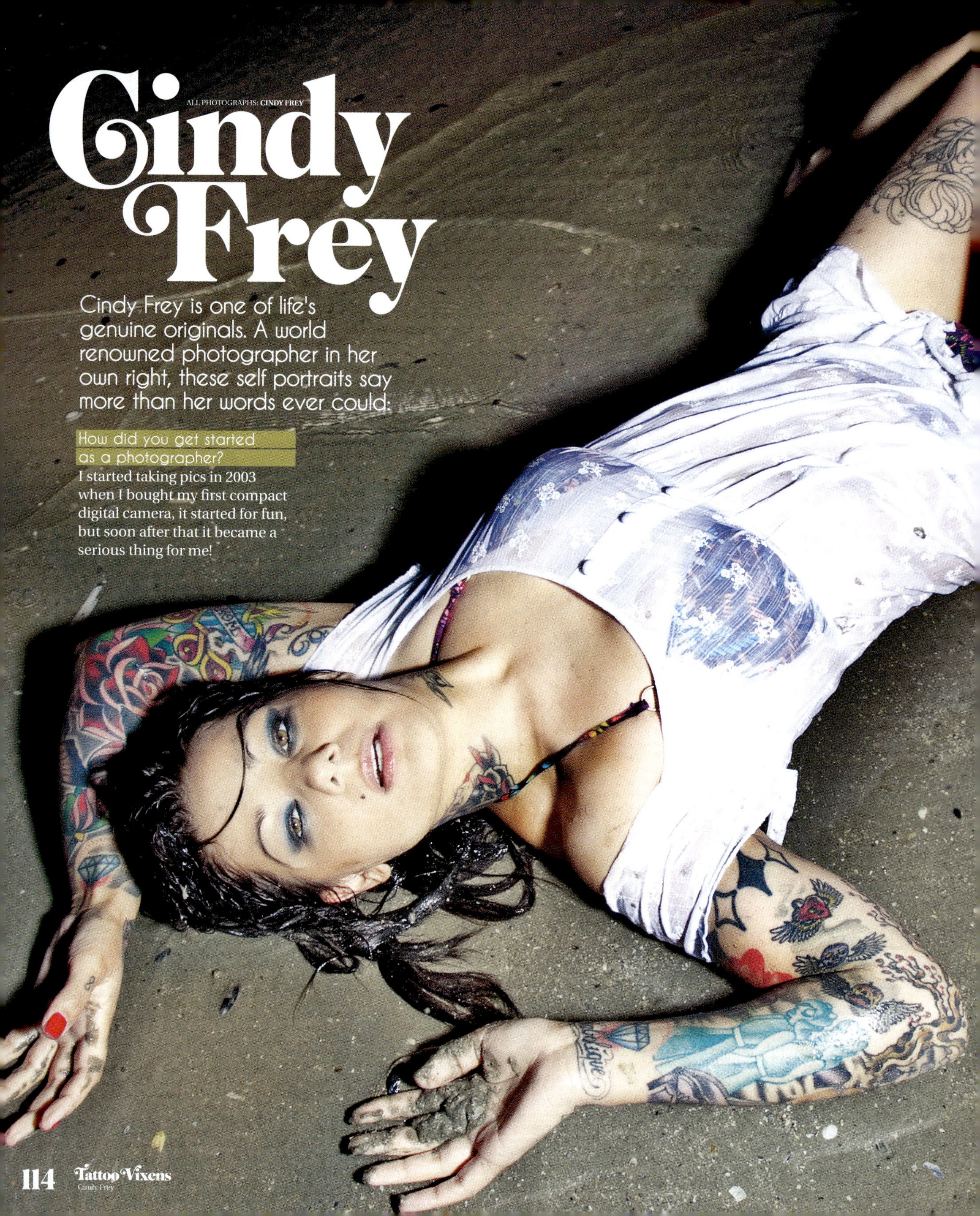

ALL PHOTOGRAPHS: **CINDY FREY**

Cindy Frey

Cindy Frey is one of life's genuine originals. A world renowned photographer in her own right, these self portraits say more than her words ever could:

How did you get started as a photographer?
I started taking pics in 2003 when I bought my first compact digital camera, it started for fun, but soon after that it became a serious thing for me!

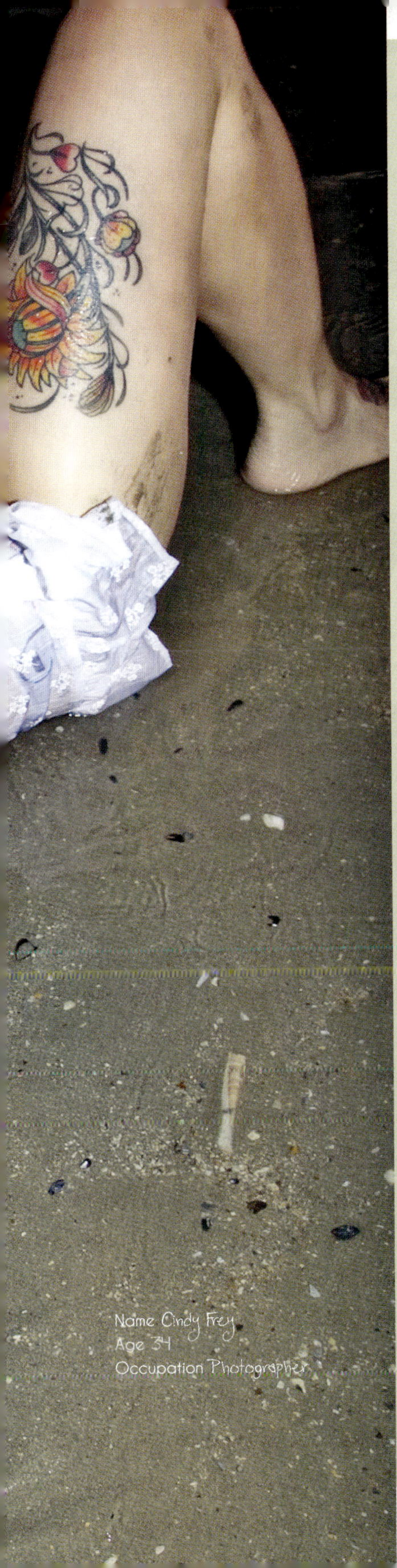

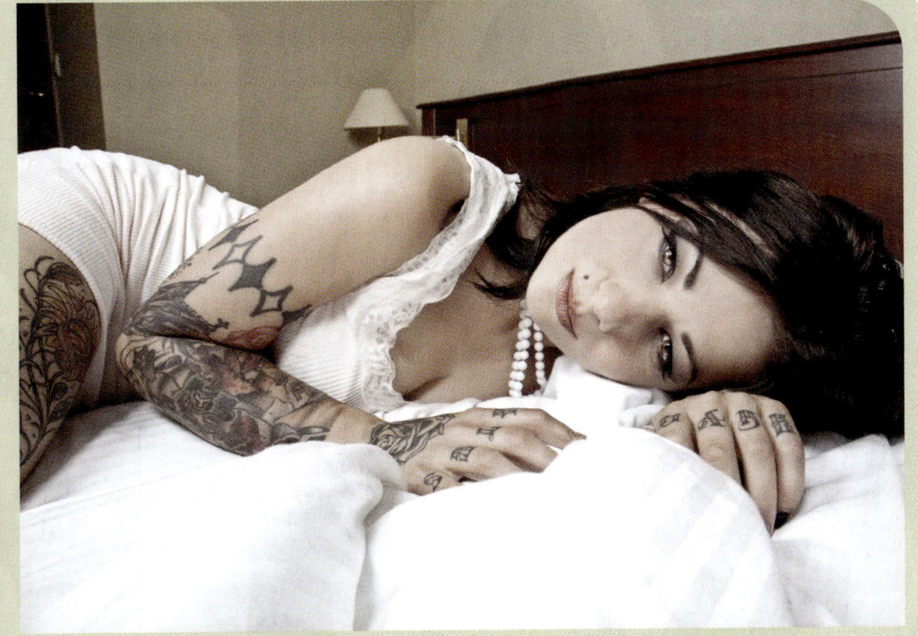

My tattoos reflect my life. I have logos and projects that I did tattooed on me, so yes, it reflects on my tattoo choices.

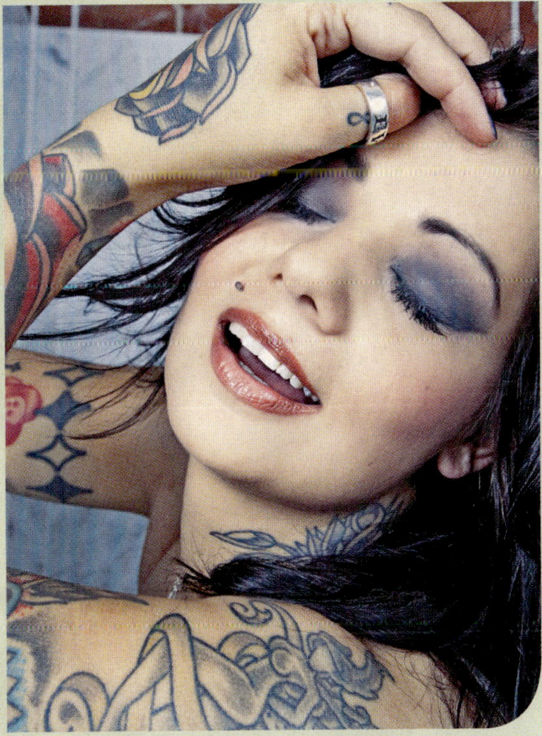

When is the next instalment of Live Evil due to go on sale?
My next book is on sale now - it came out on 31st October 2010.

When did you first take notice of tattoos?
When I was 15, I just loved it.

Is your work at all reflected in your choice of tattoo motifs?
My tattoos reflect my life. I have logos and projects that I did tattooed on me, so yes, it reflects on my tattoo choices. I want my tattoos to have a meaning.

If you could have anyone tattoo you, who would it be?
I only work with one tattoo artist, so I'm not interested in getting tattooed by someone else, even there are a lot of amazing ones.

Cindy Frey

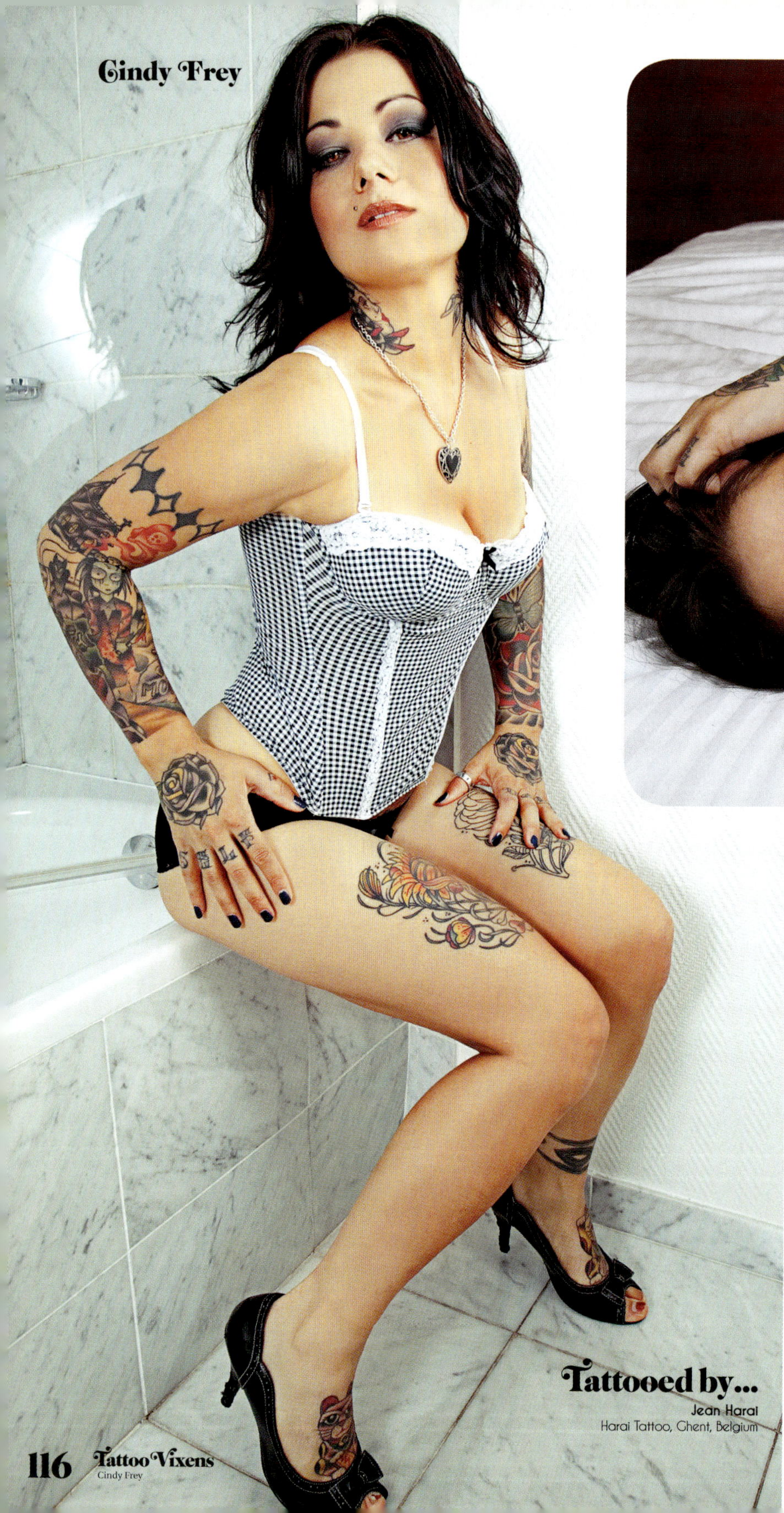

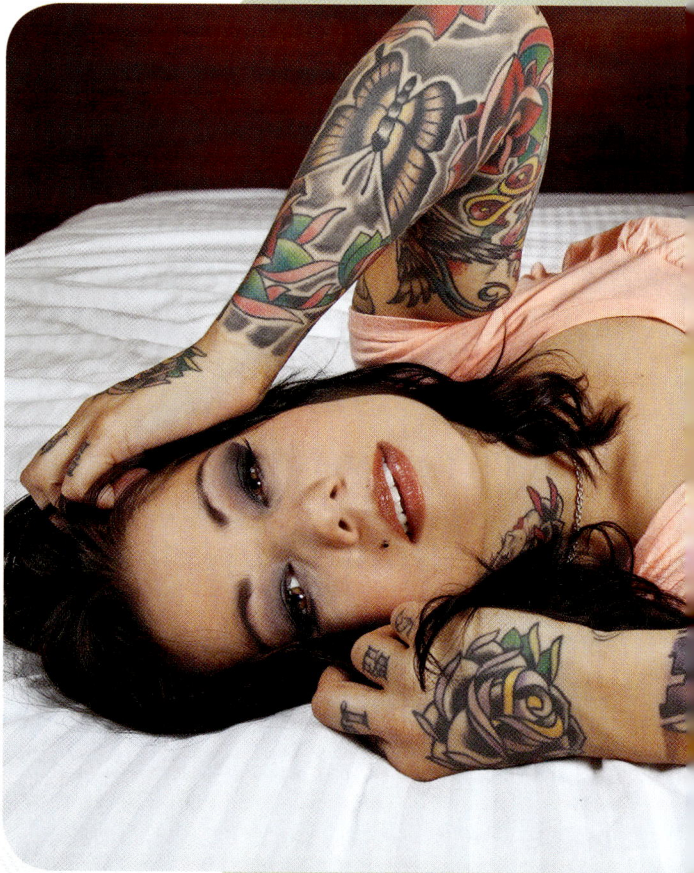

Why was the straight edge lifestyle so important to you?

To be honest, I'm not straight edge anymore. I have been drinking for a lame reason...I got heartbroken and it hit me hard. I was super down and I started drinking to forget the pain - it did help me! I was straight edge for 17 years. Now I'm in between, what should I do? Maybe I don't wanna drink anymore, don't know yet, I don't regret I did drink though; it helped me and I was doing it for myself not for others, so If I decide I don't wanna drink again, I will do it for myself. Drinking or not, people should do things for themselves, not for a trend or for others.

Tattooed by...

Jean Harai

Harai Tattoo, Ghent, Belgium

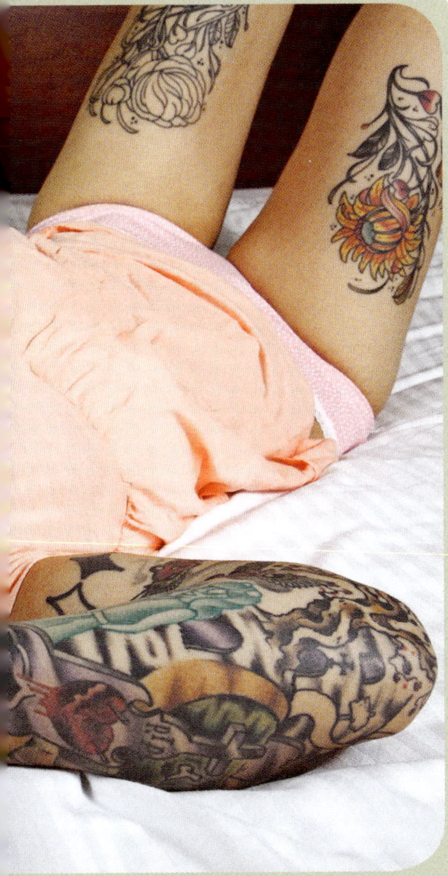

I'm not straight edge anymore. I have been drinking for a lame reason... I got heartbroken and it hit me hard.

Finally, what's the greatest gig you've ever captured on camera?
I have captured a lot of great gigs, so there 's not one favourite! Some of them are Green Day, Rammstein, Marilyn Manson, and Beastie Boys...

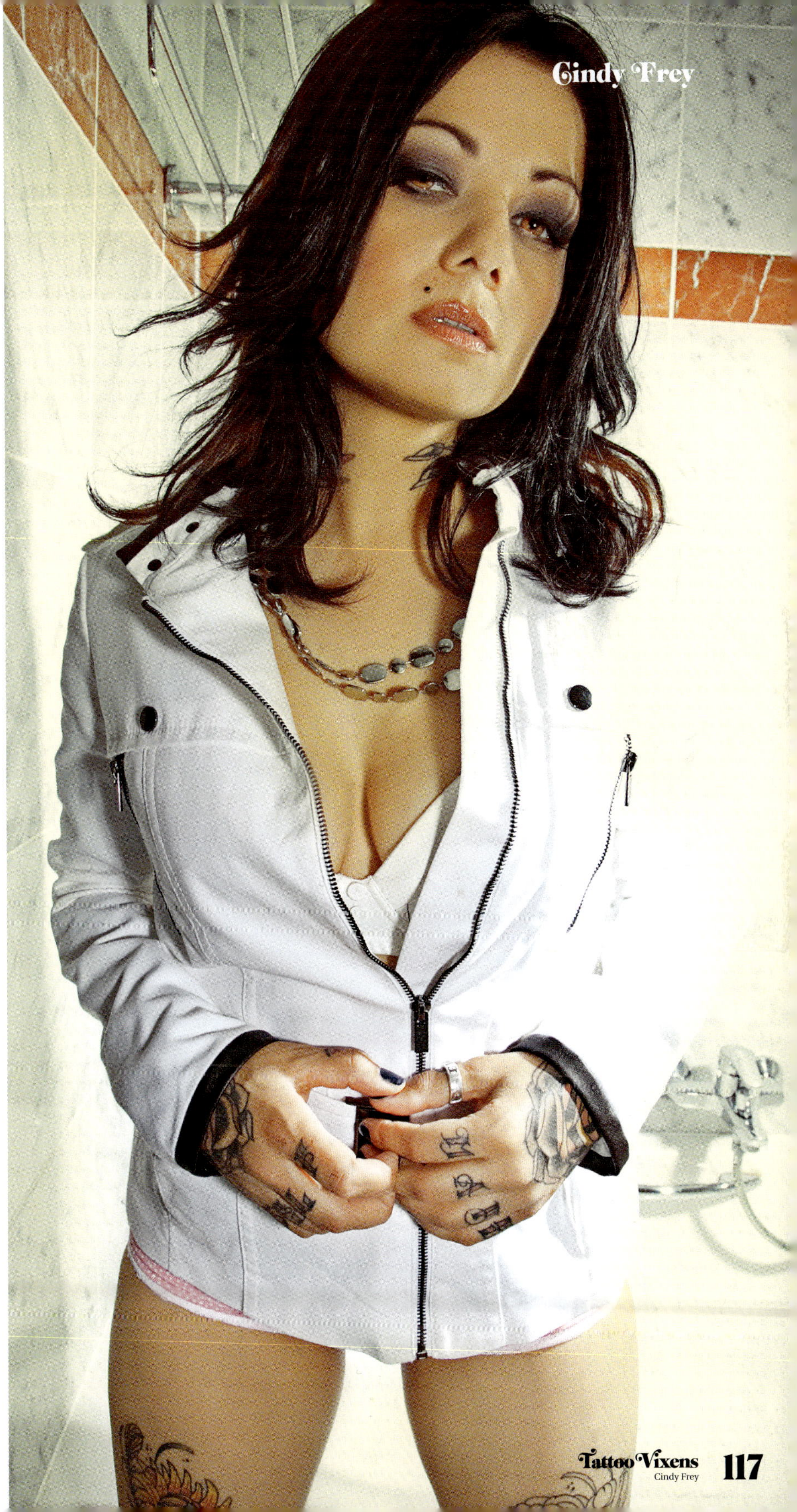

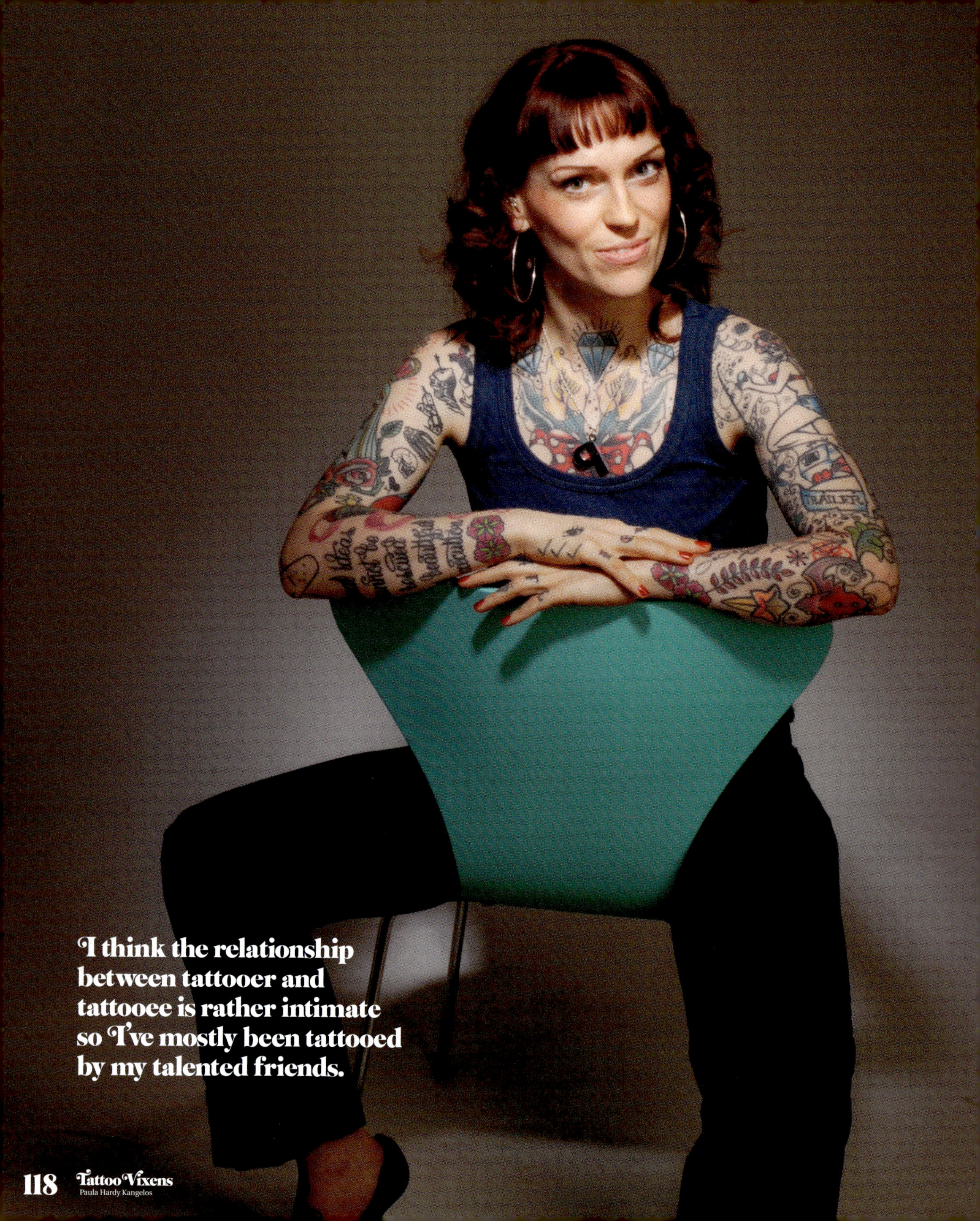

I think the relationship between tattooer and tattooee is rather intimate so I've mostly been tattooed by my talented friends.

Paula Hardy Kangelos

ALL PHOTOGRAPHS: **ANNE BURNS**

One of the staunchest defenders of the faith in the UK (and anywhere else she can get to), Paula currently writes for Skin Deep - and boy, does she ever know her stuff!

What initially attracted you towards tattoos?

The first tattoo I ever saw was the faded and blurry blue dragon on my grandfather's right forearm.

He died three weeks after my thirteenth birthday and it was only then that my Nan told me that my granddad, Len, had been an inmate in a POW camp and it was there that the tattoo had been painfully etched into his arm with a sharpened stick. He never spoke about the war and my Nan had decided that the tattoo was where my granddad had dug a hole in his flesh and buried his stories inside.

So I've always thought that tattoos were powerful, but mysterious.

What was your first tattoo?

I was 21 – quite late really. It doesn't matter what it was – it's covered with a pink rose now, my only cover-up.

Was acquiring significant tattoo coverage a conscious decision or a by-product of discovering the number of great tattoo artists available to you?

Neither! I never intended to have large-scale coverage but I've come to see tattoos as a type of narrative so the story will not end until I do.

I think the relationship between tattooer and tattooee is rather intimate so I've mostly been tattooed by my talented friends – I've got some beautiful pieces, but my interest is conceptual, rather than aesthetic.

Which of your tattoos has had the most impact, in regard to how you are perceived by other people?

My ex-husband said that he fell out of love with me when

Name
Paula Hardy Kangelos
Occupation
Artist, writer

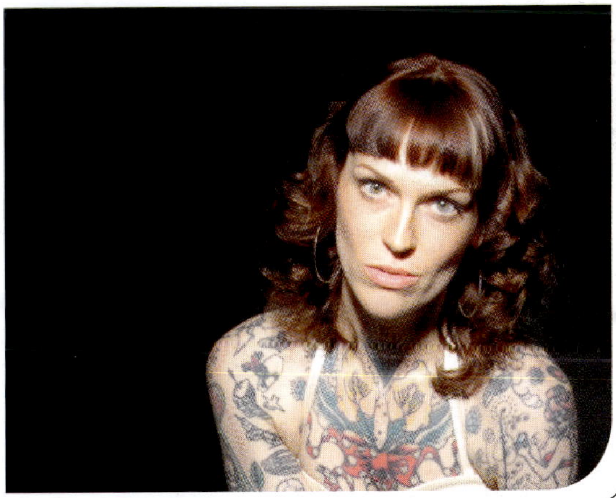

I'm marrying a tattooer - and we live a creative life of constant inspiration and tattoos and tattoo art are a massive part of that.

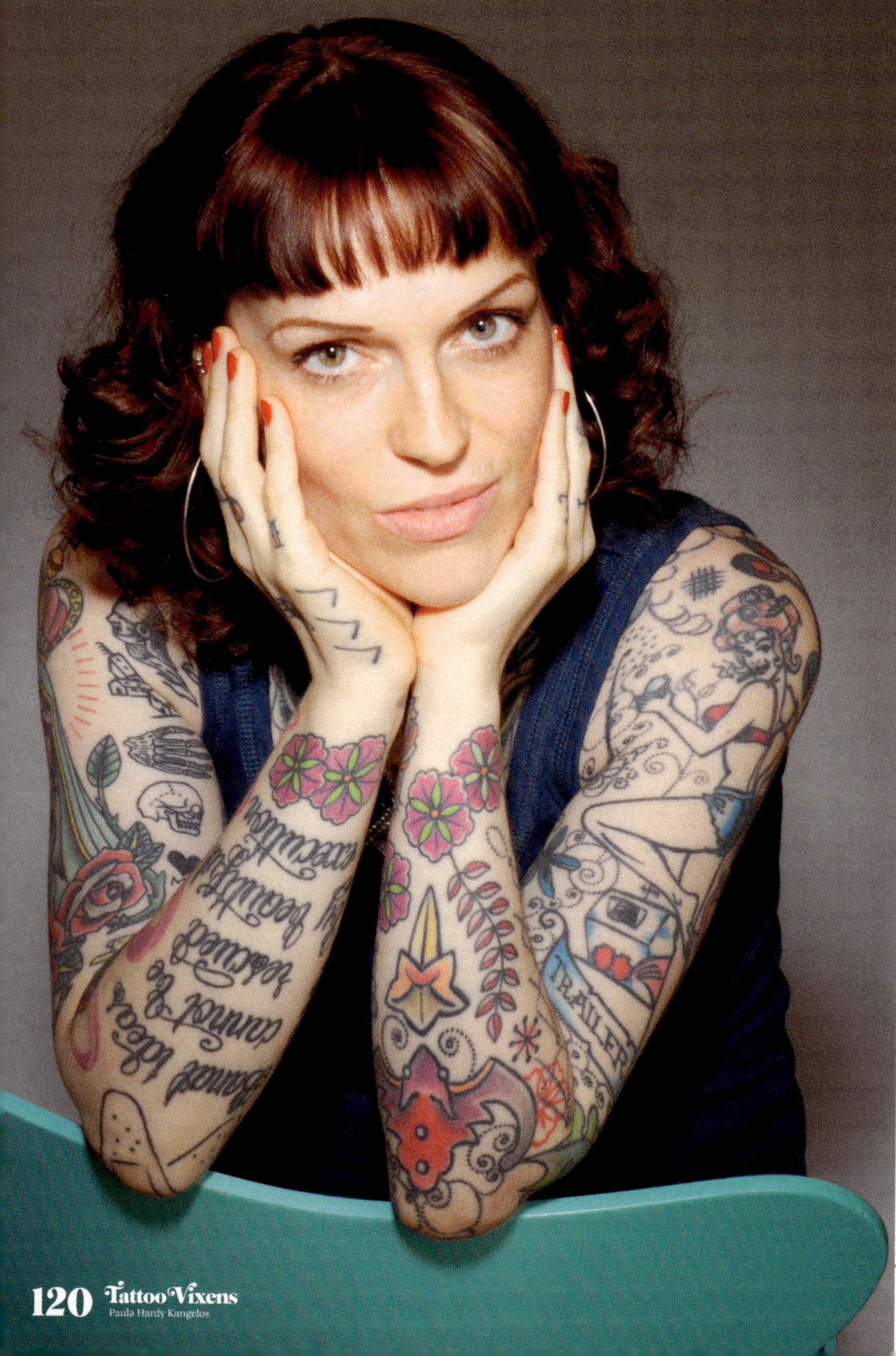

I had the diamond tattooed on my throat, that he thought it changed the angle of my face. Its public skin and a vulnerable area so could be interpreted as confrontational but I wear it instead of jewellery, so it's decorative too. Perception is informed by experience, so it's up to others to decide, tattoos always divide opinion!

What would you say is the most positive aspect of being a heavily tattooed woman?

I can't imagine my life without tattoos. They've brought me to my friends, inspired my artwork and gotten me a job. I've written about a variety of related topics at BA and MA level and I'm planning a tattoo related PhD too. I'm marrying a tattooer - and we live a creative life of constant inspiration and tattoos and tattoo art are a massive part of that.

What advice would you offer to people who are considering tattoos on public skin before they've worn much coverage elsewhere?

People must be responsible for their own decisions… But if you've only got your hands done, you'll look a bit silly naked!

If just one person could tattoo you, who would it be?

Over 30 people including Duncan X, Drew Romero, Uncle Allan and Thomas Hooper have tattooed me, so this is a difficult question to answer. Two of my best girlfriends are tattooers, as is my fiancé and I'm very proud to wear their art so I can't narrow it down to less than three: Zoe Windle, Lucy Pryor, Daniel Morris.

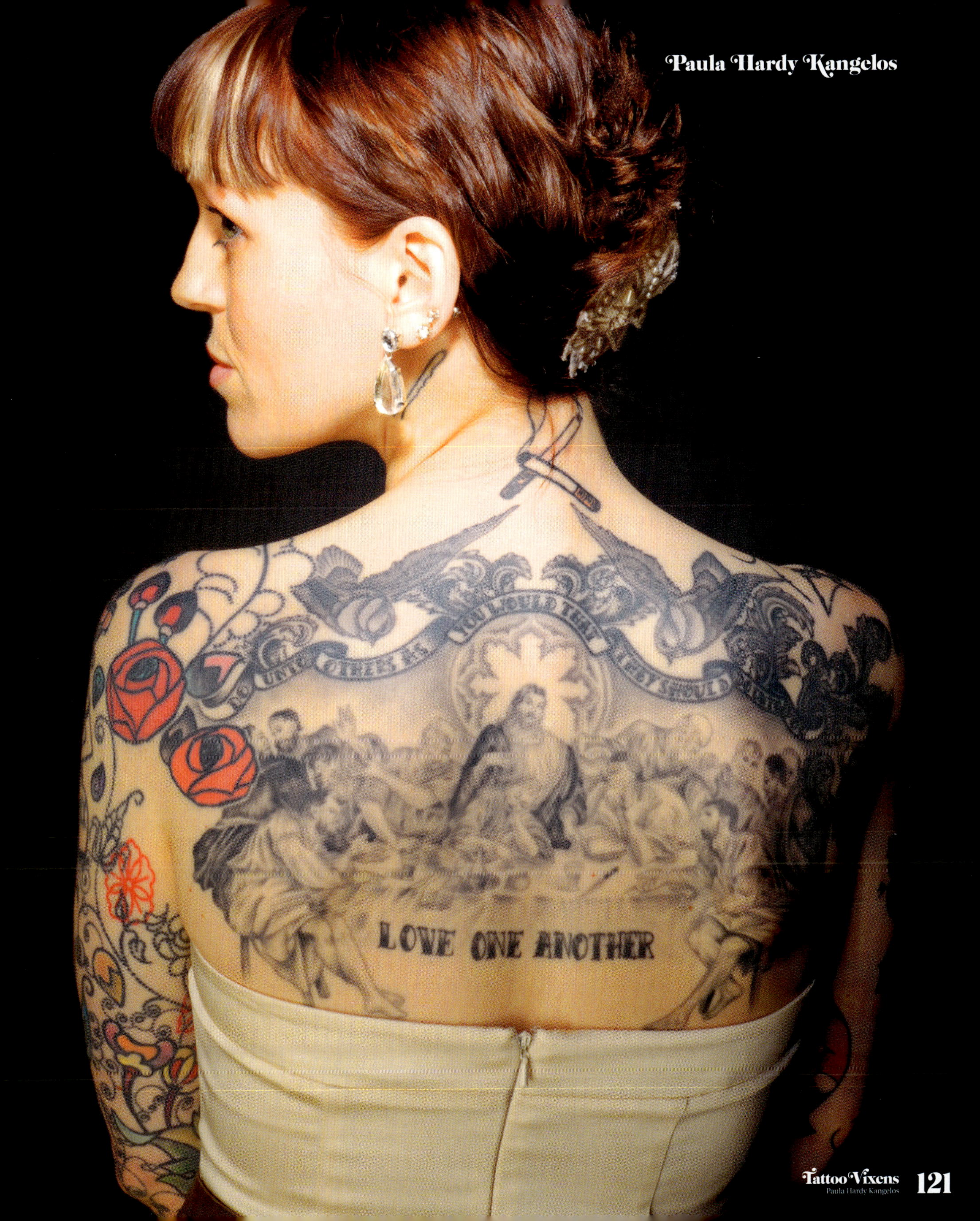
DO UNTO OTHERS AS
YOU WOULD THAT
THEY SHOULD
LOVE ONE ANOTHER

ALL PHOTOGRAPHS: **IHSAN KEMAL**

Samantha Hubbard

Exposed to tattoos and rock n roll from a young age, it's good to see Sammie keeping the flame held high.

What are you currently doing career wise or what do you aspire to be?

I'm currently doing the student thing and am studying in London. I also help lot for for my friends club nights. I currently get lost when I think of what I will do when I finish... all I think about is traveling more – or getting a cottage in Bath with ducks and reading lots of books…

Do you do any modelling in your spare time or have you ever considered becoming a full time model?

Not really... I used to do a bit for friends when I was younger but I don't think I could currently make time to do any more modelling. When I do it now I just like doing it with friends which mainly involves me doing something to do with tattoos.

Tell us something about your childhood, what ambitions you had, where did you grow up and what has inspired you?

I grew up a tiny village called Harby near Lincoln and Nottingham – nobody ever knows were Lincoln is! I was an only child and lived on a farm with my parents where I was animal crazy and was one of those kids that would rather play in mud than with dolls. My parents were big bikers and into rock and metal. So at a young age, I was listening to Sabbath and Elvis. I also had it in my head that I wanted to retire when I left school, cause retired people drove good cars. I don't think I understood what retiring actually was for a while! My parents have inspired me though most of my life.

What initially attracted you towards tattoos?

My dad had them and the singers of bands I loved had them. I was crazy about art – drawing, tattoos and body art drew me in

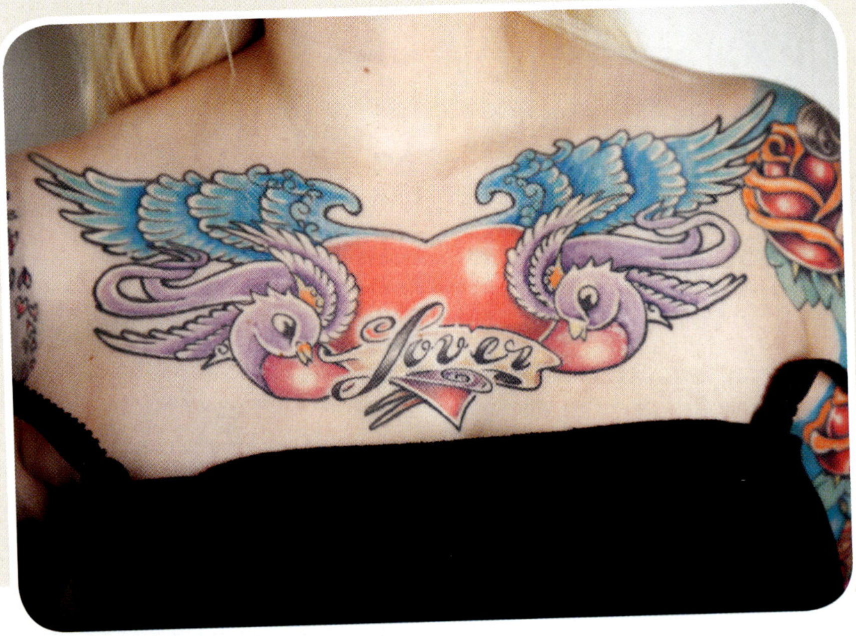

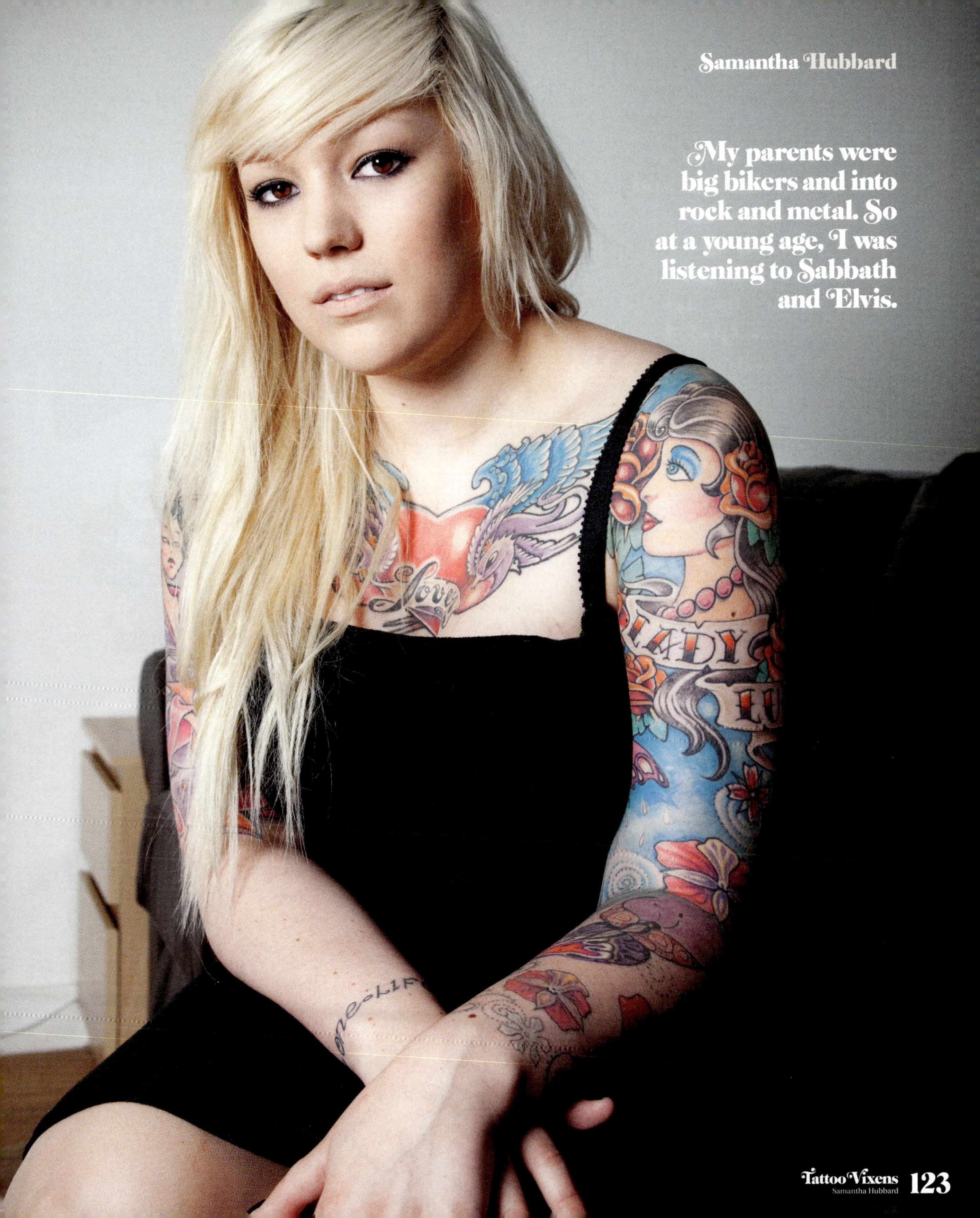

My parents were big bikers and into rock and metal. So at a young age, I was listening to Sabbath and Elvis.

Samantha Hubbard

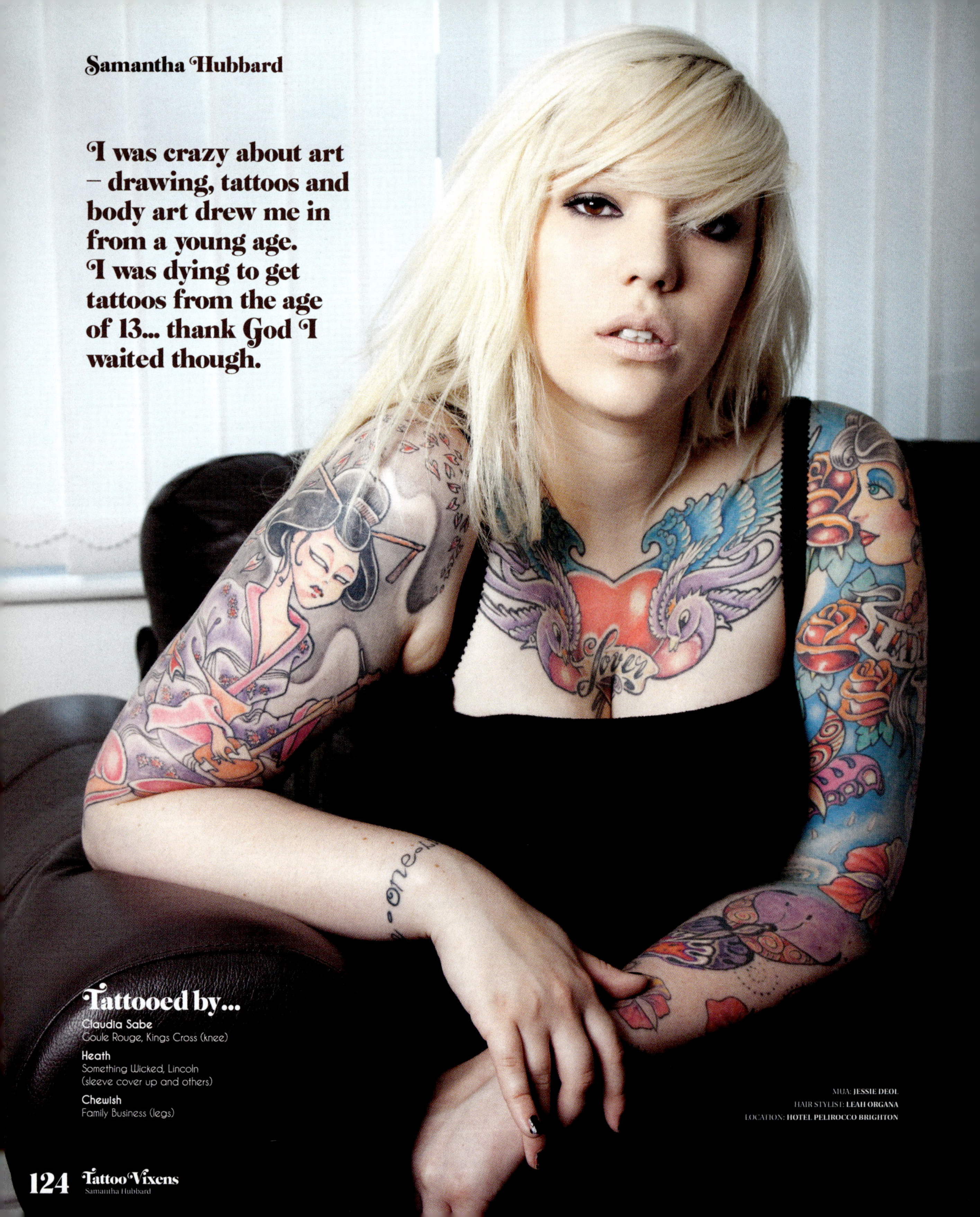

I was crazy about art – drawing, tattoos and body art drew me in from a young age. I was dying to get tattoos from the age of 13... thank God I waited though.

Tattooed by...

Claudia Sabe
Goule Rouge, Kings Cross (knee)

Heath
Something Wicked, Lincoln
(sleeve cover up and others)

Chewish
Family Business (legs)

MUA: **JESSIE DEOL**
HAIR STYLIST: **LEAH ORGANA**
LOCATION: **HOTEL PELIROCCO BRIGHTON**

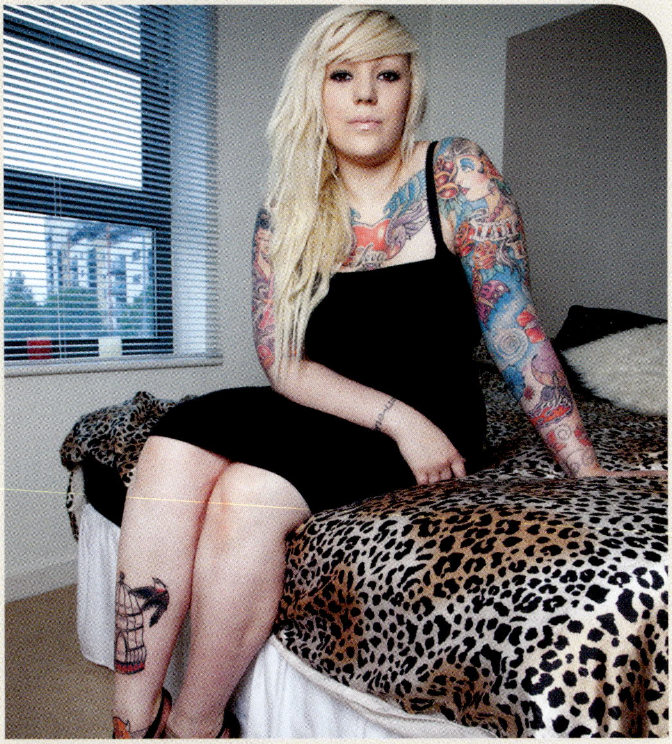

from a young age. I was dying to get tattoos from the age of 13... thank God I waited though.

Was acquiring significant tattoo coverage a conscious decision or a by-product of discovering the number of great tattoo artists available to you?
I found it was more of an addiction. Once I had my feet done I couldn't stop. I guess a bit of both because once I found an artist I was comfortable with, I just wanted to plan my sleeves.

Which of your tattoos has had the most impact, in regard to how you are perceived by other people?
I guess my chest piece... its the one you see first but I normally get nice comments if someone sees it on the underground. I'm so unaware of stares now.

Do your tattoos have any particular significance, or do you collect them purely because of their aesthetics?
Not really I have a few which mean something, but it's mostly due to the fact I hate uncovered skin. I have a few I regret though.

What advice would you offer to people who are considering tattoos on public skin before they've worn much coverage elsewhere?
Think really hard before you get it and make sure you really want it. I would also tell people to look hard for tattooist and if there is a wait then I'm sure it would be worth it.

If just one person could tattoo you, who would it be?
It would have been Claudia Sabe – she tattooed my kneecap a few months ago and it's my favourite by far. She is an amazing woman to be tattooed by and so comfortable as well.

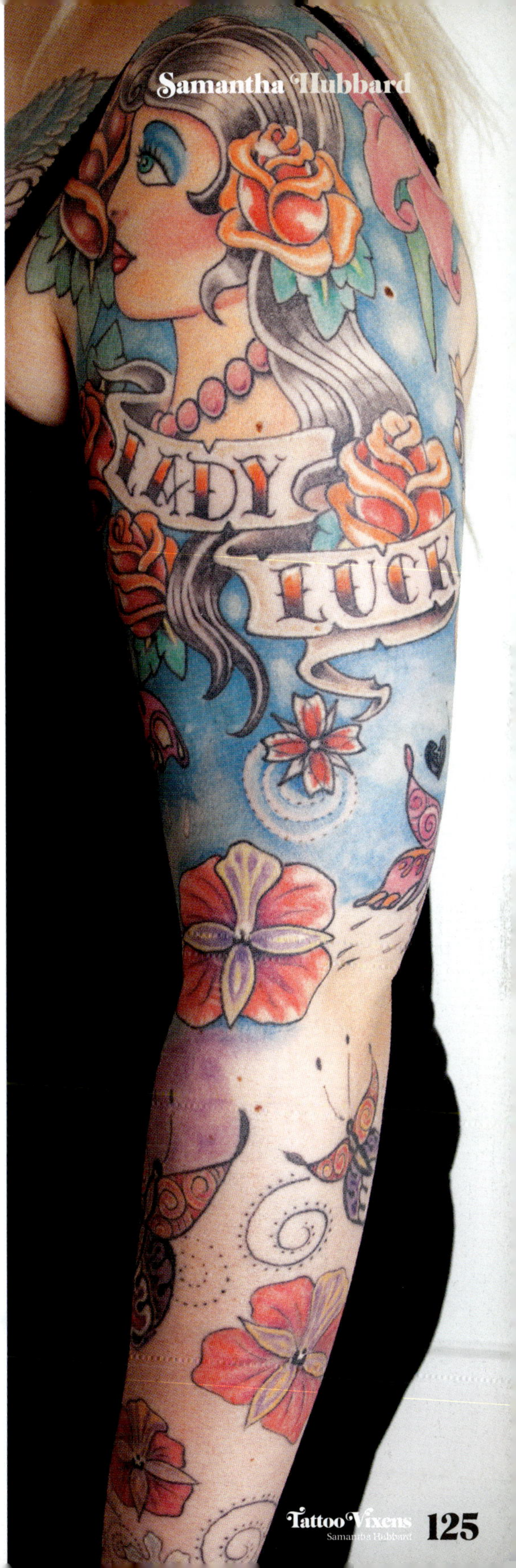

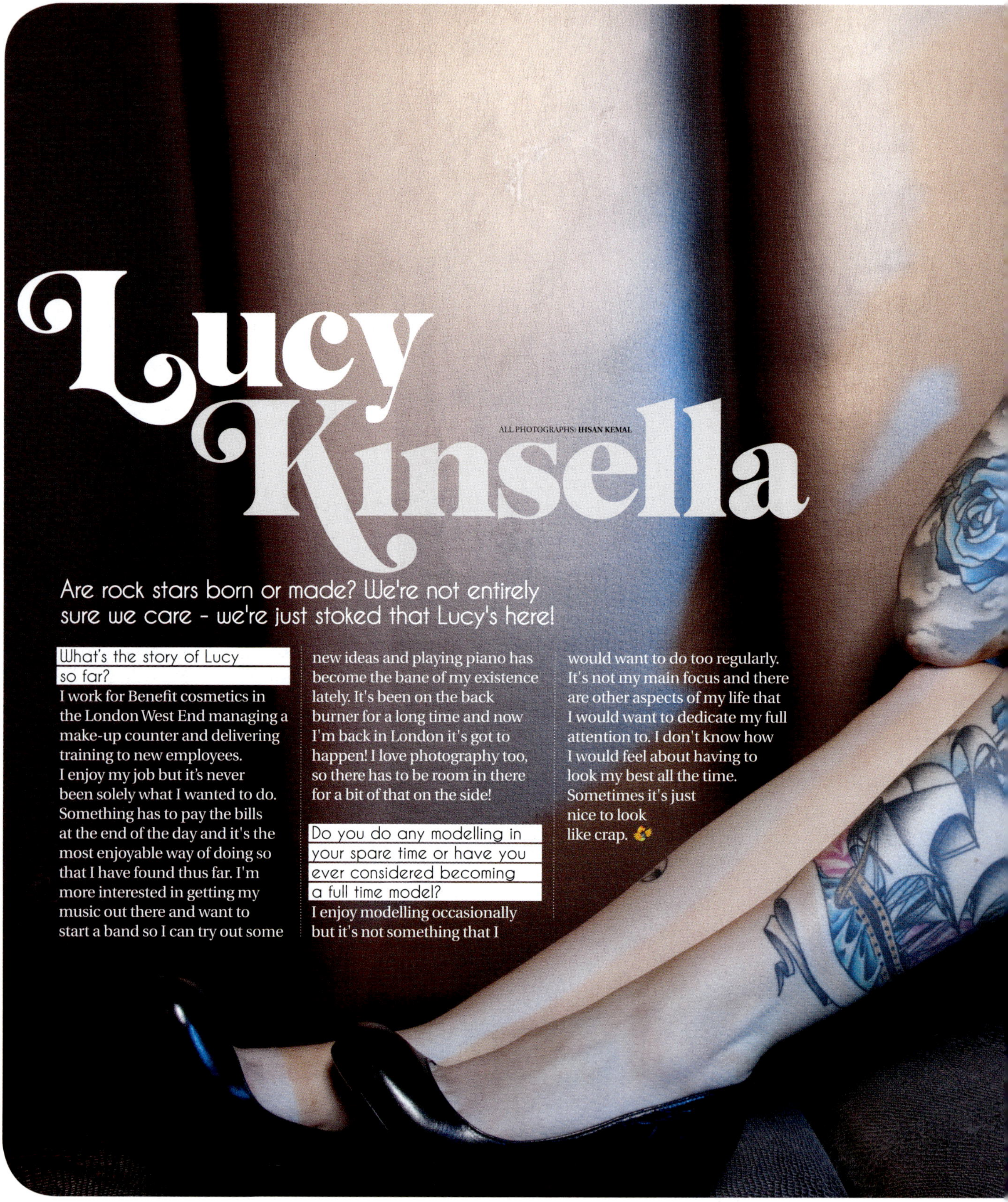

Lucy Kinsella

ALL PHOTOGRAPHS: **IHSAN KEMAL**

Are rock stars born or made? We're not entirely sure we care - we're just stoked that Lucy's here!

What's the story of Lucy so far?

I work for Benefit cosmetics in the London West End managing a make-up counter and delivering training to new employees. I enjoy my job but it's never been solely what I wanted to do. Something has to pay the bills at the end of the day and it's the most enjoyable way of doing so that I have found thus far. I'm more interested in getting my music out there and want to start a band so I can try out some new ideas and playing piano has become the bane of my existence lately. It's been on the back burner for a long time and now I'm back in London it's got to happen! I love photography too, so there has to be room in there for a bit of that on the side!

Do you do any modelling in your spare time or have you ever considered becoming a full time model?

I enjoy modelling occasionally but it's not something that I would want to do too regularly. It's not my main focus and there are other aspects of my life that I would want to dedicate my full attention to. I don't know how I would feel about having to look my best all the time. Sometimes it's just nice to look like crap.

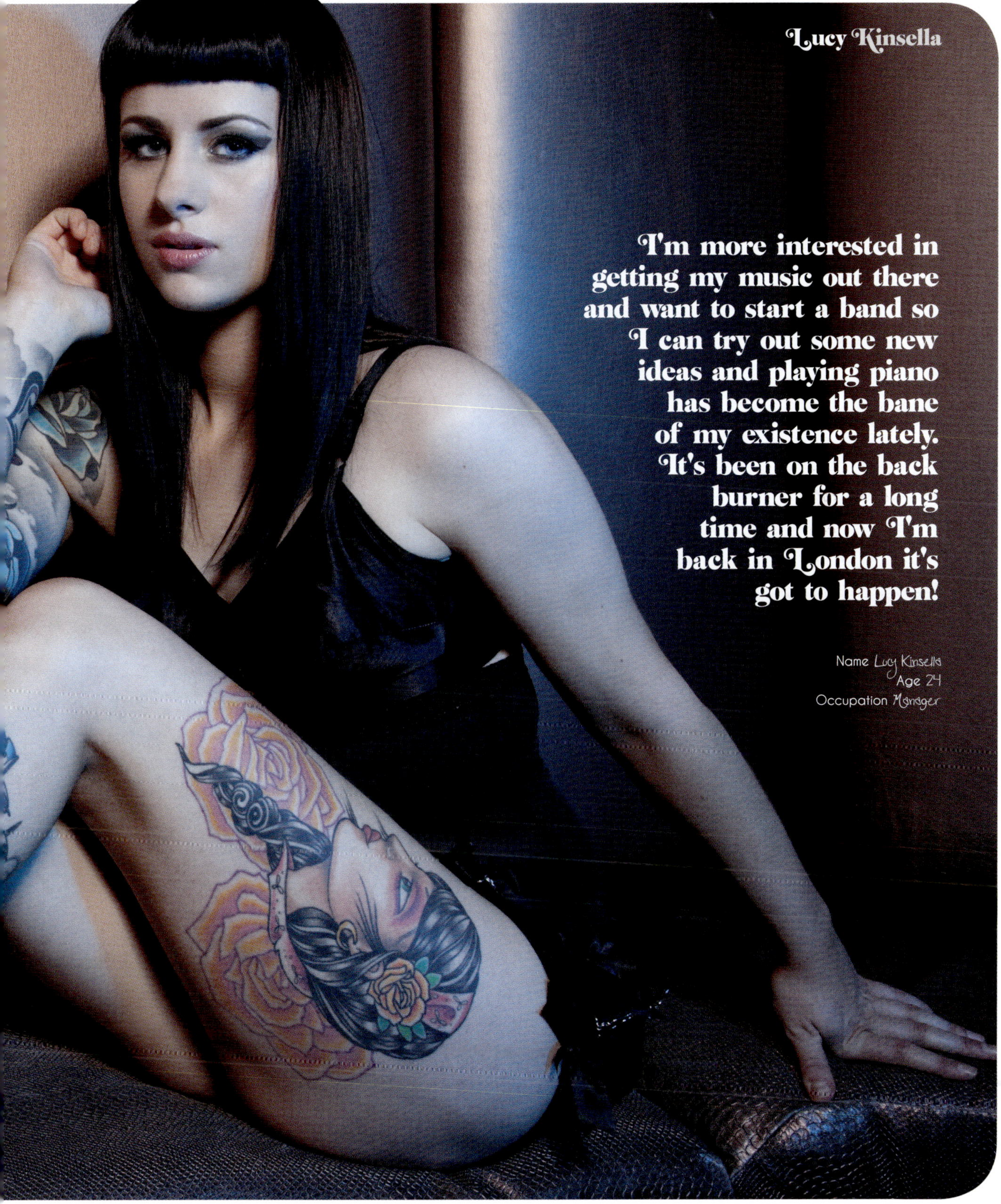

I'm more interested in getting my music out there and want to start a band so I can try out some new ideas and playing piano has become the bane of my existence lately. It's been on the back burner for a long time and now I'm back in London it's got to happen!

Name Lucy Kinsella
Age 24
Occupation Manager

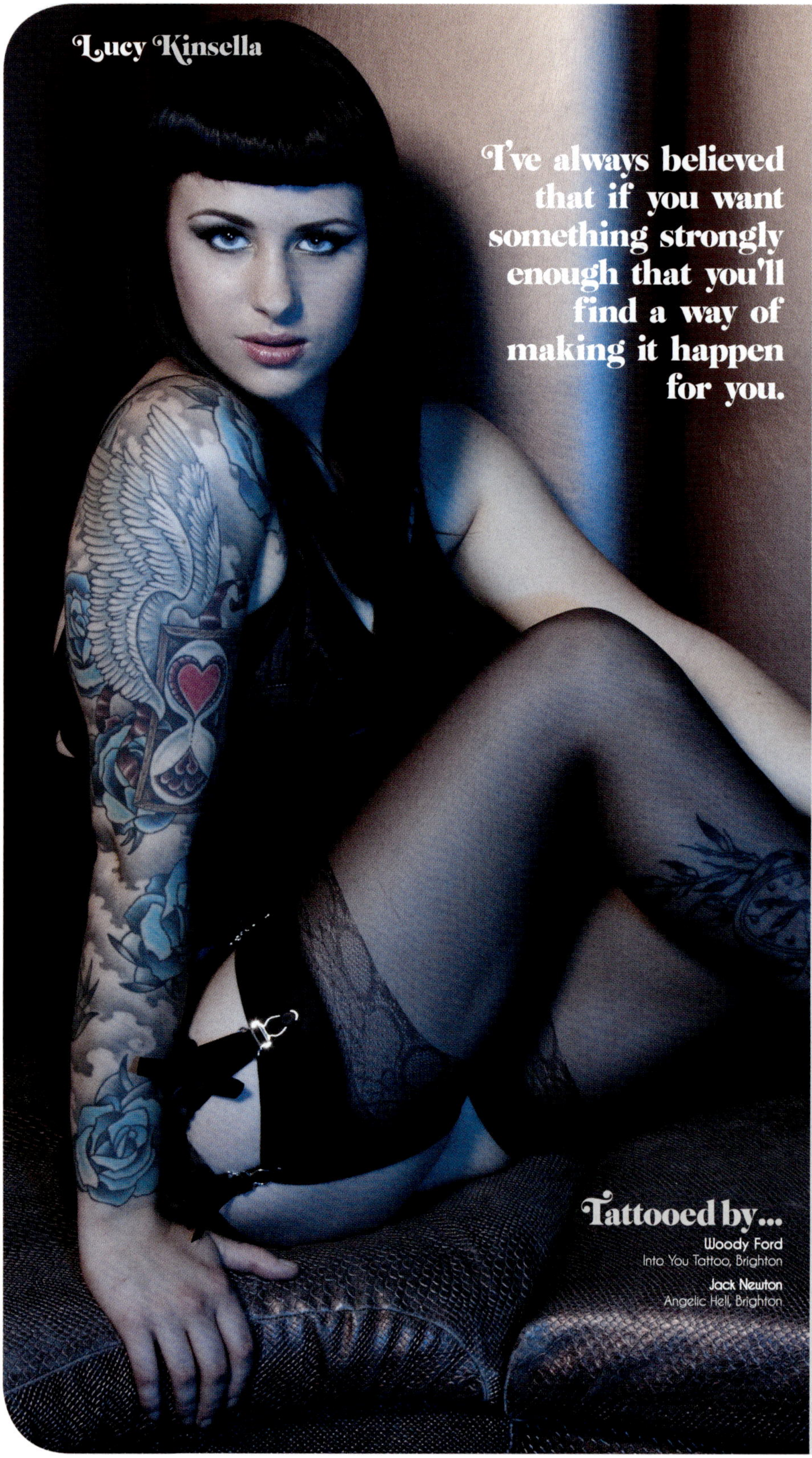

I've always believed that if you want something strongly enough that you'll find a way of making it happen for you.

Tattooed by...

Woody Ford
Into You Tattoo, Brighton

Jack Newton
Angelic Hell, Brighton

Tell us something about your childhood, what ambitions you had, where did you grow up and what has inspired you?

I grew up in London. I hated it as a kid, then again, I hated most things as a kid. I always looked around me and thought everything looked pretty run down and aspired to higher ideals I guess. I wanted more than I had and knew that the people around me weren't inspirational characters. So I moved to Brighton and went to a boarding school. Sounds simple but boarding school was a nightmare just like you would imagine it to be and girls really do some messed up and weird things!

I always wanted to be a big rock star and nothing ever changes except maybe the reality of life and the things that get in the way. However true that is, I've always believed that if you want something strongly enough that you'll find a way of making it happen for you. Unless it's something ridiculous like sprouting another head.

What was the initial attraction of tattoos?

I've had to really think about why I chose to get so many tattoos because it's something that people will always ask you. I liked the look of them and the fact that they stood for individuality initially. I loved the fact that it crossed social barriers also.

Was acquiring significant tattoo coverage a conscious decision or a by-product of discovering the number of great tattoo artists available to you?

All of my tattoos are done by the same person bar one. I decided to get so many because I loved that style and kept getting more ideas etc. I have a lot more ideas now so I guess it will result in me being more covered when I find the right person to do the work.

...and the one with most impact?

My sleeve. It is the bloody topic of conversation throughout my days and nights and drives my friends mental! I didn't consider how much it would draw people in. I thought if anything it would be something most avoided me for. It's not something I mind talking about with the right people. I just loathe getting caught up in the wrong conversations with someone who then proceeds to show me their cartoon character or tribal piece. I never really know what to say in response. It's always nice when people are genuinely curious and are thinking of getting their own done. But I enjoy the way they look on my skin and that's really the only thing that matters. It's nice to be offered different opportunities from having lots of tattoos and I would say that I'm glad it sets me aside from others.

Do any of them have any particular significance, or do you collect them purely because of their aesthetics?

They all hold strong meanings for me and echo some of my views. I do have plans to get some that are purely for aesthetic reasons – I don't think it matters why you get them done as long as you enjoy having them – but I would say you should always make sure that you're getting something that really suits you and don't be afraid to just go for it. I never imagined I would have this many tattoos and although it can be a nightmare always talking about it I don't regret my choices.

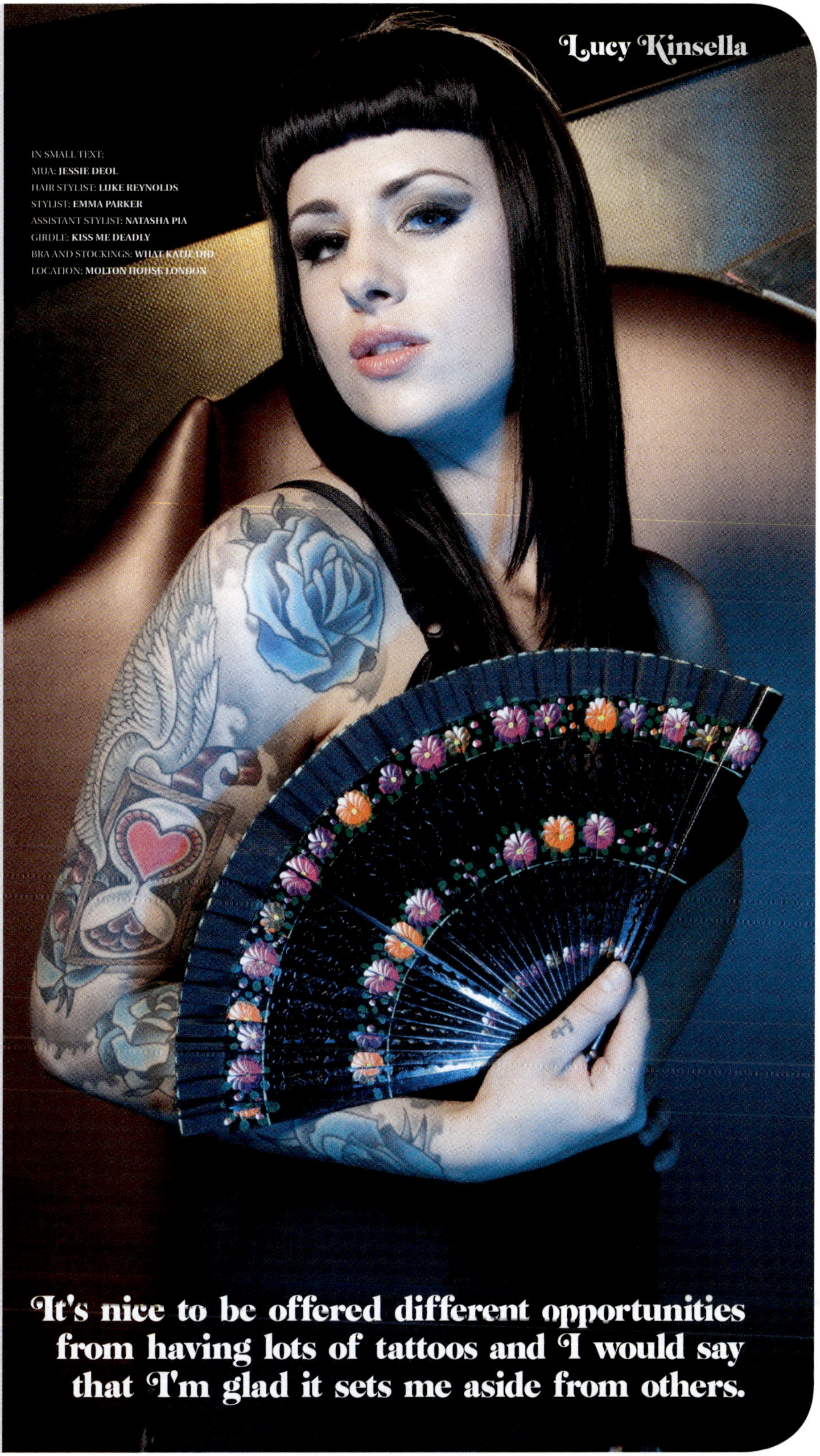

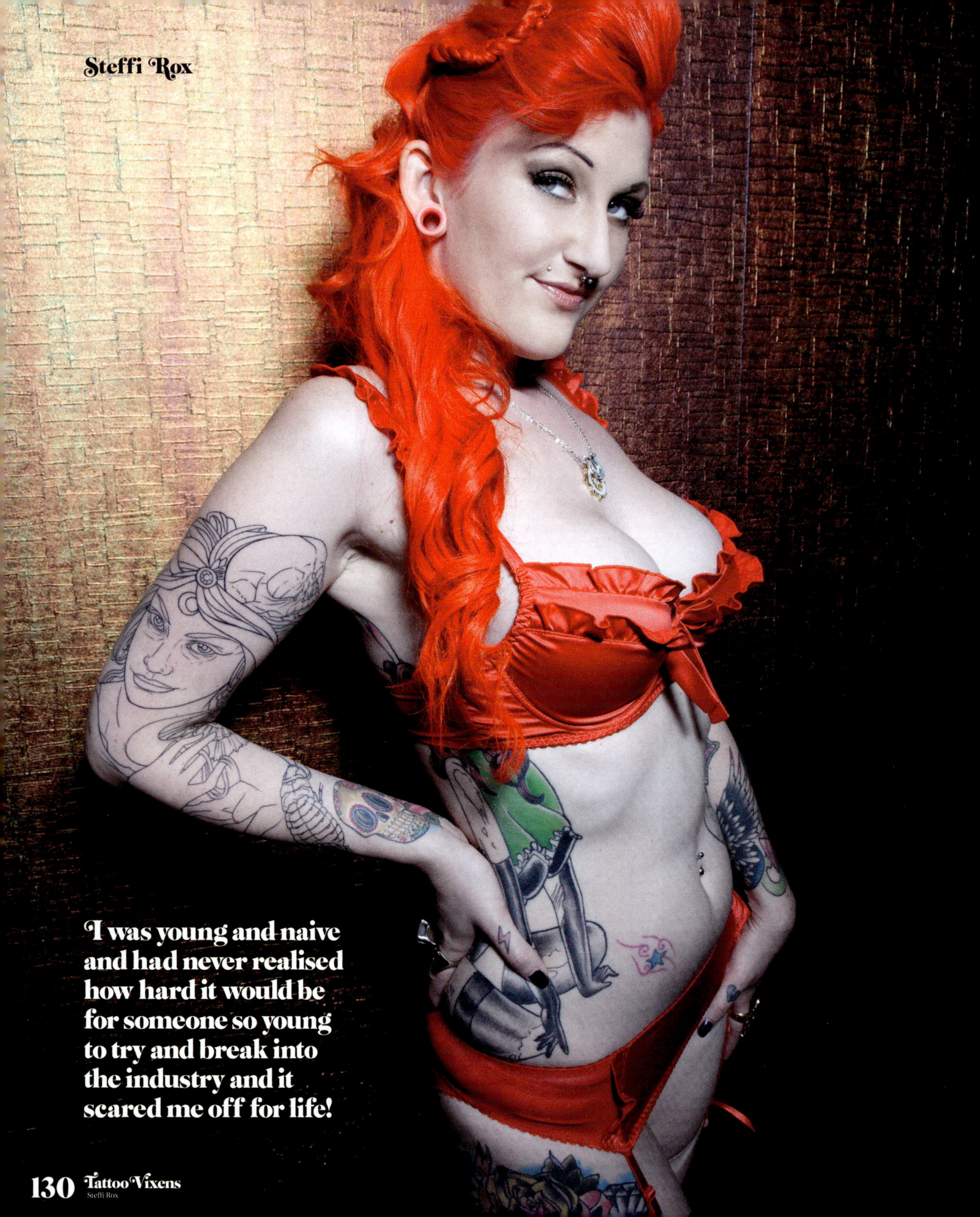

I was young and naive and had never realised how hard it would be for someone so young to try and break into the industry and it scared me off for life!

ALL PHOTOGRAPHS: **IHSAN KEMAL**

Steffi Rox

Steffi Rox is one of the better known names amongst tattooed ladies in the UK - think it's been an easy ride? Read on...

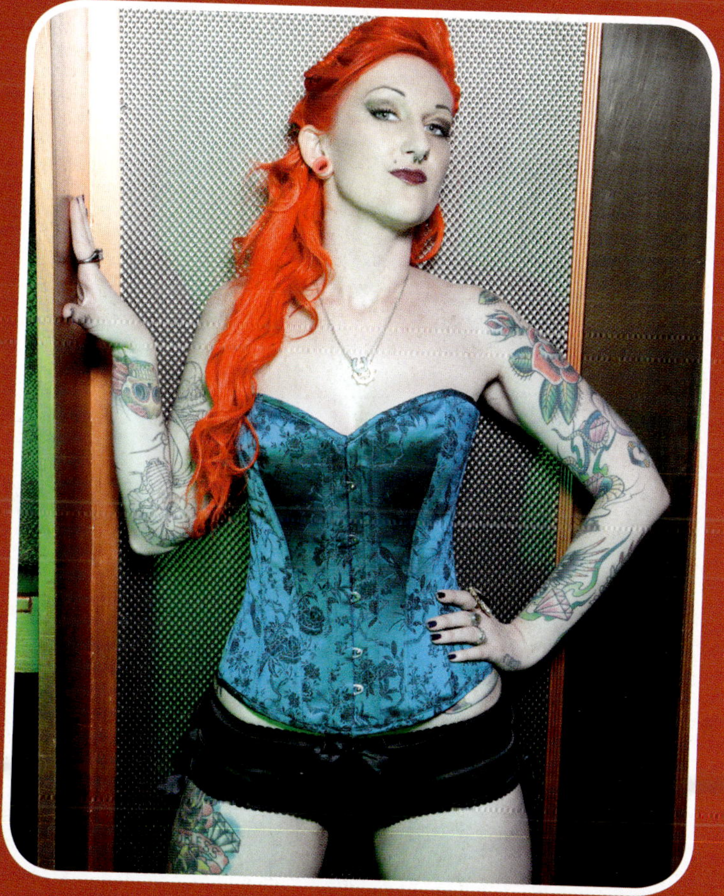

What are you currently doing career wise or what do you aspire to be?
Up until the end of 2008 I was a Senior Sales Negotiator for a large firm of estate agents but when I got fired for refusing to start covering my tattoos I decided to move to Brighton and now I work full time as an alternative/fetish model and do a bit of acting work as well. Alongside that I own property in Devon, which I have renovated and now rent out. Until recently I also worked as a receptionist in a tattoo studio which I'd love to start doing again as I really miss being in a studio environment!

Tell us something about your childhood, what ambitions you had, where did you grow up and what has inspired you?
I grew up as an only child; it was just me, Mum, Dad and my two cats in our house in Torquay so for the most it was pretty boring. I spent my time at school planning a career as a tattoo artist, so at 16 I left school and went to work in a local studio

Name *Steffi Rox*
Age *27*
Occupation
Model, Actress

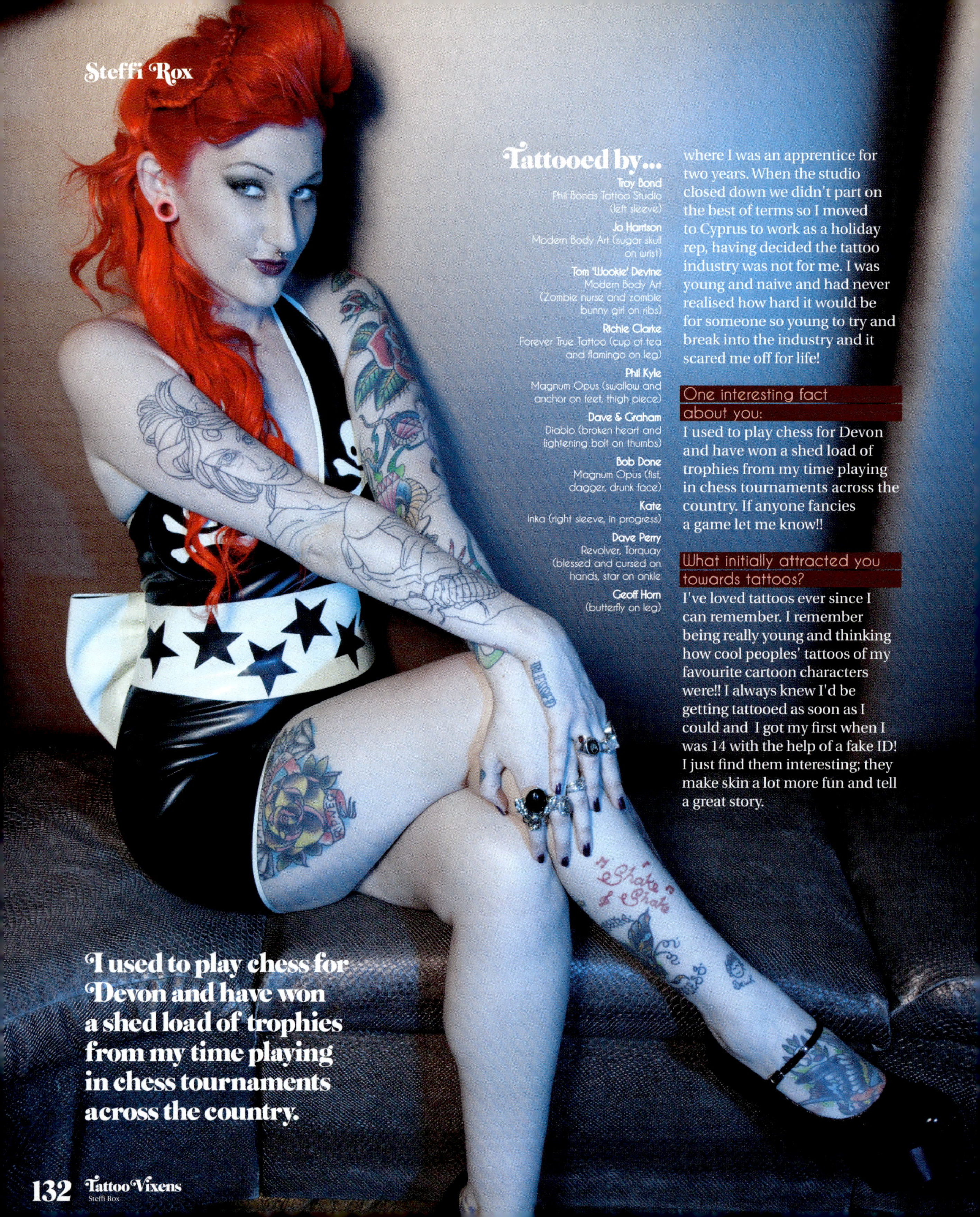

Steffi Rox

Tattooed by...

Troy Bond
Phil Bonds Tattoo Studio (left sleeve)

Jo Harrison
Modern Body Art (sugar skull on wrist)

Tom 'Wookie' Devine
Modern Body Art (Zombie nurse and zombie bunny girl on ribs)

Richie Clarke
Forever True Tattoo (cup of tea and flamingo on leg)

Phil Kyle
Magnum Opus (swallow and anchor on feet, thigh piece)

Dave & Graham
Diablo (broken heart and lightening bolt on thumbs)

Bob Done
Magnum Opus (fist, dagger, drunk face)

Kate
Inka (right sleeve, in progress)

Dave Perry
Revolver, Torquay (blessed and cursed on hands, star on ankle)

Geoff Horn
(butterfly on leg)

where I was an apprentice for two years. When the studio closed down we didn't part on the best of terms so I moved to Cyprus to work as a holiday rep, having decided the tattoo industry was not for me. I was young and naive and had never realised how hard it would be for someone so young to try and break into the industry and it scared me off for life!

One interesting fact about you:

I used to play chess for Devon and have won a shed load of trophies from my time playing in chess tournaments across the country. If anyone fancies a game let me know!!

What initially attracted you towards tattoos?

I've loved tattoos ever since I can remember. I remember being really young and thinking how cool peoples' tattoos of my favourite cartoon characters were!! I always knew I'd be getting tattooed as soon as I could and I got my first when I was 14 with the help of a fake ID! I just find them interesting; they make skin a lot more fun and tell a great story.

"I used to play chess for Devon and have won a shed load of trophies from my time playing in chess tournaments across the country.

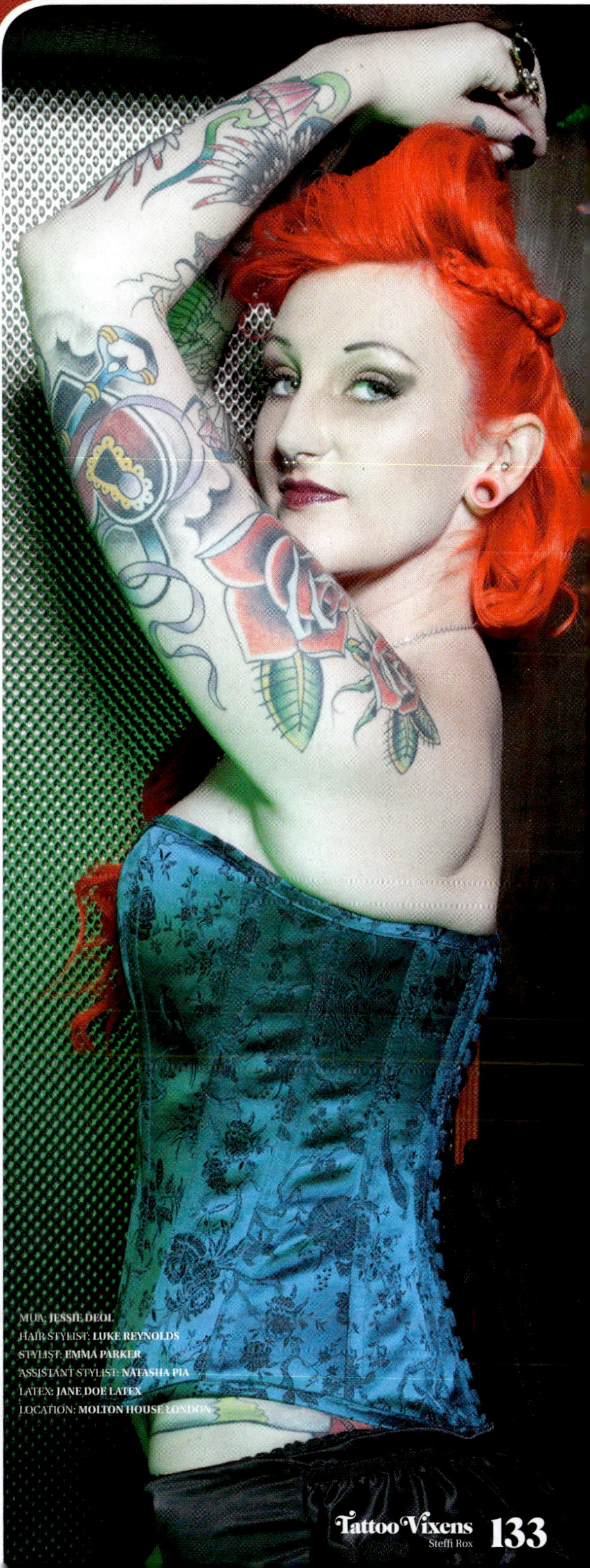

Was acquiring significant tattoo coverage a conscious decision or a by-product of discovering the number of great tattoo artists available to you?

It's been a bit of both for me really. I've always known I'll end up with a number of tattoos as I've always loved them, not getting them never seemed an option to me, but I also have tattoos that I've got purely because I've wanted certain friends to tattoo me.

Which of your tattoos has had the most impact, in regard to how you are perceived by other people?

My sleeve is the first most people notice and comment on, although when people see the zombie nurse on my ribs they're usually pretty shocked by it. I've had people say they've been surprised to find that I'm actually quite intelligent, I guess to some people tattoos make you look a bit thick haha!

What would you say is the most positive aspect of being a heavily tattooed woman?

FREE STUFF!!! I love that I'm always getting sent goodies to model for companies, like today I got a lovely mini top hat and nipple pasties in the post! I also like that having tattoos means people are always approaching me for a chat and I've got to meet so many amazing people purely because of my tattoos. And obviously thanks to my tattoos I'm able to model for a living.

Do your tattoos have any particular significance, or do you collect them purely because of their aesthetics?

Most of my tattoos have come off random ideas but the piece on my thigh means a lot to me. It says "God Bless Catastrophe" and "R.I.P Veg" The first bit is a line from an Alkaline Trio song which summed up me coming out the other side of a really troubled year and that from all the tough times I had I actually came out with a whole new outlook on life that changed things forever for the better. It reminds me that everything works out ok in the end. The second bit is for my friend Veg who died tragically during that year.

My right sleeve which I recently had started also has a lot of meaning for me, the cockroaches remind me of the days living overseas in run down apartments with no money and are there to remind me to never forget where I came from, and the girl, heart and skull represent a relationship that ended. Basically its like our relationship died but they'll always be a place in my heart for my first love.

What advice would you offer to people who are considering tattoos on public skin before they've worn much coverage elsewhere?

Basically don't do it!! Getting visible tattoos is a serious commitment and sadly limits your career options massively. I thought I'd be an estate agent forever but because one manager didn't like the 3 visible tattoos I had at the time my career was ended. I think it's really irresponsible that some artists will happily tattoo someone's neck or hands as a first tattoo. Its a life changing decision and shouldn't be taken lightly. Get tattoos where they can be covered first, get used to them and then decide if you are really committed to getting visible work.

Leah

ALL PHOTOGRAPHS: **IHSAN KEMAL**

She may be a down to earth dreamer but Leah is all there when it comes to understanding who she is...

Name
Leah Morgans
Age 30
Occupation
Hair stylist

What initially attracted you towards tattoos?

They are beautiful. I don't think I need to say any more than that really.

Was acquiring significant tattoo coverage a conscious decision or a by-product of discovering the number of great tattoo artists available to you?

I knew from a very early age that I wanted to be tattooed. When I was 23 I fell in love with someone who was incredibly creative and talented and he ended up doing a lot of work on me. Even though we are no longer together, I feel lucky to have gone on a journey with him, through 7 years of his tattooing and to watch him progress into one of the most talented artists in this country right now. I have been lucky enough to meet some amazing people over the years and get work by them too. Many have ended up being friends I will value for life.

Which of your tattoos has had the most impact, in regard to how you are perceived by other people?

Men always comment on my star wars tattoos because I guess they like it that I am a bit of a geek and they can talk to me about it, but the one that really has the

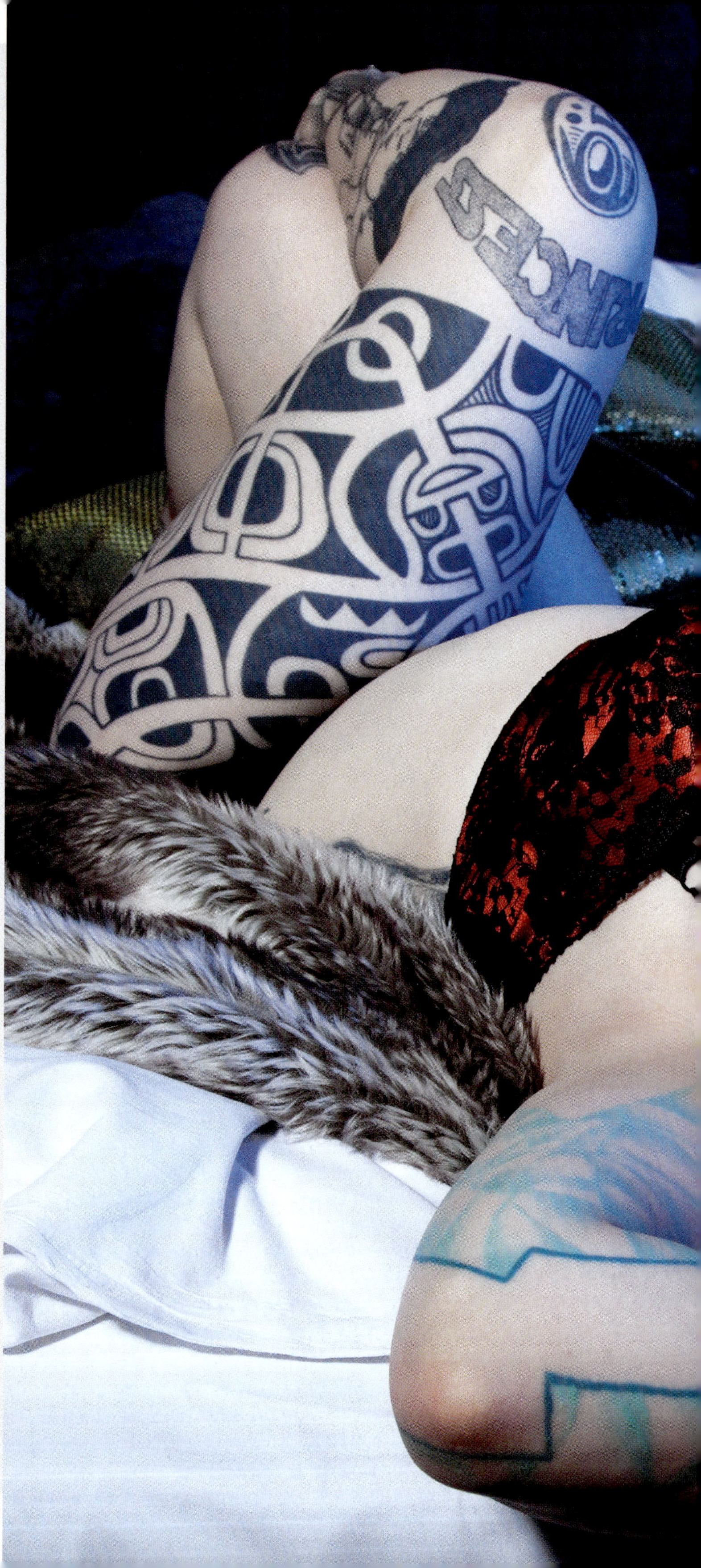

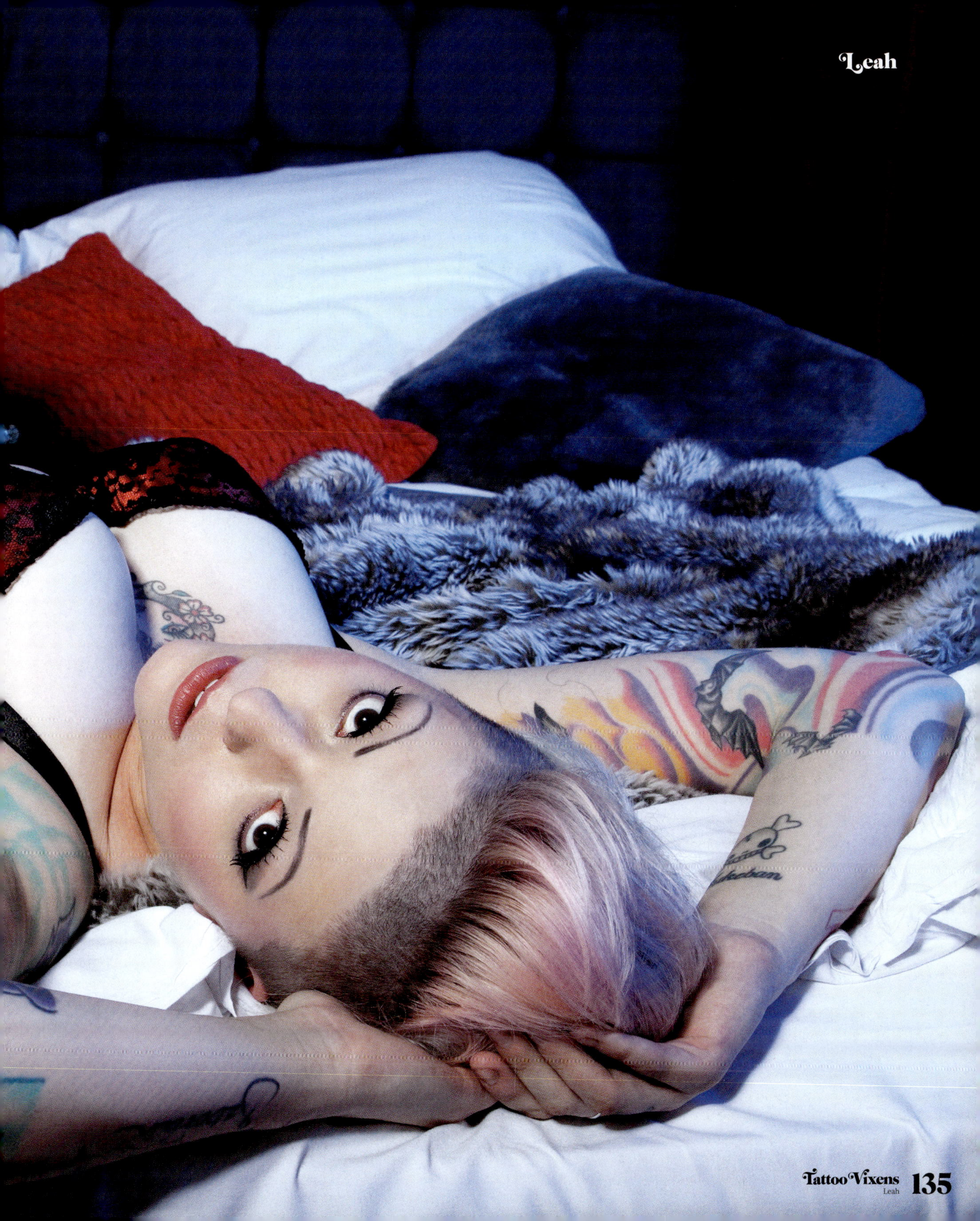

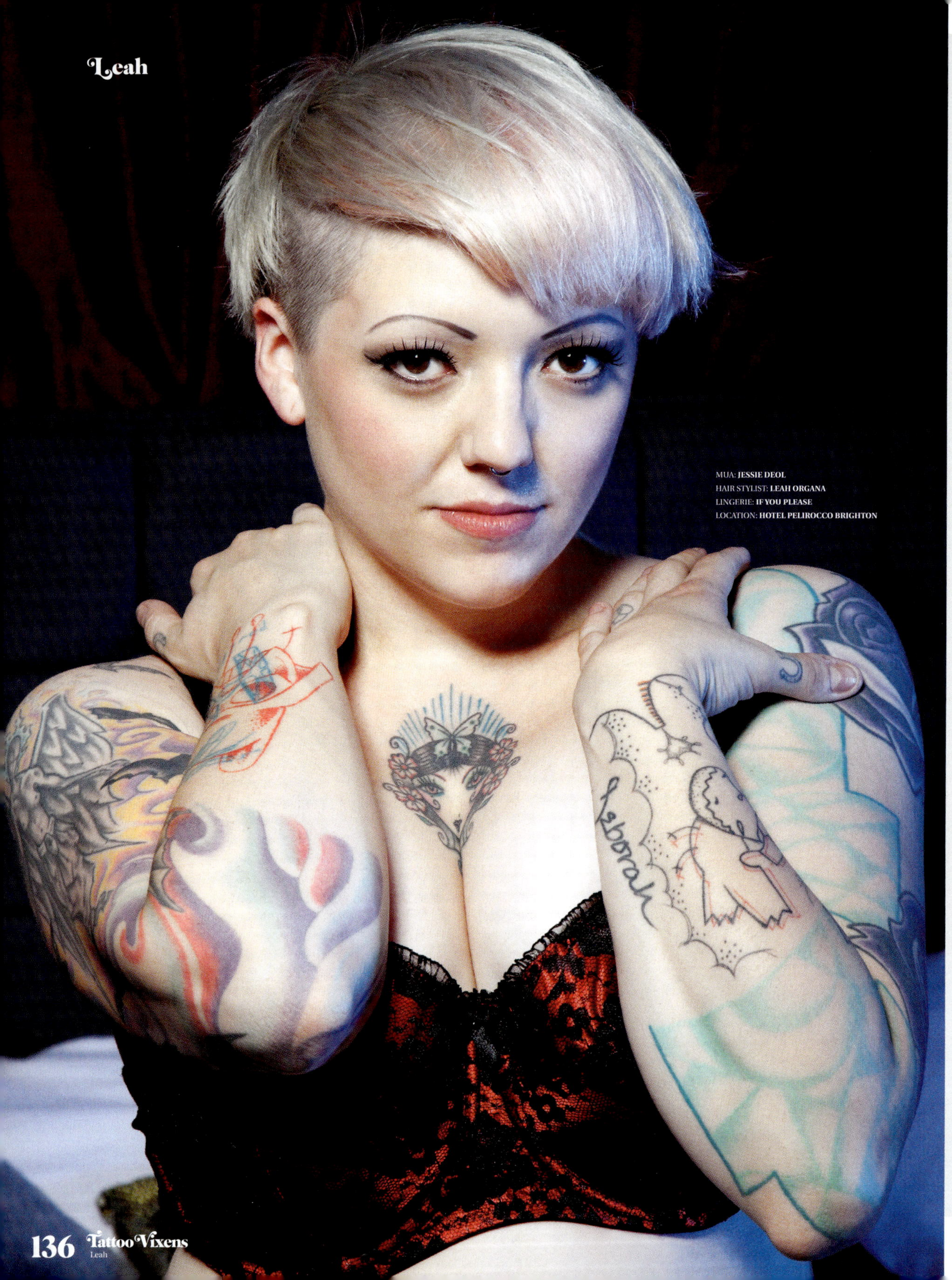

MUA: **JESSIE DEOL**
HAIR STYLIST: **LEAH ORGANA**
LINGERIE: **IF YOU PLEASE**
LOCATION: **HOTEL PELIROCCO BRIGHTON**

most impact is my thigh. In the summer when I am wearing a skirt or shorts, people feel the need to ask me lots of questions about it as it's such heavy black work that isn't seen on too many women, but generally I get a good reception. It helps when you have a smile on your face when someone wants to ask you a question about your tattoos. No matter how many times you may have been asked them before.

What would you say is the most positive aspect of being a heavily tattooed woman?

I feel happy. Relaxed in my skin. I know who I am and I've never been the sort of person to worry about how I look bothering other people. Me being tattooed doesn't change who I am or who I was before I got them. I'm not craving attention, it's just me.

Do your tattoos have any particular significance, or do you collect them purely because of their aesthetics?

Some do, some don't. Any significance is totally personal though and I don't tend to share the reasons why. Though, it's funny telling people I have a banger on my leg because I love a big sausage…

What advice would you offer to people who are considering tattoos on public skin before they've worn much coverage elsewhere?

I feel that I'm not the best person to offer advice on that subject. I believe we should be able to live in a world where, as long as we are not offending people, then so what if you want to decorate your hand or neck. However, I only just feel ready to take that step and I've been getting

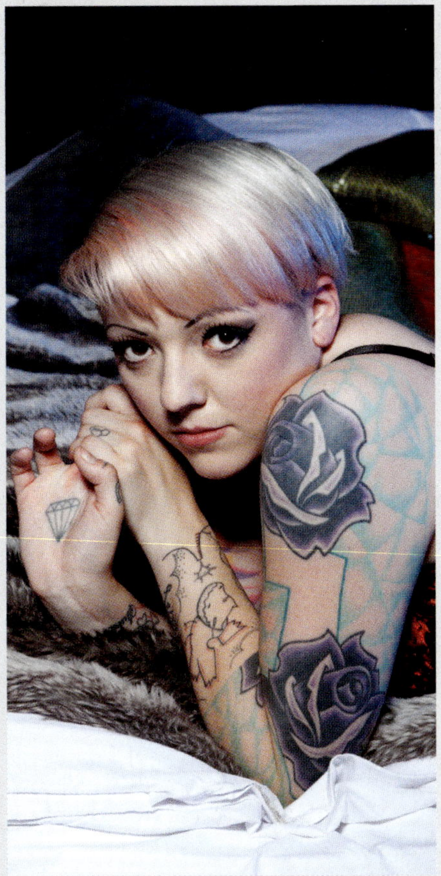

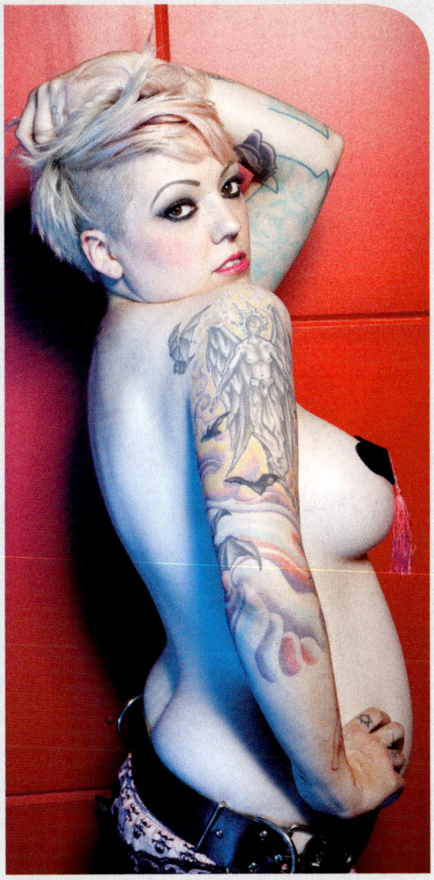

Any significance is totally personal though and I don't tend to share the reasons why. Though, it's funny telling people I have a banger on my leg because I love a big sausage...

tattooed for over 8 years now. That sense of social freedom, it's a naïve view, I'm sure, but I am a perpetual dreamer. Just always be 100% sure.

Do you share any tattoos with friends?

So many. I have a Junko Mizuno skull with my friend Dorothee, a lightning bolt with Tom and Woody. My younger brother Joshua and I have our birth dates on our kneecaps which is pretty sweet… only mine is 79 and his is 91!

If just one person could tattoo you, who would it be?

Lionel Fahey. He is the nicest person I've met through tattooing and consider him a true friend.

Tattoos by...

Lionel Fahey @ Out of Step, France- Forearms and ribs
Chris Higgins @ In2u Brighton - Thigh
Adam Sage @ In2u Brighton - Palm, kneecaps and fingers
Amanda Toy @ Frith St, London - Chest
James Woodford @ in2u Brighton- Sleeves and leg pieces
Sarah Ormond @ Intro, Brighton- Right ankle
(and hands by the time this book will be out)

ALL PHOTOGRAPHS: **IHSAN KEMAL**

SJ Whiteley

It appears that Ms Whiteley is something of an entrepreneur - watch and learn children!

Name SJ Whiteley
Age 23

What are you currently doing career wise or what do you aspire to be?

I currently run and own my own business called Built For Sin Apparel. (www.builtforsin.co.uk) Its clothing I design for people into all the same things as me! I take inspiration from rock 'n' roll, metal, hip hop, punk and tattoos. It's been going for quite a few years now and y'all should check it out! I am also a model and I love doing it. I really enjoy playing different roles in front of the camera and trying new styles. My opinion is "the more eye popping the better."

Tell us something about your childhood, what ambitions you had, where did you grow up and what has inspired you?

I am a born and bred English girl - not far from London. I come from a broken down family and was really angsty growing up in my teens. Being that way was what first got me into the rock, metal and punk scene. Anything that signified rebellion I loved, so I started playing drums so I

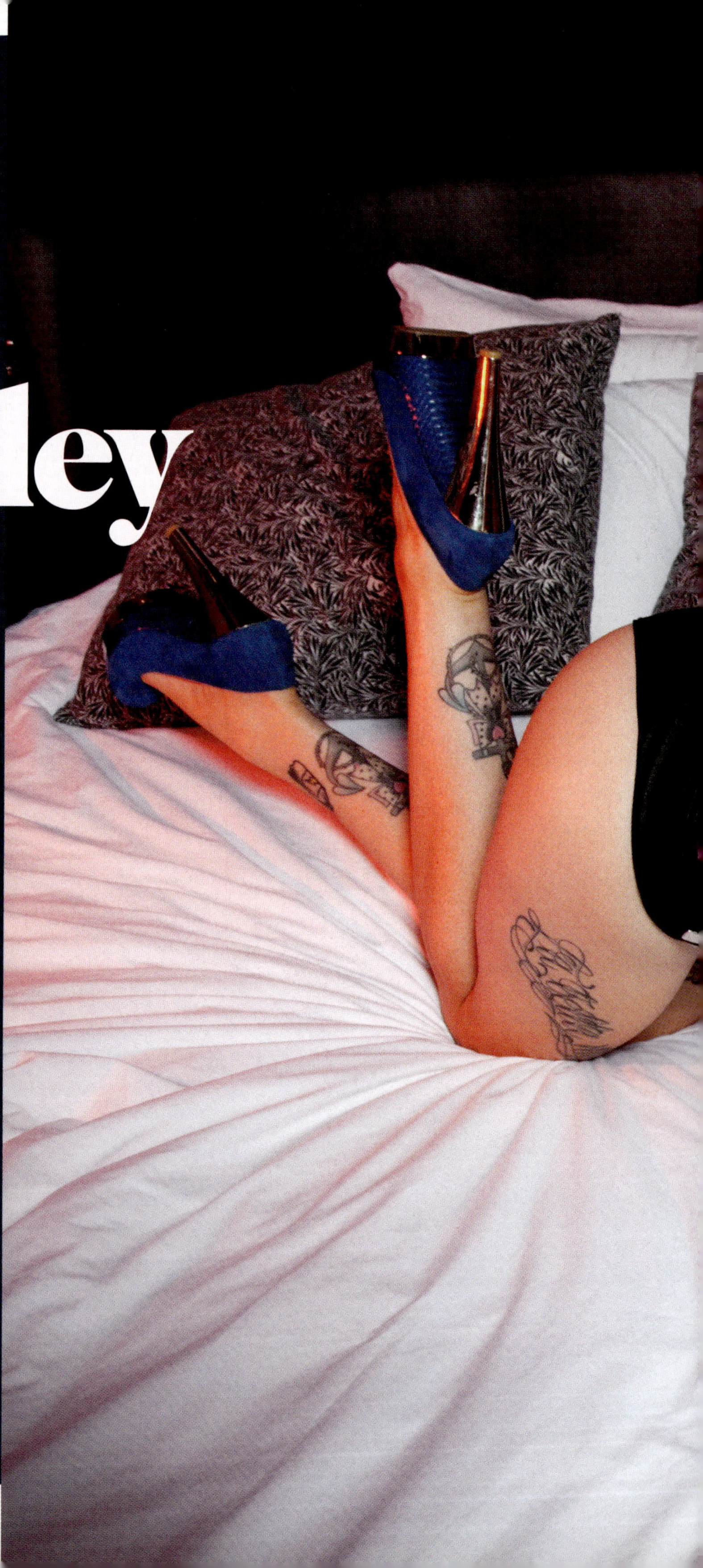

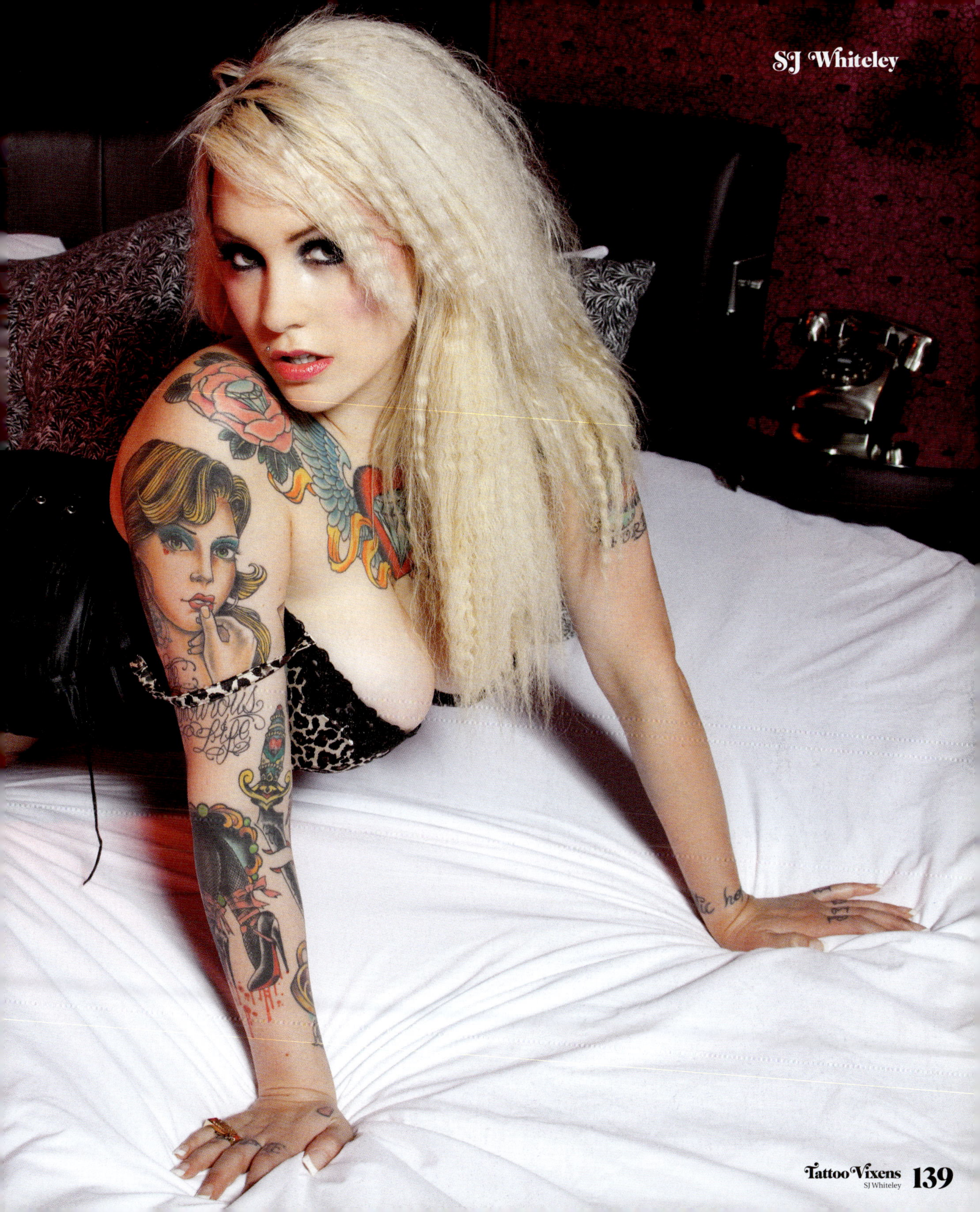

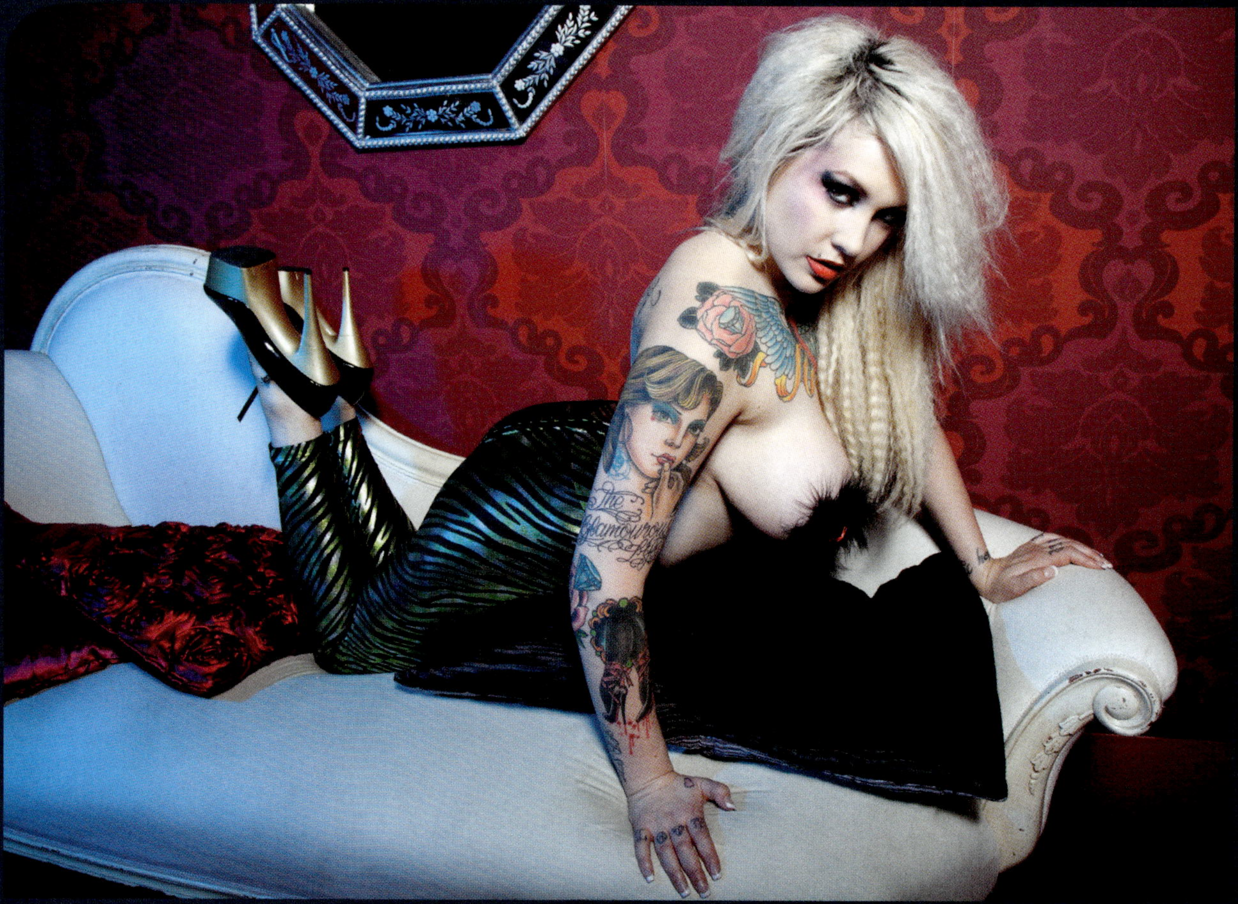

I have always been inspired by people who make their own paths in life. I think if you really want something you can work hard enough to achieve it.

could make loud noise, dyed my hair all sorts of colours and got a shit load of piercings. I wanted to tour the world singing or playing drums in a band. I have always been inspired by people who make their own paths in life. I think if you really want something you can work hard enough to achieve it.

One interesting fact about you:

I am a vegetarian and I am totally crazy about animals! Oh I also play drums in the world's first Egyptian-cider-core metal band called Scorched Flesh! Despite my girlish looks, I am a total tomboy and love hanging out with the guys doing guy things! Okay so that's a few things but never mind…

What initially attracted you towards tattoos?

I would say music initially showed me the world of tattoos. I remember watching bands on stage with sleeves and coverage and really wanted that for myself. I liked the idea of expressing yourself through artwork on your skin. I was always flicking through music mags and pointing the bands tattoos out. I liked the permanency aspect of a tattoo as well. Once you're in, you're in it for life.

Was acquiring significant tattoo coverage a conscious decision or a by-product of discovering the number of great tattoo artists available to you?

I suppose it was because of both of those reasons. I always knew I was going to get covered in tattoos but I have never wanted to rush. I was lucky enough to have been given

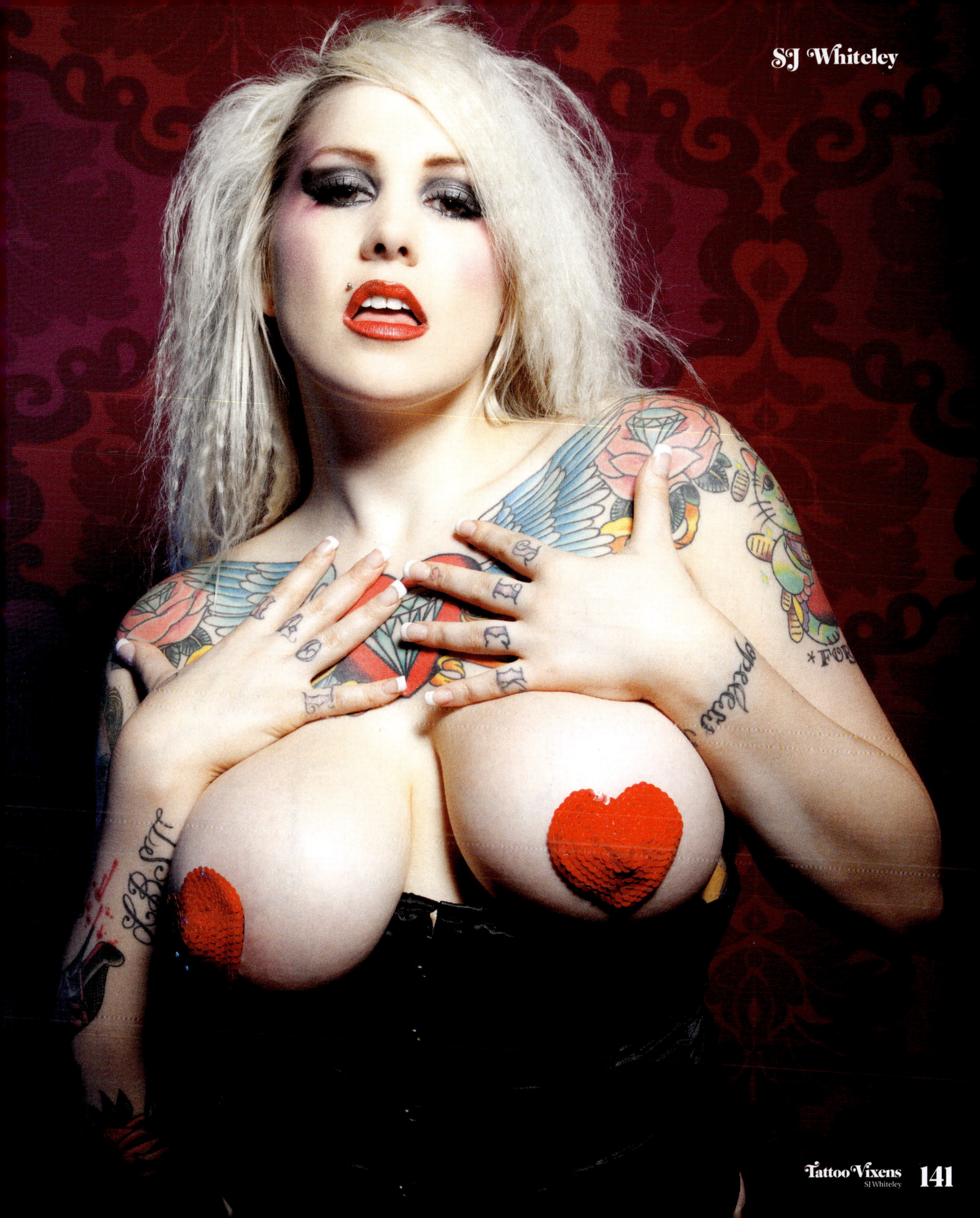

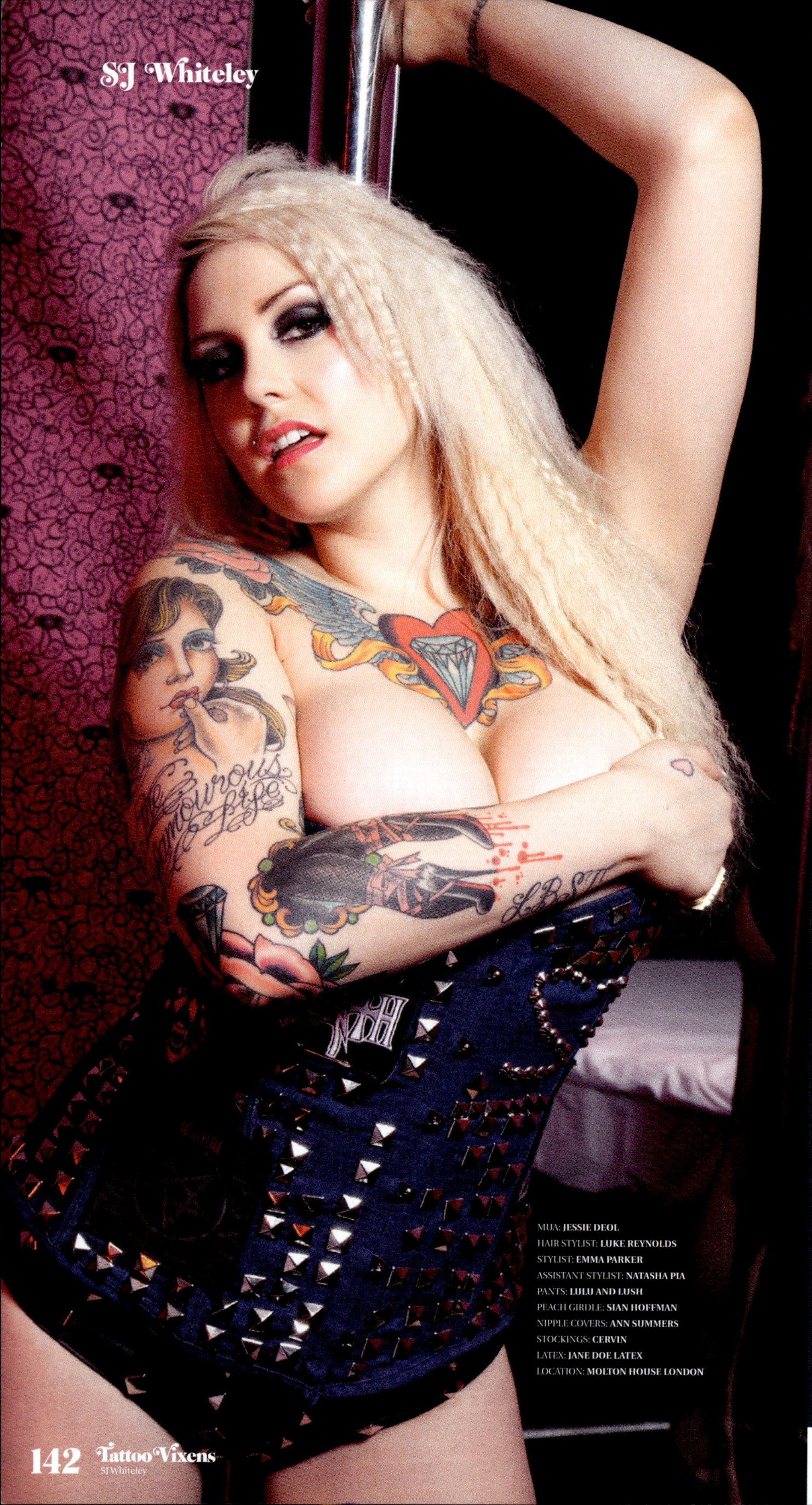

MUA: **JESSIE DEOL**
HAIR STYLIST: **LUKE REYNOLDS**
STYLIST: **EMMA PARKER**
ASSISTANT STYLIST: **NATASHA PIA**
PANTS: **LULU AND LUSH**
PEACH GIRDLE: **SIAN HOFFMAN**
NIPPLE COVERS: **ANN SUMMERS**
STOCKINGS: **CERVIN**
LATEX: **JANE DOE LATEX**
LOCATION: **MOLTON HOUSE LONDON**

After being in the scene for a little while and finding some amazing artists I'm scared I will run out of skin one day to put them all on!

good advice from other people about choosing the right artist. I can say now that I have been tattooed by some of the best people in the business. I suppose now after being in the scene for a little while and finding some amazing artists I'm scared I will run out of skin one day to put them all on!

Which of your tattoos has had the most impact, in regard to how you are perceived by other people?

My chest piece has had the biggest impact out of all of my tattoos as it's in a very personal and stand out place for a woman. I thought long and hard before getting my chest tattooed as I wanted to make sure I was ready to take that step. All of my tattoos before that were easily coverable. Although I have many tattoos now, they are always mentioned in a positive rather than negative way by other people. I get stopped every where I go with people wanting to stop and look closer at my tattoos.

What would you say is the most positive aspect of being a heavily tattooed woman?

Growing up, all of the heavily tattooed people I saw were men. I think being a tattooed women shows positively that stereotypes don't always exist. I am heavily tattooed but am also very feminine. I think I totally break down any stereotypes people might have in their head about tattoos.

Do your tattoos have any particular significance, or do you collect them purely because of their aesthetics?
All of my tattoos have significance behind them, some with more serious meanings than others though. I have had matching tattoos with my mum and my brother and then also a couple of small tongue-in-cheek in-joke type tats too! I am a very serious collector and only want to get tattooed by my favourite artists. In fact, I spend my whole time on waiting lists!

What advice would you offer to people who are considering tattoos on public skin before they've worn much coverage elsewhere?
I would highly recommend anyone against doing that. Until you have worn tattoos yourself you cannot really know how it feels. You may really enjoy having them and want more or you may think that in a few years your tastes will have changed. I know some people that have rushed in to get big pieces and now totally regret them.

If just one person could tattoo you, who would it be?
I don't know who I would choose for that, it's a tough question. I would say Xam knows what I like the best though, and he's so versatile with what he can do. I would probably pick him if I had to choose. Although the reason I go to so many different artists is because I like to pick the best for each piece. There are so many tattooists I can't wait to get tattooed by in the future.

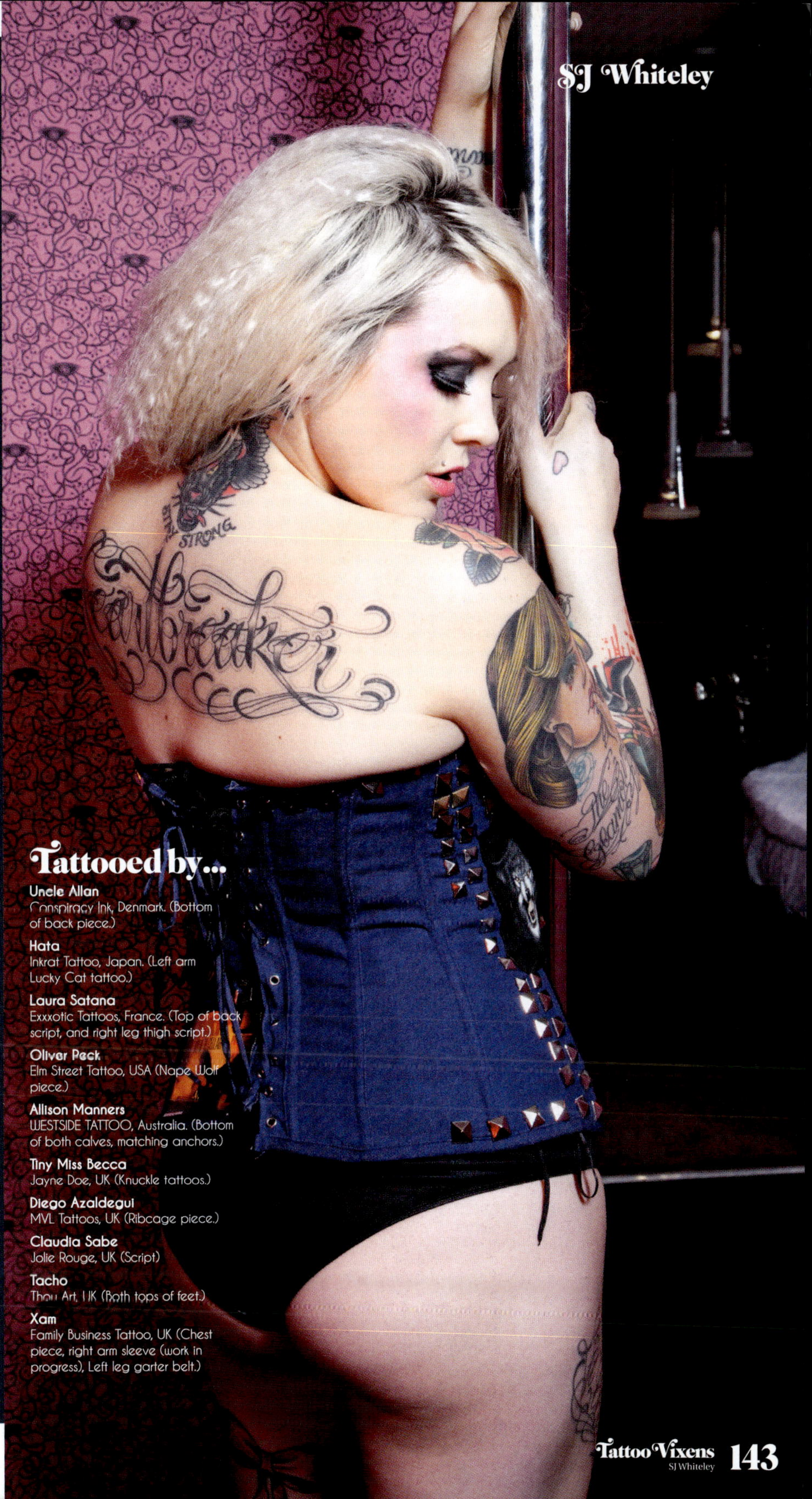

Tattooed by...

Uncle Allan
Conspiracy Ink, Denmark. (Bottom of back piece.)

Hata
Inkrat Tattoo, Japan. (Left arm Lucky Cat tattoo.)

Laura Satana
Exxxotic Tattoos, France. (Top of back script, and right leg thigh script.)

Oliver Peck
Elm Street Tattoo, USA (Nape Wolf piece.)

Allison Manners
WESTSIDE TATTOO, Australia. (Bottom of both calves, matching anchors.)

Tiny Miss Becca
Jayne Doe, UK (Knuckle tattoos.)

Diego Azaldegui
MVL Tattoos, UK (Ribcage piece.)

Claudia Sabe
Jolie Rouge, UK (Script)

Tacho
Thou Art, UK (Both tops of feet.)

Xam
Family Business Tattoo, UK (Chest piece, right arm sleeve (work in progress), Left leg garter belt.)

Hollywood Horror

ALL PHOTOGRAPHS: TAMMYNIZE GLAMOUR

Who can resist a girl in stack heels and a big Frankenstein monster inked across her chest? No, me neither:

You have really vibrant sleeve there! Can you tell us the story – how did your tattoo adventure begin?

Hmmm. The beginning – On the day of my 18th birthday, my mom let me ditch school,(it wasn't a common thing, I swear) we drove to Lodi, got tattooed together and needless to say I was hooked. I had pestered her for years about that day not coming soon enough! Shortly after, I went to Hawaii for my high school graduation, which convinced me that I had to get my arm started the minute I got back home! I have always had a love for Tiki's and anything pertaining to the oceans and beaches.. I hunted for an artist for about 4 months to design what I had envisioned and I was lucky to find Big Frank! Originally it was supposed to just be a half sleeve, which was followed by my right arm being started 8 months later...

Are they themed? Do you plan to link them up across your back or are you happy with what you've got?

Honestly, there isn't necessarily a theme, I just got crazy and spontaneous and every now and then would call Frank with an idea. Luckily he's the artist and ended creating a nice flow to both my arms, but no real theme. I am actually in the process of figuring out what the heck I want to do about linking them up though. I am torn, it's a debate I have daily with myself!

What's the story with Frankenstein's monster across your chest?

Oh, the Frankenstein tattoo! I swear that tattoo brings up a lot of different types of conversations. I am a huge horror movie fan for starters and I have always loved him, he is the "perfect monster" in my eyes. Misunderstood, terrifying yet so loving!

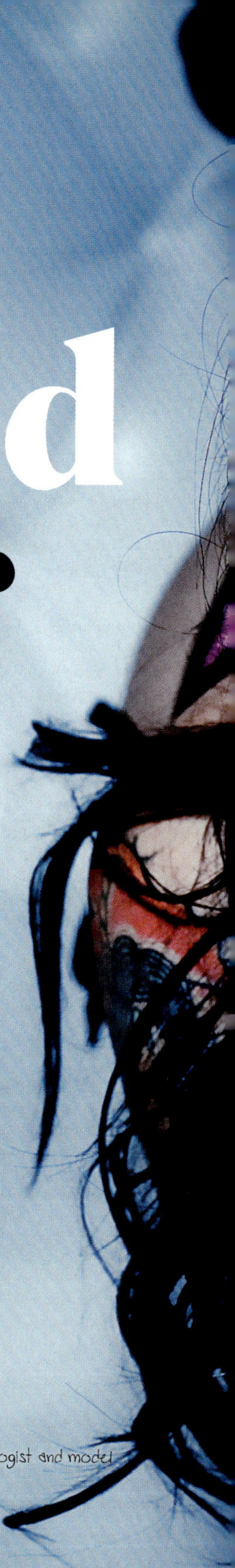

Name Hollywood
Occupation Cosmetologist and model

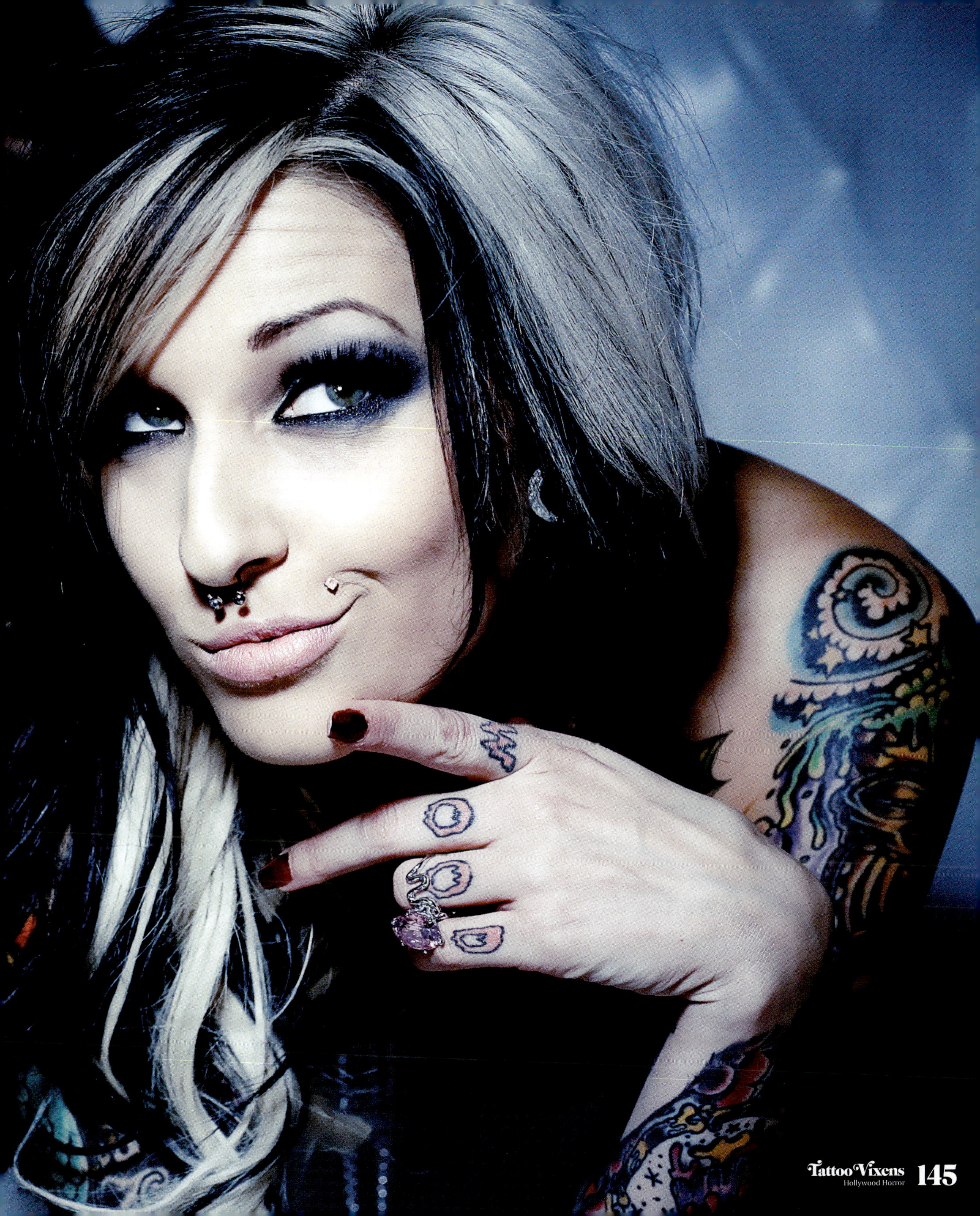

I told him if it fit between the cherries without any modifying, that he could tattoo it on me! 3 weeks later we ground it out in three and a half hours.

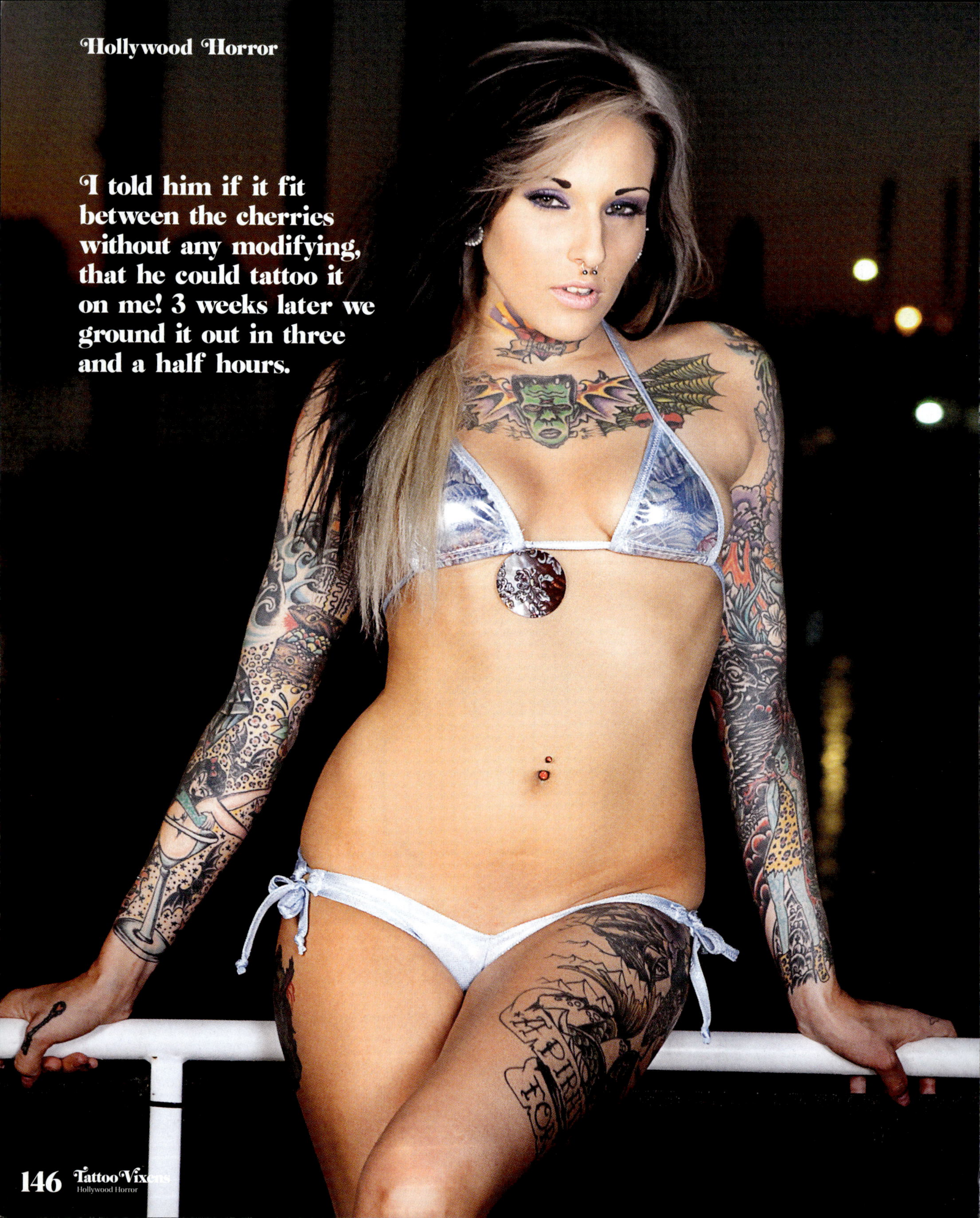

Originally, I hadn't planned that at all. I had cherries on the sides of my chest already, one day Frank was working on my sleeve and I commented about wanting horror monster tattoos - then he showed me a stencil that he drew it years ago and the guy never came for it. So at that point, I told him if it fit between the cherries without any modifying, that he could tattoo it on me! 3 weeks later we ground it out in three and a half hours. I added the webs about 2 years later.

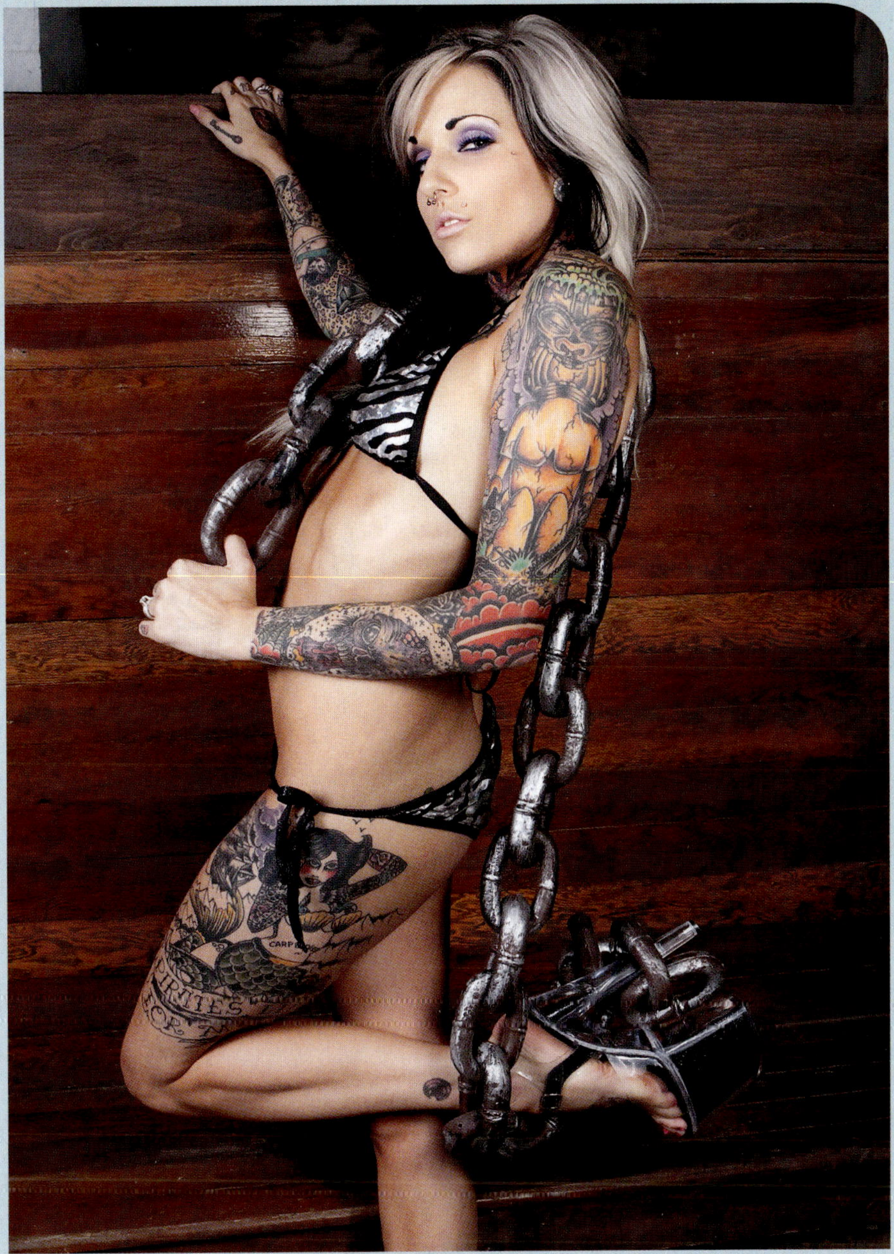

Are you a Boris Karloff fan. Do you think that DeNiro did a good job in his movie?

Boris Karloff is absolutely amazing! I swear he was the best actor of his time. I love to lay on the couch during winter and watch all his old movies, not one of them is bad. DeNiro did a great job but Boris is just perfect!!

In fact - that's quite a horror theme going on here - is this where your niche is?

I guess you could say that, I do have an extreme fascination with it - and zombies! Even my wedding, which was just this October 30th,was goth/Victorian theme at a supposedly haunted mansion. My house is full of skulls, life-size animatronics as well as random oddities and posters from movies. I have a zombie on my Tiki sleeve, my Tiki has a chain-saw in one hand, shrunken head in the other. I also have a zombie My Little Pony on my right thigh. Yeah - I guess it's my niche alright!

You're in a band - tell us a bit about that - how's it going? It's tough making it in the music industry these days.

Sigh. Bands are tough alright, it was going really great last year, but it is so hard to juggle practice and shows plus your own work and life as well as 5 others. It was fun and it is still a hobby but currently there is nothing in the works. We were a metal-core band, 2 guitarists, bassist, drummer, and my husband and I doing vocals. It was fun being on stage and seeing people getting into the music you had made. Such a unique feeling that's impossible to describe. I guarantee I was far from pretty on stage though, screaming a full set and running around made me look a bit like a monster myself at the end of a show, but it was a ton of fun!

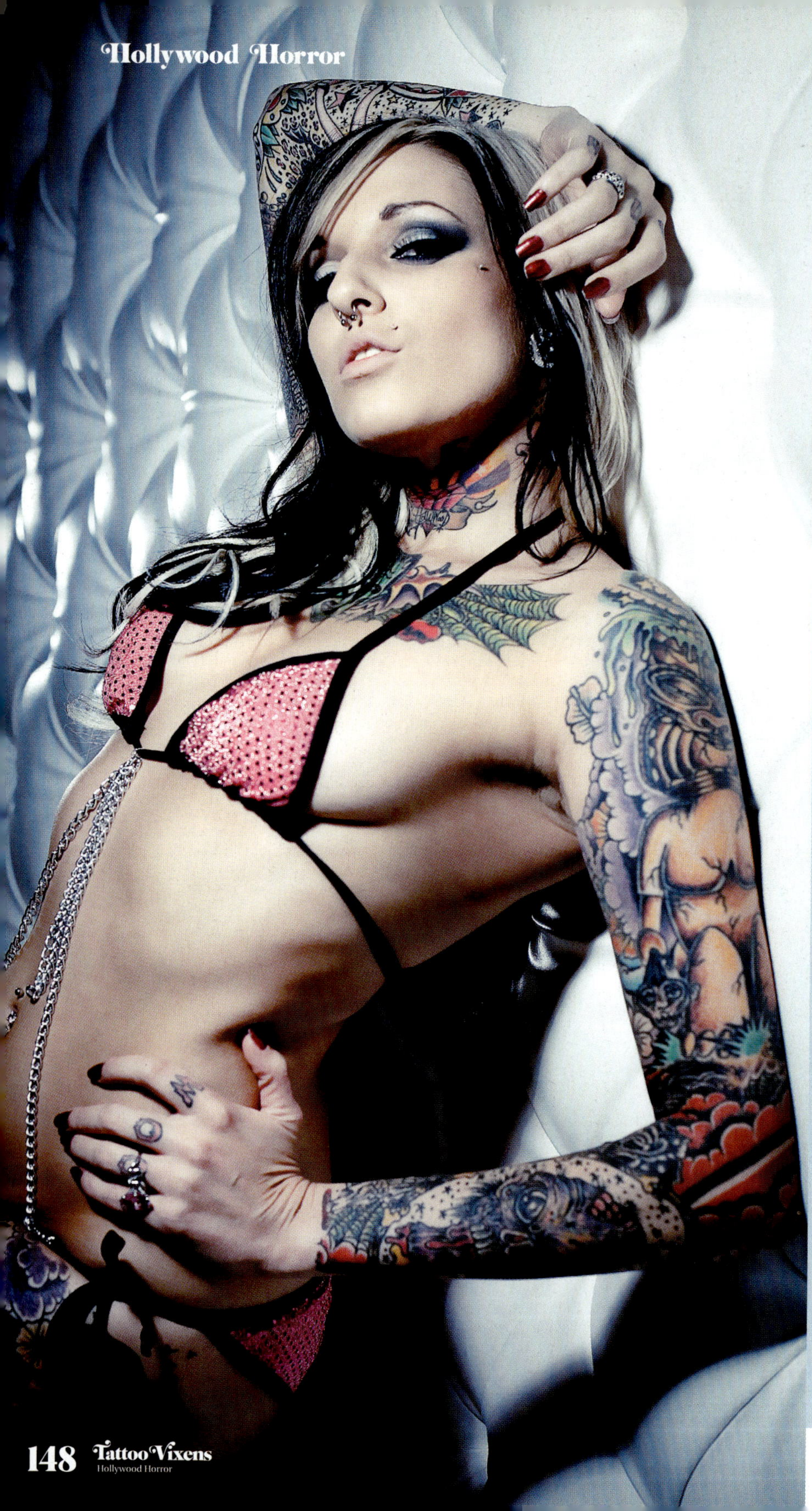

You set the boundaries and the rules and only you are responsible for yourself.

Which do you think will win - or would you prefer to keep a balanced life and be able to do both modelling and make a success of touring in a band?
At this point modelling definitely takes the cake... or lack thereof before photo shoots - that's the one hard part of modelling! Even if the band was still going the way it was last year, I would still say modelling. It's a different experience, more personal. It's you and your photographer making the images and pushing those limits. You set the boundaries and the rules and only you are responsible for yourself. Touring would have definitely been awesome, but at that time in my life I don't think I had the stability I would have needed to succeed.

Any plans to shift over to acting? There must be hundreds of opportunities in the horror world for you?
You know it crossed my mind when I first entered the modelling world almost two years ago. In school from 4th grade through high school, I was very active in the drama class. We did all sorts of plays and musicals, I loved every minute of it growing up and had hopes of possibly pursuing it one day. But once I got my cosmetology

license and started working for myself I got too busy. So right now, it hasn't completely dropped off as an option, but it's not at the top of the list at the moment.

What have you been doing in the Caribbean last week (see, you can't go anywhere without people finding stuff out?)

Darn social networking! Can't get away with anything theses days! I was actually on my honeymoon, still am - just back in the United States today with access to the world again! I love being in touch with everyone but to be honest, a week of doing nothing was insanely epic! I woke up, laid on a beach all day drank pina coladas, didn't work out once, slept and just spent 8 fabulous days with the love of my life. Couldn't have asked for more!

What was the plan when you were a little girl - this can't possibly be what you had in mind when you were 8 years old!

This is way, way more intense and amazing than anything I could have ever imagined or dreamed of! I originally wanted to be a surgeon more than anything – here I go back to the horror thing – but really, I always wanted to be a hairstylist! Man, I knew that at a really young age, but as for what I am doing now, I always wanted tattoos, knew for sure I would have sleeves, but I wasn't really thinking of the neck, chin or throat at 8 that's for sure! I feel so blessed to have had the opportunity to work with such amazing people and to constantly have nothing but love and support of others in my life.

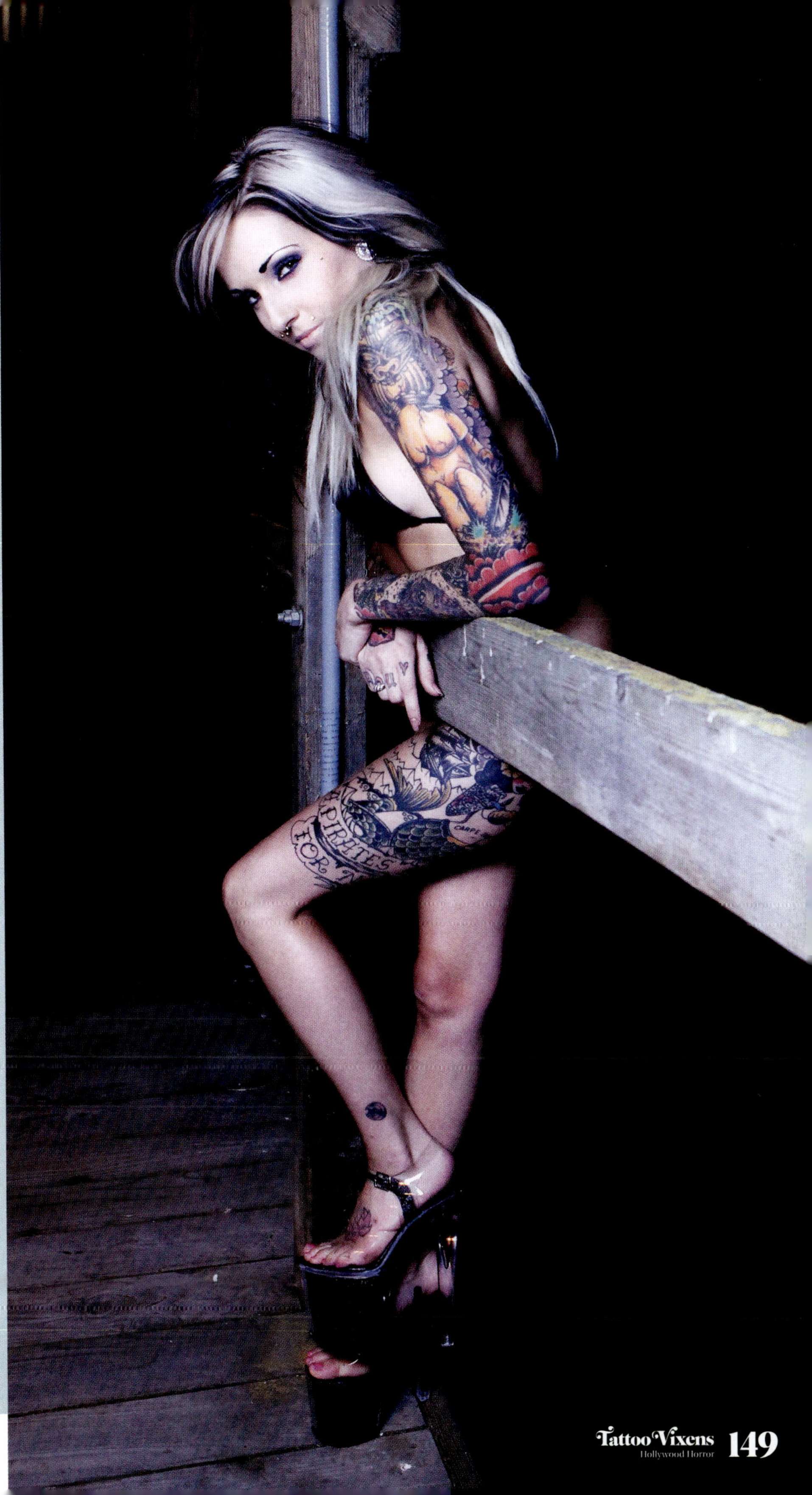

Lisa

For a young piercing apprentice, Lisa has sleeves that tell more stories than most books!

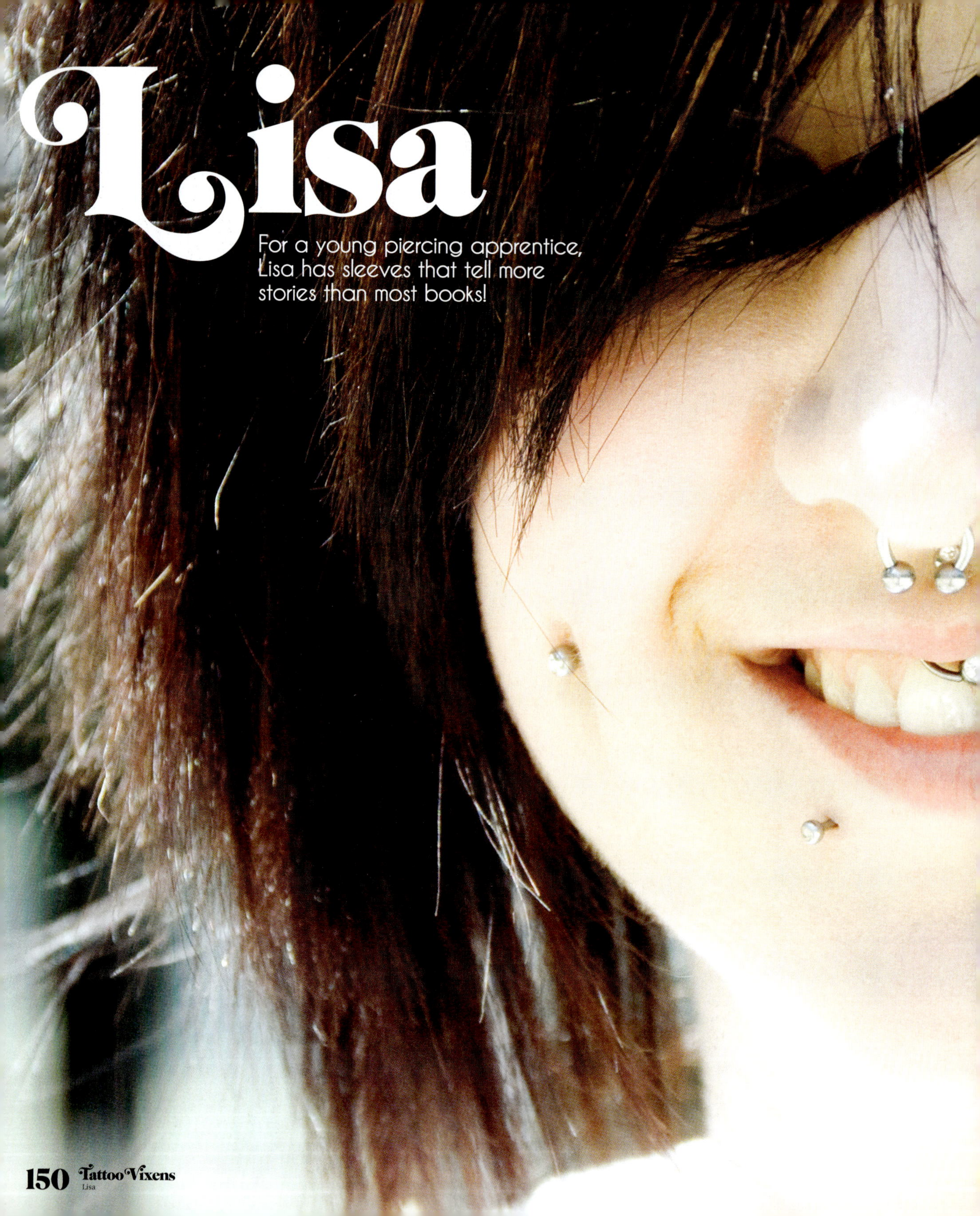

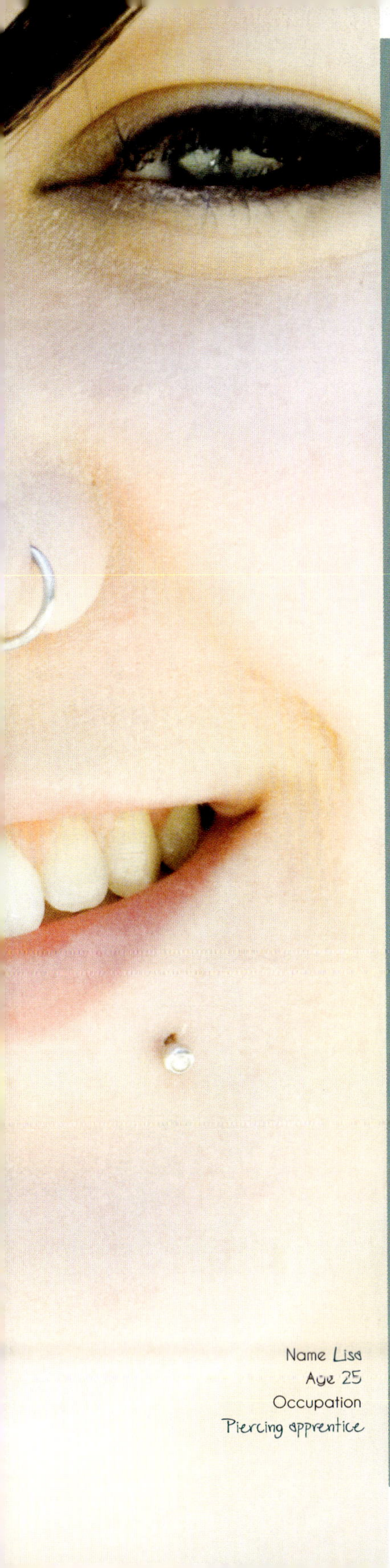

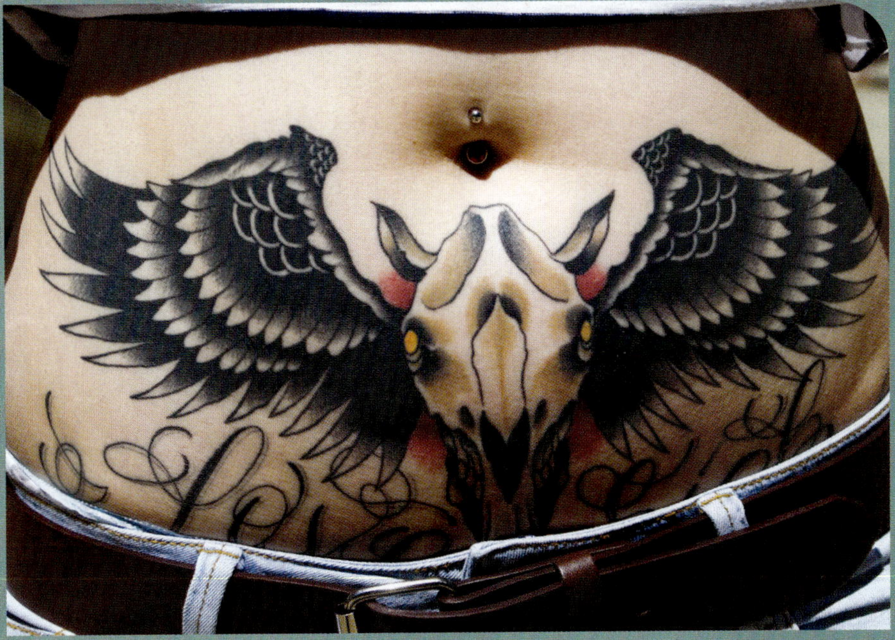

Working in the industry has given me more opportunity to meet and be tattooed by a number of amazing artists.

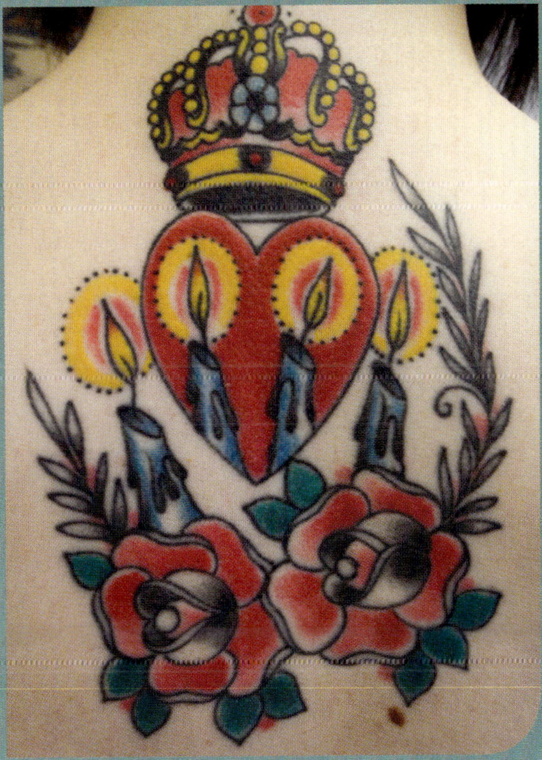

Name Lisa
Age 25
Occupation
Piercing apprentice

What initially attracted you towards tattoos?
I see skin as a blank canvas and tattooing is as a way of 'beautifying' the body. I love the way they look on skin and the fact you can decorate your body with beautiful pictures.

Was acquiring significant tattoo coverage a conscious decision or a by-product of discovering the number of great tattoo artists available to you?
I've known for a number of years that I wanted to be heavily tattooed. Working in the industry has given me more opportunity to meet and be tattooed by a number of amazing artists.

Which of your tattoos has had the most impact, in regard to how you are perceived by other people?
My arms. I think this is because

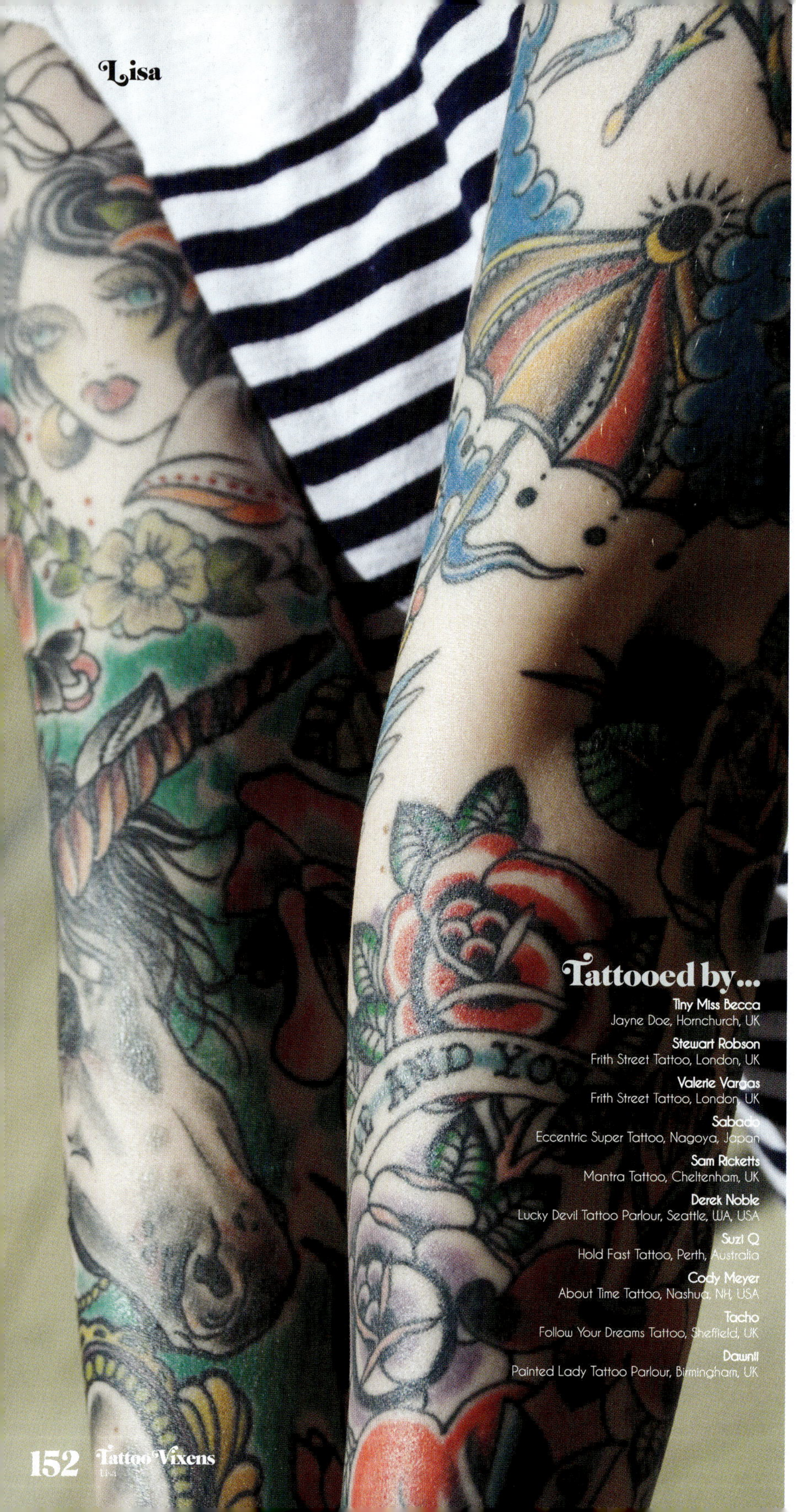

Lisa

Tattooed by...

Tiny Miss Becca
Jayne Doe, Hornchurch, UK

Stewart Robson
Frith Street Tattoo, London, UK

Valerie Vargas
Frith Street Tattoo, London, UK

Sabado
Eccentric Super Tattoo, Nagoya, Japan

Sam Ricketts
Mantra Tattoo, Cheltenham, UK

Derek Noble
Lucky Devil Tattoo Parlour, Seattle, WA, USA

Suzi Q
Hold Fast Tattoo, Perth, Australia

Cody Meyer
About Time Tattoo, Nashua, NH, USA

Tacho
Follow Your Dreams Tattoo, Sheffield, UK

Dawnii
Painted Lady Tattoo Parlour, Birmingham, UK

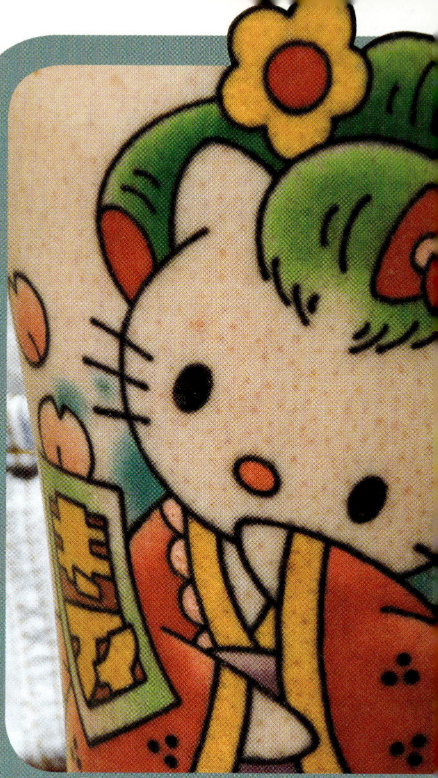

they are visible and get noticed first. I seem to get a lot of good feedback about them. Mostly people tend to be curious about them and ask questions; I think to some people, heavily tattooed girls are still a new thing.

What would you say is the most positive aspect of being a heavily tattooed woman?
I think tattooed women are perceived as strong women who have our own mind and we know what we want! I feel much happier being a tattooed lady!

Do your tattoos have any particular significance, or do you collect them purely because of their aesthetics?
Me and my boyfriend have matching diamond tattoos on our wedding fingers; this means the world to me. I also have some Smiths lyrics 'Still Ill' on the side of my hands - I had this done as a personal message/reminder for myself. Maybe the more I get tattooed, I'll collect tattoos

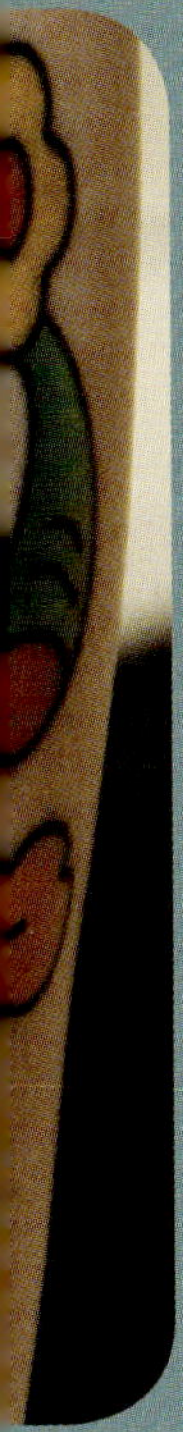

'I think tattooed women are perceived as strong women who have our own mind and we know what we want!

for specific milestones and as a tribute to family and friends, but for now I'm happy to collect pieces for aesthetic reasons.

What advice would you offer to people who are considering tattoos on public skin before they've worn much coverage elsewhere?
I don't think you have to earn tattoos or have them done in a certain order but I would advise people to think before they get tattooed. Tattooed hands or neck could stop you getting your dream job or hinder your future.

If just one person could tattoo you, who would it be?
Derek Noble!

One interesting fact about you:
My most treasured possession is my stuffed teddy cinnamon roll who I bought when I was in Japan. I love him more than life. He's my Boy!

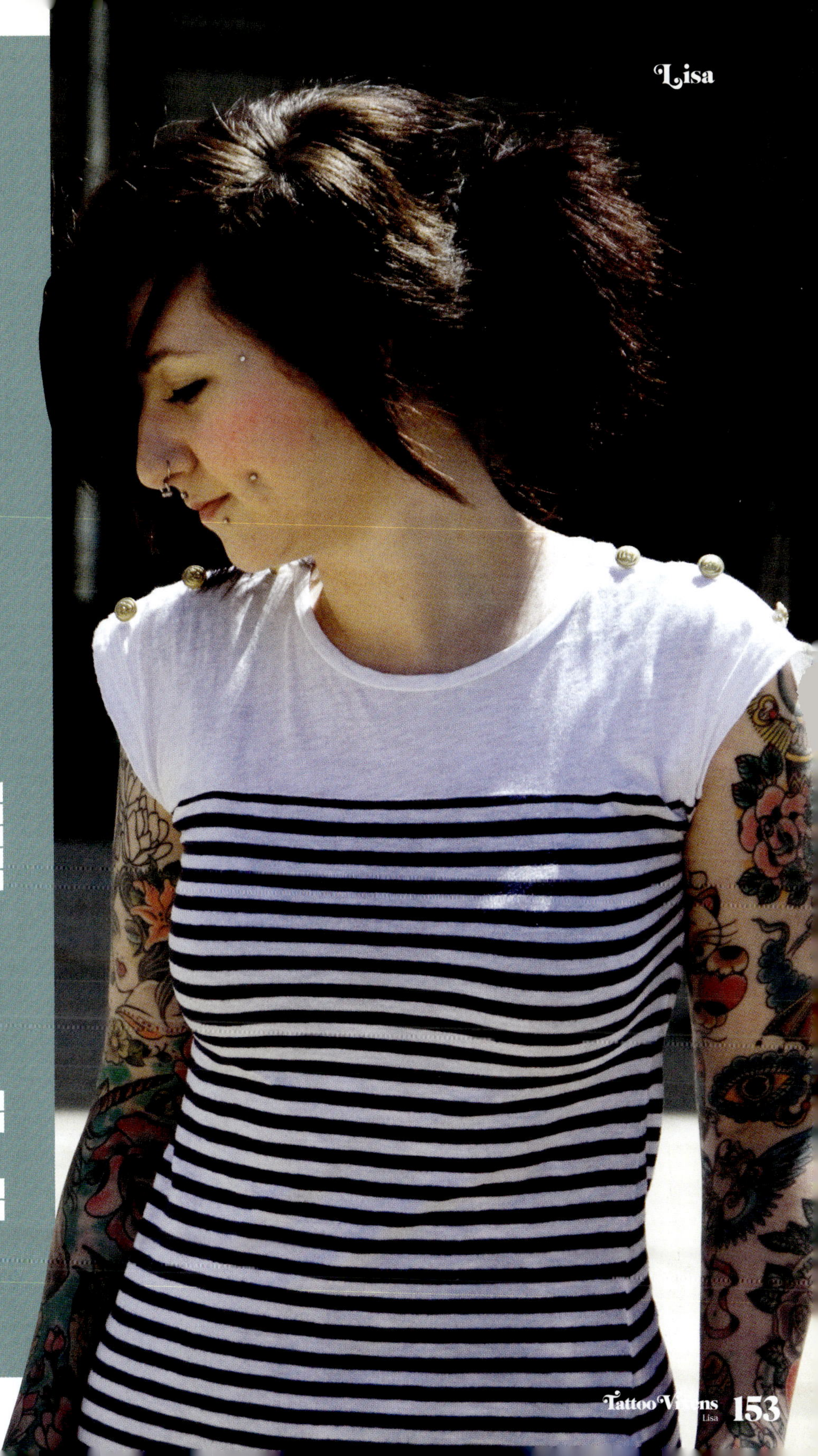

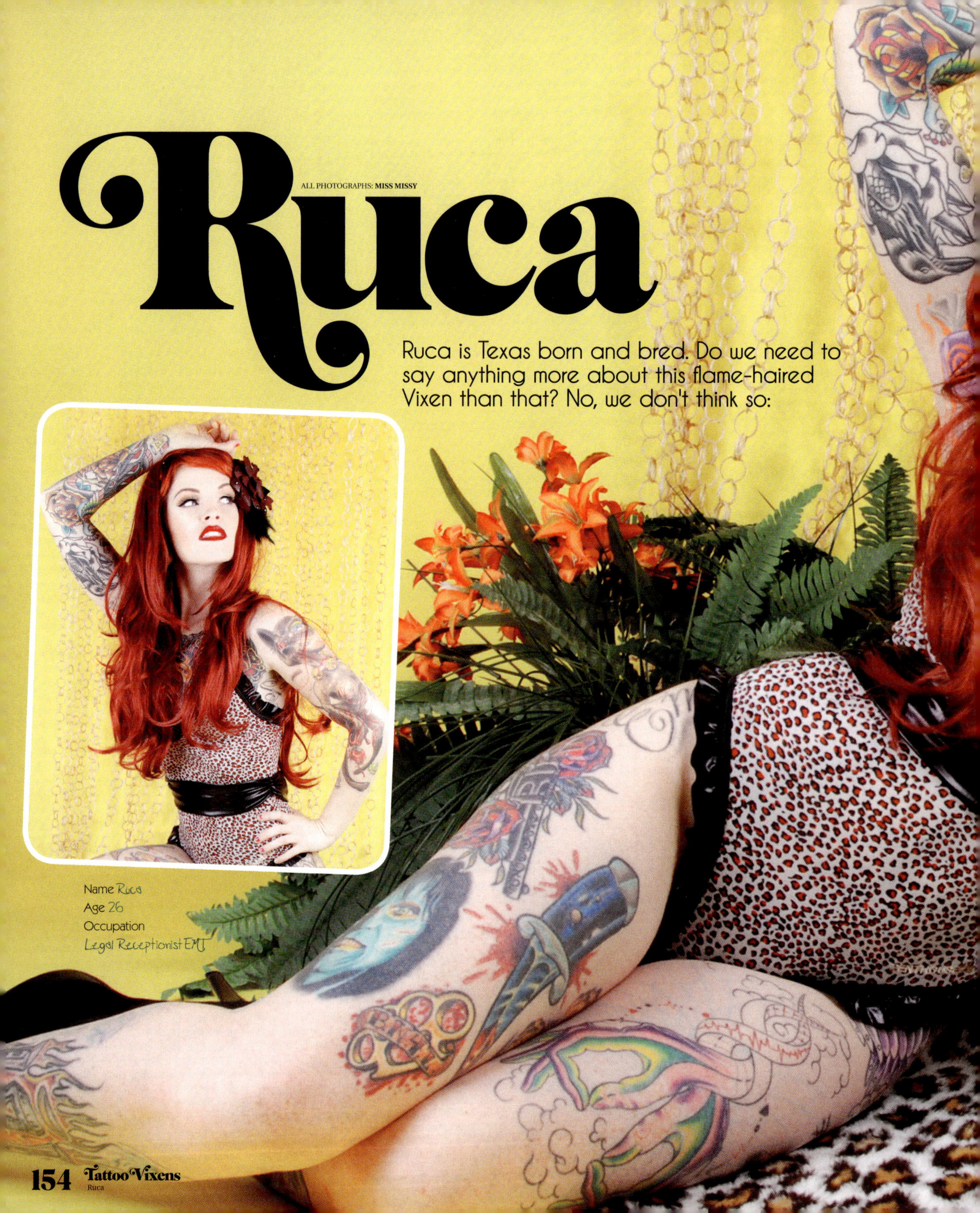

Ruca

ALL PHOTOGRAPHS: **MISS MISSY**

Ruca is Texas born and bred. Do we need to say anything more about this flame-haired Vixen than that? No, we don't think so:

Name Ruca
Age 26
Occupation
Legal Receptionist EMT

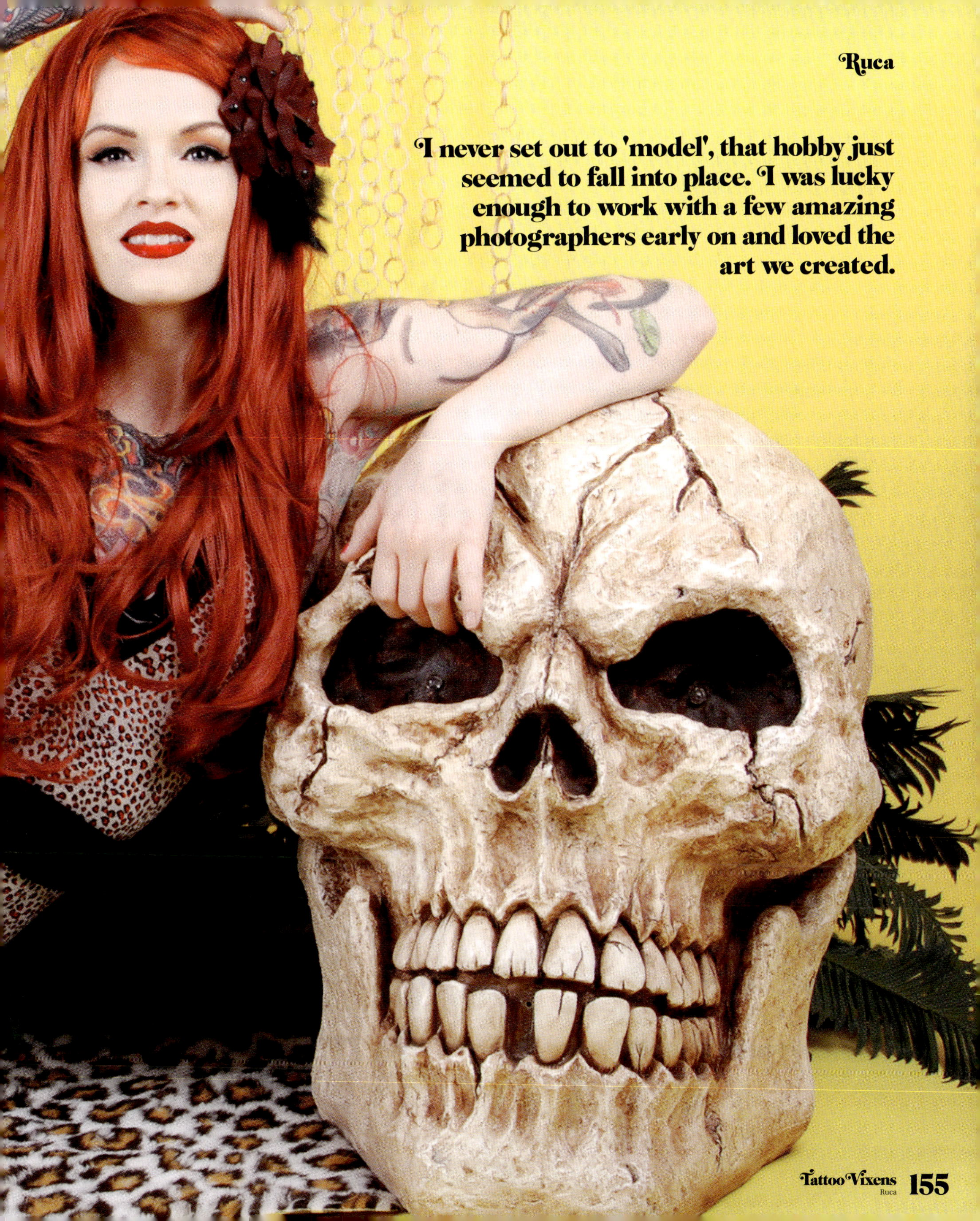

I never set out to 'model', that hobby just seemed to fall into place. I was lucky enough to work with a few amazing photographers early on and loved the art we created.

You are one of the most tattooed ladies that we have in the book! Can you tell us your story - how your journey began, your first tattoo, how long has it taken you to get this far?
I started when I was 16, which I wouldn't recommend to anyone! I sat for 3 hours to get a tribal sun in the middle of my back that I had horribly sketched up. It is now covered up by a giant snake piece thanks to a dear friend. My collection of art just snowballed from there. Decided to get my feet tattooed... then legs, then chest and then took the big leap onto my arms, back of neck, stomach, sides, etc. I've slowed down a bit recently due to lack of free skin, I'm pretty much running out of room!

Do you have any plans to link it all together?
Absolutely. After I get all of my main pieces and have them finished, I'll work on blending them all together to create my bodysuit. Only thing not tattooed will be my hands, neck and face – you're welcome, mother!

Where are you from and where do you live now? Are you the most tattooed vixen in your street?
I was born Corpus Christi, Texas, raised in Dallas, Texas and currently reside in Downtown Dallas. I live in quite the artist-thriving area so everyone seems to have a little bit of art on them.

I live in quite the artist-thriving area so everyone seems to have a little bit of art on them.

For a female though, I am very heavily tattooed.

This can't be what you wanted to do when you were a small child - can you tell us what it was that you thought you might be?
Pretty close to it!. I was a free spirited only child. Loved to paint, draw, play with my imaginary friends. I wanted to be a nurse when I grew up and am currently in school to be in the medical field. I still like to paint and create, that never left me!

Do you think you will continue with this forever in some form or maybe go back to that original dream?
I'll always be the tattooed girl, I love it too much to stop. As far as the medical field goes, I'm still pursuing my dream and will conquer it.

What's going on with that cat on your left arm? Is it scratching itself? Is there a story behind that?
Hahaha, I get more questions on her than any other! She is

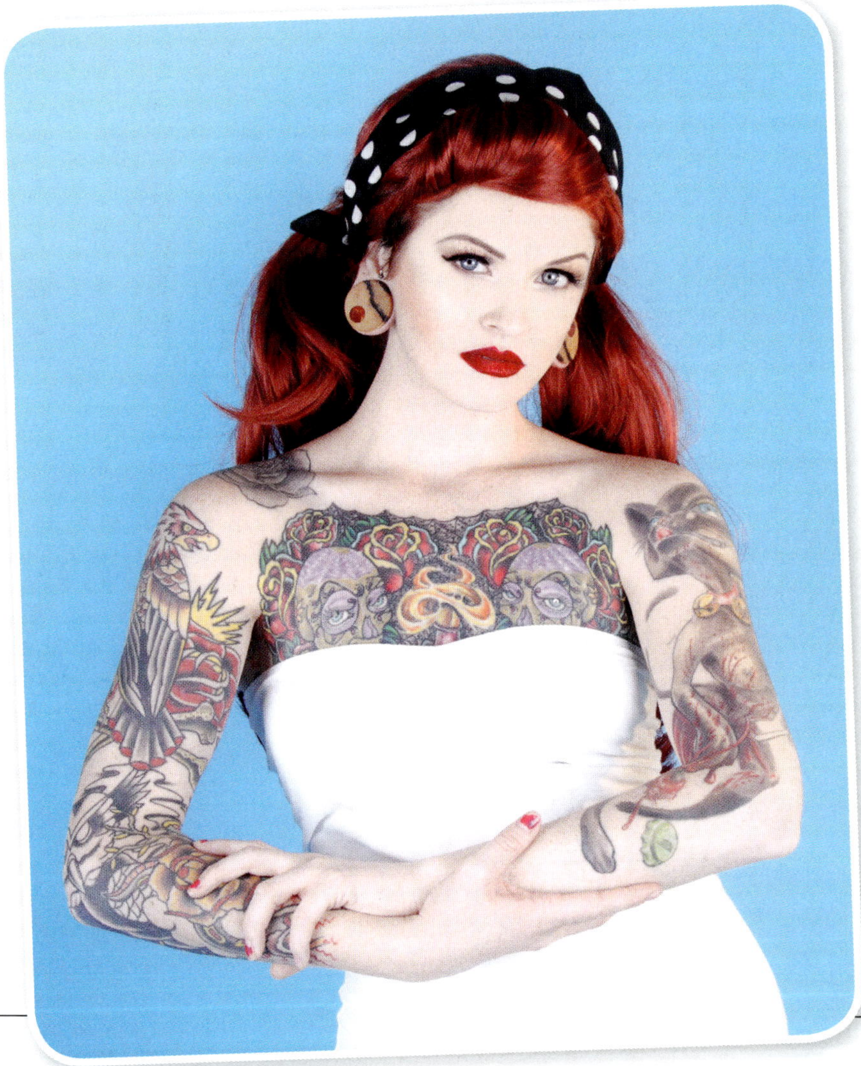

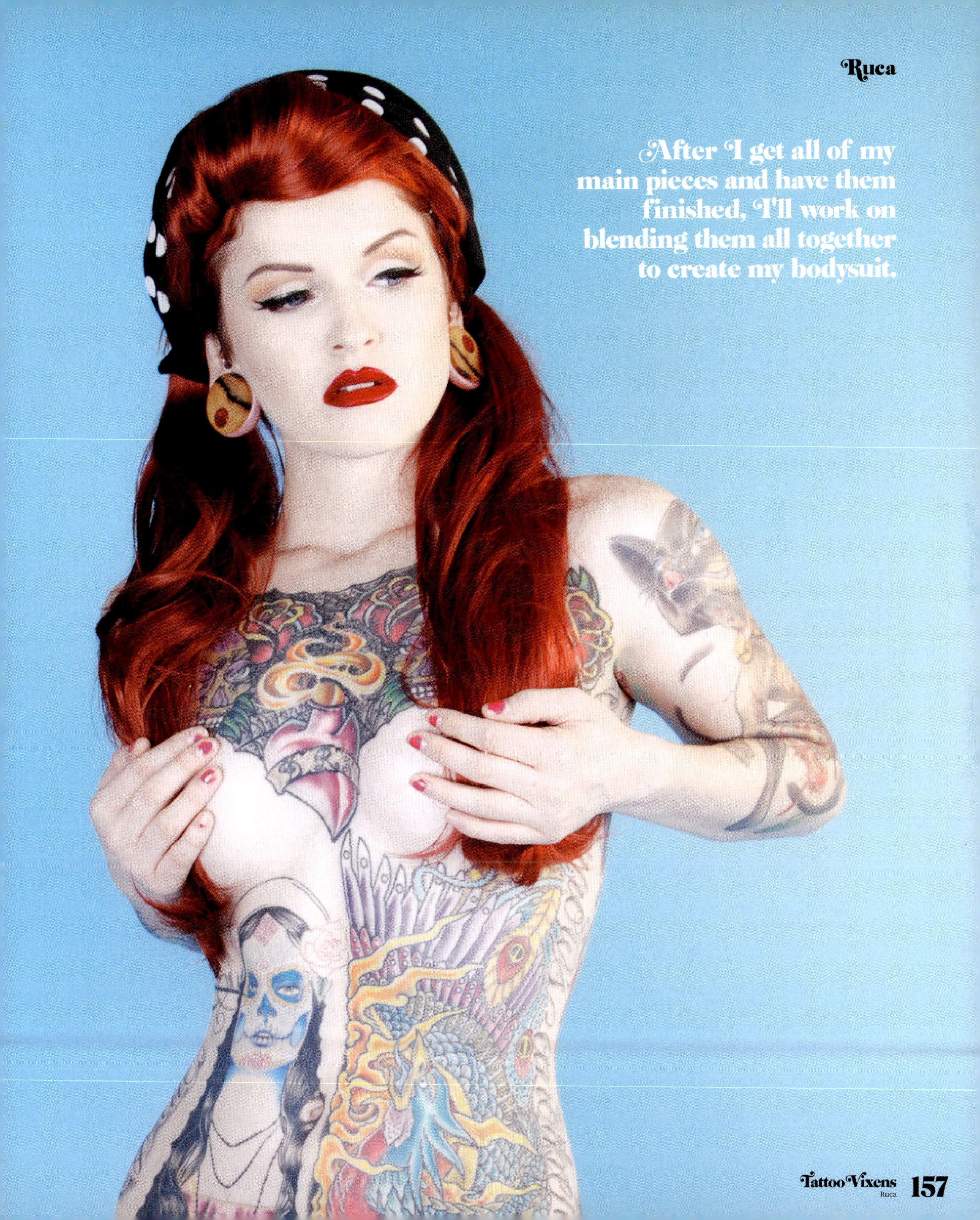

After I get all of my main pieces and have them finished, I'll work on blending them all together to create my bodysuit.

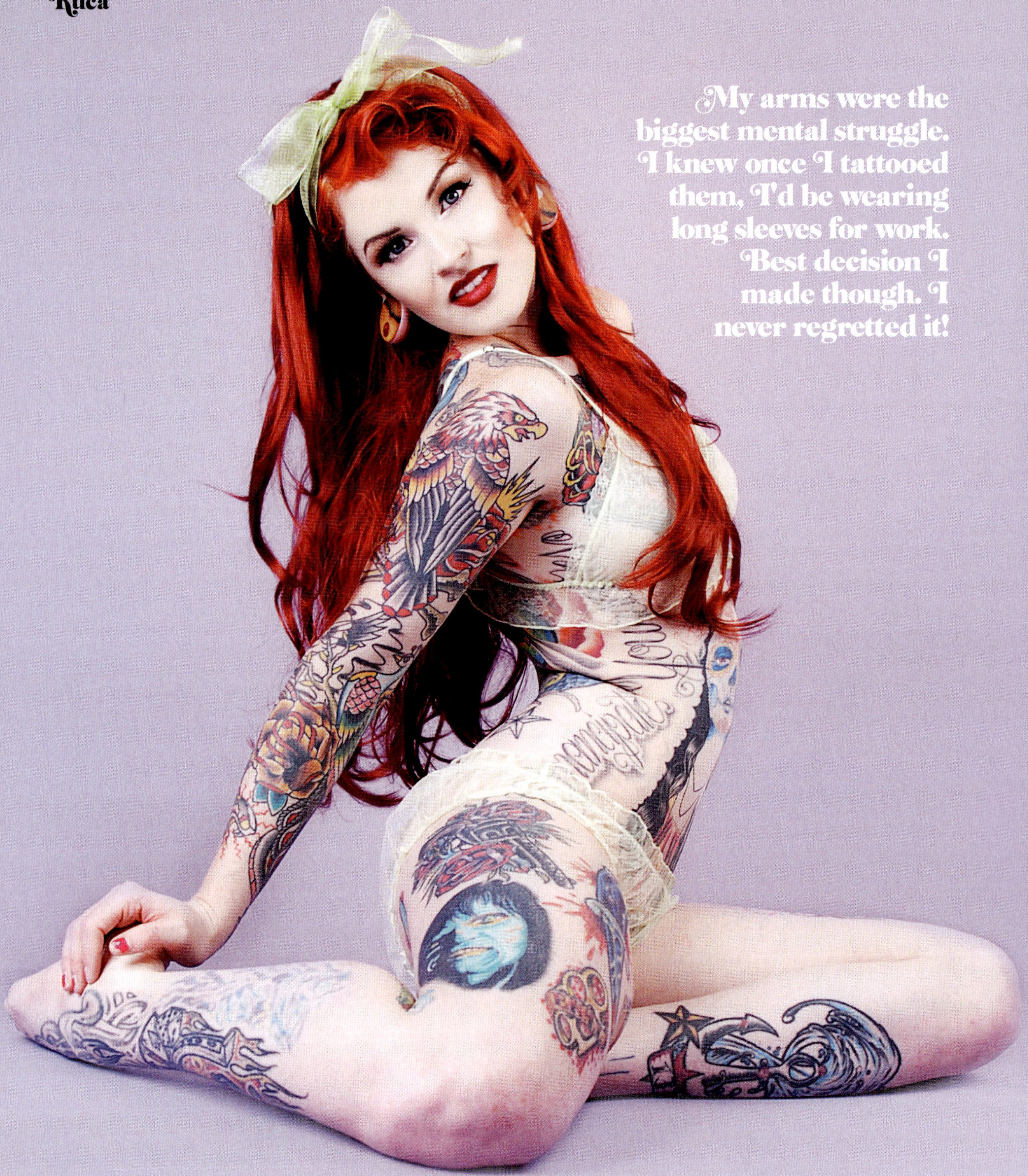

My arms were the biggest mental struggle. I knew once I tattooed them, I'd be wearing long sleeves for work. Best decision I made though. I never regretted it!

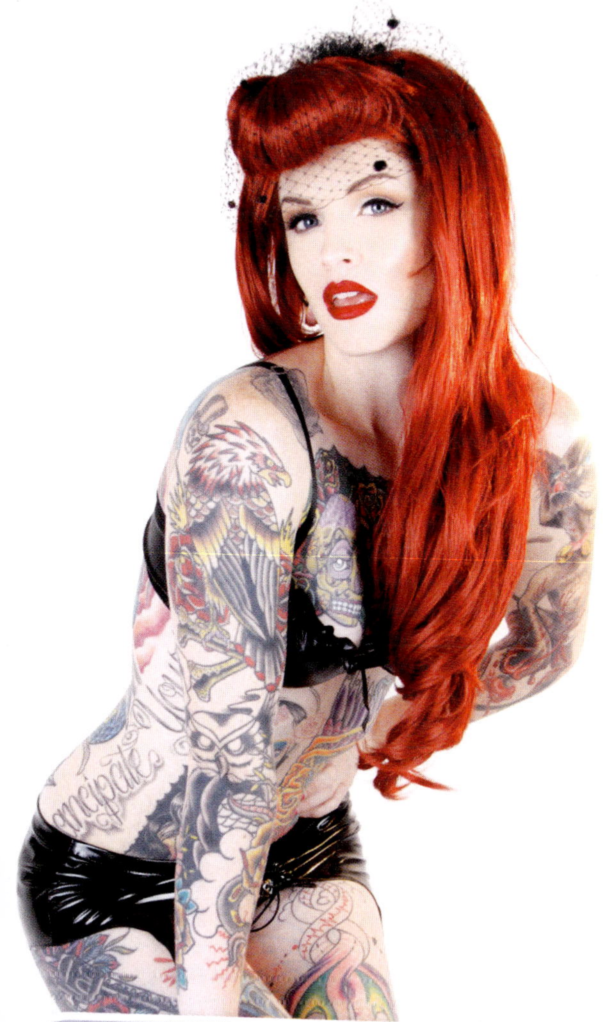

the artist's depiction of my female Siamese cat, Jinx. She has a female human form, so it makes her quite voluptuous!! She's actually playing with a toy mouse, the rest may be too graphic to write.

Was it a big decision for you to get your chest tattooed? We have seen quite a few now in this book and most have taken a long time to think about it, but have no regrets.

Chest was actually one of the easiest to decide on. I knew what I wanted and trusted my artist. My arms were the biggest mental struggle. I knew once I tattooed them, I'd be wearing long sleeves for work. Best decision I made though. I never regretted it!

I have a lot of freckles too. My tattoo artist told me that freckled skin is really tough and unforgiving – do you find that when you are having work done?

Not at all. My skin is really pale and moisturized – soaks the ink up like a sponge. I think most of the time if people have lots of freckles, their skin has sun damage, making it tough. I wear 70 spf when I go out to protect my skin and ink.

OK – I think that's about all – but would you care to give some advice to anybody thinking of going into modeling as a career – and is there something you wish somebody had told you before you started out?

I never set out to 'model', that hobby just seemed to fall into place. I was lucky enough to work with a few amazing photographers early on and loved the art we created. I do it for the art and for the creative process, so I say, do it because you love it, not because you are expecting anything from it.

Tell us a secret:

Ha! Not sure if I have too many of those! I'm super quirky though and have odd tendencies. I smell everything. It's a horrible habit.

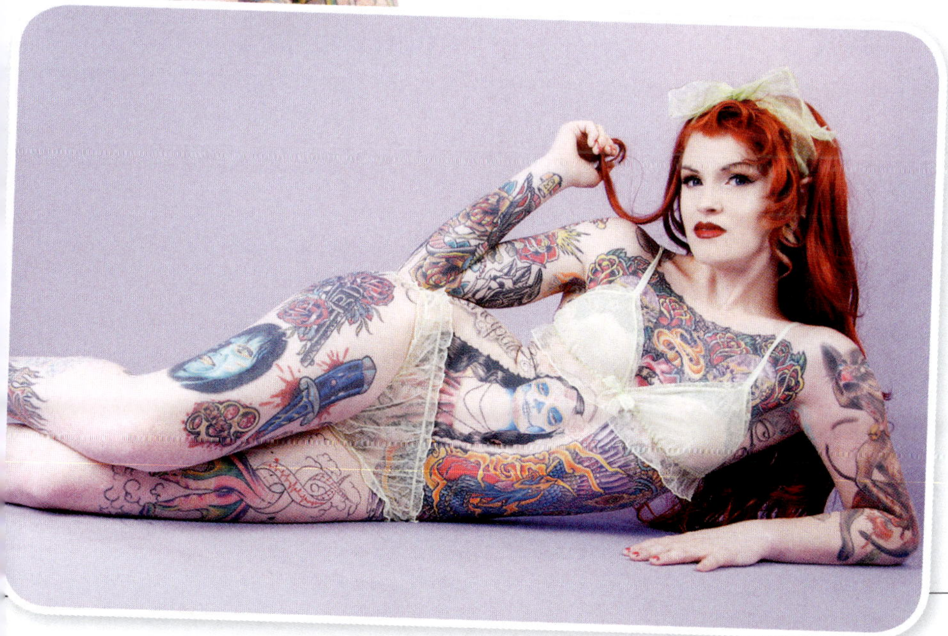

I think most of the time if people have lots of freckles, their skin has sun damage, making it tough. I wear 70 spf when I go out to protect my skin and ink.

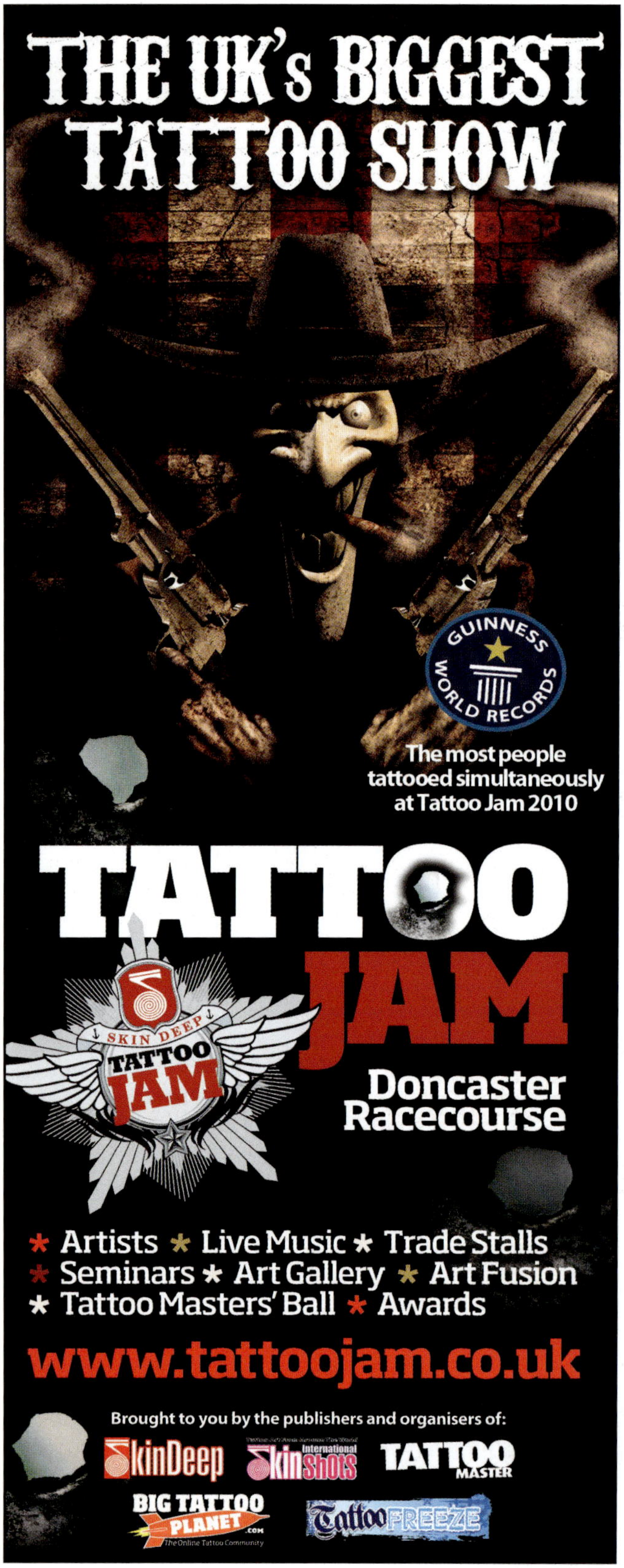
THE UK's BIGGEST TATTOO SHOW
GUINNESS WORLD RECORDS
The most people tattooed simultaneously at Tattoo Jam 2010
TATTOO JAM
SKIN DEEP TATTOO JAM
Doncaster Racecourse
* Artists * Live Music * Trade Stalls * Seminars * Art Gallery * Art Fusion * Tattoo Masters' Ball * Awards
www.tattoojam.co.uk
Brought to you by the publishers and organisers of:
SkinDeep
Skin Shots International
TATTOO MASTER
BIG TATTOO PLANET .COM
The Online Tattoo Community
Tattoo FREEZE

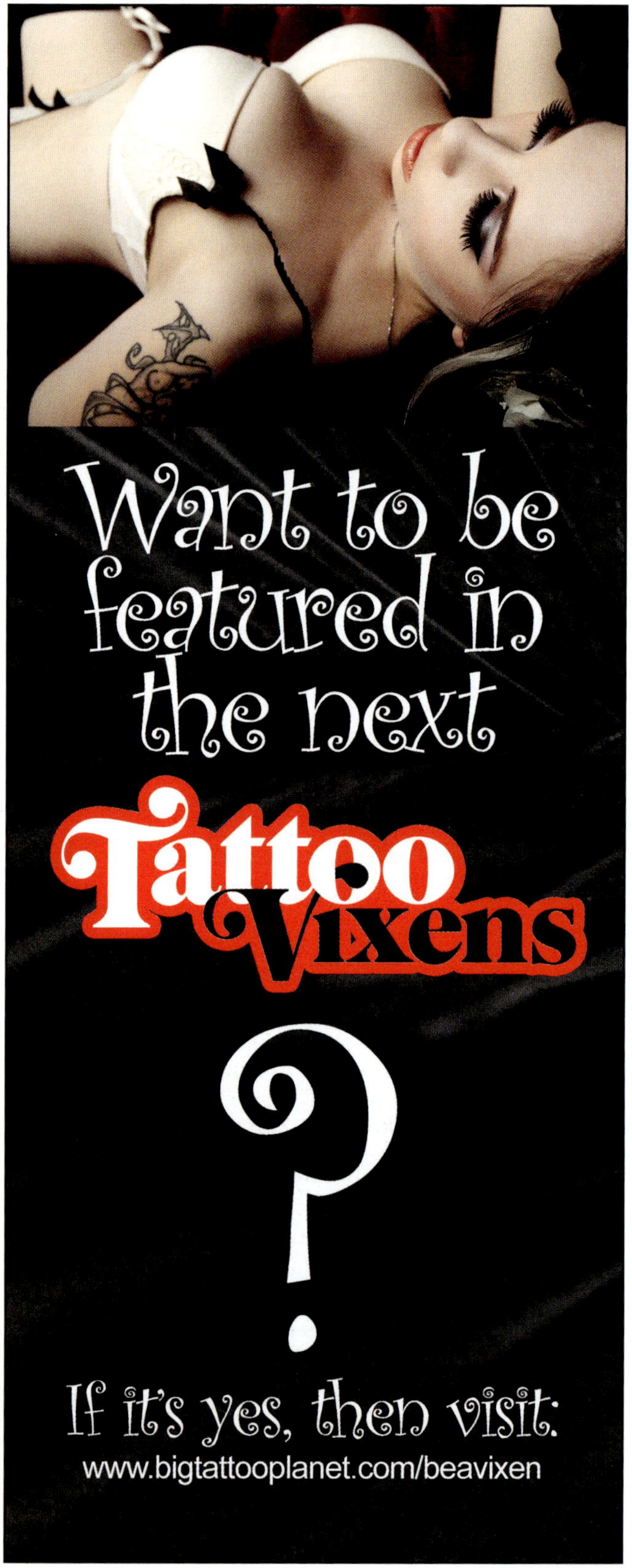
Want to be featured in the next
Tattoo Vixens
?
If it's yes, then visit:
www.bigtattooplanet.com/beavixen

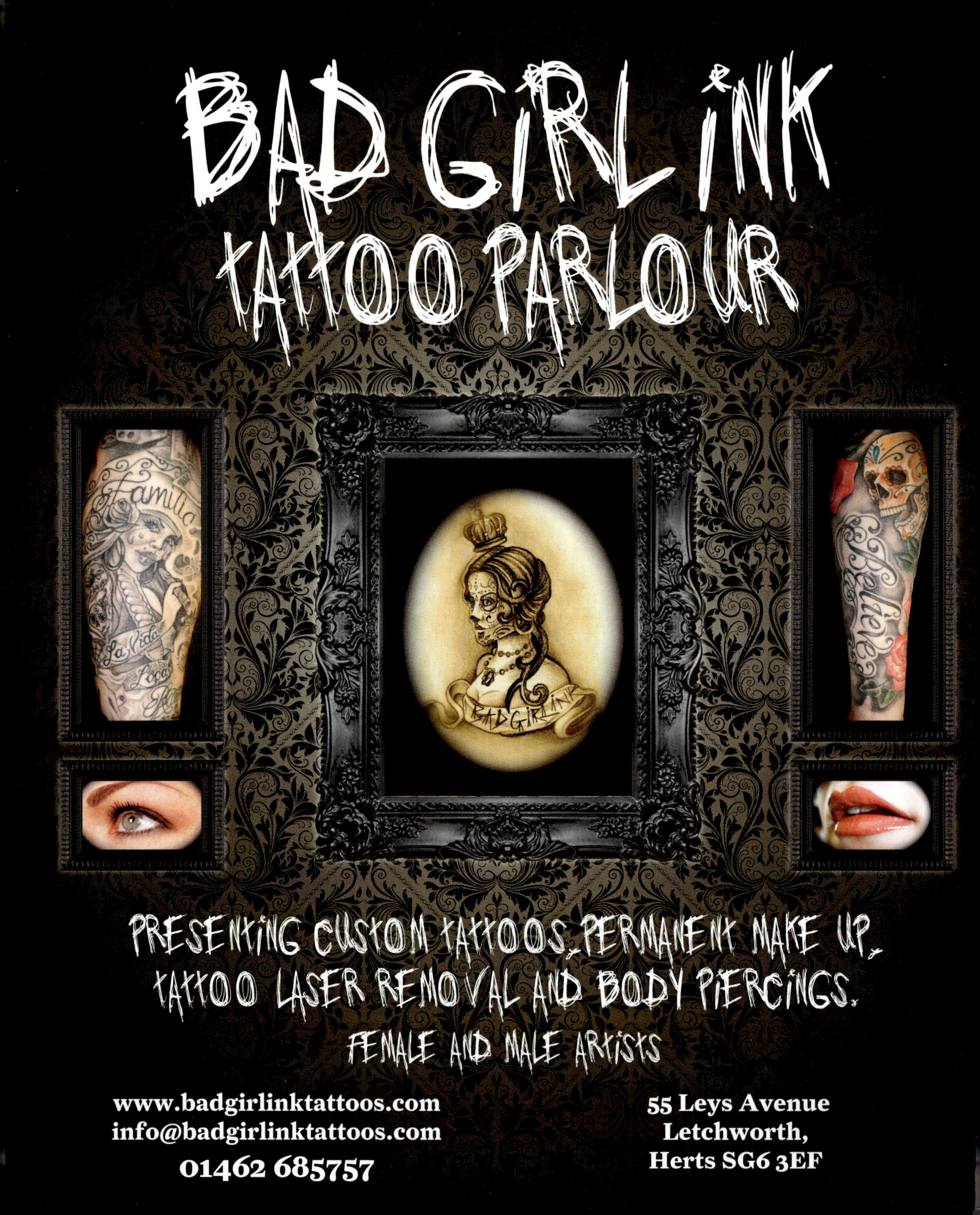